THE ARCHITECTURE OF GRASSHOPPER PUEBLO

The Architecture of Grasshopper Pueblo

Charles R. Riggs

The University of Utah Press

Salt Lake City

First paperback printing 2011

15 14 13 12 11   1 2 3 4 5

LIBRARY OF CONGRESS CATLOGING-IN-PUBLICATION DATA

Riggs, Charles R.
The architecture of Grasshopper Pueblo / Charles R. Riggs.
p. cm.
Includes bibliographical references and index.
ISBN 978-0-87480-857-5 (paperback: alk. paper)
1. Grasshopper Pueblo (Ariz.) 2. Mogollon culture. 3. Pueblo architecture.
4. Pueblo Indians—Antiquities. I. Title.
E99.M76 R48 2001
720'.89'974—dc21   2001001659

For my family,
María, Salina, and Pablo

Contents

Figures

Tables

Acknowledgments

In October of 1967, in a small town in northern Wyoming, I came into the world, at the time understandably ignorant of archaeology and the already five-year-old Grasshopper field school. That I could grow to adulthood and still participate in the fieldwork at Grasshopper, first as an undergraduate student and then as a graduate staff member, puts the span of Grasshopper research in perspective. It is impossible to thank every one of my student and staff predecessors at the field school, but they deserve the most credit for their efforts in uncovering the data used in this study. It was through the support of the White Mountain Apache Tribe and the hard work of every student, staff member, and Apache crew member that this book is even possible. I am exceedingly grateful for their labors and for the lasting friendships I have developed through my association with the Grasshopper Research Program. I hope that this book does justice to all of the effort that went into collecting the data on which it is based.

I have many individuals to thank for their help in the completion of this study, which marks the end of a nine-year personal journey. First, I extend my thanks to the members of my dissertation committee—Barbara Mills and the three Jeffs. Barbara lent her extensive knowledge of the southwestern archaeological literature and her expertise in quantitative methods, which greatly enhanced the study. Jeff Altschul provided much-needed help with my use of various statistical methods and offered insights that have helped to strengthen the book. Jeff also has my gratitude for making the computer resources of Statistical Research, Inc., available. To Jeff Dean I extend my thanks for providing excellent editorial comments on the original drafts of the work and, more important, for his inspirational work at Betatakin and Kiet Siel, which has been fundamental to many of the arguments advanced here. Finally, I could not have completed this book without the help and support of Jeff Reid. As my committee chair, Jeff has instilled in me high standards of research and an appreciation for the importance of data quality that not only has strengthened this book but also has made me a better archaeologist. Thanks also to Jeff for bringing me to the field school and for making the Grasshopper architectural data available to me.

Numerous other people are to be thanked for their roles in this work. Ray

Thompson has my thanks for his excellent choice of location for the field school. Any devotee of Grasshopper research will willingly admit that the beauty and isolation of Grasshopper is as responsible for their interests as the archaeology itself. Next, thanks to Jeff Grathwohl (Jeff no. 4) for his support. Jeff has made a potentially painful process remarkably easy through his patience and expertise, even in the face of my occasional freakouts. Thanks also to Cathy Cameron and Ruth Van Dyke, who reviewed the manuscript. They both provided insights that have greatly enhanced the book. A special thanks to Ruth for the obvious amount of time and effort she put into her comments, which served as an excellent model during the rewriting process.

Cindy Elsner Hayward's outstanding contribution is self-evident in Figures 3.3, 3.27, 3.30, 3.32, and 3.41. Susan Luebbermann has my thanks for pulling together the photographs in the Arizona State Museum (ASM) archives, despite renovations and my often vague references to cryptic Grasshopper Field School photograph numbers. Joe Abbott did an outstanding job editing the manuscript for the University of Utah Press. Thanks to John Welch for his support of my efforts and for allowing me to make numerous visits to Grasshopper when I needed to get that perfect photograph or to recheck the length of that plaza wall. Thanks to Barbara Montgomery for sharing her insights into the construction of rooms and roofs at Chodistaas and to Joe Ezzo for sharing his perspectives on bone chemistry data and local vs. nonlocal people at Grasshopper. Thanks go to Stephanie Whittlesey, who not only helped me sort out the Great Kiva floor but whose brutally honest editorial comments on my other professional writing also helped to polish the prose in this work. Thanks also to John Olsen, who provided insightful comments on my master's thesis, the bulk of which became Chapter 4 of this book. Andrew Comrie and Brigitte Waldorf have my thanks for providing me with fresh perspectives on migration studies and for their guidance and assistance in spatial analysis techniques and quantitative methods.

I could also not have completed this project without the continued support of my family. To my parents, Ross and Fran Riggs, I extend my thanks for their unwavering support and belief in my abilities. And to my in-laws, Juan and María Molina, I extend a very special thanks. Their kindness and seemingly endless generosity afforded me the time and fortitude to see this immense task through to its conclusion. Finally, my appreciation of the support of my wife and personal editor, María Molina, cannot be fully expressed in words. I am a better writer and a better person because of the many ways she has enriched my life. Without the love and support I get from her and our two children, Salina and Pablo, this work would not even have been conceivable, let alone possible.

1

Archaeology and Architecture

Architecture in general is frozen music.
—Friedrich von Schelling, *Philosophie der Kunst*

THIS BOOK TELLS THE STORY OF GRASSHOPPER PUEBLO AS SEEN THROUGH its most lasting feature, its architectural remains. The story of the interaction of traditionally defined culture groups and many of the mundane aspects of people's daily lives are captured and preserved in the walls of Grasshopper. During the early fourteenth century the Anasazi and Mogollon, the traditionally defined culture groups of the Colorado Plateau and central mountains of the southwestern United States, were living together in large numbers at places like Grasshopper, beginning their transformation into modern puebloan peoples. The architectural record of Grasshopper is valuable to archaeologists for many reasons, but the unprecedented material record it provides of community growth and change during the transition from the Pueblo III period to the Pueblo IV period, a critical time in southwestern prehistory, is quite possibly the most important.

What makes Grasshopper Pueblo and its settlement history important? By southwestern standards Grasshopper Pueblo was a large site, although by no means the largest in the Southwest. In comparison to contemporary events in world history, however, it was but a speck on the map. Its entire occupation spanned but a fraction of the seven centuries it took the Christian rulers of Spain to expel the Muslims in the Spanish Reconquest (A.D. 719–1492). It lasted, if assessed generously, as long as the Hundred Years War between England and France (A.D. 1337–1453). It was built not by kings or even great chiefs but by small individual family groups, many of whom had come to Grasshopper from other places. It was not abandoned because of a catastrophic event such as the Black Death, which swept through China (A.D. 1331) and into Europe (A.D. 1348) around the time that people began to disperse from Grasshopper Pueblo.

Why do we need to understand a site like Grasshopper Pueblo? The answer is simple: Grasshopper is, without question, remarkable, not for its grandeur or for its long occupation span but rather for its ordinariness and for the long history of archaeological exploration that has been devoted to it. When it was occupied, it was one of hundreds of large pueblos located throughout central and southern Arizona, where people came together who had never been together before. Grasshopper is important because we have recovered so much information from it and because it is accompanied by a wealth of associated material culture relative to other large sites of the same period. It has been studied intensively for almost 40 years, 30 of which were devoted to fieldwork. From 1963 to 1992 the University of Arizona Archaeological Field School at Grasshopper was the summer home to archaeologists from all over the world who unearthed 103 of the 500-plus rooms. As a well-excavated and well-reported site, Grasshopper reveals much about numerous other large fourteenth-century pueblos that have not been the subject of a 38-year research program. The excavated structures yielded not only a wealth of architectural information but also a staggering amount of artifacts, from ceramic vessels and lithic tools to exotic exchange items. The quantity or quality of artifacts found at Grasshopper has not been replicated at other important southwestern pueblo sites for which good architectural information has been reported. Together, the architecture and the artifacts from Grasshopper allow the past to be viewed from many perspectives and with confidence that the sample is a true representation of the Grasshopper community as a whole. They complement each other, serving as windows into the lives of the people who built and lived in Grasshopper Pueblo.

In addition to the body of work done there, Grasshopper Pueblo is a valuable site because its occupation was a relatively short-lived phenomenon, and the intensity of human use that took place during the fourteenth century was the only such settlement to have existed at the Grasshopper locale. Thus, unlike many large Near Eastern tells or even southwestern settlements like the Hopi pueblo of Old Orayvi, which has been continuously occupied since the twelfth century (Cameron 1999a:35), Grasshopper's architectural record is untainted by subsequent occupations. Its limited spatial extent and short occupation also ensure that many possible sources of bias are eliminated. For example, Sanders (1990:Table 5.1), in an analysis of domestic space at the Early Bronze Age site of Myrtos, on Crete, provides a useful list of the determinants for the form and use of domestic space. These include the naturally fixed elements (climate and topography), the flexible elements (available materials, level of technology, and economic resources), and the culturally fixed elements (function and cultural convention).

At Grasshopper Pueblo the naturally fixed and flexible elements can be viewed as constants. Grasshopper's core architecture is restricted to a relatively small area and is located in the middle of a dense ponderosa pine forest, on large outcrops of good quality sandstone and limestone. Thus, environmental variability was nonexistent, and construction materials were relatively abundant and probably available to all of the population. Abundant data from numerous material classes suggest that different groups of builders resided at Grasshopper. Thus, variables such as climate, topography, resource availability, and level of technological ability can be considered constants, whereas there is compelling nonarchitectural data suggesting the coresidence of different ethnic or social groups. The economic resources of the individuals may have been variable, but based on biological data, this variability may have been determined along ethnic lines (Ezzo 1993; Hinkes 1983) as a factor related to the timing of arrival at Grasshopper (Riggs 1999a). Thus, only the culturally fixed elements were variable at Grasshopper.

This architectural study represents both a conclusion and a starting point. It is the culmination of a long-term, architecturally focused research program that began in 1963 with the first attempts to generate a site plan. It builds on the work of the cornering project begun in 1967 and the growth project begun in 1971. Yet this study is the first complete examination of any material class from Grasshopper Pueblo, despite an unsurpassed catalogue of 22 dissertations, 6 master's theses, and more than 100 published books, articles, or monographs addressing Grasshopper Pueblo or sites in the Grasshopper region. It is highly unlikely that an effort of this magnitude will again be devoted to a village the size of Grasshopper because of the rising costs of fieldwork combined with a trend toward increasingly limited excavations and archaeological projects focused on salvage rather than research. All of these factors underscore the importance of the Grasshopper collection as a source of data for the Pueblo IV period.

For this reason alone this book is a significant contribution to the southwestern literature. But because of the complementary data contained in the numerous studies of Grasshopper material culture, and because of a long history of research in the American Southwest and around the world devoted to architecture and its relationship to culture and society, this book offers more than a simple description of the architecture of Grasshopper Pueblo.

It is also not a work of "household archaeology" (Steadman 1996:62) but rather a spatial analysis of Grasshopper. Many treatments of southwestern pueblo architecture examine the space enclosed by four walls and a roof as indicators of activities in the past (Ciolek-Torrello 1978; Ferguson 1996; Hill 1970a; James 1994, 1997). Although these are important considerations and are addressed to some extent here, overlooking the components of architecture limits our understanding of the behaviors related to the construction and use of an architectural space (Steadman 1996:62). The individual components of these spaces—walls, floors, and roofs—are the features that delineate boundaries and control access to a particular space; they are the architectural elements that are determined by cultural convention and contain evidence of specific technical choices.

The study of a large pueblo village like Grasshopper or its contemporary Pueblo IV neighbors requires more than a site plan to generate an informed reconstruction. The site plan of a village abandoned for centuries cannot be examined as if it captured a simple, manufactured artifact during a single moment in time. Such a one-dimensional examination of architecture misrepresents the interaction of time and human activity that generates the scatter of walls seen on the ground. Informed reconstructions of a pueblo village result from excavation and the recovery of construction and room abandonment data. These data are fundamental to an understanding of the social interactions dictated by and reflected in the architectural plan.

This book demonstrates that as people immigrated into the Grasshopper region, they brought with them subtle differences in the ways they constructed and manipulated rooms. The brief but intense experiment in ethnic coresidence at places like Grasshopper most certainly had lasting implications for southwestern pueblo society. Although the people who came together at Grasshopper might be referred to as having had an Anasazi or a Mogollon cultural tradition, the people who emigrated from the area toward the end of the fourteenth century were probably much more similar to modern western pueblo peoples. Walls built by the various inhabitants of Grasshopper contain subtle yet consistently patterned clues that people with different architectural conventions were in residence.

Numerous studies of various subsets of Grasshopper material culture provide a wealth of biological and material data to indicate occupation by ethnically diverse groups in discrete blocks of rooms within the site (Birkby 1973, 1982; Ezzo 1993; Ezzo et al. 1997; Hinkes 1983; Reid 1989, 1998; Reid and Whittlesey 1999; Shipman 1982; Triadan 1997; Whittlesey 1974). If we agree with Kent (1990:2), that structures "are conscious manipulations by humans to create boundaries where they do not exist in nature," then architecture bounds human activity in general, and different architectural units within a society of socially or ethnically diverse builders should denote the boundaries of these different groups. Did these biologically distinct builders leave markers of their culturally learned building traditions in the walls of Grasshopper? This study suggests that they did.

ARCHAEOLOGICAL PERSPECTIVES ON CONSTRUCTION, SOCIETY, AND THE USE OF SPACE

The following chapters demonstrate that people came together and built Grasshopper Pueblo with slight variations in room-construction traditions and practices that can be construed as differences in technical choices between the groups who founded various parts of the pueblo. With this fact in mind an examination of the architectural details can render a reconstruction of the settlement patterns of diverse groups of builders within the Grasshopper community. Yet looking at room function through time at Grasshopper, we find a poor fit between the architecture and the activities contained within the rooms.

How do we reconcile these seemingly contradictory statements regarding the human use of architecture? On one hand, some scholars (Hall 1959, 1966, 1968; Lemonnier 1986, 1993) suggest an intimate link between culture and architectural form, whereas others (e.g., Rapoport 1982, 1990) argue that there is only a "loose fit" between activities and architecture, or the built environment. Architectural data from Grasshopper suggest that both perspectives are correct. As an artifact architecture is the product of a series of technological choices governed by culturally specific conventions of construction and use. Thus, by focusing on the individual elements of construction, the architectural details, we can begin to identify the group or groups responsible for a specific architectural form. On the other hand, Rapoport is also correct in that architecture only contains activities loosely. Settings can be and often are changed by different constellations of semifixed cues (furnishings, floor features) and nonfixed cues (people, artifacts). In the following pages this dichotomy will be made evident at Grasshopper Pueblo.

Grasshopper Pueblo was built by those who used it and, as such, can best be understood by referencing the work of scholars who have focused on vernacular or primitive architecture, or *architecture populaire* (Rapoport 1969:3). Architecture, or the built environment, occupies many niches as a class of material culture and is a symbolic expression of the larger cultural framework as much as it is the product of an individual builder's abilities. From a functionalist perspective architecture is a shelter and a place to store household equipment, food, and valuables. As a shelter a dwelling protects its occupants from the environment. As a social construct architecture provides a sense of place by transforming open, public space into personal, private space. On a more abstract level, "human occupation of space is an act of transforming the forces of chaos into cosmological order" (Kus and Raharijaona 1990:23).

The simple act of erecting walls can produce a myriad of architectural forms, from the simple *kua* of the !Kung San (Lee 1979:273–277) to the extravagant palaces of the Minoans (Branigan 1970). Broadly speaking, architecture can be described as the product of human activity and time: a village is produced through a sequence of events determined by the actions of individual builders and the activities of various task groups, and it is influenced by the builders' culture in numerous ways. Behaviors related to the construction and use of architectural forms are conditioned by various cultural and environmental factors, including social organization, tradition, function, economics, landscape, symbolism/ideology, and ecology. Determining which factors influence and determine the form of a given architectural space within a given community is no simple endeavor. It is not surprising that a unified theory of architectural design has eluded archaeologists, given the immense range of variability in decision making and form inherent in secular architecture.

Vernacular architecture throughout the world has been examined from a variety of theoretical and methodological perspectives. Two fairly recent review articles provide in-depth discussions of how architecture has been examined by a number of different disciplines (Lawrence and Low 1990; Steadman 1996). These approaches have targeted various elements of construction, including function (Hunter-Anderson 1977; McGuire and Schiffer 1983), social organization (Flannery 1972; Hill 1970a; Layne 1987; Morgan 1965; Whiting and Ayers 1968), household studies (Blanton 1994; Clarke 1972; Wilk and Rathje 1982), symbolism (Bourdieu 1973, 1977; Hieb 1979, 1990; Kus and Raharijaona

1990; Saile 1985; Sofaer 1997; Swentzell 1990; Uphil 1972), the cultural landscape (Lefebvre 1991; Smith and David 1995), and architecture's role in reflecting and influencing human action (Donley-Reid 1990; Ferguson 1996; Hillier and Hanson 1984; Rapoport 1969, 1982; Sanders 1990). In fact, one of the central tenets of most approaches to architecture and the built environment, regardless of the approach used, is that buildings simultaneously reflect and influence social action (Hillier and Hanson 1984:2; Lawrence and Low 1990:455; Rapoport 1982, 1990), which in turn is a construct of the built environment's occupants' society or culture.

Architecture is intrinsically linked to human society. It can reflect the actions of a given society and, simultaneously, be influenced by those interactions (Hillier and Hanson 1984; Lawrence and Low 1990; Rapoport 1969, 1982; Steadman 1996). Buildings segregate external space from internal space and serve to structure interactions among members and nonmembers of a society (Hillier and Hanson 1984). In addition, the built environment has meaning not only for those who inhabit a specific building or set of buildings but also for outsiders as well. This meaning has been found to exist on many levels of society and to communicate a wealth of information about the society that occupies it. For example, in his landmark analysis of the Berber house, Bourdieu (1973) found that architecture symbolically reflects culture by means of a series of binary oppositions that serve as a metaphor for the society. As Bourdieu (1973:104) states, the house is "a microcosm organized according to the same oppositions which govern all the universe."

By transforming unclaimed, open space into bounded, architectural space, human beings in effect reproduce major themes that guide their society, if not their culture (Rapoport 1990:10). The built environment suggests the customs and restrictions of a given society through a series of design decisions that play a critical role in cueing proper behavior by encoding worldview and cultural values. Thus, "the final arrangement of the built environment is never random" (Sanders 1990:45). The form of any given society's buildings, however, amounts to much more than a nonrandom organization of space. Buildings have meaning. Through symbolic elements, the number of hallways and passages, and the size and shape of different spaces, buildings serve as a constant reminder, a mnemonic, for rules of behavior within given structures for members of a society (Rapoport 1982:56; Sanders 1990:45–46) and reflect notions of worldview and cosmology (Bourdieu 1973; Saile 1985:178). The cultural properties of architecture are captured in architectural details.

Architectural details provide clues about how Grasshopper's various immigrant communities perceived and manipulated space. Through time, as immigration rates slowed and resident households expanded, spaces within the various room blocks were altered through room remodeling and the construction of new rooms. Rooms were built around open public spaces preserved as arenas for daily interactions and ceremonial meeting spaces for village inhabitants. The construction of a great kiva after the period of rapid aggregation permitted further integration and facilitated the integration of a dispersing community prior to Grasshopper Pueblo's ultimate abandonment. As people's needs for space changed through the expansion of households and the integration of new immigrant groups, rooms were remodeled to accommodate different activities.

Thus, as Rapoport (1990:10) notes, a narrow focus on architecture alone is not adequate for an understanding of society. The built environment is but a small facet of culture and architecture only a part of the total built environment, which is composed of "systems of activities" performed in "systems of settings" (Rapoport 1990:11). Individual buildings act as one setting for a single activity in a string of activities influenced by practical and more symbolic concerns. A single building can also serve as the location of several activities through time as the semifixed and nonfixed architectural elements within it are changed (Rapoport 1982:87–101, 1990:13). Nevertheless, facets of the built environment do provide cues for proper behavior for members of a society and are a reflection of behavior, albeit a loose reflection (Rapoport 1990:18).

That architecture has meaning, informs us about the society that lives or did live within its confines, and provides culturally specific cues for proper action are not new concepts (Bourdieu 1973; Lawrence and Low 1990; Rapoport 1980, 1982). It is almost beyond refute that architecture responds to culturally specific action, which can be marked in obvious and subtle ways. The growing literature on proxemics is instructive in this regard (Hall 1966, 1968; Watson 1970). Proxemics, as applied to the built environment, examines the human need for interpersonal space within and between architectural units. Proxemics scholars suggest that people have an inborn mechanism that causes them to distance themselves from one another, a mechanism that is tempered by culture (Hall 1966:3). Thus, there are culturally specific expressions of space, and the use of space can be used as a form of nonverbal communication (Hall 1959; Rapoport 1982). Much of this behavior has been found to arise from unconscious spatial manipulation resulting from learned conventions of use of space (Hall 1966:43), and as a result the organization of the built environment comes to reflect culturally specific, yet unconscious, decisions regarding the socially proper use of space (Sanders 1990:48).

The role of unconscious, innate, culturally determined behaviors in construction decisions suggests another way of looking at architectural variability in the archaeological record. Based on the work of Pierre Lemonnier (1986, 1993), a number of scholars have begun to focus on the concept of technological style (Childs 1991; Pfaffenberger 1992; Stark 1998). Technological style stands in marked contrast to those approaches that view style as a conscious attempt to display identity (Wobst 1977). Lemonnier (1986:153) focuses instead on techniques that "manifest the choices made by societies from a universe of possibilities," what Sackett (1990:33) refers to as "isochrestic variation." Thus, techniques inform all aspects of the manufacturing process, from the selection of materials to the completion and subsequent use of the item.

A careful observation of the manufacturing process can reveal the steps in manufacturing and the technical choices made by the manufacturer. Because many choices are culturally determined, the presence of technical variants can be used to differentiate peoples with different social realities (Lemonnier 1986:155). Finally, as with proxemic behavior, technical choices are often unconscious but can be observed in the material culture (Lemonnier 1986:155; Wiessner 1984:161). These traces then reflect the different social realities of groups with differing cultural traditions. Thus, examining technological style is a useful technique for differentiating social boundaries in the archaeological record (Cameron 1998; Stark 1998; Stark et al. 1998).

A detailed look at the individual elements of construction at Grasshopper reveals that the individual room blocks, especially those of the main pueblo, were constructed by groups of builders with differing "social realities" who expressed their architectural technology in subtly different yet archaeologically visible ways. This is evident from their selection of different construction materials, their standards for doorway and wall-feature size, their perceptions about room size, and their use of specific types of semifixed floor features. On one hand, this analysis supports Lemonnier's (1986:149) assertion that the entire operational sequence—the *chaîne opértoire*—needs to be observed in order to understand the technical choices that were available to the builders of Grasshopper. In Chapter 3 the detailed description of architectural elements approximates the actual observation of the manufacturing process as closely as is possible using archaeological data.

On the other hand, this analysis also demonstrates that architecture at Grasshopper probably did contain activities only loosely (Rapport 1990:18). Rooms were remodeled at a relatively high rate, suggesting that systems of activities took place in different rooms at different times. Little evidence for specific types of domestic activities is found in the fixed architectural elements—the walls and room form—at Grasshopper. Instead, patterned associations of semifixed and nonfixed feature elements marked the activities contained within rooms (see Ciolek-Torrello 1984, 1985; Reid and Whittlesey 1982). The data described in Chapter 5 suggest that these associations changed through time. This was probably a result of changing functional and symbolic needs of the occupying groups as the Grasshopper community developed.

The latest rooms constructed at Grasshopper seem to have contained activities even more loosely than the first rooms built. A reduced commitment to construction and a decline in the formality of building practices indicate a differently organized Grasshopper community after A.D. 1330 (Reid 1989). This architecture contrasts starkly with the more formal rooms of the early period and emphasizes how the Grasshopper community changed markedly just prior to its abandonment. The literature on the transition from pit house to pueblo suggests that a shift to a more impermanent type of structure reflects a concomitant decrease in commitment to full-time occupation.

Hunter-Anderson (1977), building on Flannery's (1972) classic comparative study of house form in Mesoamerica and the Near East, approaches the pit house–to–pueblo transition from the perspective that houses are containers of objects and activities. Sedentism is directly related to the level of differentiation of activities (Hunter-Anderson 1977:304), and the transition from pit house to pueblo is seen as a response to a perceived increase in the number and diversity of activities (including the number of actors). Gilman's (1987) cross-cultural study of dwelling use, similarly found that pit structures are direct indicators of the level of seasonality and of mobility patterns (Gilman 1987:560).

The less substantial structures of the late period at Grasshopper, although not pit houses, were an impermanent type of structure, similar to pit houses in that they had a superstructure of brush or *jacal* rather than full-standing masonry walls and formal pueblo roofs. Further, the elements and artifacts preserved on the floors of these later rooms suggest that activities were loosely assigned to rooms, similar to the more generalized use associated with pit houses. Late-period activities came to be contained by more informal settings, related to a decreased commitment to full-time occupation of the Grasshopper locale. McGuire and Schiffer (1983) have related house form to considerations of anticipated use life. Societies with a high level of mobility perceive a shorter anticipated use life for their dwellings and tend to build informal structures requiring less labor and lower construction costs; more sedentary societies, anticipating an extended stay, tend to favor houses with high construction costs but low maintenance requirements. Thus, the architectural evidence suggests that prior to abandonment of the Grasshopper community, people had switched to a more mobile settlement system. Continued organization of the community into discrete architectural units, room blocks, implies that social differences were still being maintained during the late period. The informal nature of the architecture, however, and the smaller number of late rooms mask many of the architectural details that allow us to recognize different groups of builders.

GRASSHOPPER PUEBLO'S PLACE IN THE HISTORY OF SOUTHWESTERN PUEBLO ARCHITECTURAL STUDIES

The transition from pit house to pueblo is but one example of a number of recent studies in the American Southwest that examine more closely the relationship between people and their dwellings. These recent studies, including this book, draw on a long history of scholarly concern with the intimate link between southwestern people and their built environments. In another recent example Ferguson (1996) combines Giddens's (1979) structuration theory with a space-syntax approach to emphasize that public space at Zuñi does indeed act to integrate society by fostering interactions among social groups. Ferguson's study was the first of many recent works in the Southwest to take a space-syntax approach to architecture (Clark 2001; Cooper 1995; Potter 1998; Shapiro 1997; Van Dyke 1999).

Pots and houses, as well as other structures—mounds, ball courts, kivas—have been major diagnostic components of southwestern archaeology. Thus, along with ceramics, architecture has always been an important material class in the Southwest. Throughout the history of southwestern archaeology, its role has shifted along with the various paradigms within the discipline. A brief review of this history, however, reveals a consistent emphasis on linking pueblo architecture to culture. Although this emphasis has taken many forms, its persistence in the Southwest, despite a diverse array of approaches, further informs this study.

Early investigators, most trained in ethnology, saw archaeology simply as the prehistoric component of ethnography (Longacre 1970b). As a result puebloan material culture was interpreted through direct analogy with modern pueblo peoples. The ruined pueblos of the Southwest were considered direct antecedents to the modern pueblos, related by an unbroken chain of events traceable through history (Cushing 1896; Fewkes 1900; Hewett 1993:95–104; Mindeleff 1891). Activities related to architectural form were considered self-evident and could be reconstructed through close observation of modern pueblo societies. Prudden's (1903:234–235) recognition of the "unit type" pueblo complemented the contemporary work of Cosmos Mindeleff (1900:649), who postulated that architectural units in precontact pueblo society were directly related to the activities of individual clans. Thus, architectural forms were linked to specific social groups by even the earliest southwestern explorers (Fewkes 1911:79–80; Mindeleff 1900:649; Prudden 1903:234). In fact, Cosmos Mindeleff's (1900) discussion of Hopi clan localization provides an excellent ethnographic model for the settlement of Grasshopper Pueblo by different groups of builders. The association between social groups and architecture in the earliest constructions at a Hopi village describes precisely the early settlement history of Grasshopper Pueblo (Chapter 4; Riggs 1999a).

Later, archaeologists' focus shifted from defining past behavior based on references to modern societies to an attempt to fill in the gaps of prehistory (Brew 1946; Haury 1928, 1936, 1985; Kidder 1962; Reed 1956; Wheat 1955), and architecture became more significant as a marker of cultural differences. Prehistoric "cultures" were defined as sets of traits, and change through time was marked by shifts in the constellation of these traits and by innovations in artifact styles (Longacre 1970b:5). For all practical purposes archaeological cultures consisted of suites of material traits. Scholars of this period posited that culturally determined activities created differences in artifact styles that changed through time and could be used to delineate cultural boundaries. These cultural-historical approaches were criticized heavily by later scholars (Binford 1962; Kluckhohn 1940; Taylor 1948), yet they remain the foundation of most archaeological research conducted in the Southwest. That we can pick out peoples with either a Mogollon tradition or an Anasazi tradition at places like Grasshopper (Reid and Whittlesey 1999) and Point of Pines (Haury 1958; Lindsay 1987) speaks to the persistence and efficacy of these approaches. As Dean (1988b:199) notes, "The fact that the components of this interactional network are archaeologically recognizable suggests that Mogollon and Anasazi are two different sociocultural entities that persisted even into the late 13th century."

Presaged by the work of Julian Steward (1955) and by the pioneering efforts of Martin and Rinaldo (1950:536–570), processual archaeology viewed architecture as linked to numerous facets of society. Population density (Cook and Hiezer 1968), social group affiliation (Dean 1969, 1970; Hill 1970a; Longacre 1970a), and household identification (Ciolek-Torrello 1978, 1984, 1985) all were important social variables reflected in the architectural record and were exceedingly important to Grasshopper research throughout the 1970s. Room function, although not a new concern (Beaglehole 1937; Forde 1931; Mindeleff 1891), became an especially important consideration in reconstructing households and other corporate groups (Ciolek-Torrello 1978, 1984, 1985; Dean 1969, 1970; Hill 1970a; Rohn 1965, 1971). The ethnographic pueblos were evoked once again, but under this perspective they were a source of social theory and provided hypotheses that could be tested empirically using archaeological data (Cook and Heizer 1968; Hill 1970a, 1970b; Longacre 1970a; Whiting and Ayres 1968).

In tandem with a long history of concern with architecture, ethnographic data has been a mainstay in southwestern archaeology. Several ethnoarchaeological studies reflect a growing concern with documenting architectural details, providing a great deal of data on the use of space and construction techniques in currently inhabited pueblo villages that can be used to help interpret archaeological data (Adams 1983; Cameron 1999a; Reynolds 1981). These approaches to puebloan architecture strengthen inferences about past behaviors by using ethnographic data to develop principles or analogs for relating human action and society to architecture (James 1994, 1997). Data from these ethnographic studies inform the architecture of Grasshopper in numerous ways in the following pages.

CONCLUSION

This book examines the link between architectural variability and culturally fixed determinants of form and use of space, namely cultural convention as expressed through architectural style. Although several studies have addressed aspects of architecture at Grasshopper (Ciolek-Torrello 1978, 1984, 1985; Graves 1991; Reid 1973; Reid and Shimada 1982; Reid and Whittlesey 1982; Scarborough and Shimada 1974; Sullivan 1974), a systematic analysis of all amassed architectural data has yet to be completed. Thus, the focus of this book is to provide a comprehensive architectural description of Grasshopper Pueblo as a means of addressing issues of migration and community organization and their importance in the founding and growth of Grasshopper Pueblo.

Much of the story of Grasshopper's establishment, growth, and abandonment is reflected in its architecture. By drawing on other classes of information recovered from Grasshopper and a rich history of research relating architecture to society in general, but with specific reference to the Southwest, this book provides an informed and relatively complete picture of room construction and use and of the social realities of the diverse builders of Grasshopper Pueblo as imprinted in its architecture. The interpretations made about the builders of Grasshopper are reliable because they draw on an unprecedented sample of a large pueblo, a sample that has yielded a wealth of architectural and associated artifact data.

2

Grasshopper Region and Research Overview

Grasshopper, though many things, is not a bug.
—J. Jefferson Reid, *Growth and Response to Stress at Grasshopper Pueblo, Arizona*

THE FIELD PROGRAM AT GRASSHOPPER GENERATED AN ABUNDANCE OF ARCHitectural and other data concerning settlement dynamics at a critical period in the development of southwestern pueblo culture. Numerous lines of material evidence have been brought to bear on processes of community development in the Grasshopper region in the fourteenth century. These data suggest that local people and various immigrant groups founded Grasshopper Pueblo.

The influx of these immigrants and their interactions with the region's local inhabitants had serious implications for room construction and use. Migration and community organization influence architectural diversity and provide a structure for understanding pueblos as living entities that reflect the behaviors of their builders. The data presented here speak to these issues and provide some of the strongest evidence available for addressing them. Migration, aggregation, community organization, and abandonment are currently fashionable as research domains in southwestern archaeology (Cameron 1993, 1995; Clark 2001; Cordell et al. 1994; Crown and Kohler 1994; Duff 1998; Fish et al. 1994; Herr and Clark 1997; Potter 1998; Stark et al. 1995). These topics have always been central to Grasshopper research (Reid 1998) and are addressed in this work; indeed, this chapter demonstrates that much of the data collection and research at Grasshopper has focused on these themes.

The Grasshopper region and Grasshopper Pueblo have been the focus of intensive research since 1963, when Raymond Thompson founded the University of Arizona Archaeological Field School there. Prior to work by the University of Arizona, Walter Hough had visited the site on two occasions and published some brief accounts of Grasshopper and other ruins in the area (Hough 1919, 1920, 1930). Leslie Spier was also an early visitor to Grasshopper (Spier 1919).

The Grasshopper region is located in the western part of the Fort Apache Indian Reservation in east-central Arizona and is part of a mountainous transition zone between the Colorado Plateau on the north and the basin and range province to the south (Figure 2.1). The boundaries of the Grasshopper region consist of Cibecue Creek on the east, Canyon Creek on the west, the Mogollon Rim to the north, and the Salt River to the south (Figure 2.2).

The history of Grasshopper research is, in many ways, a history of staged architectural data collection. Early on, the generation of an architectural plan was an important objective of fieldwork (Longacre and Reid 1974:18; Thompson and Longacre 1966:271). Attempts to produce an accurate site plan inspired the cornering and growth projects (Longacre and Reid 1974:20, 22; Reid 1973:2; Reid and Shimada 1982:12–13; Wilcox 1982:19–20), which in turn shifted the focus to satellite communities with better preserved architecture, such as Red Rock House and Canyon Creek Pueblo (Graves 1982, 1983; Haury 1934; Reid 1989; Reynolds 1981). Finally, an extensive survey of the region was undertaken as a means of understanding variability in regional architecture and settlement (Reid and Whittlesey 1990; Tuggle 1970; Tuggle et al 1984; Welch 1996).

Much of the data collection and research was devoted to collecting architectural data that could be used specifically to address these issues of community growth and organization. Architectural data from several Pueblo III period sites, such as Chodistaas, and Pueblo IV period cliff dwellings, such as Canyon Creek Pueblo, help to flesh out the picture of community development by providing analogues for those data that do not exist for Grasshopper Pueblo.

GRASSHOPPER PUEBLO

Grasshopper Pueblo is a large masonry pueblo on the Grasshopper Plateau, 17.4 km west of the modern Apache community of Cibecue. The site is at an elevation of 1829 m (6000 ft) and straddles the old channel of Salt River Draw, a south-flowing tributary of the Salt River. Salt River Draw flows through the largest expanse of agricultural soils in the Grasshopper region, and Grasshopper Pueblo is located in the middle of these soils (Tuggle et al. 1984:Figure 1). The underlying topography consists of a flat expanse of alluvial soils ringed to the north and east by several low hills. The core of the site is located in the flat along Salt River Draw (Figure 2.3), whereas several of the outliers are situated on the adjacent hills overlooking the site core (Figure 2.4).

Grasshopper Pueblo consists of 447 ground-floor room spaces, 103 of which were excavated (Table A.1). Of these 447 room spaces 68 are interpreted to have had two stories (Chapter 3), for a total of 515 room spaces. These room spaces are distributed among 13 numbered room blocks and 20 small units or single rooms scattered in the flat and along the hill slopes on both sides of the old channel of Salt River Draw (Figure 2.4). Grasshopper's architecture was arrayed around three large room blocks on either side of the draw, referred to collectively as the main ruin or main pueblo (Longacre and Graves 1982:1;

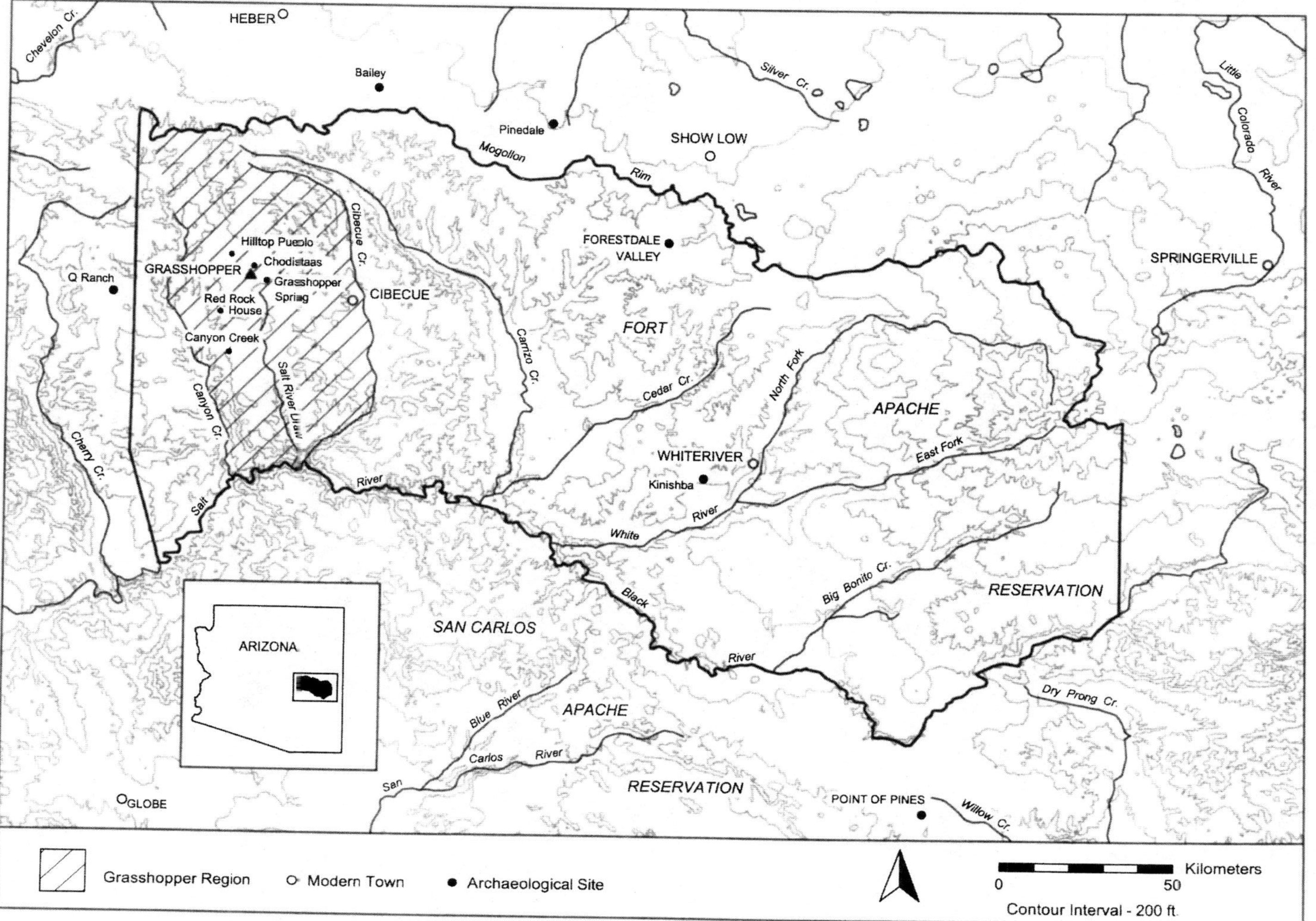

FIGURE 2.1. The Grasshopper region in east-central Arizona.

FIGURE 2.2. Salt River Canyon and the Mountain Transition Zone. Photograph by the author.

FIGURE 2.3. Overview of Grasshopper Pueblo. View looking north along the old channel of Salt River Draw. The mound on the right is Room Block 1, and Room Block 2 is to the left. Photograph by the author, 1999.

Longacre and Reid 1974:12; Reid 1989:83). The two room blocks on the west side of the draw (Room Blocks 2 and 3) formed the West Village; Room Block 1 to the east constituted the East Village (Reid and Whittlesey 1999:20). The remaining 10 room blocks and isolated rooms are referred to collectively as the outliers and, except for Room Blocks 5 and 7, typically date later in the occupation than the main pueblo.

For this study the traditional division of the site into the main pueblo and the outliers is further subdivided. Room Blocks 5 and 7 have always been classified as outliers by Grasshopper scholars, but, as demonstrated in the following

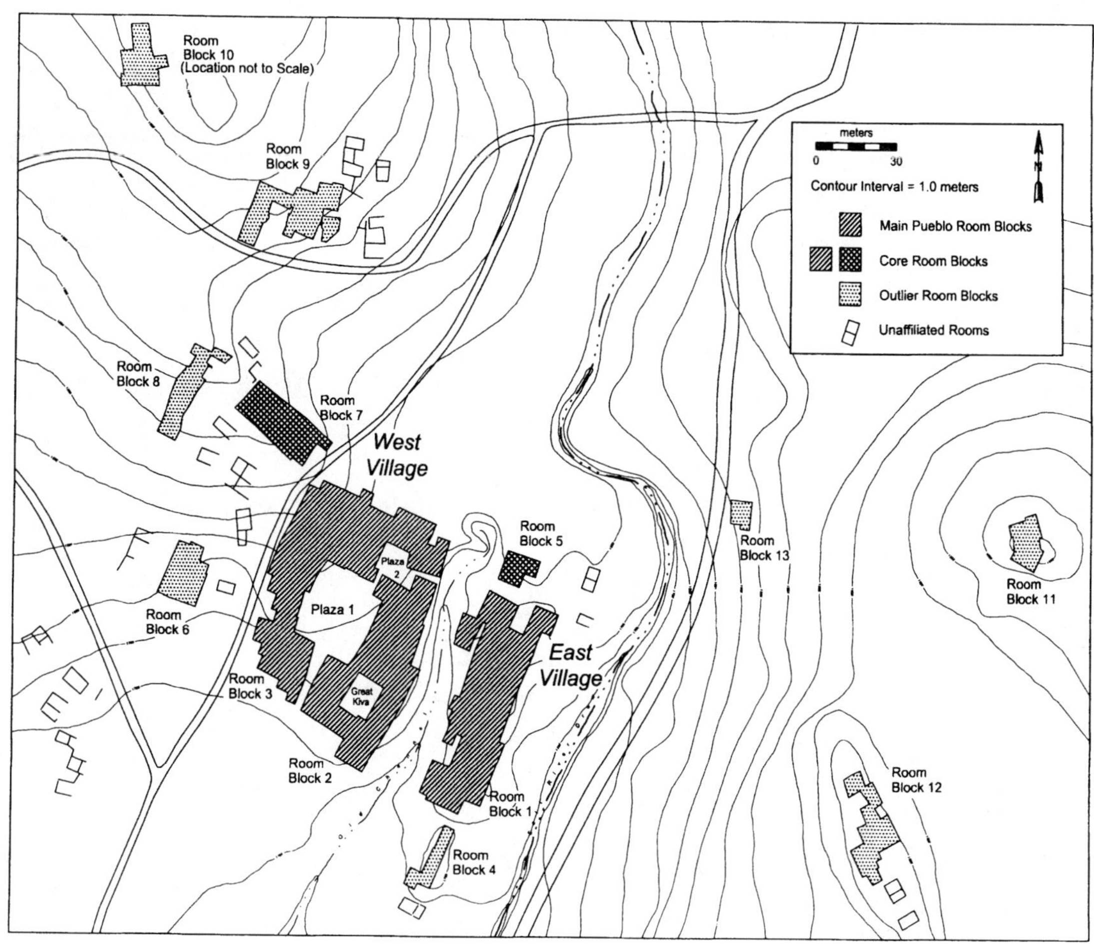

FIGURE 2.4.
Analytical and behavioral divisions within the Grasshopper site.

pages, their architectural characteristics are more similar to the room blocks of the main pueblo in several ways, including their relatively early construction dates and their having been constructed with full-standing masonry walls rather than with the low masonry walls of the other outliers. This distinction allows a third spatial category of community layout, the "site core." The "site core" or core room blocks consisted of the main pueblo (Room Blocks 1, 2, and 3) and Room Blocks 5 and 7, which were more similar to the main pueblo than to the outliers. In fact, Room Block 7 may even have been attached to Room Block 3, but a modern road between these two room blocks has obscured any surface evidence of this connection (Figure 2.4).

PUEBLO PERIOD SETTLEMENT IN THE GRASSHOPPER REGION

Chronologically Grasshopper Pueblo was bracketed by two well-investigated sites within the Grasshopper region that serve as architectural analogues (Figure

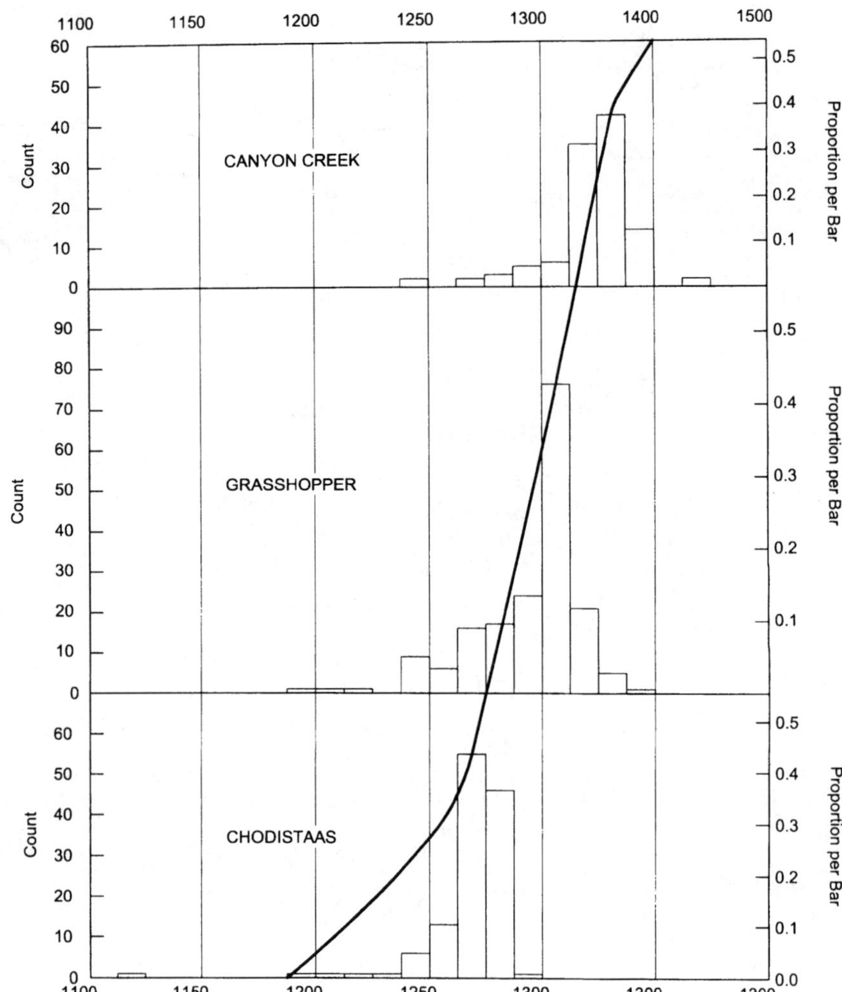

FIGURE 2.5. Tree-ring dates from selected Pueblo III and Pueblo IV period sites in the Grasshopper region.

2.5). Combined with the early work of Emil Haury (1934) at Canyon Creek Pueblo, the Grasshopper research program collected a wealth of information about architectural change during the critical transition from the Pueblo III to Pueblo IV period, concluding with the eventual dispersion of the population and ultimate abandonment of the region. Data from the Pueblo III period sites of Chodistaas, located approximately one mile north of Grasshopper, and to a lesser extent Grasshopper Spring Pueblo, located approximately one mile east of Grasshopper, serve as analogues for the Pueblo III period architecture of Grasshopper Pueblo, which was obscured by the construction of the large Pueblo IV period village that is the subject of this book (Figure 2.1). On the other end of the sequence, the well-preserved Canyon Creek Pueblo, a 120-room cliff dwelling (Reid and Whittlesey 1999:21) constructed in a shallow alcove in a side canyon of Canyon Creek (Haury 1934:23–24; Figure 2.1), serves as an architectural analogue for elements of construction that did not survive the passage of time and as a model of settlement practices during the dispersion of the population into outlier room blocks and satellite communities prior to the abandonment of the region (Reid and Whittlesey 1999:21). The overview presented in this section places the architecture of Grasshopper Pueblo into a regional context by focusing on the temporal and social history of regional settlement with an eye toward architectural diversity and population dynamics beginning in the late Pueblo III period and ending with the abandonment of the Grasshopper region.

CULTURE HISTORY AND SETTLEMENT DYNAMICS

For the purposes of the current analysis Grasshopper prehistory began in the late Pueblo III period (see Reid 1989 and Reid et al. 1996 for a discussion of earlier materials). Reid et al. (1996:77) have described the basic settlement pattern during this period:

> The regional pattern is for sites to cluster on the Grasshopper Plateau and the Cibecue Creek Valley. . . . Individual sites are located on terraces above creeks, on the pediment overlooking the Cibecue Valley, and on moderately high land forms such as prominent ridges and hill tops. . . . Intensive survey coverage around Grasshopper Pueblo has revealed a spatial clustering of sites adjacent to agricultural soil with the largest settlements functioning as focal settlements. Three settlement clusters have been proposed—one at Chodistaas, one at Grasshopper Spring, and one at Grasshopper Pueblo. . . . The arrangement is a local expression of the long-term pattern of settlements dispersed around a focal settlement. In the eastern mountains focal settlements generally contain a great kiva (Haury 1985), while those in the Grasshopper and Q Ranch regions commonly have a plaza or courtyard.

The overall picture of the Pueblo III period is one of a dispersed, highly mobile, horticultural settlement system (Welch 1996). Through time, however, because of demographic shifts on the Colorado Plateau, people in the region became increasingly sedentary and by the late Pueblo III period began to intensify activities at focal communities such as Grasshopper and Chodistaas (Reid 1989:77–78; Reid et al. 1996:77). Studies of this period suggest that it was a time of increased uncertainty in which a growing number of people competed for the same resources. The burning of Chodistaas, Grasshopper Spring, and AZ P:14:197, located northeast of Grasshopper, during this period suggests a heightened level of conflict prior to aggregation into large villages in the Pueblo IV period (Reid 1989:81).

Immigrant groups moving into the mountains around A.D. 1300 impacted the long-term local pattern of high residential mobility in the region (Reid 1989; Reid et al. 1996). In many ways events that took place at Grasshopper

Pueblo are typical of the Pueblo Southwest, resulting from abandonment of the San Juan drainage (Dean 1988a; Dean et al. 1994). From A.D. 1280 to 1300 there was a restriction in local residential mobility that was accompanied by the burning and abandonment of several Pueblo III period villages. This was followed by a tenfold increase in the number of constructed rooms (Longacre 1975, 1976; Reid 1973, 1989) and more than a threefold increase in the amount of formal public village space in the Grasshopper region (Reid and Riggs 1995). Before A.D. 1300 the largest site in the region had fewer than 20 rooms. After aggregation ten sites on the Grasshopper Plateau had 35 or more rooms (Reid 1989:81; Reid and Whittlesey 1990:187). Although these numbers reflect a lower population density than other parts of the Southwest at this time (Cordell et al. 1994:115–118; Dean et al. 1994:64, 68; Kintigh 1985:1), these increases point to a significant population surge in the Grasshopper region after A.D. 1300. As demonstrated in Chapter 5, immigrants were a significant driving force in this population increase and were pivotal in shaping the architecture of Grasshopper Pueblo.

Aggregation at Grasshopper Pueblo itself occurred rapidly (Longacre 1975, 1976; Riggs 1994a) and was probably largely a defensive response to local competition and aggregation in adjacent areas (Reid 1989:81; Reid et al. 1996:77). The vast body of material culture recovered over the 30-year field program provides a unique perspective on life in this rapidly growing pueblo community. What follows is a brief settlement history of the Grasshopper region with a focus on the Pueblo III and IV periods and evidence supporting the hypothesis, based on a number of lines of data, that different ethnic or social groups were present within the region. This discussion frames later chapters by highlighting the evidence for different groups of people within the region and places the architectural data and analyses into a regional and historical perspective.

Establishment (A.D. 1275–1300)

Data suggest that after a long history of shared, although sporadic, use of the mountain region by different ethnic groups (Reid 1989:80–81), people from the Colorado Plateau began to settle in earnest during the late Pueblo III period at Chodistaas and Grasshopper Spring. Replacement of Cibola Whiteware by Roosevelt Redware at Chodistaas over a very short period in the A.D. 1290s indicates the introduction of new manufacturing technology (Montgomery and Reid 1990:89) and perhaps new people. This development coincided roughly with the construction of four large storage rooms (Reid 1989:77). Ceramic compositional analysis by Zedeño bolsters this interpretation by indicating that locally and nonlocally produced ceramics were present in the area as a result of any one of three mechanisms: long-distance exchange trips, trade between mobile groups, and the movement of migrants into the region (Zedeño 1994:101).

Mortuary data for this period are silent on the issue of migrants. Both Grasshopper Spring and Chodistaas were largely excavated after a policy of not disturbing burials had been implemented (Reid and Whittlesey 1999:61). As for architectural data, a detailed comparison between Chodistaas and Grasshopper Spring has yet to be made, and some differences in layout may indicate other, yet unobserved, architectural differences.

We do know that architectural styles consisted of low-walled, informally roofed structures at all of the Pueblo III period sites investigated (Reid 1989:76). Architecture at Grasshopper Spring Pueblo was similar to that at Chodistaas; rooms were large and informally constructed, suggesting a less-sedentary adaptation by their builders. Room excavations, however, documented two different styles of hearth on room floors. Square masonry-lined hearths were relatively frequent at Chodistaas but were absent at Grasshopper Spring (Lowell 1994:Table 1), suggesting that the inhabitants of the two sites had different traditions of hearth construction and cooking.

Painted ceramics at Chodistaas and Grasshopper Spring appear to have been identical, suggesting that both communities had access to the same decorated ceramic types and participated in exchange relationships with the same, or similar, nonlocal groups (Zedeño 1994:101). Other material classes, however, including corrugated ceramics, provide evidence that different social or ethnic groups inhabited the two sites. At Chodistaas, corrugated cooking and storage vessels were manufactured from brown-firing clays, typical of traditional Mogollon ceramics. At Grasshopper Spring, however, the utilitarian ceramics were manufactured from orange-gray firing clays used by potters working in a plateau ceramic tradition (Reid and Montgomery 1998; Reid and Whittlesey 1999:41–42).

In addition to different styles of utilitarian ceramics, the inhabitants of the two sites also used different styles of projectile points, suggesting different hunting traditions. Differences in the size and weight of projectile points recovered from the two sites indicate that the inhabitants of Grasshopper Spring hunted with the atlatl, whereas Chodistaas's inhabitants relied on the bow and arrow (Lorentzen 1993:21–22).

The similarity in painted ceramics between these two sites with otherwise dissimilar material culture implies that exchange networks were established between settlements and different ethnic groups. As a whole these data suggest that a plateau Anasazi population, who had been utilizing the mountains sporadically, settled Grasshopper Spring in the A.D. 1280s. The inhabitants of Chodistaas, however, seem to have been a Mogollon population with strong Anasazi ties and influences who had likewise been utilizing the mountain and plateau environments until intensifying their settlement at Chodistaas in the A.D. 1290s (Reid and Whittlesey 1999:43–44).

Aggregation and Expansion (A.D. 1300–1330)

The beginning of the fourteenth century marked a time of significant change in the Grasshopper region. The small villages characteristic of the late Pueblo

III period were all burned and abandoned, and new, larger communities were formed elsewhere. People who probably already resided at Grasshopper founded the largest of these communities, Grasshopper Pueblo, sometime around A.D. 1300 (Riggs 1994a:75). Wall stubs and ceramics from under the fourteenth century pueblo indicate that the locale was occupied during the Pueblo III period (Reid 1989:83; Riggs 1999b:194). These initial inhabitants built the first 21 rooms in Room Block 2 (Reid and Whittlesey 1999:65–66; Riggs 1994a:75; Chapter 4) atop the wall stubs of the older village. As for the other main pueblo room blocks, Reid and Whittlesey (1999:66) suggest that people from Grasshopper Spring founded Room Block 1 and that people from Chodistaas founded Room Block 3. The Chodistaas group seems to have been more closely linked to the local founders of Room Block 2. The existing ties of the three founding communities to people outside of the region might have served as social corridors along which potential migrants moved into the growing community.

Community organization during founding and early growth reflects a mix of social groups from areas within and outside the Grasshopper region. Architectural and biological evidence suggests that these different groups were localized within spatially discrete room blocks. Growth patterns indicate that newly arriving immigrants built their dwellings near those of former immigrants with whom they shared some social tie (Chapter 4). The social differentiation of the community resulted from at least two, and possibly three, social groups. Bone chemistry analysis by Ezzo et al. (1997) finds three primary sources of population. One group exhibits a local dietary signature, suggesting that they had always lived at the Grasshopper locale. Another group exhibited a chemical signature, suggesting that they came to Grasshopper Pueblo from elsewhere within the Grasshopper region. The third group was found to have bone chemistry indicating origins outside of the Grasshopper region. This third group might have traveled from more than one source location, including areas within the mountain province, the Mogollon Rim area, and the Tonto Basin area to the west (Ezzo et al. 1997:461).

Biological Data. Additional skeletal data and architectural evidence reinforce this interpretation. Analyses of the individuals buried at Grasshopper have established that at least two distinct social groups were in residence (Birkby 1973, 1982; Shipman 1982). The presence of two different biological populations inhabiting the East and West Villages is supported by the analysis of discrete cranial traits from burials on both sides of Salt River Draw (Birkby 1973:100–103). Birkby's analysis of discrete cranial traits is further supported by Shipman's (1982) analysis of discrete traits of the axial skeleton, which found an identical divergence between the East and West Villages (Shipman 1982:180). Individuals buried under Room Block 1 have also been found to exhibit higher frequencies of dietary stress markers (Hinkes 1983:156), suggesting limited access to cultigens, a higher reliance on gathered foods (Ezzo 1993:83), and a high frequency of nonlocal diets (Ezzo et al. 1997:456–457). West Village (Room

Blocks 2 and 3) patterns differ markedly from those seen in Room Block 1, and some evidence suggests that Room Block 3 had at least a partially nonlocal population (Ezzo et al. 1997:457).

Architectural Data and Social Implications. The biological diversity of the population is reinforced by the fact that architectural variability is more extreme in Room Block 3 than in either of the other two main pueblo room blocks. This variability probably results from a mix of local and nonlocal builders (Chapter 5).

Architectural differences between the three room blocks of the main pueblo were expressed in numerous ways, including the proximity to plaza areas, the size and orientation of rooms, the frequency and metric characteristics of wall features, and patterns in the use of local building materials (Chapter 5). In keeping with the evidence for different social groups, the gradual unification of spatially distinct architectural units suggests an increase in community social integration through time. A certain level of village cooperation is also indicated by the maintained sanctity of central communal space (cf. Ferguson et al. 1990:114–115). Village growth around these public areas was rapid and directed toward the delineation of plaza spaces, involving at least two distinct social groups—the inhabitants of Room Blocks 2 and 3. Even during the closure of the large plaza (Plaza 1) and the construction of the great kiva in Plaza 3, which marked the apex of community growth, the three large room blocks remained distinct.

Social organization during the early occupation was probably grounded in kinship-based leadership roles and the ethnic differentiation of the community; later, relationships and ties within the community probably became more complex, as is evident in the formation of sodality groups. Evidence in the mortuary assemblage for membership in different sodality groups (Reid 1989:87; Reid and Whittlesey 1982:700) that crosscut these local and nonlocal groups (Ezzo et al. 1997:457–458) further points to the development of sociopolitical institutions that also provided community leadership. Community concerns such as the closure of the public areas were likely addressed by the leaders of these ethnic groups and by the various sodalities.

The demarcation of public areas indicates a higher level of cooperation than would typically be expected for a community of unrelated immigrants. The sodalities provided a means of crosscutting different social groups and for providing additional levels of decision making. The fluidity of the social environment would have made centralized political control impractical, whereas a communally based heterarchical structure (Crumley 1995; Ezzo 1999) with leadership grounded in different social groups, crosscut by sodalities, better fits the reconstruction of the community as a village of immigrants.

Ceramic Data. Ceramics reflect local and nonlocal manufacture in the Pueblo IV period. Locally and nonlocally produced White Mountain Redware were common. In addition, a crude local copy of Fourmile Polychrome known as Grasshopper Polychrome was also prevalent, but more so in the period from

A.D. 1320 to 1340 (Triadan 1997:3, 78). Gila Polychrome has also been demonstrated to have been manufactured locally and nonlocally (Whittlesey 1974:110). Other imports included shell, obsidian, macaws and parrots, copper bells, and a variety of other nonlocally produced ceramics including Kinishba Polychrome, and some Jeddito wares (Graves et al. 1982:115). These trade items indicate ties to other areas of the Southwest that were probably built along immigrant lines. Because immigrant groups were small households or extended family groups (Duff 1998:44), exchange relationships and migrant sponsors remained on a low organizational level controlled and implemented by family heads.

Dispersion and Abandonment (A.D. 1330–1400)

Given the model of migration and community organization sketched here, the abandonment of the Grasshopper region was predictable. The social networks that were so critical for bringing people into the community were probably also an important force in its eventual abandonment. The establishment and growth of contemporary settlements in other parts of the Southwest (Adams 1998; Creamer 1993; Duff 1998; Kintigh 1985) reinforce the fact that Grasshopper was but one of many large pueblos occupied at this time. Some of these settlements may have been linked through interpersonal ties to Grasshopper and other large villages. Newly formed enclaves in other areas may have been attractive to prospective emigrants whose traditional homelands, to which they once had ties, were now depopulated. This latter fact may have been exacerbated by a 30-year period of below-average precipitation after A.D. 1325 (Reid 1989:89). Communities like Grasshopper may have been nodes in a network of shifting social relationships at a time of significant demographic change tempered by environmental events. At first, some of the population tried to revert to old patterns of land use in the area (Chapter 5). The outliers and satellite communities like Canyon Creek and Red Rock House are our best evidence for a process whereby people attempted to bring more land under cultivation in the face of increasing agricultural shortfalls (Reid and Whittlesey 1999:20). Despite these attempts, the decrease in annual precipitation may have combined with demographic variables, namely newly formed ties to people moving out of the area and into newly established communities elsewhere, to draw people into other communities. People may have felt pressure to leave the area or to adopt a less-sedentary lifestyle, allowing them to (1) meet basic subsistence needs and (2) access social networks and obtain nonlocal exchange items through seasonal movement or emigration.

GRASSHOPPER PUEBLO: A STRONG ANALYTICAL CASE

For several reasons Grasshopper Pueblo's architectural record offers a strong analytic case (Montgomery and Reid 1990:88–89) for evaluating architecturally defined questions: the pueblo's excavation ratio of nearly one in every four rooms, the strength of the cornering data from the majority of the remaining rooms, the spatial and temporal representativeness of the excavated sample, and the incorporation of architectural details from Canyon Creek Pueblo and other well-preserved sites.

Despite architecture's complexity as a material class, the strength of the sample permits a highly confident and detailed description of the founding, growth, and decline of the community. The large size and the spatial and temporal representativeness of the architectural sample ensure that inferences drawn from the data are much more reliable than those drawn from site plans, from test excavations, or from small samples of large sites. Artifacts left on room floors as de facto refuse, almost 700 burials, and extensive extramural excavation largely support these inferences and in almost every instance provide independent verification of the architectural reconstruction detailed in this analysis. These data testify to the importance of using multiple lines of evidence to solve problems about the past, an approach that has always been critical to Grasshopper research (Reid 1998:633–634).

They also underscore the importance of high-quality, representative excavation data. The 30-year field program generated the necessary information to elevate this study above a simple treatment of an archaeological site map. These data allow the exploration of Grasshopper Pueblo's occupation, including the shifting parameters of community organization and the physical remains of various social groups that settled and built the pueblo. From this strong sample Grasshopper Pueblo can be viewed not as a static object, manufactured as an event and frozen in time as an archaeological site plan, but rather as a dynamic village where people came, lived their lives, buried many of their dead, and left a record of architectural change that ultimately came to us as mounds of rubble.

ASSESSING THE EXCAVATED SAMPLE

Exploration of the sample of excavated rooms bears out the following statements: (1) the various means of deriving room area do not introduce bias into the sample; (2) the excavated sample of rooms is representative of the sample of all rooms with respect to room size; (3) the sample from the main pueblo is, for the most part, representative of construction through time; and (4) the spatial sample is an adequate representation of variability among the numerous room blocks. The significance of these results is enhanced by the large size of the excavated sample (23 percent). The various scales at which the data are measured—temporal, spatial, and behavioral—all confirm that the room excavations generated a representative sample of the overall variability encapsulated within Grasshopper Pueblo.

In addition to the 103 excavated rooms,[1] several other portions of the site have been excavated (Figure 2.6). The southern corridor into Plaza 1, an

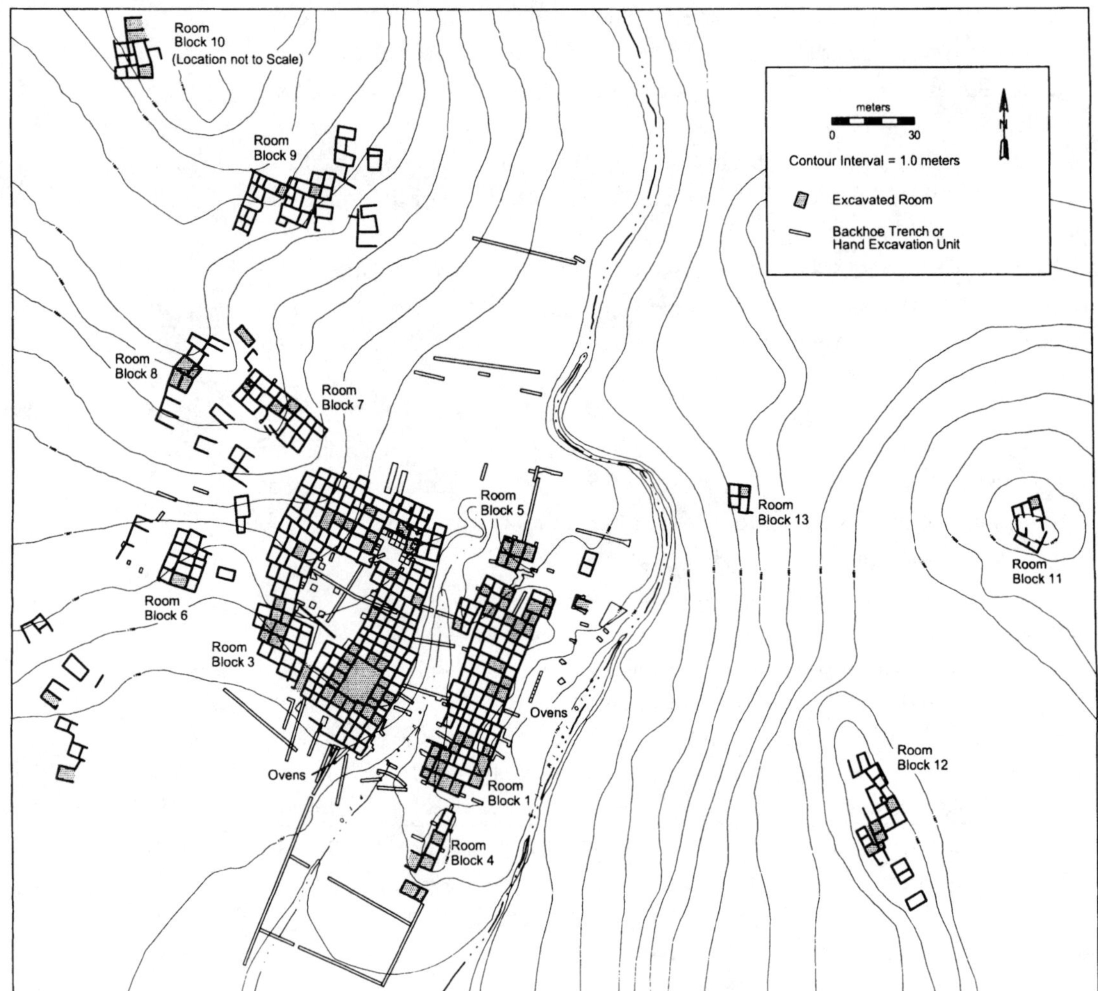

FIGURE 2.6.
Excavations at
Grasshopper Pueblo.

important feature in the construction history of the community, was completely excavated and has been tree-ring dated (Chapter 5). The Great Kiva was also completely excavated, yielding numerous burials recovered from the subfloor excavations, tree-ring dates, and information about ceremonial activities. Extramural areas have also been sampled quite extensively and include over 700 linear meters of backhoe trenching, 80 m^2 of backhoe excavations in the form of broadsides and other nonlinear excavations, 120 m of hand trenches and 205 m^2 of hand excavations (Figure 2.7). These extramural excavations were largely concentrated in the areas around the main pueblo, including Plazas 1 and 2 and the area between Room Blocks 1 and 2 (Figure 2.6). Trenching in the area to the north of the main pueblo recovered evidence of a prehistoric pond, reservoir, or walk-in well (Longacre and Graves 1982:1; Olsen 1982:61), probably like similar features documented in the Point of Pines region (Wheat 1952). Finally, a bank of 13 masonry-lined ovens located to the

FIGURE 2.7. Backhoe trench 73, located north of Room Block 1. Photograph by P. Bion Griffin, 1968. Courtesy of the Arizona State Museum, University of Arizona; neg. no. 18527.

east of Room Block 1 was also excavated as part of the extramural sampling of the site (Thompson and Longacre 1966:261).

Despite the large size of the sample, the 103 excavated rooms are but a portion of the architectural data still buried beneath tons of wall-fall debris. Inferences drawn from the data discussed in the following chapters are strengthened by the size and representativeness of this sample. The cornering project provides a baseline for assessing how these excavated rooms reflect room variability in the unexcavated portions of the rubble mound by generating room-size data for each of the 447 room spaces.

Testing for Bias in Wall Measurement Techniques

Prior to a characterization of the excavated sample, the various types of wall measurements used to obtain room-size data are assessed for bias. Room size was measured from three different sources. Room walls were measured from fully excavated rooms (n = 103), from excavated corners (n = 179), and from surface indications (n = 165) (Table 2.1). Room size varied from 2.96 m^2 to 43.84 m^2, with a mean of 16.27 m^2. A density histogram of room size (Figure 2.8) demonstrates graphically that room-size data are not normally distributed. In fact, a Kolmogorov-Smirnov one-sample test for normality indicates that

TABLE 2.1.
Room Area Confidence Ranks and Distribution of Wall Measurement Types

Rank	n	%	Description
1	103	23	Excavated rooms
2	179	40	Cornered rooms
3	165	37	Rooms measured from surface indications

they deviate significantly from a normal distribution ($n = 447$, maximum difference = 0.998, $p = 0.000$). Similar tests run on other ratio scale variables (e.g., wall height) produced similar results. Because the architectural data are not normally distributed, nonparametric statistics were relied on for all analyses.

To assess bias in room measurement types, a Kruskal-Wallis one-way analysis of variance was first run on the entire population of rooms, grouped by the three measurement types.[2] Results do not allow rejection of the null hypothesis that the three groups are drawn from the same population (0.05 significance level), suggesting that there is no systematic bias introduced by measurement type when the entire site is viewed as a whole (Table 2.2).

The main pueblo (Room Blocks 1, 2, and 3) was separated from the outliers, and a Kruskal-Wallis test was run on the main pueblo and on the outliers to test the reliability of different measurement types in these two groups of rooms. Tests on the main pueblo and the outliers echo the tests run on the entire site and do not allow rejection of the null hypothesis (0.05 significance level), suggesting that each measurement type reflects the same continuous population (Table 2.2).

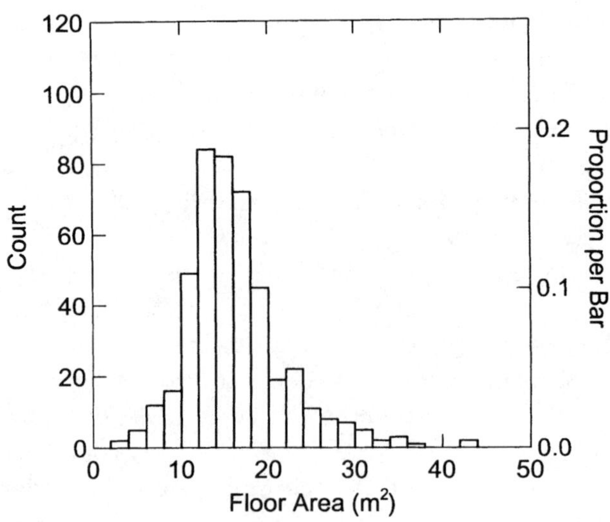

FIGURE 2.8.
Frequency histogram of room floor area.

TABLE 2.2.
Kruskal-Wallis Tests for Room Area Grouped by Measurement Type

	n	Kruskal-Wallis Statistic	Probability
All rooms	447	1.56	0.46
Main pueblo	287	3.61	0.16
Outliers	160	0.30	0.86

Testing the Excavated Sample's Representativeness

The types of wall measurement do not introduce bias into the room-size sample. This section uses these measurements to address the representativeness of the excavated room sample. Room area is measured for every room and can be used as a gauge of other variables. In other words, if it can be demonstrated that the excavated sample accurately reflects room size, then it can be argued that the sample is representative of other room parameters and, by extension, the activities that took place prehistorically (Reid and Whittlesey 1982:690).

To determine if the excavated sample from each of these areas is representative of room size, a series of Mann-Whitney tests (Blalock 1972:255–262) were run on various subgroups. The Mann-Whitney test is the nonparametric equivalent of the two-sample t-test and tests the null hypothesis that two independently drawn samples come from the same population (Blalock 1972:255–260). Again, the 0.05 significance level was used to assess whether test values exceeded critical limits. These tests of sample representativeness build on the work of Reid and Whittlesey (1982:690), who used t-tests and F-tests to obtain results identical to those described below.

To characterize the sample adequately, the excavated rooms from a given area (site, main pueblo, or outliers) were compared to a randomly drawn sample (sampling with replacement) from that area. Excavated rooms from each area were compared to five different randomly drawn samples to address variability within each area. For the entire site Table 2.3 indicates that in five runs the null hypothesis that excavated rooms reflect the same population cannot be rejected at a 0.05 significance level. This result suggests that the excavated rooms, when viewed as a whole, are representative of variability in room size.

Tests focusing on only the core room blocks (Room Blocks 1, 2, 3, 5, and 7) yield similar results (Table 2.4), as do tests of the individual room blocks of the main pueblo (Room Blocks 1, 2, and 3; Table 2.5). Tables 2.4 and 2.5 indicate that there are no biases in the size of the excavated rooms within the population of core room blocks or within each of the three main room blocks. Thus, patterns in room size, and by extension in other architectural variables, are not biased by the excavated sample.

Finally, the null hypothesis cannot be rejected for excavated rooms in the outliers (Room Blocks 4, 6, 8, 9, 10, 11, 12, and 13), suggesting, once again, that

TABLE 2.3.
Mann-Whitney Tests Comparing Excavated Room Size to a Randomly Drawn Sample of Rooms from the Entire Site

Run	Sample Group	Count (*n*)	Mean	*SD*	Rank Sum	*U* Statistic	Probability
1	Excavated	103	16.47	5.12	11148.00	5792.00	0.254
	Random	103	15.74	5.42	10173.00	—	—
2	Excavated	103	16.47	5.12	11287.50	5931.50	0.143
	Random	103	16.16	7.37	10033.50	—	—
3	Excavated	103	16.47	5.12	10843.00	5487.00	0.670
	Random	103	16.51	4.90	10478.00	—	—
4	Excavated	103	16.47	5.12	10829.00	5473.00	0.694
	Random	103	16.58	5.67	10492.00	—	—
5	Excavated	103	16.47	5.12	11213.50	5857.50	0.196
	Random	103	15.92	5.87	10107.50	—	—

TABLE 2.4.
Mann-Whitney Tests Comparing Excavated Room Size to a Randomly Drawn Sample of Rooms from the Core Room Blocks

Run	Sample Group	Count (*n*)	Mean	*SD*	Rank Sum	*U* Statistic	Probability
1	Excavated	77	16.04	4.35	6221.50	3218.50	0.359
	Random	77	15.63	4.15	5713.50	—	—
2	Excavated	77	16.04	4.35	6049.50	3046.50	0.767
	Random	77	16.14	4.39	5885.50	—	—
3	Excavated	77	16.04	4.35	6189.50	3186.50	0.422
	Random	77	15.59	3.80	5745.50	—	—
4	Excavated	77	16.04	4.35	6371.00	3368.00	0.145
	Random	77	15.11	3.93	5564.00	—	—
5	Excavated	77	16.04	4.35	6455.50	3452.50	0.078
	Random	77	14.99	4.84	5479.50	—	—

TABLE 2.5.
Mann-Whitney Tests Comparing Excavated Room Size to a Randomly Drawn Sample of Rooms from the Main Pueblo

Run	Sample Group	Count (*n*)	Mean	*SD*	Rank Sum	*U* Statistic	Probability
RB1–1	Excavated	32	16.16	4.15	1099.00	571.00	0.428
	Random	32	14.92	3.14	981.00	—	—
RB1–2	Excavated	32	16.16	4.15	1058.50	530.50	0.804
	Random	32	15.89	4.05	1021.50	—	—
RB1–3	Excavated	32	16.16	4.15	1096.50	568.50	0.448
	Random	32	15.32	2.78	983.50	—	—
RB2–1	Excavated	20	14.19	3.45	387.50	177.50	0.543
	Random	20	15.45	5.31	432.50	—	—
RB2–2	Excavated	20	14.19	3.45	421.50	211.50	0.756
	Random	20	13.55	2.73	398.50	—	—
RB2–3	Excavated	20	14.19	3.45	421.00	211.00	0.766
	Random	20	14.08	5.19	399.00	—	—
RB3–1	Excavated	16	18.31	3.85	281.00	145.00	0.522
	Random	16	17.44	3.98	247.00	—	—
RB3–2	Excavated	16	18.31	3.85	295.50	159.50	0.235
	Random	16	16.42	5.23	232.50	—	—
RB3–3	Excavated	16	18.31	3.85	282.50	146.50	0.486
	Random	16	17.19	3.93	245.50	—	—

TABLE 2.6.
Mann-Whitney Tests Comparing Excavated Room Size to a Randomly Drawn Sample of Rooms from the Outliers

Run	Sample Group	Count (n)	Mean	*SD*	Rank Sum	U Statistic	Probability
1	Excavated	26	17.75	6.88	715.50	364.50	0.628
	Random	26	16.48	6.77	622.50	—	—
2	Excavated	26	17.75	6.88	733.00	382.00	0.421
	Random	26	16.18	8.25	645.50	—	—
3	Excavated	26	17.75	6.88	735.50	384.00	0.400
	Random	26	17.62	9.78	643.00	—	—
4	Excavated	26	17.75	6.88	685.50	334.50	0.949
	Random	26	18.58	8.76	692.50	—	—
5	Excavated	26	17.75	6.88	694.50	343.50	0.920
	Random	26	17.30	7.41	683.50	—	—

the excavated rooms are representative of the population of rooms (Table 2.6). No tests of intraroom-block variability were attempted for the outliers because of a tendency toward small sample sizes.

Temporal and Spatial Representativeness of the Excavated Sample

Having demonstrated that the excavated sample of rooms is an adequate representation of intrasite variability, I now address the spatial and temporal representativeness of the sample. First, an assessment of the sample's temporal representativeness can be made using the construction sequence as a rough measure of time (Chapter 4). Table 2.7 shows the temporal sampling of the main pueblo, where 68 (24 percent) of the 287 rooms were excavated. The

TABLE 2.7.
Excavated Rooms from the Main Pueblo by Construction Phase

Construction Phase (CP)	Rooms in CP	Excavated Rooms	Percentage of All Rooms Excavated	CP Sample Size (%)
1	63	15	22.06	23.81
2	33	6	8.82	18.18
3	35	6	8.82	17.14
4	33	8	11.76	24.24
5	47	13	19.12	27.66
6	23	6	8.82	26.09
7	16	6	8.82	37.50
8	9	3	4.41	33.33
9	9	2	2.94	22.22
10	6	0	0.00	0.00
11	4	1	1.47	25.00
12	4	1	1.47	25.00
13	4	1	1.47	25.00
14	1	0	0.00	0.00
Totals	287	68	100.00	23.69

TABLE 2.8.
Excavated Rooms by Room Block

Room Block (RB)	Rooms in Room Block	Excavated Rooms in RB	Percentage of All Rooms Excavated	Room Block Sample Size (%)
0	37	6	5.83	16.22
1	94	32	31.07	34.04
2	92	20	19.42	21.74
3	101	16	15.53	15.84
4	6	3	2.91	50.00
5	6	6	5.83	100.00
6	13	1	0.97	7.69
7	21	3	2.91	14.29
8	10	4	3.88	40.00
9	26	2	1.94	7.69
10	11	3	2.91	27.27
11	9	1	0.97	11.11
12	17	5	4.85	29.41
13	4	1	0.97	25.00
Totals	447	103	100.00	23.04

number of rooms per construction phase decreases through time (Chapter 4). Thus, a representative sample of earlier construction phases requires the excavation of more rooms in earlier construction phases than in later ones.

Of the 68 excavated rooms, 48 come from construction phases 1 through 5. In fact, as Table 2.7 demonstrates, most of the construction phases in the main pueblo are adequately sampled (i.e., greater than 20 percent). Although construction phases 10 and 14 ($n = 7$) were not sampled at all, and construction phases 2 and 3 yielded sample sizes under 20 percent, in general, when viewed from the perspective of relative time, the sample looks to be generally representative of temporal variability in construction. Whether the excavated sample of all rooms is temporally representative is partially determined by the extent of sampling in the later outliers. Thus, on a community scale the temporal sample is partially influenced by the spatial sample.

The 103 excavated rooms are well distributed among the various room blocks. This represents a 23 percent sample of rooms from the entire site and includes excavations in all of the 13 defined room blocks and several of the unaffiliated outlier rooms (Table 2.8). As Table 2.8 demonstrates, sample size within individual room blocks varies from 8 percent in Room Blocks 6 and 9 to 100 percent in Room Block 5. Of the three room blocks of the main pueblo, Room Block 1 is most thoroughly sampled (34 percent), whereas Room Block 3 is the least well sampled (16 percent). In all, 8 of the 14 spatial divisions listed in Table 2.8 yield an excavated room sample of greater than 20 percent, and all but two room blocks (Room Blocks 6 and 9) have a sample size of 10 percent or greater.

FIGURE 2.9. Excavation in a cluster of rooms in Room Block 3. Room 218 is in the foreground, and Rooms 215 and 210 are beyond. Photograph by Susan E. Luebbermann, 1972. Courtesy of the Arizona State Museum, University of Arizona; neg. no. 31606.

One limitation of the excavation data is a tendency for spatial clustering of excavated rooms (Figure 2.6). This is especially apparent in Room Block 2, where the bulk of the sample is concentrated around the great kiva. Room Block 1 also exhibits spatial clustering of excavated rooms with the north and south ends being well represented. Room Block 3 has perhaps the most dispersed coverage, although excavations were biased toward clusters of earlier rooms (Figure 2.9). This clustering results largely from attempts to target the founding of the community (Longacre and Reid 1974:22; Reid and Shimada 1982:12–13) and from efforts to delineate social groups and households in the main pueblo (Ciolek-Torrello 1978; Rock 1974). Despite this clustering in excavation coverage, the assemblage of excavated rooms appears to be representative of room construction and use activities; and if the outliers are considered, it adequately represents the temporal depth of the occupation.

CONCLUSION

The sample of excavated rooms from Grasshopper Pueblo is representative of room-size variability and is spatially representative. All of the outliers were sampled, and all but two of the construction phases in the main pueblo produced excavated rooms. In addition to the large representative sample of excavated rooms from Grasshopper Pueblo, 30 years of fieldwork and the impressive compendium of Grasshopper literature have revealed much about human behavior in the Grasshopper region from the mid-1200s until abandonment by A.D. 1400. Two Pueblo III period sites, Grasshopper Spring and Chodistaas, were intensively excavated and provide a reliable picture of life in the Grasshopper region just before people began to settle there in large numbers beginning around A.D. 1300. Data from these two communities suggest that both Anasazi and Mogollon groups, who participated in farther-reaching exchange relationships that extended to the Colorado Plateau and perhaps to other areas, utilized the Grasshopper region sporadically.

Just before A.D. 1300 these groups began to intensify their use of the Grasshopper region. By A.D. 1300, or slightly thereafter, their villages had been abandoned and burned, and the former occupants of Grasshopper Spring and Chodistaas were residing at Grasshopper Pueblo along with people who had been living there prior to A.D. 1300. In the fourteenth century the exchange relationships of these people introduced nonlocal items to Grasshopper and served to bring new people into the community. The immigrants and locals at Grasshopper can be identified because of their biological characteristics, because they continued to manufacture ceramics in traditional ways, and because they left subtle yet indelible signatures through their construction of walls.

At the other end of the occupation, two well-preserved and well-dated cliff dwellings provide a model for Grasshopper regional settlement as people began to disperse into outlier room blocks and satellite communities prior to abandonment of the region. These sites suggest that people may have been attempting to compensate for environmental shortfalls by bringing more land under cultivation. The architecture of the latter part of the occupation is reminiscent of that of the preceding Pueblo III period. It has a more impermanent appearance and suggests a higher level of mobility than that of the early-fourteenth-century occupation of Grasshopper Pueblo.

3

Architectural Description and Analysis

> That is how architecture is meant to be known. As the material theater of human activity, its truth is in its use.
>
> —Spiro Kostof, *A History of Architecture*

THE DESCRIPTION AND ANALYSIS OF THE ARCHITECTURAL DATA PROVIDED here serves as a compendium of the technical choices (Lemonnier 1986) made by the builders of Grasshopper. More than this, however, these data also demonstrate the complex nature of the archaeology of pueblo architecture. For example, an extended discussion of blocked doorways highlights issues of equifinality for one class of architectural information and questions the assumption that doors simply connect two interior spaces, which is logical but may be unfounded in some cases. The issue of estimating second-story rooms, even in excavated spaces, is also discussed. The nature of wall collapse and room construction, combined with variables such as sedimentation rates, trash disposal rates, and underlying topography, complicates what seems to be a relatively straightforward relationship between standing wall height and the number of stories. This analysis demonstrates that assessing the number of stories in a ruined pueblo is conjectural at best unless excavation data are available.

Another component of this descriptive section is a series of predictions about architectural forms using data from other ruined and modern pueblos. Incorporation of these data helps to fill gaps in the architectural record and allows a more complete reconstruction of the architecture of Grasshopper Pueblo.

This chapter serves two purposes: to describe the architectural data and to generate a set of low-level inferences relating to the activities of Grasshopper's builders. These activities include, for example, the use of doorways, roof-construction techniques, and the estimation of the number of two-story rooms. To accomplish this second goal, it is necessary to refer to other excavated and better-preserved sites in the Southwest to obtain those elements of construction not preserved at Grasshopper. As mentioned in Chapter 2, Canyon Creek Pueblo has long served as an analogue. Because of its proximity and its close temporal relationship to Grasshopper, it is thought to be the best single example of the types of construction data that did not survive the passage of time at Grasshopper and is drawn on extensively for comparative purposes. Drawing comparisons between the architectural details preserved at both sites reinforces the strength of Canyon Creek as an architectural analogue.

SITE LAYOUT

Grasshopper conforms to Reed's "plaza-multiple court" layout type (Reed 1956:13). It had an inward or central focus rather than the unidirectional orientation characteristic of traditional Anasazi pueblo layouts, where storage rooms were at the back of the pueblo, habitation rooms were in front of these, and kivas were located in front of the habitation rooms. The room blocks of the West Village, located on the west side of Salt River Draw, enclosed two plazas and a great kiva plaza. Plazas 1 and 2 were fully enclosed between Room Blocks 2 and 3 and were entered prehistorically through a long roofed corridor to the south of Plaza 1 and a shorter roofed corridor to the east of Plaza 2 (Longacre and Reid 1974:12). The two plazas were connected by a narrow passage between Room Blocks 2 and 3. Plaza 3 was enclosed entirely within Room Block 2 and was converted into the Great Kiva around A.D. 1330 (Chapter 4). Room Block 1, the third large room block of the main pueblo, was constructed entirely on the east side of Salt River Draw and constitutes the East Village. Finally, Room Blocks 5 and 7 completed the site core. Located directly north of Room Block 1, Room Block 5 appears to have been closely associated with the East Village. Room Block 7 was probably part of the West village and may have been attached to Room Block 3, the evidence for which may have been obliterated by a modern road that runs between the two room blocks.

The remainder of Grasshopper Pueblo consisted of eight formal room blocks and 20 isolated rooms and small masonry units scattered among them. Most of these outliers are situated on the hill slopes to the west and northwest and to the south and east of the main pueblo (Figure 2.4). In general, the outliers were constructed of low masonry walls with brush or *jacal* superstructures; the five core room blocks were composed of rooms with full-standing one- and two-story masonry walls. No three-story rooms existed at Grasshopper, and two-story rooms were restricted to the three room blocks of the main pueblo (Longacre and Graves 1982:1; Longacre and Reid 1974:12; Reid 1989:83).

For the most part rooms were larger and less substantial with increased distance from the core of the site (Table A.2). This pattern was likely a result of the gradual abandonment of the area and changing commitment to agriculture (Welch 1996:167), accompanied by more informal, generalized patterns of room use reflected in a more informal architectural style (Reid and Whittlesey 1982:696). Hence, habitation spaces served more general needs and were occupied on a seasonal or part-time basis (Reid 1989:85). Other notable characteristics of site layout include the frequency of three-walled rooms open to the east on the west side of Salt Draw and their absence to the east side of the draw, the tendency to locate outliers on hill slopes and hilltops, and the overall dispersed appearance created by the location of later outliers compared to the more compact site core.

WALL CONSTRUCTION

Before proceeding, a methodological note concerning the nature of pueblo walls and the way they were recorded is in order. As obvious as it sounds, it must be stated that walls define rooms, and in pueblo architecture, as in other architectural traditions, the bounding of room spaces is achieved by erecting walls. On a basic level a wall is itself a feature. As a feature it is a nonportable aggregate of disparate elements built for a specific purpose. Unlike most archaeological features, a wall is not unique to an individual space but defines one or more rooms or exterior spaces. One face of a given wall was recorded during excavation of one room, the other face during excavation of an adjacent room. In addition to this, the Cornering Project provided metric data for all of Grasshopper's 447 rooms on a wall-face by wall-face basis. As a result most walls were counted twice in the construction and manipulation of the database.

There is no simple solution for the problems this creates in the database. A wall database that assigns feature numbers to each wall could be constructed. The problem then becomes linking the walls to their related rooms and/or exterior spaces. This is a daunting task in a site of Grasshopper's size, where thousands of walls were constructed to demarcate room spaces. Assigning feature numbers to individual walls is further complicated by the fact that many rooms were added to existing rooms by appending wall segments of varying length to existing walls. For example, two or more rooms could share a single, continuously bonded wall segment, or they could be added as individual units. The complexity of wall additions makes a feature-based approach unwieldy and was not used in this analysis. As a partial solution each wall face was assigned its own number (corresponding to its associated room) so that walls could be linked to individual rooms more easily for analysis (cf. Morris 1986:27).

Wall Foundations and Leveling

Wall foundations typically consisted of a course of larger stones, probably set into a trench or on leveled soil (Figure 3.1). Foundation courses and leveling techniques were often difficult to identify during excavation because the high clay content of the soil caused the walls to settle and has obscured evidence of foundation trench excavation. Another problem is related to community burial practices.

Many rooms in the main pueblo were constructed over old burial areas, resulting, in some instances, in the construction of walls on top of burial pits.

FIGURE 3.1. South wall of Room 35, in RoomBlock 1, showing two subfloor excavation units with foundation course of larger stones visible. Wall is a Type 1 wall. Photograph by Susan E. Luebbermann, 1971. Courtesy of the Arizona State Museum, University of Arizona; neg. no. 31126.

As burials settled under the weight of walls, the walls became more prone to collapse. In addition, many burials were interred in log cribs covered with earth (Whittlesey 1978:271). As the wooden material in the grave decayed, the burial pit slumped, further exacerbating wall collapse over these types of burials.

Walls were built on top of alluvium, trash, or bedrock, with sporadic evidence (i.e., larger stones) of formalized foundations. In certain areas of the site, like the northern end of Room Block 1, rapid alluviation from runoff into Salt River Draw necessitated construction on alluvial soils. In contrast, much of Room Block 3's core was constructed on or just above the underlying bedrock. Similar construction on or near the bedrock was also evident in many of the outlying room blocks on the hill slopes surrounding the site core. In some cases trash fill was used to level surfaces with excessive slopes, and the outliers, often constructed on hill slopes, typically required this type of construction. For example, the floor of Room 414 in Room Block 10, added to the north of existing architecture, was constructed on top of approximately 0.50 m of imported fill. This trash fill was used to level the surface between the existing rooms downhill and an outcrop of bedrock uphill to the north. Overall, most rooms were built on relatively level surfaces, although other types of unidentified leveling strategies may have been employed.

Room 39 in Room Block 1 provides a good example of two different types of wall foundations (Figure 3.2). The east wall of the room was constructed earlier, as part of Room 40, and its foundation consisted of three courses of large squarish stones. The remaining walls of Room 39, all bonded together,

FIGURE 3.2. South wall of Room 39 in Room Block 1, showing different depth of walls and trash buildup under south wall. Photograph by Susan E. Luebbermann, 1970. Courtesy of the Arizona State Museum, University of Arizona; neg. no. 27409.

represent a different foundation technique. These walls were constructed some 0.30 m above the base of the west wall, and small chinking stones were used as a foundation to level the ground prior to construction. This room is representative of the diversity of wall foundation practices that form a continuum from formal construction techniques to the seemingly expedient wall construction technology exemplified by Room 39's enclosing walls.

One possible leveling feature has been documented in Room 45 in Room Block 1. A "wall-like" alignment of stones running from the east wall to the room's center was found on the floor of the room. This wall followed the natural slope of the underlying, preroom trash deposit. The room's excavators hypothesized that this feature was used to level the floor behind it, much like a check dam. This seems a dubious interpretation, however, given the evidence found in other rooms that floors were leveled with imported fill. If, however, the room was flooded by occasional runoff, the wall may have served to divert water from the room's hearth.

The addition of new rooms to existing architecture, the accumulation of debris, and the remodeling of floor surfaces in long occupied rooms in the main pueblo sometimes created the illusion of subfloor wall foundations. In many cases one or two room walls extended to a great depth below the floor surface, which was not uncommon in the main pueblo. For example, the south wall of Room 43 in the north end of Room Block 1 extended to a depth of more than a meter below the floor surface; the remaining walls extended to only about 0.30 m below the floor. This particular room is located in an area where alluviation was a problem and where soil probably accumulated more rapidly than in other parts of the site. The reason for the variation in wall-base depth is that the room was added to a core construction unit to the south, around which soil and trash had accumulated to a depth of approximately 0.70 m before the construction of Room 43.

Masonry

Walls were largely constructed with a wet-laid masonry technique and a clay-based mortar. Wall stones were either well dressed or partially shaped on at least one edge to provide a straight line for wall construction. The local availability of tabular limestone and sandstone allowed builders to prepare stones for construction with little effort.

In a study of the geological composition of walls from excavated rooms, Scarborough and Shimada (1974) found that Grasshopper's walls were constructed of limestone and sandstone from four sources in the proximity of the pueblo. The spatial distribution of each type of raw material was assessed throughout the excavated rooms. Scarborough and Shimada noted that wall rocks usually came from the closest possible sources and that, in general, people selected stones based on a least effort criterion (Scarborough and Shimada 1974:58–59). Scarborough and Shimada's (1974:Figure 2) four quarry areas included Area 1 limestones, which occur to the south of the site and were less frequently used than any other type of stone, constituting only 4 percent of the sample (Scarborough and Shimada 1974:Table 2). Area 2 sandstones occur in a thin ribbon running from the northeast to the southwest through the middle of the site and were used fairly extensively (22 percent of the sample) by the builders of Room Blocks 1, 2, 6, and 7. Area 3 limestones are the closest source and were the most commonly used construction stone, making up 46 percent of the sample (Scarborough and Shimada 1974:Table 2). Finally, Area 4 sandstones, the most distant source of wall rocks, are located approximately one mile to the northeast of the site.

Area 4 sandstones made up 28 percent of the sample, indicating that they may have been prized for their higher quality (Scarborough and Shimada 1974:62). It is also noteworthy that in Room Block 2, which made use of all four quarry areas, 42 percent of the wall rock samples came from Area 4. In contrast, the builders of Room Block 1 only used Area 4 rocks in 10 percent of the sample taken by Scarborough and Shimada. Thus, it appears that the builders of Room Block 2 (identified as locals) may have had preferential access to the best quality building stones. The pattern in these data supports a substantial body of architectural evidence suggesting that inhabitants of the various room blocks used different construction techniques (Chapter 5).

Wall face data. The masonry types defined at Grasshopper differ from the extravagant masonry styles at Chaco Canyon (Hawley 1938; Judd 1927, 1964; Lekson 1984:17) and other sites in the Southwest (Clark 2001) for which distinct masonry types are either intentional expressions of identity or symbol-

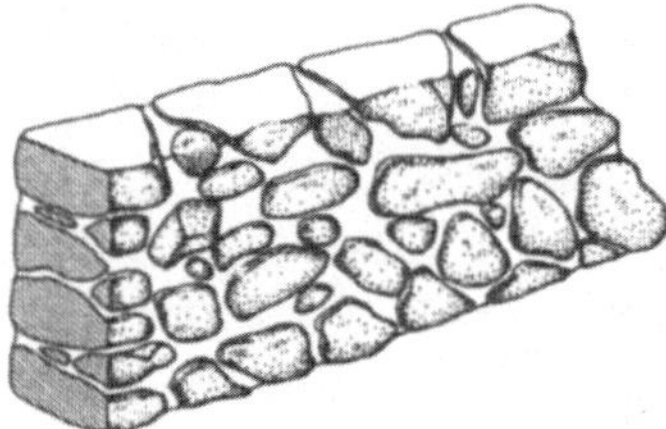

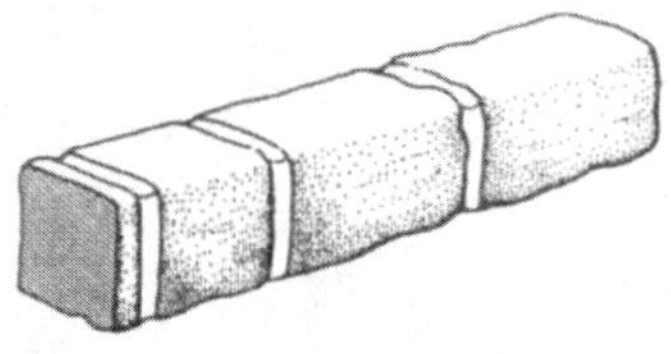

FIGURE 3.3.
Wall face types, after Scarborough and Shimada 1974:Figure 1.

ism or are temporal indicators. Scarborough and Shimada (1974:Figure 1) note four types of masonry construction (Figure 3.3). These masonry types were all variations of a single style and reflect the orientation of the wall with respect to a room's interior or exterior. They are described as follows:

> The Type I wall face has been simplistically described as a smooth-faced, chinked wall. Some of the formal attributes outlined for the Type I wall face include (1) the consistent use of shaped stones and horizontal chinking material between every course and (2) lines of direction that run along each course of the wall and do not intersect. A Type II wall face is similar to a Type I wall face except that the former does not make consistent use of chinking material. Type III has been called a rough-faced wall and essentially constitutes the opposite (face) of the Type I. The definition of a Type IV wall face is currently undergoing revision. This type is rarely known to occur. It characteristically exhibits only one or possibly a few courses of stones that have a length/width ratio of less than two [Scarborough and Shimada 1974:50].

Following Metzger et al. (1989), Scarborough and Shimada's Type I walls would be referred to as "coursed-patterned," Type II walls would be considered "fully coursed," and Type III walls would be called "uncoursed" (Figures 3.4 and 3.5; Metzger et al. 1989:Figure 6). All of the walls at Grasshopper can be described as single-coursed, double-coursed, or compound when viewed in cross section (cf. Metzger et al. 1989:Figure 5).

FIGURE 3.4. North wall of Room 218 in Room Block 3, showing the abutment of a Type 2 wall to a Type 1 wall. Photograph by Susan E. Luebbermann, 1972. Courtesy of the Arizona State Museum, University of Arizona; neg. no. 31373.

FIGURE 3.5. South wall of Room 210 in Room Block 3, showing a typical example of a Type 3 wall and a blocked doorway. Photograph by Susan E. Luebbermann, 1972. Courtesy of the Arizona State Museum, University of Arizona; neg. no. 31685.

At Canyon Creek Pueblo Haury (1934) documented two masonry styles identical to those at Grasshopper. The predominant style at Canyon Creek, consisting of tabular sandstone set in courses without chinking (Haury 1934:32), corresponds to Grasshopper Type II masonry. The second type, also constructed of tabular sandstone but more regularly coursed with extensive use of chinking spalls between horizontal and, less frequently, vertical masonry courses (Haury 1934:34), corresponds to Type I masonry at Grasshopper. The similarities in wall-construction styles between Canyon Creek Pueblo and Grasshopper further support the idea that the two sites were part of the same overall group of builders.

No rubble core walls have been noted at Grasshopper and most walls conform to what Metzger et al. (1989:Figure 5) refer to as different types of flagged masonry. The wall face types described by Scarborough and Shimada (1974) are essentially the two sides of a simple flagged wall. The front is a smooth face (Type 1 or 2) that was once an exterior room wall, and the back, the flagged face of the same wall, is an interior (Type 3) wall face (Figure 3.3). These three wall face types occurred in all of the room blocks. Type 4 walls were restricted entirely to the low-walled outliers and were typically only one or two courses high. These walls probably represent an expedient foundation for a brush/*jacal* room.

One of the many goals of the Growth Project was to collect wall face information from the cornered rooms (Chapter 4). The location of interior and exterior wall faces was critical to the identification of construction units (Reid and Shimada 1982:14). Rinaldo (1964:49), in his analysis of the architecture of Carter Ranch Pueblo, was one of the first to note that exterior wall faces were smoother than interior wall faces because walls were laid out and constructed from the outside of the room rather than the inside. Thus, the exterior face was smooth by virtue of its role as a plumb line in wall construction (also Rohn 1971:45), and a smooth-faced wall found within a room indicates that the enclosed space was once exterior to the wall bearing the smooth face, although perhaps only briefly. Early work with wall faces in the main pueblo confirmed that, in keeping with Rinaldo's findings, walls exterior to rooms tended to be smooth, whereas interior room walls were rough (Figures 3.6 and 3.7). Later work in the outliers used Scarborough and Shimada's typology and identified the four wall face types. Wall face data are available for all of the room blocks, although not all of the room blocks were fully documented, partly because the low height of the outlier walls made identification of the masonry type difficult. The collection of this information, in conjunction with bond-abut data, became crucial in building a construction sequence for the community (Chapter 4).

Bond-abut data. The identification of corner relationships between individual walls is also crucial to the demarcation of construction units and an understanding of community growth (Figure 3.8). Figures 3.9 and 3.10 depict the

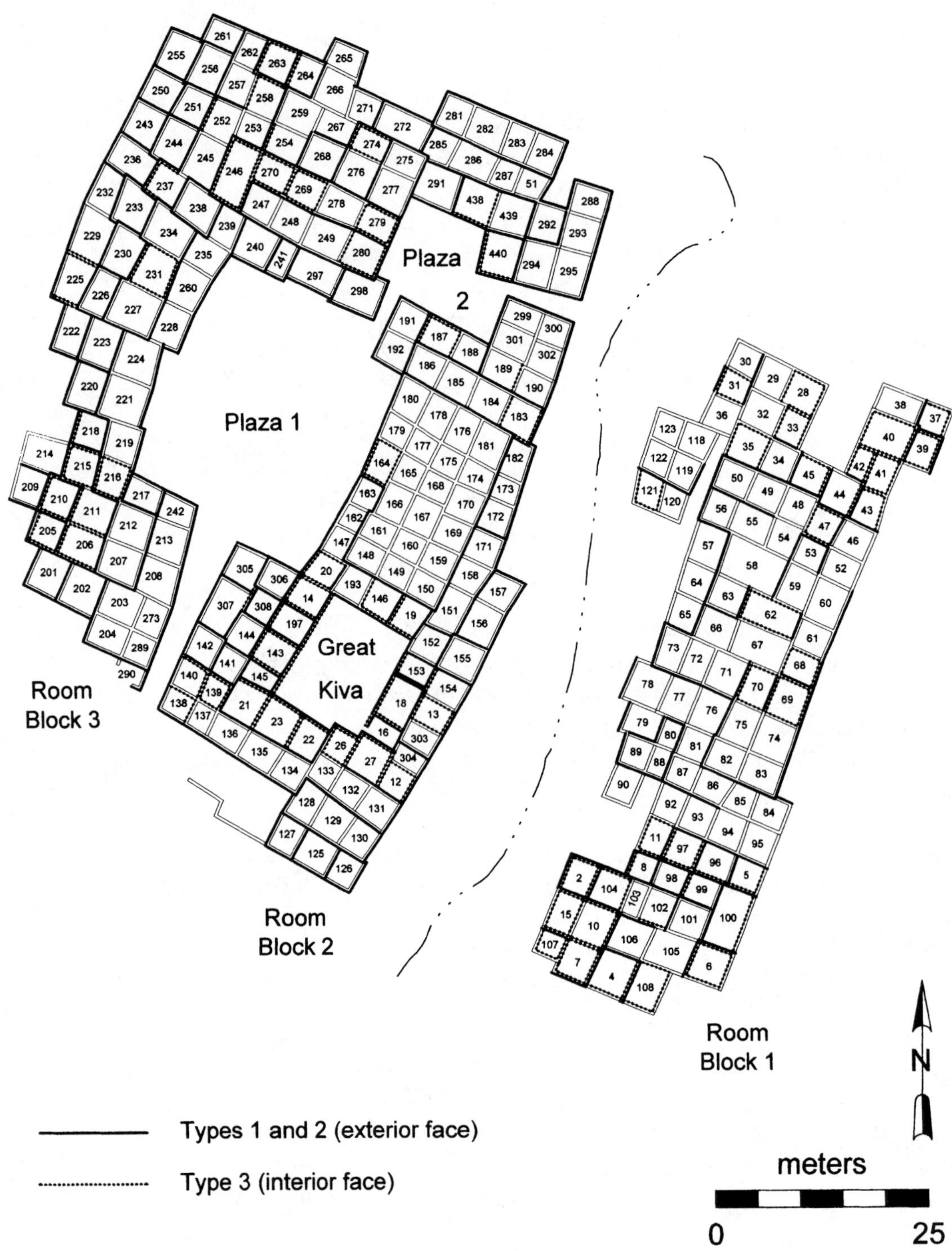

FIGURE 3.6.
Wall faces in the main pueblo.

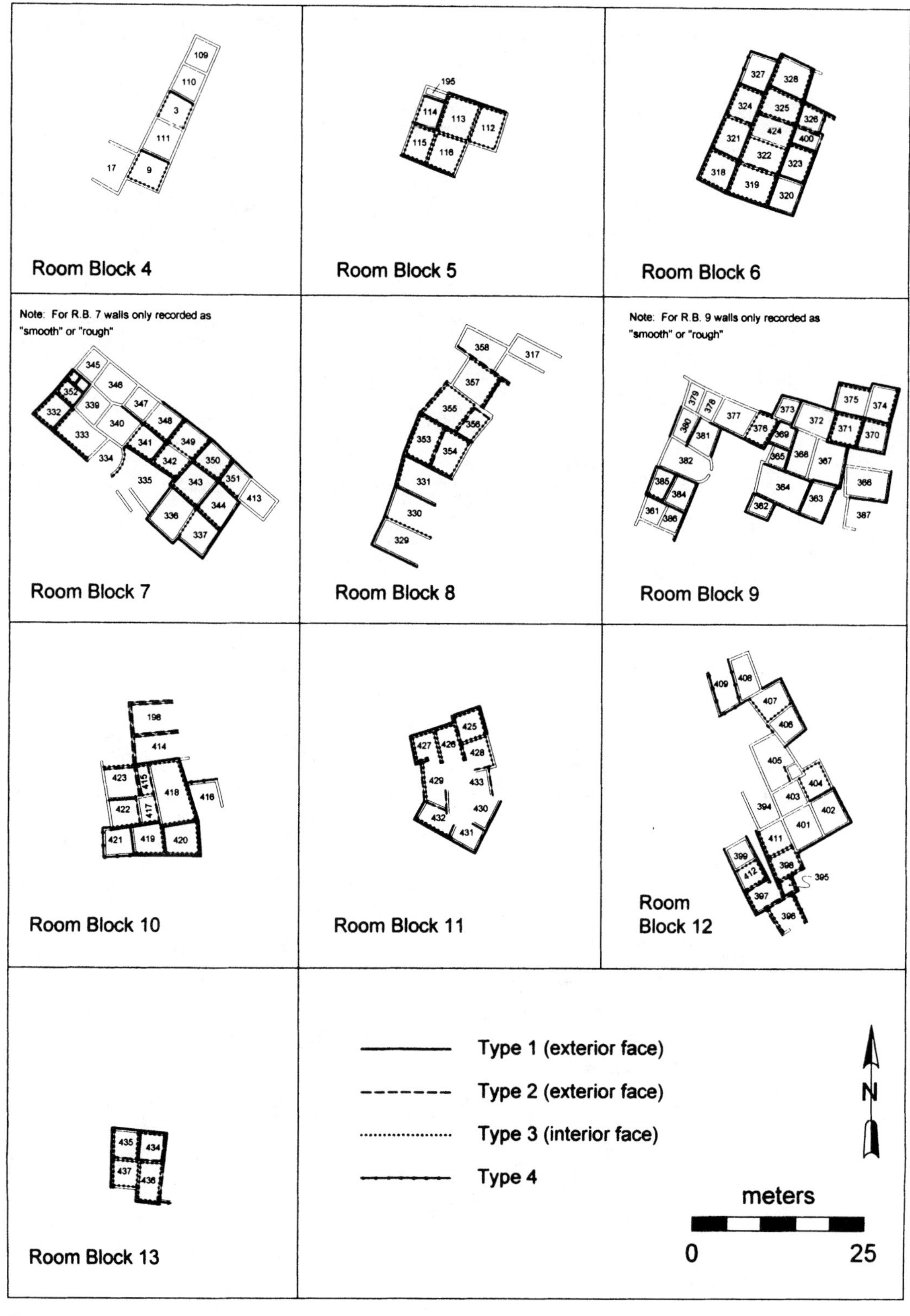

FIGURE 3.7.
Wall faces in the outliers.

FIGURE 3.8. West wall of Room 44 in Room Block 1, showing the abutment of two Type 1 walls, a blocked doorway, and excavations in Room 45 beyond. Photograph by Susan E. Luebbermann, 1971. Courtesy of the Arizona State Museum, University of Arizona; neg. no. 31129.

relationships derived from the Cornering Project and from room excavation records. Once again, the confidence in the higher walls of the site core, especially the main pueblo, make corner assessments from these rooms more reliable than those from the outliers, where the low walls often made corner relationships difficult to ascertain. The bond-abut and wall face data and their roles in building a construction sequence are discussed in more detail in Chapter 4.

Wall types and the division of space. As an outgrowth of the Cornering and Growth Projects, this analysis divides walls into two classes, bounding walls and partition walls, based on how they delimit space. A bounding wall is any wall that turns exterior space into interior space. For example, a new room constructed in isolation from any other architecture is said to consist of four bounding walls. Partition walls subdivide existing interior space by converting an interior space into two or more interior spaces. Although wall face and corner relationships form the basis for defining wall types, they are not synonymous with these categories. For example, partition walls were often bonded to exterior bounding walls and can be either smooth or rough faced. In addition, two or more bounding walls that define an interior space can either be bonded or abutted to one another. In general, bounding walls most often have rough interior faces and smooth, well-dressed exterior faces. In contrast, partition walls often have two rough faces, as if stacked in an expedient manner, although typical smooth exterior/rough interior walls exist, as do a few walls with two smooth faces.

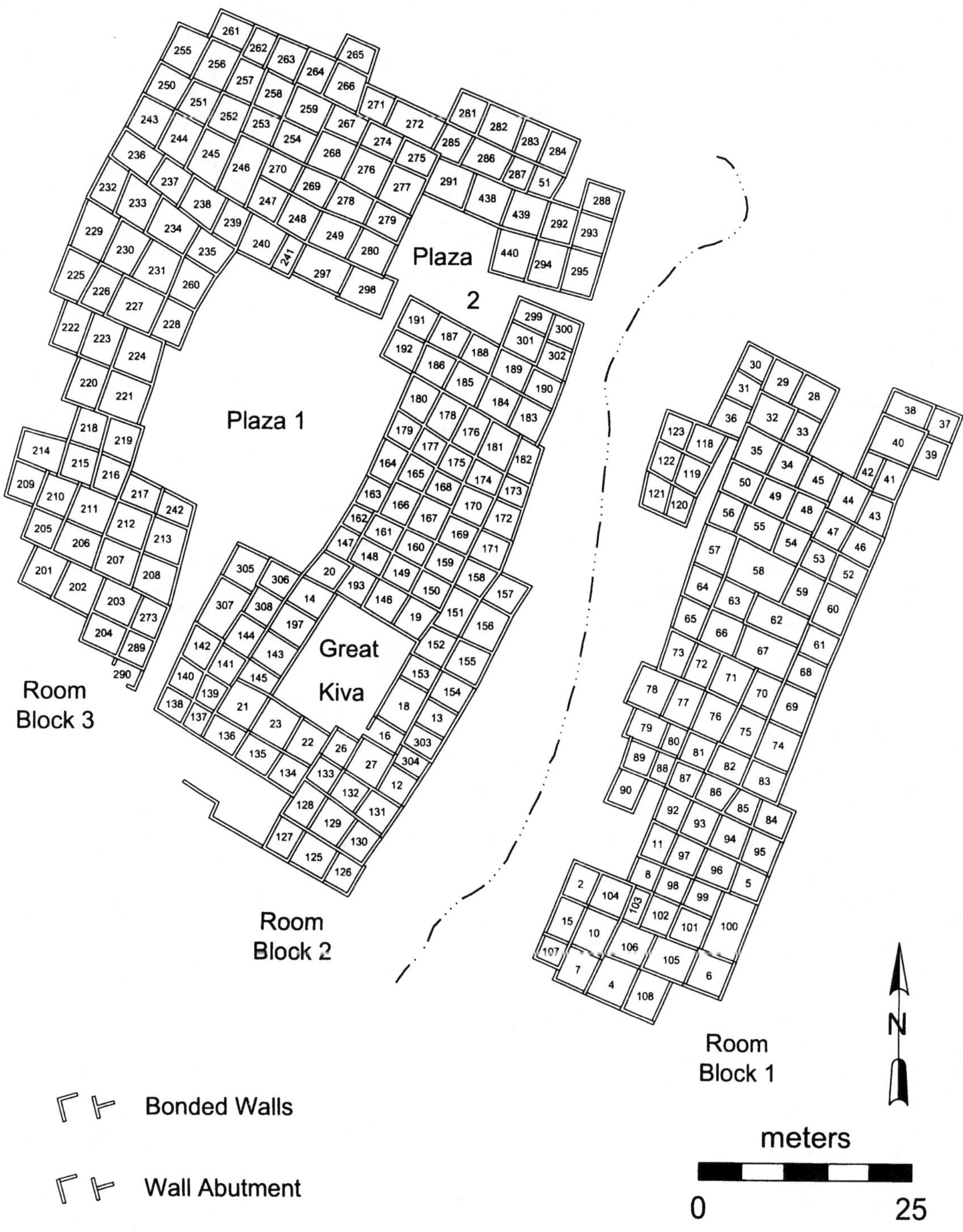

FIGURE 3.9.
Bond-abut map for the main pueblo.

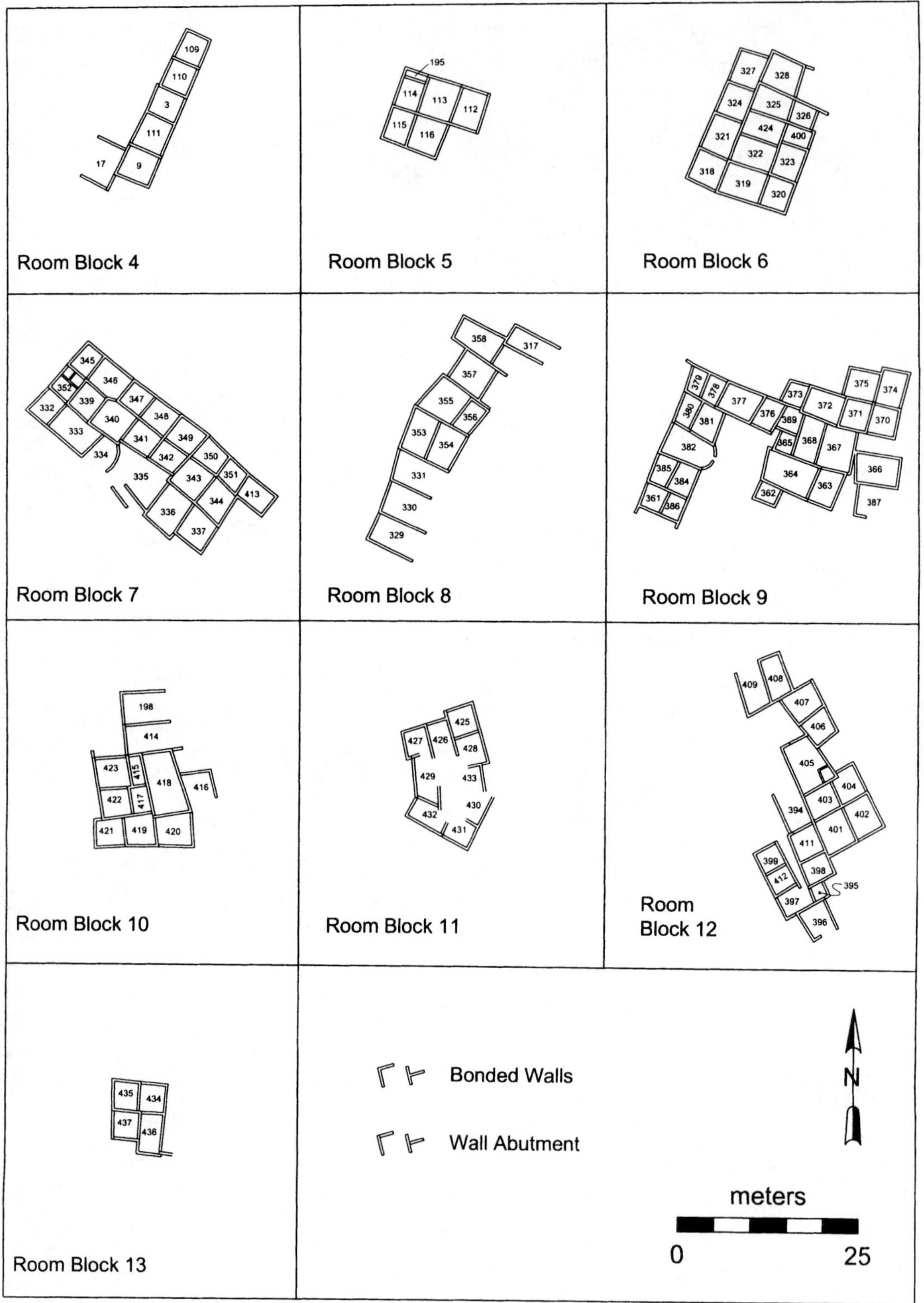

FIGURE 3.10.
Bond-abut maps for the outliers.

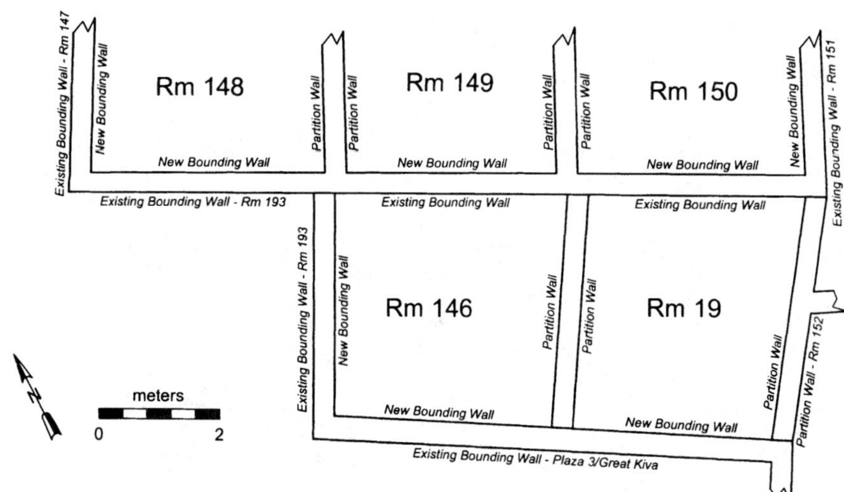

FIGURE 3.11. Examples of bounding and partition walls from Room Block 2.

This analysis makes a further distinction in wall types to facilitate data manipulation. Because it is too complicated to number individual walls and associate them with the many spaces (rooms) that they enclose or partition, a four-class typology was implemented to clarify these relationships. These types are (1) new bounding walls, (2) existing bounding walls, (3) partition walls, and (4) mixed walls in which both types were used (for example the west wall of Room 187). The two classes of bounding walls reflect the context in which a particular wall is discussed (Figure 3.11).

Existing bounding walls are walls that existed before the construction of a new room, whereas new bounding walls separate a new room from exterior space. For example, the north wall of Room 146 in Room Block 2 was defined as an existing bounding wall because it once defined one or more rooms in the large core unit to the north. The south and west walls of Room 146 were classified as new bounding walls because they separated the room from exterior space (from Plaza 3/great kiva in this case). Finally, the east wall of Room 146 was a partition wall because it separated Room 146 from other rooms but did not bound exterior space (Figure 3.9). The broad categories of bounding and partition walls are never altered, regardless of their ultimate relationship to other surrounding rooms within a room block.

Whether a bounding wall is classified as a "new bounding wall" or an "existing bounding wall" depends entirely on the context within which it is being discussed (Figure 3.11). Because the distinction between new and existing bounding walls is room specific, new bounding walls are most often classified as rough faced, and existing bounding walls are largely smooth faced (Figure 3.12). This is because the walls in question incorporate interior space in the former case and a previous exterior wall in the latter case (Table 3.1).[1]

Although bounding walls deep within the core of the room block serve to partition interior space once incorporated into the room block, they still serve to delineate boundaries between architecturally defined units such as house-

FIGURE 3.12. West, Type 3 and Type 1, wall of Room 41 in Room Block 1 with an open doorway. Room was enclosed by adding a new bounding wall to an existing bounding wall. Photograph by Susan E. Luebbermann, 1970. Courtesy of the Arizona State Museum, University of Arizona; neg. no. 27416.

holds or other corporate groups. There are many more bounding walls than partition walls. This is a logical consequence of a room construction sequence in which sets of rooms are added to existing architecture, incorporating new interior space, rather than through the construction of large blocks that are then subdivided by means of partition walls. In addition, partition walls may be overrepresented in the sample because every one is, by definition, counted twice. Only bounding walls adjacent to other rooms are counted twice, whereas those adjacent to plazas or extramural areas are counted once.

The distribution of these wall types sorted by room block indicates some interesting points about construction (Table 3.2). As expected, most room blocks have considerably more bounding walls than partition walls. Room Block 2, however, stands out for having an extraordinarily high number of partition walls. This results from its initial rapid construction, consisting of

TABLE 3.1.
Cross-Tabulation of Wall Types by Wall Face
(Expected Values Shown in Parentheses)

	Smooth	Rough	Total
Existing bounding walls	79 (29.12)	3 (52.88)	82
New bounding walls	6 (37.65)	100 (68.35)	106
Partition walls	18 (36.23)	84 (65.77)	102
Total	103	187	290

Note: $\chi^2 = 187.94$; $df = 2$; $p = 0.000$; $\phi = 0.81$; Cramer's V = 0.81

TABLE 3.2.
Distribution of Bounding Walls and Partition Walls by Room Block

Room Block	Bounding Walls		Partition Walls		Mixed Walls		Total	
	n	%	*n*	%	*n*	%	*n*	%
1	278	74	95	25	3	1	376	100
2	204	55	160	43	4	1	368	100
3	313	77	85	21	6	1	404	100
4	21	91	2	09	—	—	23	100
5	16	67	8	33	—	—	24	100
6	46	88	6	12	—	—	52	100
7	69	83	14	17	—	—	83	100
8	29	88	4	12	—	—	33	100
9	79	82	14	15	3	3	96	100
10	37	90	3	07	1	2	41	100
11	25	83	5	17	—	—	30	100
12	43	68	15	24	5	8	63	100
13	12	75	4	25	—	—	16	100
Total	1172	73	415	26	22	1	1609	100

few large architectural units (Chapter 4). Other room blocks that grew relatively rapidly, given their size, exhibit this same pattern (Room Blocks 5, 12, and 13). Room blocks with low percentages of partition walls are either linear, such as Room Blocks 4 and 8, or were constructed in several small-room-set additions (Room Blocks 6 and 10). The distinctions between these wall types provide rough estimates of pueblo growth, which are discussed in more depth in Chapter 4.

Curved walls. Another feature noted at Canyon Creek has a parallel at Grasshopper, although the similarity may be coincidental. Haury found the remains of a curved masonry wall below the floor in Room 19 at Canyon Creek. This wall is described as an arc running from northeast to southwest with a height of 0.61 m (2 feet) (Haury 1934:52). A similar wall exists at the southern end of Room Block 7 (Figure 3.10). This example comes from Room 334, where the eastern wall is an arc curving from northeast to southwest. The height of this wall is unknown because the associated room was never excavated. Another documented example at nearby Hilltop Pueblo (AZ P:14:12) (Figure 2.1; Spier 1919) implies that it was an uncommon, yet periodically occurring, component of pueblo architecture in the Grasshopper Region during the Pueblo IV period.

ROOM SIZE, SHAPE, AND ORIENTATION

Data from the Cornering and Growth Projects, room excavation, and surface mapping have been combined to produce metric information for all of the

447 *room spaces* at Grasshopper (Table A.3). Following Wilcox (1982:23–24), it is necessary to make the distinction between a *room* and a *room space* when discussing Grasshopper's architecture. The room space was simply the area defined by four walls within which one or more rooms, defined as a space bounded by four walls, a floor, and a roof, was constructed. Given this, the numbers on the site maps in this work refer to room spaces, each of which housed one or more rooms between the erection of the bounding walls and the abandonment of the pueblo.[2] Many room spaces also had more than one story; thus, the 447 room spaces on the site map reference an unknown number of rooms, both through remodeling of floors and through the addition of a second story. Therefore, we are not really analyzing rooms (activities) but rather room spaces (techniques) when discussing fixed architectural elements.

Size, shape, and orientation, the three room form variables, offer one means of understanding construction practices and have a rich history of research in the Southwest. Room size has long been an important means of determining room function (Hill 1970a:37–47; Lowell 1991:17) and has also been used to detect the presence of different cultural groups (Baldwin 1987:166; Haury 1958:2) or residence and descent patterns (James 1994). Researchers have used room shape in similar ways, although with more limited applications. The most notable use of the room shape variable was Haury's (1958:2) observation that the nonlocal, Maverick Mountain rooms at Point of Pines Pueblo were rectangular, in contrast to the square rooms typical of the region. Similarly, Lekson (1983:42) finds that Chacoan rooms were typically rectangular, with a long axis dimension almost twice that of the short axis. Room orientation has seen even less use; however, it has been applied as one criterion for differentiating between various cultural groups. For example, the entryways of Mogollon pit houses consistently point east or southeast or sometimes northeast (Haury 1985:181; Reed 1956:13; Wheat 1955:40–53). This pattern contrasts with structures in the Hohokam region, which often faced one another in courtyard group configurations (Wilcox et al. 1981), or the typical Anasazi house, which, not necessarily oriented to a given direction, typically faced trash areas. Later, trash areas, kivas, and pueblos came to be arranged in a linear fashion (Prudden 1903:234–235; Reed 1956:11).

At Grasshopper, where high immigration rates and a significant amount of remodeling occurred, the relationship between variables such as room size and room function are difficult to see archaeologically. These variables, however, do seem to indicate some subtle differences in perceptions of space that were probably culturally determined. For example, as demonstrated in Chapter 5, Haury's finding that larger rectangular rooms are associated with people from the Colorado Plateau seems to be supported at Grasshopper, where Room Blocks 1 and 3, thought to be the domains of nonlocals (Reid and Whittlesey 1999:116), had higher frequencies of large rectangular rooms that stand in stark contrast to the small square rooms of Room Block 2. Patterns in room shape, orientation, and room size also support the contention that room construc-

TABLE 3.3.
Descriptive Statistics for Room Size Measures ($n = 447$)

	Length (m)	Width (m)	Area (m^2)
Minimum	1.87	0.78	2.96
Maximum	8.65	5.28	43.84
Range	6.78	4.50	40.88
Median	4.25	3.60	15.53
Mean	4.46	3.58	16.27
SD	0.93	0.64	5.63
Variance	0.87	0.41	32.69

tion parameters changed as people began to live at Grasshopper on a more sporadic basis and began constructing the outlying room blocks (Reid 1989; Chapter 5).

Overall, five measures of room form have been derived from cornering and excavation data: length, width, size, shape, and orientation. Room length was determined by averaging the length of the two parallel long walls, and room width was generated by averaging the two parallel short walls. Room length in this analysis is simply the length of the room's long axis, whereas room width is the length of its short axis. Room length varies between 1.87 m and 8.65 m, with a mean of 4.46 m. Width has a tighter range, between 0.78 to 5.28 m, with a mean of 3.58 m (Table 3.3). Neither of these measures is used extensively for this analysis, but both are important for calculating other estimates of room form. As a measure of general trends, however, the difference between mean room length and room width is less than 1 m, indicating that the majority of rooms were square.

Room size is the area of the floor space in square meters as determined by multiplying room length by room width. The average room size was 16.27 m^2 when the site is considered as a whole (Chapter 2:Figure 2.8). Rooms in the main pueblo averaged 15.42 m^2, rooms in Room Blocks 5 and 7 averaged 16.62 m^2, and the outliers had an average room size of 18.02 m^2. By comparison, average room size at Canyon Creek Pueblo was 11 m^2, with the largest rooms measuring 19 m^2. These numbers are lower than those at Grasshopper; however, the restrictions on space imposed by Canyon Creek Pueblo's alcove location were likely a significant limiting factor in the determination of room size.

Other measures of room form generated from the length-width data are room shape and orientation. Room shape was derived by dividing the long axis of the room by its short axis. Rooms in which the length exceeded the width by a factor of 1.2 or greater were classified as rectangular. Room orientation, although somewhat categorically defined, was calculated by dividing a room's average north-south wall length by its east-west wall length. Hence, this measure actually refers to the room's long-axis orientation rather than to the orientation of the room entrance. In this measure, values of less than 1.0 were classified as north-south oriented rooms, and spaces with a value greater

TABLE 3.4.
Number and Percentage of Square and Rectangular Rooms

	Square	Rectangular	Total	North-South	East-West	Total
N	243	204	447	227	213	440
%	54	46	100	52	48	100

Note: Seven rooms had identical length and width measurements and could not be measured for orientation.

than 1.0 were classified as east-west oriented rooms. Thus, even rooms classified as square using the room shape index are given an orientation in this study.

The long-axis orientation measure was a practical decision based on four factors. First, azimuths referencing true or magnetic north could not be used because the entire pueblo is oriented in roughly the same direction, probably influenced by the course of Salt River Draw. Second, doorway placement within rooms could not be used because some rooms had as many as four doorways, one on each wall, and because this would have limited the analysis to only those rooms that were completely excavated. Third, this use of the measure permitted the inclusion of all cornering data and could be applied to all 447 room spaces. Finally, this measure provided a quick and entirely objective means of determining the orientation of the rooms without having to gather new data. The one drawback of this measure is that it includes rooms that were classified as square. Initial work with the data, however, demonstrated that results of statistical tests were not affected when square rooms were included in the sample, and this solution was used, again, so that all rooms could be assessed for orientation.

Just over half (54 percent) of the rooms were classified as square. Generally rooms in the main pueblo (Room Blocks 1, 2, and 3) were more often square than those in the outliers (Room Blocks 4, 6, 8, 9, 10, 11, 12, 13, and unaffiliated rooms), which were more often rectangular. The remaining two core room blocks (Room Blocks 5 and 7) more closely parallel the main pueblo, with a majority of square rooms.

Room orientation breaks evenly into north-south and east-west oriented rooms, with only a slightly larger percentage of north-south rooms (Table 3.4). Seven rooms (1.6 percent) in the sample were truly square, with identical long-and short-axis dimensions and are not classified by orientation. Room orientation was also generally patterned by site divisions. The main pueblo contained a larger percentage of north-south oriented spaces (54 percent) than east-west aligned rooms (45 percent) and contained three of the truly square spaces (1 percent). The outliers had more east-west spaces (54 percent) than north-south (43 percent), and Room Blocks 5 and 7 were equally split with 13 (48 percent) east-west rooms, 13 (48 percent) north-south oriented rooms, and one truly square room (4 percent).

WALL WIDTH AND HEIGHT

Wall width was not recorded as consistently as other wall metrics. All wall widths were recorded in meters, and few were measured in terms of the number of horizontal courses. In all, only 256 (63 percent) of the 408 excavated walls provided width data. The width of the walls varied between 0.20 m and 0.79 m with a mean of 0.37 m. Wall width at Canyon Creek Pueblo corresponds with that documented for Grasshopper (Table 3.5), ranging from 0.30 m to 0.61 m, with an average width of 0.41 m (Haury 1934:30). Because wall width was not consistently measured at the same vertical position in the wall at Grasshopper, it is difficult to use it for any substantive analyses. In general, there is a great deal of variability in wall width, suggesting the presence of single coursed and compound walls (cf. Metzger et al. 1989:Figure 5), as well as variability in the location at which the measurement was taken. Measures taken closer to the base of the wall should be greater than those taken at the top; however, because the number of vertical courses was not typically recorded, this relationship is unknown. Given the variability introduced by the number of courses and measurement location, wall width is not used in subsequent analyses. All that can be said concerning this variable is that the outliers have neither consistently narrower nor consistently wider walls than the main pueblo. In addition, in contrast to Chacoan masonry, where wall width decreases relative to increasing wall height (Lekson 1984:15), there is also no relationship between the height of a wall and its width at Grasshopper.

Wall height data are available for all of the 103 excavated rooms, totaling 408 measurements. Wall height is recorded as the maximum height of the standing wall above the floor or the wall base.[3] Although minimum wall height was recorded for many walls, this analysis uses only maximum wall height because it is a closer approximation of original wall height. The preserved height of Grasshopper walls ranges from 0.10 to 3.55 m with a mean of 1.38 m (Table 3.5). Outliers generally represent the low end of the height range, being composed largely of low-walled structures. The high end of the wall height range occurs only in room spaces in Room Blocks 1, 2, and 3, several of which were two-story (Figure 3.13; Longacre and Graves 1982:1; Longacre and Reid

TABLE 3.5.
Descriptive Statistics for Wall Height and Width Measures

	Wall Width (m)	Max. Wall Height (m)	Floor to Wall Base (m)
N	256	408	113
Minimum	.20	0.10	– 0.75
Maximum	.79	3.55	1.01
Range	.59	3.45	1.75
Median	.35	1.30	0.28
Mean	.37	1.38	0.26
SD	.09	0.67	0.19
Variance	.01	0.45	0.04

FIGURE 3.13. South wall of Room 270 in Room Block 3, showing the preserved height of a two-story Type 3 wall measuring 2.8 meters. Note the blocked doorway. Photograph by Susan E. Luebbermann, 1972. Courtesy of the Arizona State Museum, University of Arizona; neg. no. 31315.

1974:12; Reid 1989:83). Room Blocks 5 and 7 (and perhaps 13) fall between the low-walled outliers and the main pueblo, consisting solely of one-story rooms with full-standing masonry walls (Table 3.6).

Regarding the question of wall height, published comparative data from Canyon Creek is not available. The height of only a single wall is reported

TABLE 3.6.
Maximum and Average Standing Wall Height Statistics by Room Block

Room Block	Maximum Standing Wall Height				Average Standing Wall Height			
	Min.	Max.	Mean	*SD*	Min.	Max.	Mean	*SD*
1	1.00	3.55	1.77	0.60	0.50	3.10	1.53	0.56
2	1.22	3.30	2.19	0.61	1.03	2.67	1.84	0.49
3	1.18	3.05	1.98	0.54	0.66	2.87	1.71	0.59
4	0.70	0.95	0.82	0.13	0.53	0.88	0.70	0.18
5	1.40	2.00	1.56	0.23	1.17	1.55	1.34	0.13
6	0.88	0.88	0.88	0.88	0.77	0.77	0.77	0.77
7	1.34	1.53	1.40	0.11	1.09	1.29	1.20	0.10
8	0.34	0.95	0.68	0.28	0.28	0.84	0.60	0.26
9	1.16	1.29	1.23	0.09	0.95	0.99	0.97	0.03
10	0.50	0.80	0.60	0.17	0.43	0.68	0.54	0.13
11	0.85	0.85	0.85	0.85	0.67	0.67	0.67	0.67
12	0.42	1.10	0.72	0.28	0.26	0.70	0.50	0.20
13	1.35	1.35	1.35	1.35	1.19	1.19	1.19	1.19
0	0.37	1.10	0.59	0.27	0.30	1.03	0.52	0.27

TABLE 3.7.
Kruskal-Wallis Analysis of Standing Wall Height Grouped by Intrasite Divisions

Group	Count	Rank Sum	Kruskal-Wallis Statistic	Probability
Main Pueblo	68	4513.50	56.140	0.000
Outlier	26	384.00	—	—
Room Blocks 5 and 7	9	458.50	—	—

(Haury 1934:30), and its excessive dimension of 7 m is well beyond that documented for two-story rooms, rendering it a poor analogue for wall height.

Inspection of the maximum wall height data presented above indicates clear variability in standing wall height by room block (Table 3.6). Maximum standing wall height for the site separates into a multimode distribution with the primary mode being in the 1.5 m range, about what would be expected for a collapsed single-story room (Riggs 1999b:Figure 4.12). To test whether these modes reflect differences in wall heights between the core and the outliers, a Kruskal-Wallis one-way analysis of variance was run using three spatial divisions—the main pueblo, Room Blocks 5 and 7, and the outliers (Table 3.7). The results are depicted graphically in a notched box-and-whisker plot, which definitively portrays a three-way division in standing wall height (Figure 3.14).

The nonoverlapping notches indicate that the three groups reflect three separate populations within the data. The main pueblo rooms have a higher median wall height (approaching 2 m) with a greater range of variability than the other two subdivisions. The outliers exhibit the lowest median, less than

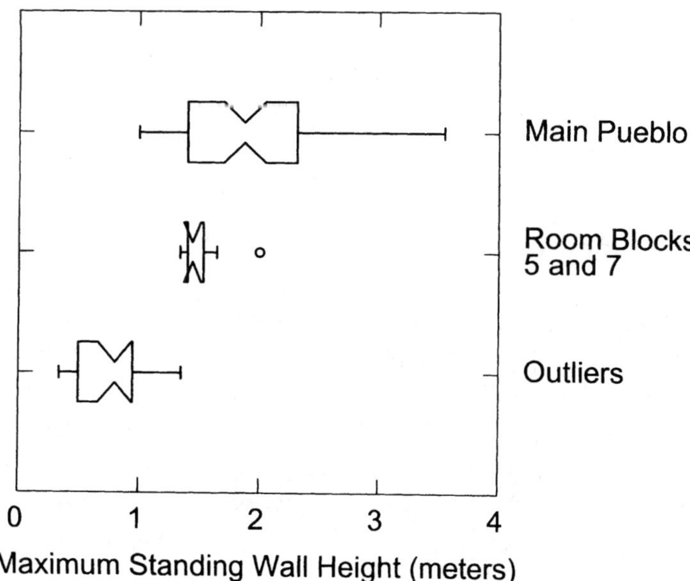

FIGURE 3.14. Notched box plots comparing standing wall height grouped by intrasite divisions.

FIGURE 3.15. North wall of Room 411 in Room Block 12. Note diminished height of preserved wall, which measured only 0.40 meters. Photographer unknown, 1976.

1 m (Figure 3.15). Finally, Room Blocks 5 and 7 have the tightest range in wall height and measure somewhere between the two other areas. These data reinforce the long-held interpretation that the main pueblo contained one- and two-story rooms with full-standing masonry walls, whereas the outliers consisted of rooms with low masonry walls and nonmasonry superstructures. Room Blocks 5 and 7 stand out as a separate group because they were made up solely of one-story rooms, and unlike the other outliers, they had full-standing masonry walls.

Stone Use and Implications for Construction

The total mass of wall rock used to build Grasshopper can be estimated at 8,428,269 kg (9,290 tons) of rock. Of this, almost 5,506,321 kg (6,070 tons) were used to construct the site core. The sheer amount of rock manipulation suggests a strong labor commitment for construction during the early part of Grasshopper Pueblo's occupation. Room construction was likely a household endeavor in which individual families or other small corporate groups built rooms based on changing needs. Early on, when groups arriving at the site were typically larger, building may have been a cooperative activity including several households that worked in tandem to erect a block of rooms (construction unit, Chapter 4). Drawing from Hopi and Zuñi ethnography, Grasshopper society may have been organized matrilocally, and women may have owned the houses. If this was the case, women were probably largely responsible for most of the construction (James 1997:439; Mindeleff 1891:100–101), whereas men may have been responsible for procuring the stone and roof beams and for setting the large roof timbers in place.

Regardless of how construction was organized, an assessment of stone use reinforces a settlement pattern of changing commitment to full-time occupation. The contrast in material use for construction between the site core and the outliers provides additional evidence for the change in settlement patterns. Compared to the estimated 5,506,321 kg used to build the site core, only an estimated 1,729,500 kg (1,906 tons) of rock was used to build the outliers.

Wall weighing experiments. During the 1980 field season, sections of the walls from Rooms 309 and 312, located in the unaffiliated group of rooms in the far southwestern portion of the site (Figure 2.4), were dismantled and weighed to determine the percentage of different rock types and the amount of material used to build the walls, and to provide data on the height of walls (Table 3.8). In all, 1,278.70 kg (2,819 lbs.) of wall rock were removed from 0.745 m^3 of wall, resulting in an average of 1,716.37 kg (3,783.9 lbs.) of rock per cubic meter of standing wall. A difference of 442.26 kg (975 lbs.) per cubic meter was found between Rooms 309 and 312; this may result from the differential mass of sandstone and limestone (Table 3.8). Despite this difference, the data from these rooms provide an average weight for wall materials that can be used to predict standing height.

Wall rocks from the fill of Room 309 were also weighed during the 1980 field season. In all, 770.67 kg (1,699 lbs.) of sandstone and 6,085.50 kg (13,416 lbs.) of limestone were recovered from the room fill, totaling 6,856.16 kg (15,115 lbs.) of wall rock. An estimate of 1,611.38 kg (3,552.4 lbs.) of rock per cubic meter derived from the measurement of wall sections yields 4.25 m^3 of rock recovered from the fill. Adding this figure to the 3.82 m^3 of existing standing wall in the room reveals that over 8 m^3, or 13,003.84 kg (28,668.26 lbs.), of rock were used to build the three low walls of Room 309. This number does not reflect any wall material that may have fallen outside of the room, which would require a further adjustment. When used to determine the original height of the room's masonry, this reconstruction suggests that the individual walls were 0.59 m higher than recorded during excavation prior to their collapse. Based on an average standing wall height of 0.53 m, a total wall height of 1.12 m is derived. This figure is well within expected wall height for the outlier rooms. In addition to confirming that the outliers were low-walled structures, these data can be used to predict total site wall mass and to make assessments of expected wall fall debris within one- and two-story rooms.

Estimates of total wall mass for rooms throughout the site can be calculated using the average figure of kilograms of rock per cubic meter of wall derived from the weight experiments above. A sample of two blocks of excavated, contiguous, single-story rooms was used to provide estimates of the quantity of wall material and wall fall debris for all rooms. Room Block 5 and the southern core unit (Chapter 4) of Room Block 1 allowed for a determination of wall mass, without having to account for problematic unexcavated shared walls. The estimates of total wall mass are based on an average one-story wall height of 2.37 m (see roof height discussion below; Table 3.9). These figures suggest that an average of more than 10.22 m^3, or 17,541.3 kg (38,671.55

Table 3.8.

Results of Wall Weighing from Rooms 309 and 312 with Sandstone (ss) and Limestone (ls) Weight Given Separately

	Width	Height	Length	m^3 of Wall	m^2 of Wall	kg ss	kg ls	Total kg	kg/ m^3	/kg m^2	% ss
Room 309 Wall Sections											
North	0.27	0.37	1.05	0.105	0.389	123.83	93.90	217.73	2073.60	559.71	56.90
West	0.40	0.43	1.10	0.189	0.473	2.27	267.17	269.44	1425.60	569.64	0.84
South	0.37	0.50	1.30	0.240	0.650	0.00	373.31	373.31	1555.47	574.33	0.00
Totals	1.04	1.30	3.45	0.534	1.511	126.10	734.38	860.48	1611.38	569.48	14.70
Room 312 Wall Sections											
North	0.37	0.36	1.00	0.133	0.36	132.90	109.77	242.68	1824.63	674.10	54.77
West	0.27	0.29	1.00	0.078	0.29	97.98	77.57	175.54	2250.55	605.32	55.81
Totals	0.64	0.65	2.00	0.211	0.65	230.88	187.34	418.22	1982.08	643.41	55.20
Total	1.68	1.95	5.45	0.745	2.161	356.98	921.72	1278.70	1716.37	591.72	27.9

TABLE 3.9.
Wall Weight Predictions for Two Areas of Contiguous Excavated Rooms

	Total Length	Avg. Width	Avg. Height	m^3	kg	kg/Room	m^3/Room
Room Block 5 (6 rooms, 16 walls)							
Actual	67.17	0.38	1.36	35.17	60,365	10,061	5.86
Predicted	67.17	0.38	2.37[a]	60.49	103,823	17,304	10.00
Predicted Wall Fall				25.32	43,458	7,243	4.22
Room Block 1, Southern Core Unit (6 rooms, 17 walls)							
Actual	68.97	0.38	1.22	31.97	54,872	9,145	5.33
Predicted	68.97	0.38	2.37[a]	62.11	106,604	17,767	10.35
Predicted Wall Fall				30.14	51,731	8,622	5.02
Totals							
Actual	—	—	—	67.14	115,237	9,603	5.59
Predicted	—	—	—	122.60	210,427	17,536	10.22
Predicted Wall Fall	—	—	—	55.46	95,190	7,932	4.62

[a]Based on mean predicted wall height for single-story rooms.

lbs.), of rock went into the construction of a single-story room. Based on these estimates, one would expect to remove, on average, 4.62 m^3 (over 7,929.63 kg [17,481.66 lbs.]) of wall fall per single-story room in the site core and, depending on the extent of wall collapse, anywhere from 5 m^3 (8,581.85 kg [18,919.55 lbs.]) to as much as 14 m^3 (24,029.18 kg [52,974.73 lbs.]) of rock from a two-story space (Figure 3.16).

FIGURE 3.16.
East wall of Room 269 in Room Block 3. Note the preserved height of the wall, which measured 2.16 meters. A blocked door and two niches are also visible. Photographer unknown, 1975.

TABLE 3.10.
Predicted Weight and Volume of Rock Used in the Construction of Grasshopper Pueblo

Site Area	Rooms	Total kg	Total m^3
Core (ground floor)	314	5,506,321	3208.12
Outliers	133	1,729,500	1007.65
2d story	68	1,192,448	694.75
All rooms	515	8,428,269	4910.52

The amount of rock used to build Grasshopper Pueblo was assessed by combining these estimates of rock use for the site core with projections from the outliers based on Room 309 (Table 3.10). The numbers given above are meant to be an approximation of rock use. Several issues affect the extent to which these estimates accurately reflect actual rock use. First, the sample of experimentally weighed wall sections is small (five sections from two rooms) and comes entirely from the outliers. Second, no estimates were ever made for rocks in the fill of site core rooms. Third, the 2.37 m average wall height estimate may or may not be accurate (although see below for its determination). Fourth, the assessment for the outliers is a projection based on a single, three-walled room (Room 309) rather than on a sample of several excavated rooms, although the longer than average walls of the room probably make up for this deficiency. Fifth, the walls in the core room blocks were generally better constructed than the outliers, relying more frequently on thinner, shaped stones. This procedure probably made walls in the site core denser. Finally, although the measurements used for Rooms 309 and 312 are outside wall measurements, the rooms from the two sample areas are inside wall measurements and, if anything, underrepresent the total amount of wall material. In total, the issues affecting the accurate prediction of wall mass bias the estimate toward an underestimation of rock use.

WALL FEATURES

The four major types of wall features include doorways, crawlways, vents, and niches. In addition, beam sockets, masonry seams, and benches were also documented, but only beam sockets are discussed in detail here. These wall openings are differentiated based on size, as well as on their construction techniques, which are elaborated below.

Doors/Doorways

Doorways are defined as large wall openings that were constructed contemporaneously with the wall in which they occurred. Because the excavation of two adjacent rooms resulted in the duplication of doorways in some cases, a distinction is made between a door, which is the exposure of a doorway in an excavated wall face, and a doorway that connected two rooms or a room and an exterior space. All doors signify doorways, but only the excavation of adjacent rooms recorded the entire doorway. Typically, doorways were built at or just above the floor surface and often had a stone sill. Doors for which the entire height was preserved indicate that stone lintels were used quite frequently, although wooden lintels may also have been used at Canyon Creek Pueblo (Graves 1982:110; Haury 1934:40; Reynolds 1981:184, 186), where the doorways exhibit numerous similarities to Grasshopper doorways.

In all, 161 doors were recorded in the 103 excavated rooms (Table A.4). Of these, 39 doors were duplicated between adjacent excavated rooms, leaving 122 recorded doorways. Average door height was 0.88 m, and average width was 0.56 m. Doorways were constructed between 0.21 m below the floor and 1.80 m above room floors and averaged 0.42 m above the base of the wall (Table 3.11). Most doorways were located in the center of the wall; however, they also occurred in high frequency to the left and right of center (Table 3.12). All recorded doorways except for the doorway in the south wall of Room 70 in Room Block 1 were associated with the first story. The bottom of this latter doorway was located 1.80 meters above the final room floor.

In comparison, doors at Canyon Creek were typically constructed with stone sills, masonry door jambs, and lintels composed of four to six poles of

TABLE 3.11.
Descriptive Statistics for Doors (n = 163)

	Height	Width	Distance to Floor	Distance to Wall Base	Area
n^a	125	157	114	61	125
Minimum	0.45	0.26	– 0.21	– 0.01	0.16
Maximum	1.74	1.16	1.80	1.05	1.62
Range	1.29	0.90	2.01	1.06	1.46
Mean	0.88	0.56	0.17	0.42	0.52
SD	0.20	0.13	0.27	0.24	0.22
Variance	0.04	0.02	0.07	0.06	0.05
Median	0.88	0.55	0.00	0.40	0.46
Mode	0.90	0.50	0.00	0.30	0.62

[a]Values in this row refer to the actual number of doors measured for the corresponding variable.

TABLE 3.12.
Number and Percentage of Wall Feature Locations in Walls

	Left		Center		Right		Total	
	n	%	n	%	n	%	n	%
Doors	41	30.5	57	42.5	36	27.0	134	100.0
Crawlways	1	11.0	3	33.0	5	56.0	9	100.0
Vents	14	32.0	13	29.0	17	39.0	44	100.0
Niches	36	49.3	12	16.4	25	34.3	73	100.0
Total	92	35.0	85	33.0	83	32.0	260	100.0

approximately 0.08 m (3 inches) in diameter. Doors ranged in size from 0.41 by 0.51 m to 0.64 by 1.02 m, well within the range of door sizes at Grasshopper (Table 3.11). Canyon Creek's doors also fit within the range noted at Grasshopper with respect to door location (Table 3.12). The sills were typically constructed between 0.30 and 1.02 m above the floor. Although Haury (1934:42) did not provide counts, subsequent work by Reynolds (1981:Figures 24 and 25) suggests that approximately 39 percent of the doorways at Canyon Creek were sealed. These occurred throughout the site, including second-story rooms. One of Haury's blocked doors was T-shaped and was located on the second story of the cliff dwelling.

As at Canyon Creek, the vast majority of doorways at Grasshopper were rectangular. The two notable exceptions were a pair of T-shaped doors from Room 113 in Room Block 5. One was in the southern wall and connected Room 113 to Room 116; the other connected Room 113 to Room 114 through the west wall (Figure 3.17). The southern doorway measured 0.92 m tall by 0.63 m wide with a 0.30 by 0.42 m notch in the bottom. The west door was similar in size, measuring 0.95 m tall by 0.75 m wide. Its bottom notch was 0.21 m high by 0.41 m wide, and a small niche was left open in the door. Like the example from Canyon Creek, both were sealed with masonry.

The presence of T-shaped doorways in Room 113 is consistent with other evidence from Room Block 5 pointing to construction by inhabitants with a northern material culture tradition (Triadan 1989:45–47). T-shaped doorways were common in the Southwest during the Pueblo II and Pueblo III periods in the San Juan Basin, and several examples can be found in the literature (Fewkes 1909:16, 1911:34; Lekson 1984:25; Rohn 1971:50–52). T-shaped doors were also common at Casas Grandes, in Chihuahua, Mexico (Di Peso et al. 1974:236), and in the cliff dwellings of the Sierra Madre (Sánchez 1986). Based on recent revisions in site dating (Dean and Ravesloot 1993:96), the Casas Grandes doors were roughly contemporary to those at Grasshopper.

T-Shaped doorways are rare in the central mountains of Arizona and occur primarily in areas where other evidence suggests the presence of immigrants from the Colorado Plateau (Ezzo et al. 1997:461; Haury 1958; Lindsay 1987). As noted, Haury (1934) recorded one T-shaped doorway at Canyon Creek, and another occurred at Pine Flat Cave in the Point of Pines region to the south (Gifford 1980:149). The correlation between these features and other architectural data described below suggests habitation of the East Village and Room Block 5 by immigrants with differing construction traditions (Chapter 5).

The data above indicate an overwhelming number of doorways in the main pueblo, where all of the excavated rooms but two (Rooms 11 and 108) had one or more doorways. By contrast, only 17 out of 34 excavated rooms in the outliers contained doorways (Figures 3.17 and 3.18). Of the 122 (161 doorway faces) recorded doorways, 113 (149 doorway faces), or 93 percent, were blocked with masonry by Grasshopper's inhabitants, cutting off access routes to adjacent rooms or to extramural spaces.

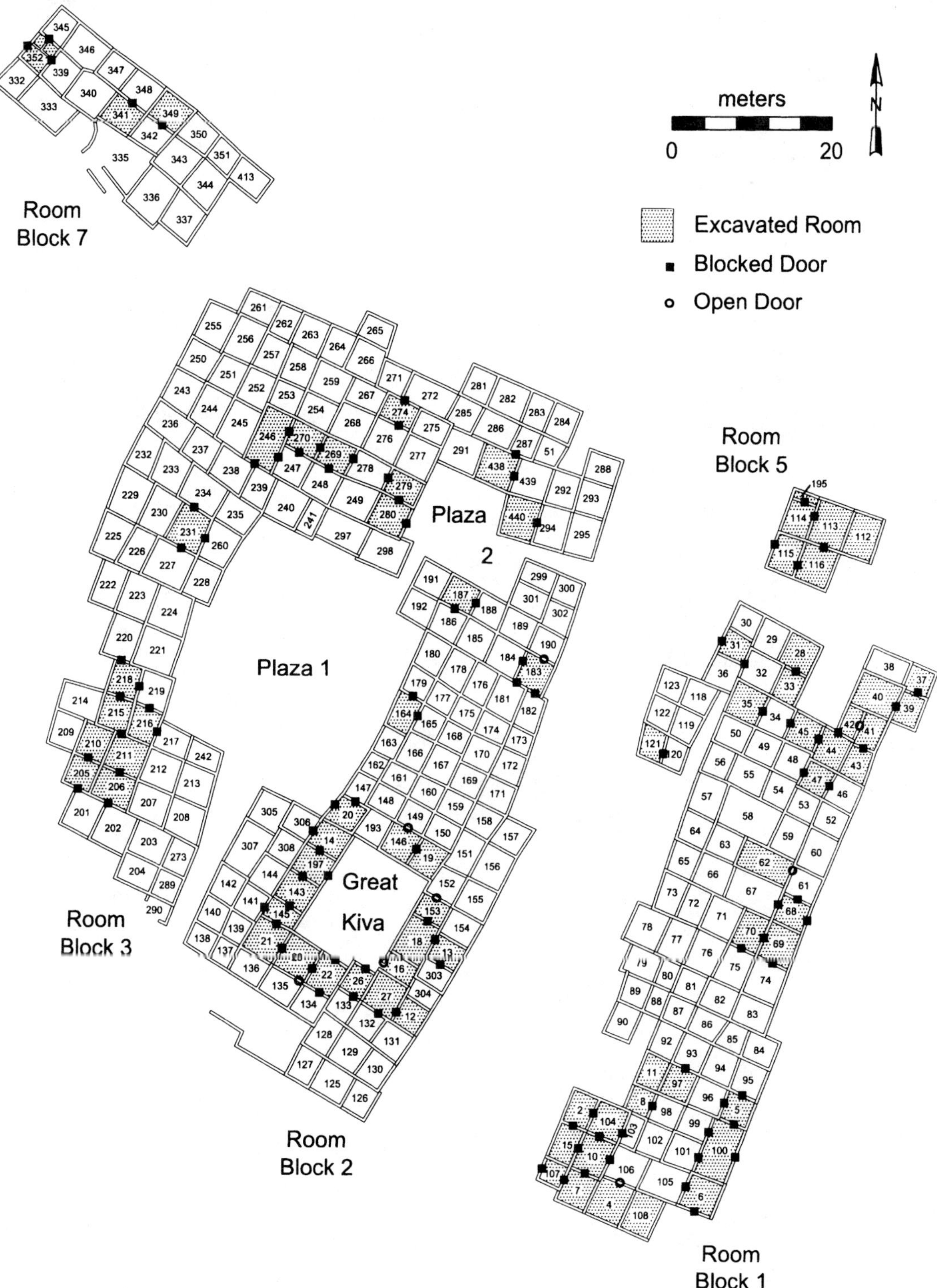

FIGURE 3.17.
Doorways recorded in excavated rooms in the core room blocks.

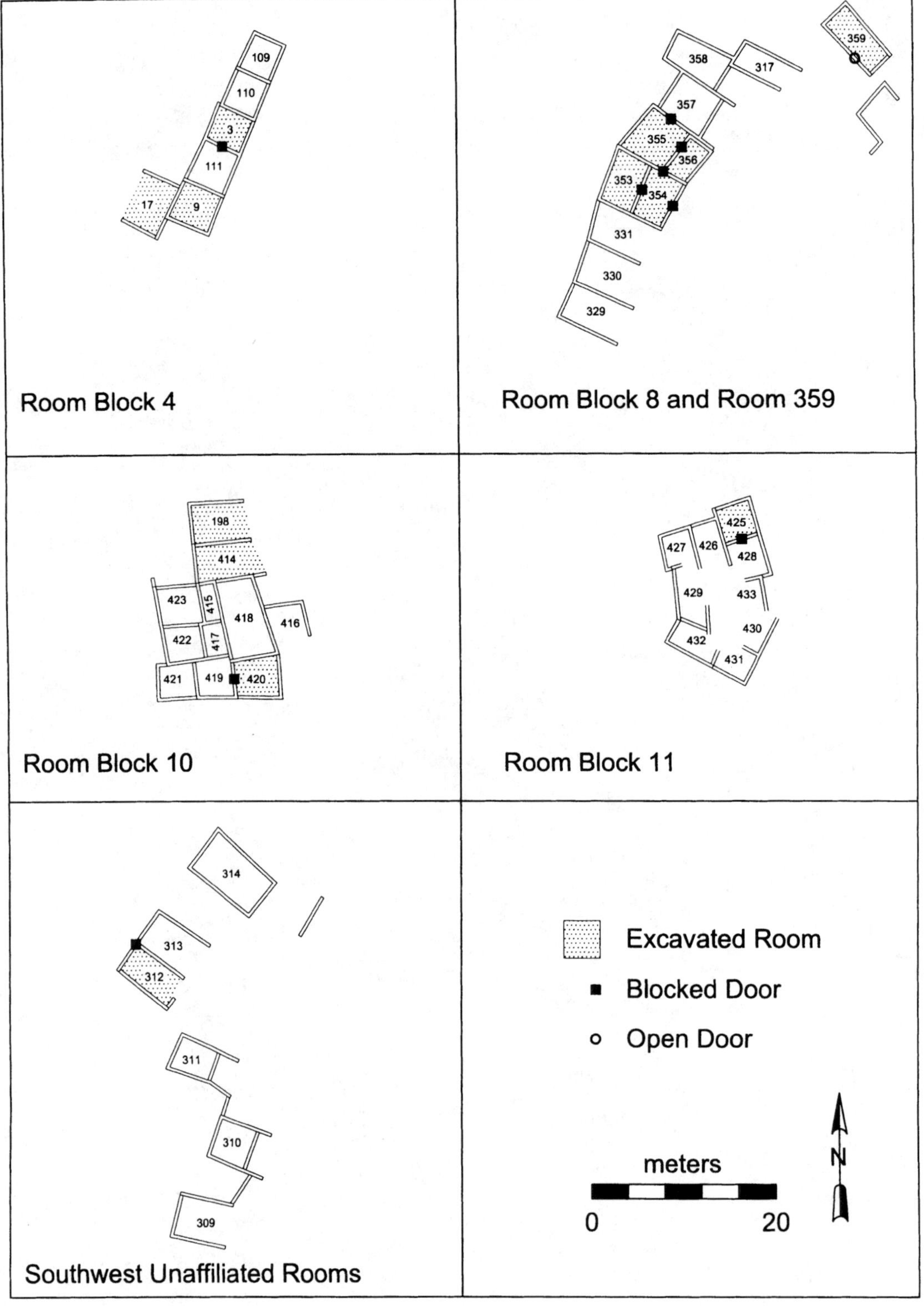

Figure 3.18.
Doorways recorded in excavated rooms outside of the core room blocks.

Blocked doorways are more common than open doorways at sites throughout the prehistoric Southwest. For example, at Arroyo Hondo 68 percent of the doorways were blocked (Creamer 1993:Tables 2.4 and 3.6). Two sites in the Hay Hollow Valley further indicate the prevalence of blocked doorways. Investigations at the Pueblo III period Joint Site revealed that 53 percent of the doorways, including portals, were blocked (Wilcox 1975:149, Table 10), whereas data from Broken K Pueblo (Martin 1967:20) indicate that 61 percent of the doorways were sealed. The two large cliff dwellings in the Grasshopper region diverge in relation to the blocked-door pattern. The pattern at Red Rock House matches the aforementioned findings, with 56 percent of its doorways blocked (Reynolds 1981:Figure 15). In contrast, only about 39 percent of the doorways at Canyon Creek were blocked (Reynolds 1981:Figures 24 and 25), suggesting patterns of social interaction, use, and abandonment that differed from those at Red Rock House and Grasshopper.

These limited examples indicate that Grasshopper fits a general trend in prehistoric southwestern architecture with respect to sealed doorways. Conventional wisdom suggests that as rooms were occupied for longer periods, they were remodeled more often and doorways were sealed with higher frequency. Although this makes logical sense and may partially explain the prevalence of blocked doorways in puebloan sites, the contrast between the frequency of door closure at Canyon Creek Pueblo versus that at Red Rock House suggests that occupation span is not the only explanation for sealed doorways. Red Rock House has been estimated to have been occupied for approximately 30 years (Reynolds 1981:165), and Canyon Creek Pueblo was occupied for approximately 35 years (Reynolds 1981:232). Thus the length of occupation for both was approximately the same, yet the frequency of blocked doorways at the two sites was different, with the longest occupied site having the lower percentage of blocked doorways.

Turning to Grasshopper, which was occupied intensively for no more than 50 to 75 years, the frequency of blocked doorways is much higher than expected given only a 40 percent room remodeling rate (Chapter 5). The number of blocked doorways could be a result of the local settlement history, during which groups of immigrants entered the community throughout its occupation, continually altering intrasite spatial relationships between the various households (Chapters 4 and 5). There may be a simpler explanation, however. Despite several other possible factors, which are reviewed below, the most parsimonious explanation for doorway phenomena is that doorways were built in rooms as standard construction features that allowed easy passage into and out of the room during construction (Mindeleff 1891:182) and enabled more flexibility in structure use through time.

Blocked doors, room construction, and room connectivity. Whereas changes in intrasite social relationships related to new room construction and room remodeling seems to be the most logical explanation for the frequency of blocked doorways at Grasshopper and at other sites in the Southwest, there are numerous other possibilities. The treatment of blocked doorways that follows demonstrates (1) that the issues of equifinality related to blocked doorways make them unreliable indicators of these relationships and (2) that doorway construction in pueblo rooms was probably a standard component of room construction. Following from this second point, doorways functioned primarily as temporary access routes during construction that were then sealed but that could have been left open or reopened at any time if necessary.

Many doors at Grasshopper were sealed during room use rather than after rooms had fallen into disuse. Several doorways extended below the last room floor or were blocked by wall abutments (Figure 3.17), implying that they were closed while the room was in use. For example, the doorway in the west wall of Room 32 in Room Block 1 and the doorway in the north wall of Room 274 in Room Block 3 were sealed and abutted by masonry walls exterior to the rooms (Figure 3.17). In Room Block 7 the construction of the two storage bins in Room 352 involved blocking the doors and abutting masonry against the former openings in the north and east walls. These two cases suggest that some doorways may never have been used to connect two room spaces, at least in the context of Rooms 32 and 274, where once exterior doorways were rendered unusable by abutting masonry. These blocked interior-exterior doorways suggest another scenario.

In his classic study of puebloan architecture V. Mindeleff (1891:182) noted that many doors were used as temporary openings during room construction and were sealed at the completion of the room. If this activity were responsible for the frequency of blocked doorways at Grasshopper, we would expect doorways in newly constructed rooms to open onto exterior space to allow passage of people and materials into the room during construction. Several construction units (Chapter 4) containing or abutted by excavated rooms were selected to assess this hypothesis with respect to room construction.

The number of excavated rooms at its north end renders Room Block 1 the best example for discussing the pattern of room construction and doorway use. Figure 3.19 illustrates the trend in door placement through seven construction episodes in the northern end of Room Block 1. As expected, all of the excavated rooms in the core construction unit had doorways opening onto exterior space. This trend continued throughout the construction sequence. Almost every added construction unit with an excavated room contained one or more doorways opening to an external space. Further, every excavated, single-room construction unit except Room 37 contained a doorway opening to an exterior space.

These data suggest that doorways at Grasshopper were indeed used as temporary passageways during construction. The opening in an exterior wall provided easy access from the inside to the outside of the space being built. This passage would have been especially useful for allowing the builders to easily move in and out of the room during the placement of large primary roof

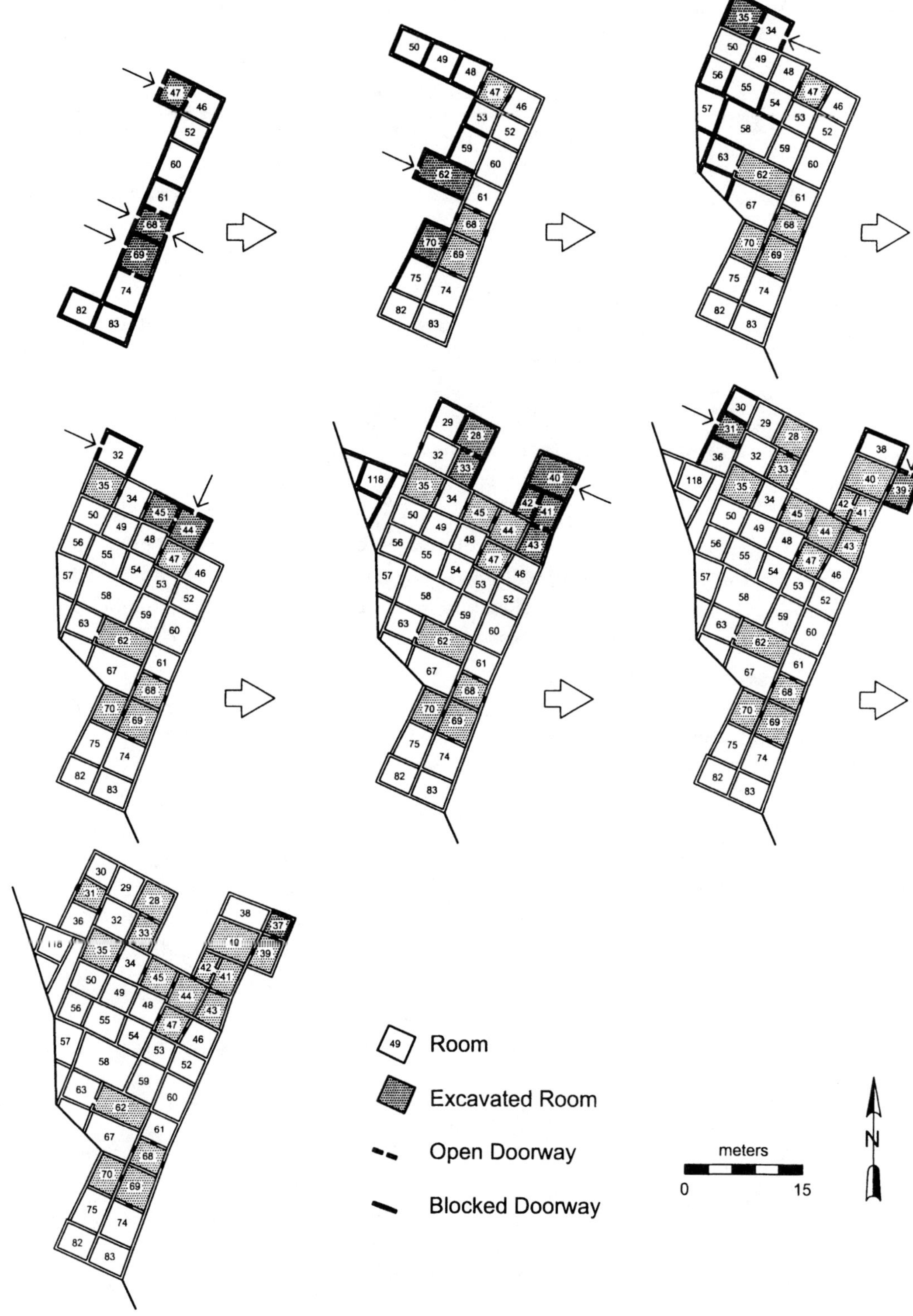

FIGURE 3.19.
Relationship between doorways and room additions in the north end of Room Block 1.

beams. The passage was probably left open until the roof and roof hatch were completed. At this point many doorways would have been blocked and covered with plaster.

Another possible explanation is that doorways were constructed expressly to access exterior space. If this were the case, the doorways were likely blocked when a room was added to the wall containing the door, unless the added room was built as an addition to the original household. An argument against the idea that doorways were built to access exterior space is that no doorways opening onto a plaza or extramural area were ever recorded (Room 16, the vestibule of the Great Kiva, is an obvious exception; see below). By contrast, sites of the Pueblo III period such as Chodistaas had doorways that opened onto exterior space and remained open after site abandonment. This tendency can be explained if the Grasshopper community aggregated partially as a defensive response (Reid 1989:81); doorways that opened out to exterior space would have compromised the safety of room contents and would have been sealed. There is ethnographic support for this hypothesis from Santo Domingo Pueblo, where Morgan attributed the lack of doorways in the ground floor to a defensive response to raiding (Morgan 1965:144), and other investigators have reached similar conclusions (Cameron 1999a:25; Ferguson and Mills 1987:249–250; Ferguson et al. 1990:106; Mindeleff 1891:182). The possibility also exists that doors in the earlier construction units did open onto plaza and exterior spaces but were later closed for defensive reasons. This is impossible to detect archaeologically at Grasshopper, where an absence of cutting dates limits the resolution to which we can resolve individual room additions and because it is impossible to tell how long a given doorway was open before its closure.

Doorways blocked on final room abandonment or for seasonal abandonment could also explain the number of blocked doors. Rooms that were abandoned early and used for trash disposal would certainly have their doorways blocked as a means of keeping refuse out of adjacent occupied rooms (Cameron 1999a:59). This pattern is not supported at Grasshopper because there were as many open doors associated with early abandoned as with later abandoned rooms (Table 3.13). This indicates that rooms were abandoned and never used again or that doors were purposefully left open to allow for easy refuse disposal from adjacent rooms. In either case there appears to be no clear-cut rule

TABLE 3.13.
Distribution of Open and Closed Doorways in Relation to Abandoned Rooms (Expected Values Shown in Parentheses)

	Open Door	Blocked Door	Total
Late abandoned	5 (8.26)	128 (124.74)	133
Early abandoned	5 (1.74)	23 (26.26)	28
Total	10	151	161

Note: $\chi^2 = 7.89$; $df = 1$; $p = 0.005$; $\phi = -0.22$; Yule's Q $= -0.69$

for assessing the relationship between early abandoned rooms and blocked doorways.

Rooms with assemblages of de facto refuse (Schiffer 1987:89, 1995:29) present a slightly different situation. In these cases it is plausible that the doorways were temporarily sealed during seasonal or short-term room abandonment to protect the items left in the room (Mindeleff 1891:183). The distinctive ways that doors were blocked at Grasshopper provides limited support for this interpretation. Although never quantified, the data indicate that the formality of door closure varied. Some doors were sealed with well-coursed, dressed masonry with a more stable, permanent appearance, whereas others were blocked informally, suggesting a temporary closure. Because these data were not always collected, it is difficult to assess the spatial distribution of these two practices or even to determine whether they are simply differences in technique or differences in function. The distinction, however, supports the argument for temporarily sealed doors.

The few open doorways suggest that there was some horizontal connectivity between the rooms. Connectivity between rooms of a single household or other cooperative social group could also explain the presence of doorways (Dean 1969; Rohn 1971). If doorways were constructed to allow access between rooms in a single household, one would expect doors to occur in walls that subdivided architectural units associated with households. At Grasshopper this was the construction unit (Chapter 4). The dichotomy of bounding walls and partition walls allows this expectation to be tested. If one function of doorways was to connect rooms in a construction unit, then doorways would be located in partition walls more often than in bounding walls. This pattern does seem to hold up at Grasshopper where 106 of 111 partition walls (95 percent) contained doorways. By contrast, only 132 of 196 bounding walls (67 percent) contained doorways (Table 3.14). These data support the interpretation that doorways were constructed to provide access between rooms within discrete architectural units. It is not clear, however, whether these doorways served as temporary passages to aid in construction, as actual access routes between rooms in a household, or were simply a standard component of wall construction. The fact that most of these doorways were sealed makes any statement of function unreliable.

Despite the numerous explanations for the frequency of blocked doorways, the discovery of doorways in virtually every excavated room in the main pueblo

TABLE 3.14.
Distribution of Doors by Wall Type (Expected Values Shown in Parentheses)

	No Door	Door	Total
Bounding walls	64 (44.05)	132 (151.95)	196
Partition walls	5 (24.95)	106 (86.05)	111
Total	69	238	307

Note: $\chi^2 = 32.22$; $df = 1$; $p = 0.000$; $\phi = 0.32$; Yule's Q = 0.82

(66 of 68 excavated rooms) suggests that doorways were a requisite feature of room construction. Mindeleff's observations at Hopi strengthen this interpretation, which is further bolstered by the analysis of the subset of constructions from the northern end of Room Block 1. Building doorways as a regular element in wall construction allowed more flexibility in the use of the architectural spaces. Doorways could be left open to allow internal circulation or could be sealed to restrict access. As just demonstrated, there are many possible explanations for the preponderance of blocked doorways at Grasshopper. Any of the interpretations discussed above could also have been contributing factors in producing the number of blocked doorways. Nevertheless, if doorways were, as argued here, a standard component of room construction, regardless of whether they were ever intended to connect two room spaces, then Mindeleff's notion of temporary passages is probably the most likely explanation for blocked doorways.

The frequency of blocked doorways implies that most rooms were entered through the roof and that people and materials moved through the site on the rooftops rather than between the rooms through doorways. This pattern of structure use has been well documented for the historic and modern pueblos (Dohm 1996; Mindeleff 1891:201; Morgan 1965:144). If second-story doorways had survived at Grasshopper, we would see numerous doorways opening onto exterior roof spaces (Mindeleff 1891:182). Further, if these second-story doorways were blocked, some of the hypotheses discussed above could be discounted or confirmed. For example, blocked second-story doorways would provide additional support for the hypothesis that doorways were temporarily sealed to protect their contents. The single second-story doorway that was preserved was blocked. It did not, however, connect a second-story room to an open roof area but rather two second-story rooms (Rooms 70 and 75 in Room Block 1), one of which was not excavated. Because it did not open onto the roof area, it does not provide data to confirm the temporary closure hypothesis. Instead, it suggests that the doorway was either sealed through changing use of the associated rooms through time or was constructed as a temporary access passage.

The numerous issues of equifinality related to blocked doorways underscore the complexity of human behavior in relation to a single class of architectural information. They also point out one of the problems with applying approaches that depend on the interconnectivity of internal space in a pueblo community. The Grasshopper data call into question the assumption that doorways existed simply to provide access between adjacent rooms.

Crawlways

In most respects crawlways were identical to doorways. They allowed passage of people or material between rooms. Crawlways, like doorways, were large wall openings but often had a height of less than 0.5 m. Also, unlike doorways,

FIGURE 3.20.
East wall of Room 215 in Room Block 3, showing a crawlway. Photograph by Susan E. Luebbermann, 1972. Courtesy of the Arizona State Museum, University of Arizona; neg. no. 31596.

crawlways were knocked through walls after the wall was built rather than during wall construction (Figure 3.20). Typically, crawlways were wider than they were tall and were largely restricted to the main pueblo (Figure 3.21). In general, they were located higher in the wall than doorways, although several occurred at the floor surface, suggesting that some could have been large vents. The locations of crawlways within walls were also different from doors in that crawlways were more often located either to the left or right of the wall centerline (Table 3.12).

Eleven crawlways were recorded, and four of these were duplicated between excavated rooms, yielding a total of nine of these features. Crawlways occurred between 0 and 0.63 m above the floor and averaged 0.58 m above the base of the wall (Table A.5). Crawlways had a more restricted size range than doorways and smaller mean dimensions (Table 3.15). Their distribution within the

TABLE 3.15.
Descriptive Statistics for Crawlways (n = 11)

	Height	Width	Distance to Floor	Distance to Wall Base	Area
n[a]	11	11	9	4	11
Minimum	0.31	0.32	0	0.36	0.16
Maximum	1.10	0.80	.63	0.95	0.99
Range	0.79	0.48	.63	0.59	0.83
Mean	0.57	0.55	0.15	0.58	0.43
SD	0.25	0.16	0.22	0.26	0.29
Variance	0.06	0.02	0.05	0.07	0.08
Median	0.51	0.56	0.05	0.50	0.34
Mode	0.52	0.65	0	—	0.34

[a]Values in this row refer to the actual number of crawlways measured for the corresponding variable.

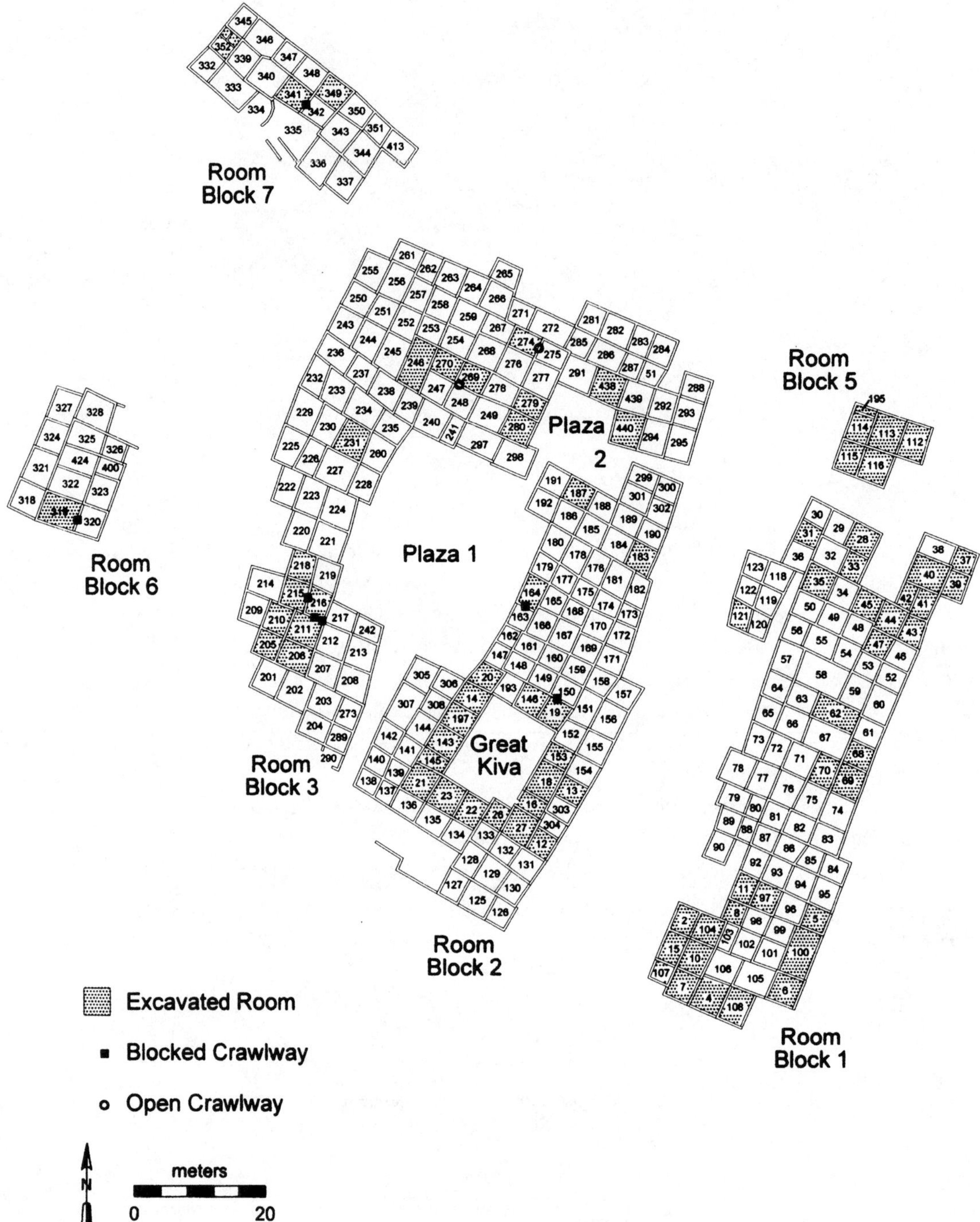

FIGURE 3.21.
Crawlways recorded in excavated rooms.

FIGURE 3.22.
North wall of Room 146 in Room Block 2, showing an open doorway, two niches, and a vent. Note wall collapse resulting from breakage or decay of door lintel. Photograph by Susan E. Luebbermann, 1971. Courtesy of the Arizona State Museum, University of Arizona, neg. no. 31181.

site was also more restricted. Crawlways occurred only in Room Blocks 2, 3, 6, and 7 and were most abundant in Room Block 3 (Figure 3.21). Like doorways, the majority of crawlways were sealed, and only two of the nine recorded were left open (Table A.5). Interestingly, although the sample of crawlways is small, they occurred only in the West Village and not in Room Blocks 1 and 5.

The limited use of crawlways suggests that openings between rooms were sometimes added after the construction of a wall. Crawlways were most often added to walls without doorways, although some were punched through walls with existing doorways such as between Rooms 248 and 269 in Room Block 3. Unlike doorways, crawlways most often occurred in previously exterior walls and may be more reliable than doorways as indicators of changes in intrasite relationships. On the other hand, because crawlways were also frequently blocked, they too may have been temporary access corridors.

Vents

Vents are small, squarish wall openings that allow for air circulation, light, and possibly communication between rooms. Typically, they were constructed with a small lintel stone set atop one to three courses of masonry or in some cases vertical slabs (Figure 3.22). Like doorways and crawlways, vents on single wall faces represent ventilators that extended through the wall and connected two rooms. Because recording varied through the years, however, an assessment of shared features between rooms is not possible, and each vent (on a wall face)

TABLE 3.16.
Descriptive Statistics for Vents ($n = 50$)

	Height	Width	Distance to Floor	Distance to Wall Base	Area
n[a]	41	43	35	8	41
Minimum	0.08	0.12	– 0.21	0.15	0.12
Maximum	0.30	0.53	2.28	1.30	0.90
Range	0.22	0.41	2.49	1.15	0.78
Mean	0.30	0.53	2.28	1.30	0.90
SD	0.06	0.09	0.65	0.50	0.22
Variance	0.00	0.01	0.43	0.25	0.05
Median	0.17	0.20	0.15	0.44	0.32
Mode	0.20	0.15	0.00	1.23	0.17

[a]Values in this row refer to the actual number of vents measured for the corresponding variable.

was counted separately. Figure 3.23 displays the location of all recorded vents and provides a partial estimate of vents shared between rooms. Fifty vents were found, and these occurred only in the five room blocks constituting the site core (Room Blocks 1, 2, 3, 5, and 7). Unlike doorways and crawlways, vents were almost never sealed, and only two have been identified as blocked.

Vent size ranged from 0.08 to 0.30 m in height and from 0.12 to 0.53 m in width (Table 3.16). Vents were constructed at all elevations (– 0.21 to 2.28 m above floor) in the wall but were most common at the bottom, ostensibly to provide air for the room's hearth (Table A.6). They also occurred almost equally in the center, to the left, and to the right of wall midlines (Table 3.12). This category of wall features also includes several openings that, because of their location toward the top of the wall, could have served as roof beam sockets. These were included with vents above but are also discussed below along with several niches, which were also possible beam sockets.

Niches

Niches are small, often more informally constructed, wall openings that did not extend through the wall and were probably used for the storage of small items. Hill (1970a:53) notes that at Broken K Pueblo these features were strongly correlated with kivas and that the modern Hopi use them to store "idols" (Donaldson 1893:55). Seventy-eight niches were recorded during room excavations (Table A.7); however, no such ceremonial association has been noted for these features (Chapter 5). Niches were found at all elevations in the walls but were most often located toward the middle and top of the walls. These features ranged from 0.10 to 0.45 m high and from 0.10 to 0.42 m across with an average area of 0.33 m^2 (Table 3.17). In contrast to vents and doorways, niches occurred to the left and right of the wall center more often than in the middle of the wall (Table 3.12). In addition, they were much more likely to be present in pairs on a single wall (Figure 3.24).

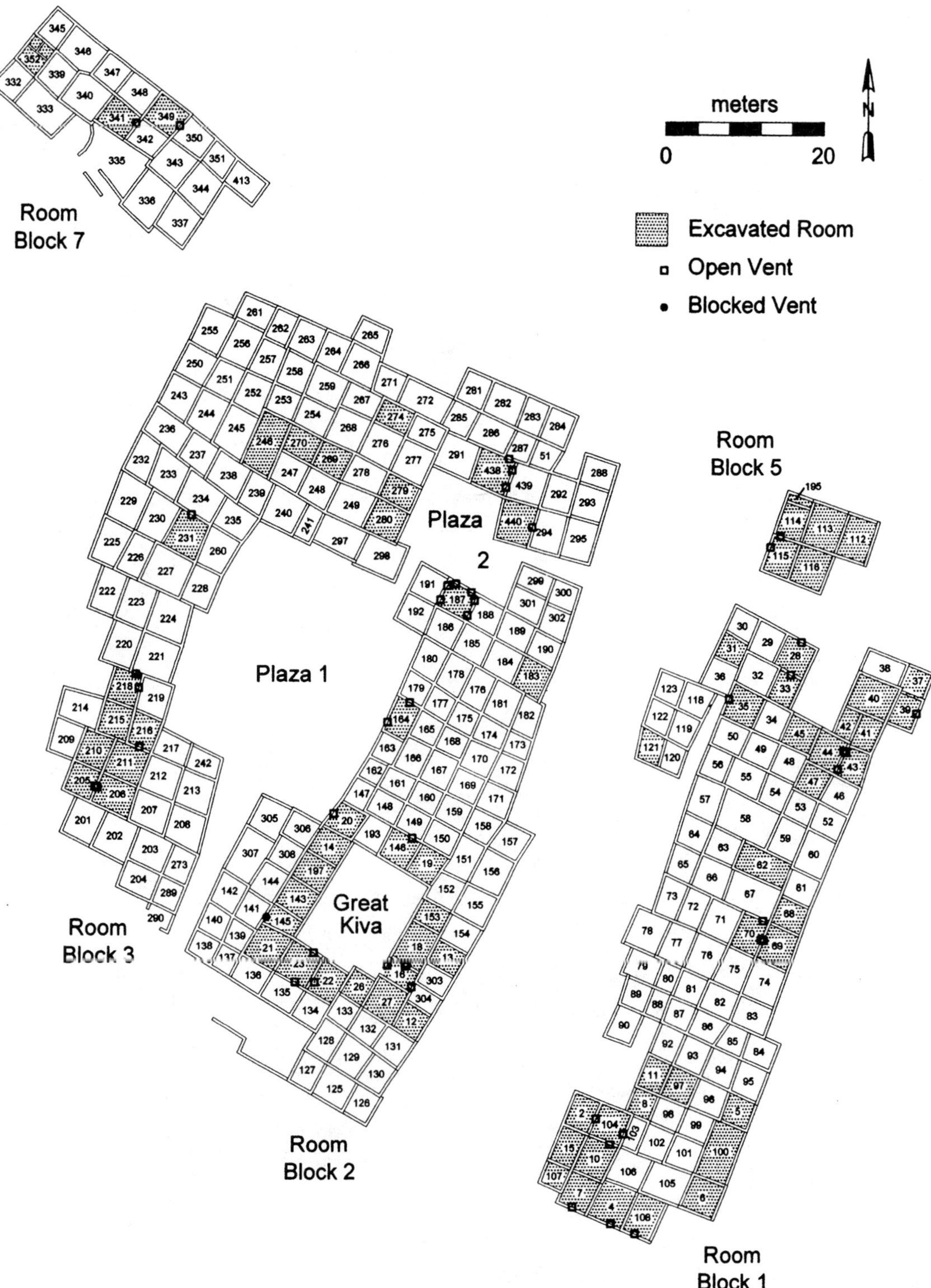

FIGURE 3.23.
Vents recorded in excavated rooms.

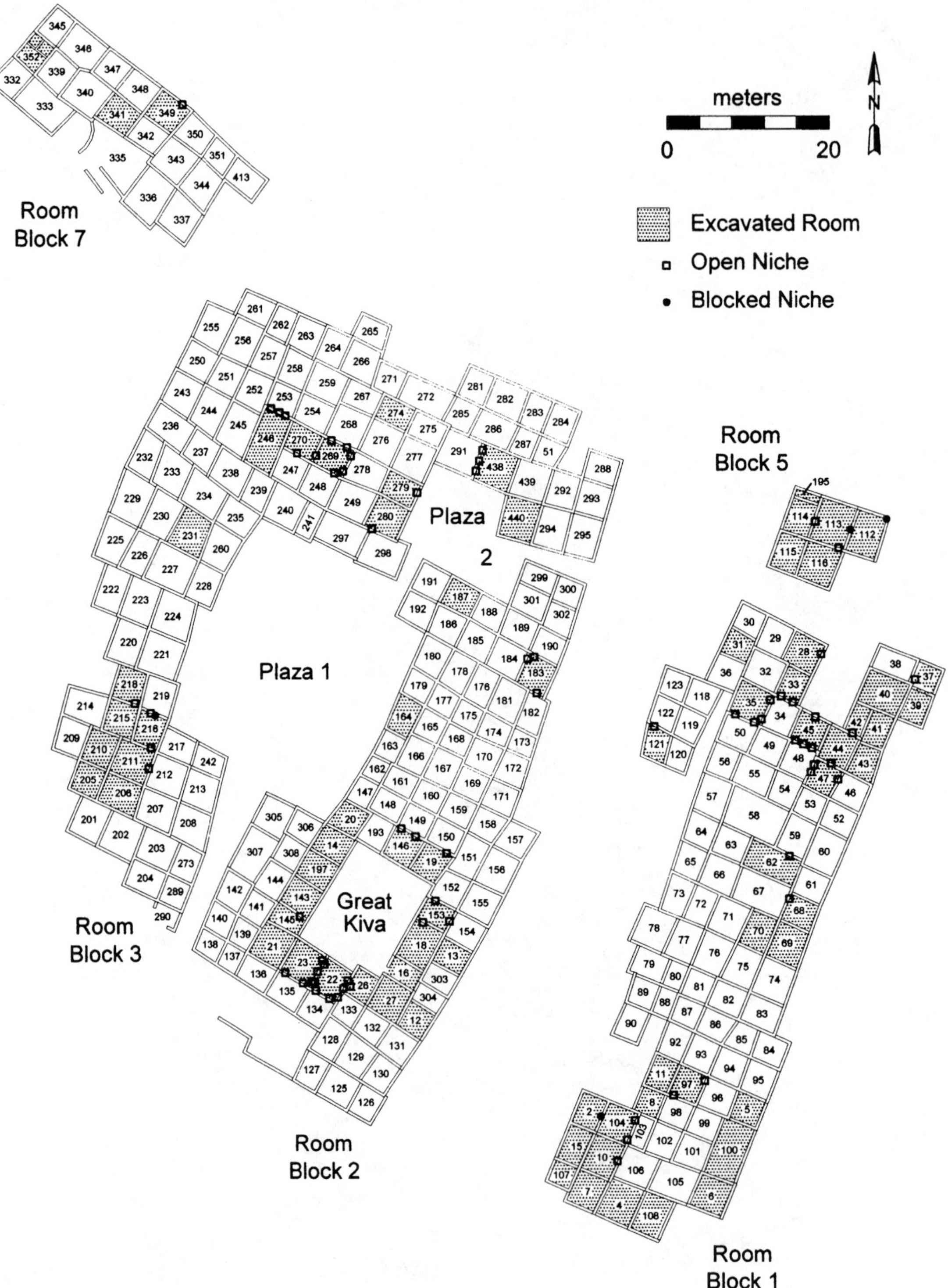

FIGURE 3.24.
Niches recorded in excavated rooms.

TABLE 3.17.
Descriptive Statistics for Niches (n = 78)

	Height	Width	Distance to Floor	Distance to Wall Base	Area
n[a]	56	60	52	18	56
Minimum	0.10	0.10	0.00	0.00	0.02
Maximum	0.45	0.42	2.49	2.74	0.90
Range	0.35	0.32	2.49	2.74	0.88
Mean	0.19	0.21	0.94	1.18	0.33
SD	0.07	0.07	0.53	0.71	0.19
Variance	0.01	0.01	0.28	0.51	0.04
Median	0.17	0.18	0.98	1.24	0.29
Mode	0.15	0.18	1.25	1.28	0.22

[a]Values in this row refer to the actual number of niches measured for the corresponding variable.

Niches were only found in the core room blocks (Room Blocks 1, 2, 3, 5, and 7). As with vents, most niches were open, and only four (5 percent) were recorded as blocked. Like vents, several niches could have been beam sockets, based on their location. These features were retained in the data as niches but are also discussed in the following section.

Beam Sockets

Features in walls were most often classified either as vents or niches, although some of these represent sockets for primary roof-support beams. Three definite beam sockets were observed during room excavation; two occurred in Room 146 in Room Block 2 and one in Room 68 in Room Block 1. All three were located at 1.8 m above the floor of their associated room. Data from Canyon Creek Pueblo, with an average primary beam height of 1.83 m (6 feet) (Haury 1934:38), support the consistency and deliberateness of this placement.

This information suggests strongly that some of the features designated as vents or niches were actually the remains of roofs, second-story floors, or possible second-story floor vents. To determine which of these features were most likely to be beam sockets, data from several well-preserved southwestern sites were used to generate a range of beam socket height variability that was then used to predict whether given wall features represent beam sockets at Grasshopper. Table 3.18 provides the floor-to-ceiling height of vigas from several sites with published measurements, including data from Canyon Creek and the three known beam sockets from Grasshopper. From these data a mean height of 1.82 m above floor with a standard deviation of 0.30 m was derived. The possible beam sockets were identified by using this information as a guide for separating the distribution in wall features' height above floor. Figure 3.25 displays the distance from the floor to the bottom of all niches and vents that were measured to floor (rather than to wall base). The distribution of feature height is trimodal, with modes at 0.10 m, 1.0 m, and 1.8 m. The two lower

TABLE 3.18.
Multisite Sample of Viga Height above Room Floor.

Site	Space	Height Above Floor
Grasshopper	Room 146	1.80
	Room 146	1.80
	Room 68	1.80
Canyon Creek	Site average	1.83[b]
Mug House	Room 10/1[a]	1.79[b]
	Room 11/1[a]	1.74[b]
	Room 12/1[a]	1.77[b]
	Room 15/1[a]	1.71[b]
	Room 36/2	1.83[b]
	Room 37/1	1.92[b]
	Room 42/1[a]	1.76[b]
	Room 46/1[a]	1.98[b]
	Room 57	1.52[b]
	Room 70	2.13[b]
Montezuma Castle	Room 1, Lvl 1	1.30
	Room 1, Lvl 2	1.78
	Room 2, Lvl 2	1.56
	Room 3, Lvl 2	1.95
	Room 1, Lvl 3	1.85
	Room 3, Lvl 3	1.63
	Room 4, Lvl 3	1.70
	Room 5, Lvl 3	1.87
	Room 6, Lvl 3	1.77
	Room 1, Lvl 4	1.90
	Room 2, Lvl 4	2.59
	Room 3, Lvl 4	2.90
Gila Cliff Dwellings	Cave 2, Room 4	1.70
	Cave 3, Room 9	1.88
	Cave 3, Room 10	2.00
	Cave 3, Room 10A	2.00
	Cave 4, Room 17	1.88
	Cave 4, Room 18	1.96
	Cave 4, Room 24	1.60
	Cave 4, Room 25	1.20
	Cave 4, Room 25A	1.50
	Cave 5, Room 27	1.90
	Cave 5, Room 32	1.50

Sources: Grasshopper (this study); Canyon Creek (Haury 1934); Mug House (Rohn 1971); Montezuma Castle (Wells and Anderson 1988); Gila Cliff Dwellings (Anderson et al. 1986).

Note: Mean 1.82 m; *SD* 0.30 m.

[a]Average height in room.

[b]Measures converted to metric from English units.

modes reflect associations with room floors (ground floors) in the first case and with general wall area in the second. The isolation of the third mode from the remainder of the distribution suggests that these features are distinct from other wall features and may reflect beam seats or vents in the upper-story wall. The case is further strengthened by the observation that the distribution falls

-0		2
-0		11
0	H	00000000000011111111
0		2222223
0		4445
0		666677777
0	M	8888888999999
1	H	000000000011111
1		22223
1		
1		677
1		88889
2		0
2		2
Outside Values		
2		4

FIGURE 3.25. Stem-and-leaf plot showing floor to bottom-of-feature distance for vents and niches.

almost entirely within one standard deviation of the mean (1.52 to 2.12 m) generated from the multisite sample. Expanding to two standard deviations (1.22 to 2.42 m) encompasses all of these cases. The highest of these features reflect either tall roofs or features associated with second-story room walls.

This analysis, based partially on a sample of preserved roofs, indicates that beam sockets and second-story vents most likely occurred at a height of between 1.52 and 2.12 m (1 standard deviation) with a mean of 1.82 m above room floors. Because there were no preserved/intact roofs at Grasshopper, it is difficult to ascertain which of these features were niches or vents in the ground-story room wall, which were beam sockets, and which were openings in the wall of the upper story. Table 3.19 provides a list of the three features that were identified as beam sockets and those predicted to be beam sockets or second-story floor vents.

Wall Feature Correlations

The next task, after describing the general distributions and intricacies of various wall features, is to determine to what extent they correlated with each other. The co-occurrence of certain wall feature types would provide information about construction practices, such as room function, that treating each feature class as isolated may not. For example, did the presence of a doorway in a given wall dictate the placement of niches within the same wall? Did it negate the necessity for a vent in that wall? Were beams seats placed in the same wall as a doorway? To address these types of questions, a series of binary correlation matrices was generated to assess whether the four main wall feature types co-occurred (Table 3.20).[4] The data used for the correlations were organized by wall, not by room, so that the relationship between features on given walls could be assessed. Correlations were run on the data at various spatial scales to ensure that areas posited as socially distinct were adequately tested for wall feature correlation. As Table 3.20 indicates, there are no strong

TABLE 3.19.

Definite and Possible Beam Sockets or Second-Story Vents ($n = 12$).

Room	Wall	Room Block	Horizontal Location	Feature Type	Distance to Floor	Distance to Wall Base	Height	Width	Description
35	E	1	Left	Niche	1.68	—	0.12	0.19	Possible beam socket
47	E	1	Left	Niche	2.49	2.74	0.12	0.18	Possible second-story vent/niche
47	W	1	Center	Niche	—	2.28	0.14	0.16	Possible second-story vent/niche
68	W	1	Right	Niche	1.8	2.03	0.24	0.24	Definite beam socket
70	E	1	—	Vent	1.96	—	—	—	Possible beam socket/second-story vent
70	N	1	Right	Vent	2.28	—	0.26	0.20	Possible beam socket/second-story vent
23	S	2	Right	Niche	2.05	—	—	0.20	Possible beam socket
23	S	2	Left	Niche	1.86	—	—	—	Possible beam socket
146	N	2	Left	Niche	1.8	—	0.16	0.18	Definite beam socket
146	N	2	Right	Niche	1.8	—	0.15	0.17	Definite beam socket
187	N	2	Right	Vent	1.72	—	0.12	0.12	Possible beam socket
187	N	2	Left	Vent	1.75	—	0.11	0.15	Possible beam socket

TABLE 3.20.
Jaccard (S3) Binary Correlation Matrices for All Wall Features at Various Spatial Scales

All Excavated Walls (n = 204)				
	Doors	Crawlways	Vents	Niches
Doors	1.00			
Crawlways	0.01	1.00		
Vents	0.12	0.04	1.00	
Niches	0.16	0.05	0.05	1.00
Walls from Core Room Blocks (n = 190)				
	Doors	Crawlways	Vents	Niches
Doors	1.00			
Crawlways	0.01	1.00		
Vents	0.13	0.04	1.00	
Niches	0.17	0.05	0.06	1.00
Walls from the Main Pueblo (n = 171)				
	Doors	Crawlways	Vents	Niches
Doors	1.00			
Crawlways	0.02	1.00		
Vents	0.13	0.02	1.00	
Niches	0.17	0.06	0.06	1.00
Walls from Room Block 1 (n = 75)				
	Doors	Crawlways	Vents	Niches
Doors	1.00			
Crawlways	0.00	0.00		
Vents	0.09	0.00	1.00	
Niches	0.12	0.00	0.03	1.00
Walls from Room Block 2 (n = 54)				
	Doors	Crawlways	Vents	Niches
Doors	1.00			
Crawlways	0.00	1.00		
Vents	0.16	0.00	1.00	
Niches	0.24	0.06	0.11	1.00
Walls from Room Block 3 (n = 42)				
	Doors	Crawlways	Vents	Niches
Doors	1.00			
Crawlways	0.06	1.00		
Vents	0.17	0.08	1.00	
Niches	0.18	0.13	0.05	1.00

correlations between any feature types on any walls viewed at the four analytical scales selected. The strongest correlation is between niches and doors in Room Block 2, and a value of 0.239 does not present a strong correlation. Finding that there was no correlation between any of the wall feature types paves the way for analyzing the spatial distributions of these features by eliminating one possible source of bias—that related to patterns of feature correlation determined by room function. Distribution patterns of wall feature types and sizes are one line of evidence linking different groups of builders to the architecture of Grasshopper. Eliminating the possibility that these wall features correlate because of room function strengthens the idea that they are reflections of the construction techniques of the different social groups (Chapter 5).

OCCUPATION SURFACES

This analysis addresses only those aspects of activity surfaces that can be classified as architectural. This includes floor preparation, roof and second-story floor construction, and to some extent preroom activity surfaces. These latter types of occupation surfaces are briefly discussed because their presence or absence has direct bearing on some of the architectural evidence discussed in the following chapters. In general, artifacts and features on room floors are outside the scope of this work unless they provide evidence to corroborate or contradict the findings of the architectural analysis. Several studies have been completed using floor feature and artifact data from Grasshopper room floors (Ciolek-Torrello 1978, 1984, 1985; Reid and Whittlesey 1982; Rock 1974; Whittlesey et al. 1982; Wilcox 1982). These have addressed the systems of activities that took place during the occupation and are discussed in more detail in Chapter 5 to explain the disjunction between room construction variables and room use over time.

Roofs

No intact, preserved roofs were recovered from Grasshopper. The remaining roof construction details are drawn from the position of wall features, beam impressions, charred beam fragments, and roof features recovered during excavation. Data from nearby cliff dwellings, Canyon Creek (Graves 1982, 1983; Haury 1934; Reynolds 1981) and Red Rock House (Reynolds 1981) enhance the reconstruction of roofing strategies at Grasshopper.

Roofing methods in the site core. The preceding discussion of beam sockets suggests that primary beams were typically placed at least 1.6 m above the floor with an average height of 1.82 m above floor. This number is identical to the average distance of 1.83 m (6 feet) from floor to primary beams noted by Haury (1934:38) at Canyon Creek. As at Canyon Creek, the available evidence suggests that two primary beams were most often used in roof construction and that these primary beams paralleled the long axis of the room (Haury 1934:38). Evidence for secondary beams has also been noted at Grasshopper, further reinforcing the parallels to Canyon Creek roofing methods. As an example, excavation of Room 183 in Room Block 2 revealed a pattern of beam impressions associated with the collapse of the roof (Figure 3.26). The primary beam impressions were oriented parallel to the long axis of the room

FIGURE 3.26. Beam impressions, collapsed hearth, and a broken vessel from the roof of Room 183 in Room Block 2. Photograph by Susan E. Luebbermann, 1972. Courtesy of the Arizona State Museum, University of Arizona; neg. no. 31612.

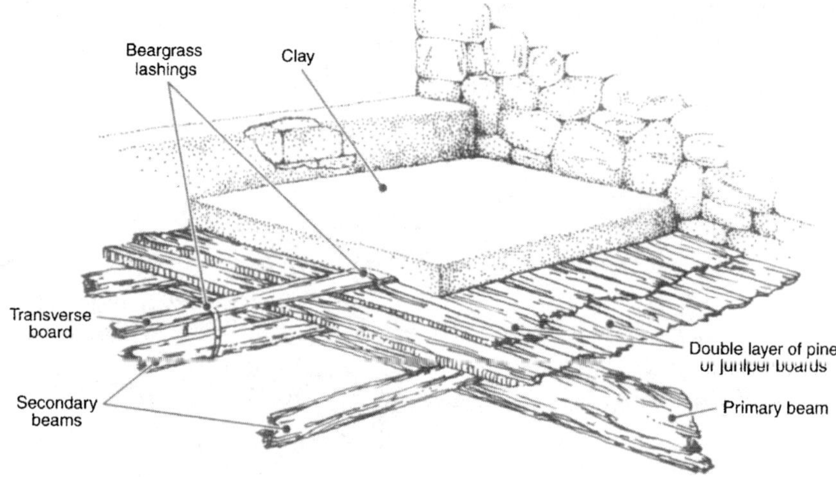

FIGURE 3.27. Roof construction details (after Haury 1934:Figure 8).

and were spaced approximately 0.90 m apart. The secondary beams ran perpendicular to these (across the short axis of the room) and were spaced about 0.20 to 0.25 m apart. The remaining details about roof construction were not preserved, but Haury's description of Canyon Creek serves as an analogue for the construction of Grasshopper roofs and is similar to other descriptions of pueblo roof construction (Figure 3.27; Ahlstrom et al. 1991:629–630; Lange et al. 1993):

> Roofing methods uniformly followed the same plan. Across the longest axis of the room were laid two pine beams averaging one foot in diameter. These were placed from two to four feet away from the walls which they paralleled. Beam ends were imbedded in the masonry and allowed to project a few inches on the outside.... At right angles to the large beams there were next laid juniper poles from three to five inches in diameter, and spaced at about one foot intervals.... Ends of these secondary beams were usually imbedded in the wall, but do not show on the outside. Across the juniper poles there was spread a layer of boards split out of either juniper or pine logs which had a particularly even grain.... Both single and double layers of these planks were used. Cross pieces were laid parallel and directly above every fifth or sixth secondary beam. Leaves of beargrass were next passed over the cross pieces, down between the boards, and tied on the under side of the secondary beam.... The final step in roofing was the ten to twelve inch layer of clay that was evenly spread over the wooden foundation. It was not unusual to put flat rocks in with the roofing clay. [Haury 1934:38].

To differentiate between collapsed roofs and second-story floors, the original excavation notes were first consulted. In many cases both were documented in a single room, and the observations of the excavators were used to determine which was recorded. It was common to find a collapsed roof or second-story floor that fell almost intact into the room. In these cases features and artifacts that once resided on the room's roof were found in relatively good condition close to their original positions on the roof surface (Figure 3.28). In all, 39 roof features were recorded in 26 of the excavated rooms. This undoubtedly underrepresents the features from excavated rooms because, in the early days, roof features may not have been recorded in all cases. Nevertheless, 25 percent of all excavated rooms had roof features. Eliminating the excavated outliers, which did not have full-standing walls and usable roofs, a full 34 percent of the excavated rooms produced roof features, indicating an extensive use of pueblo roofs for habitation. Other researchers have noted the intensive use of roof surfaces; it appears to be a common feature of prehistoric and historic pueblo life (Cameron 1999a; Ciolek-Torrello 1978; Dohm 1996; Lekson 1984; Martin and Rinaldo 1960:284; Mindeleff 1891; Morgan 1965).

The most common feature noted on Grasshopper roofs was the rectangular slab-lined hearth or cooking hearth (Figure 3.29; Table A.21). These features were the same in all respects to hearths found on room floors at Grasshopper and at sites throughout the Pueblo Southwest (for example see Rinaldo 1959:Figure 80; Wendorf 1950:Plate VIII). Mealing bins were also common on room roofs. Although these were not preserved as well as hearths, it can be assumed that they too were identical to their ground-floor counterparts (Figure 3.30).

The final feature often associated with roofs was the entry hatch. Only two were recorded, although every room entered through the roof presumably had one. By comparison, hatchways at Canyon Creek were found in all preserved roofs and were always located near one of the walls, depending on the configuration of

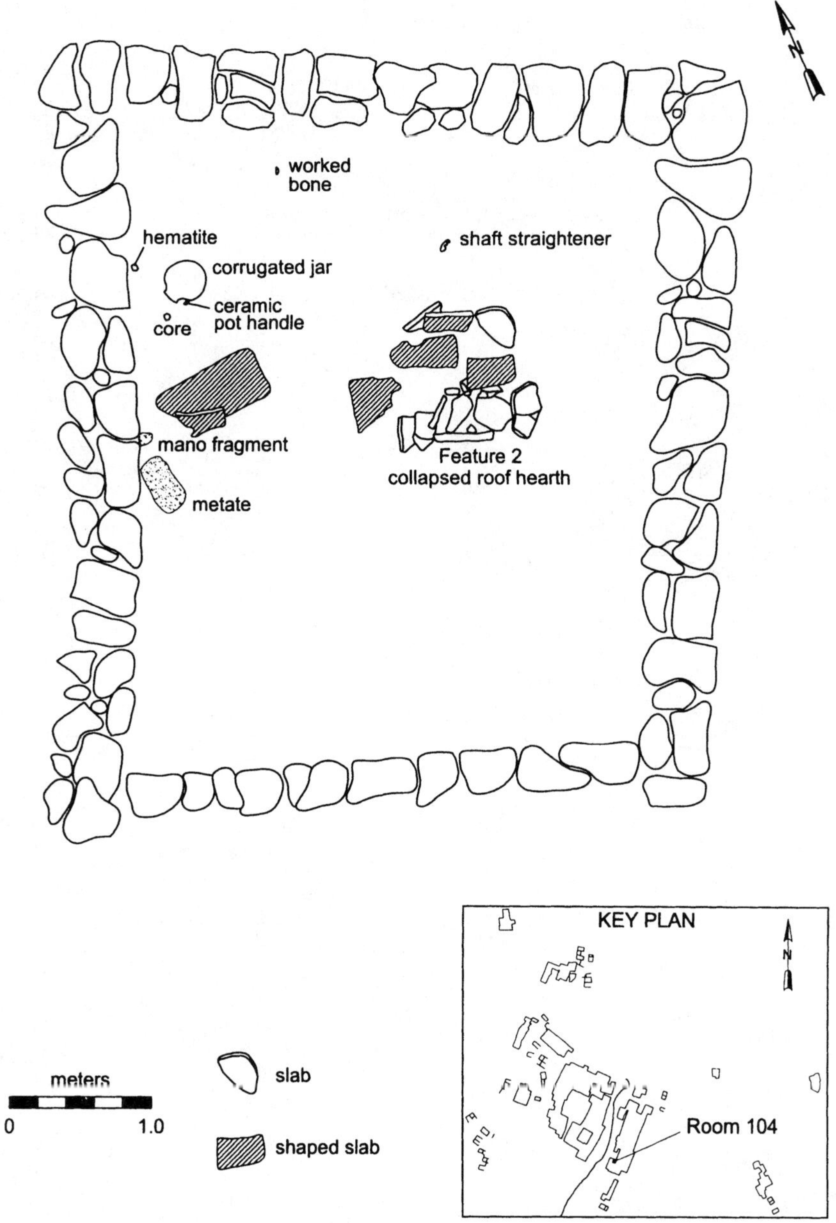

FIGURE 3.28. Materials found on collapsed roof in Room 104 in Room Block 1.

the beam structure of the roof (Haury 1934:43). This location, if it was a common practice at Grasshopper, may explain why so few were recorded. It is not possible to definitively locate the entry hatch in any room at Grasshopper, but based on its normal position nearer to the walls at Canyon Creek, it is likely that the slabs composing the roof entry may have been indistinguishable from the wall fall debris.

At Canyon Creek the long axis of the hatchway was always oriented perpendicular to the nearby wall, and roof hatches and second-story hatches were

FIGURE 3.29. Collapsed roof hearth from Room 104 in Room Block 1. Photograph by Barbara K. Montgomery, 1992.

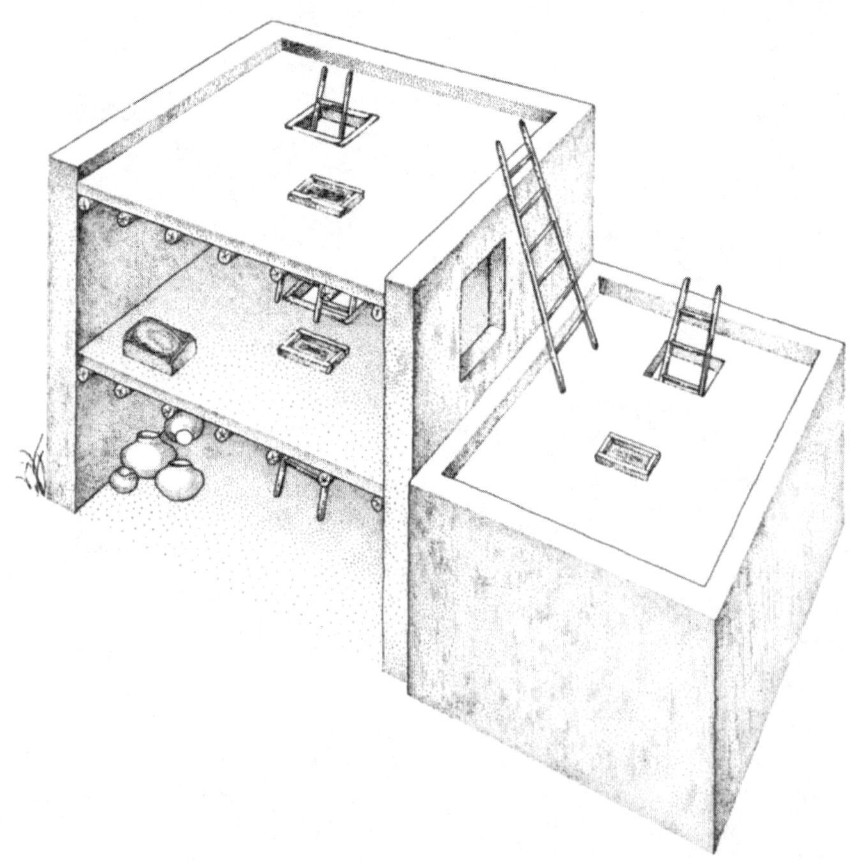

FIGURE 3.30. Schematic rendering of room floor and roof relationships.

always in direct vertical alignment. This presumably allowed light to more effectively reach the lower room and may also have allowed smoke to vent from the ground-floor room. Haury reports that hatchways at Canyon Creek were more regular in size than the doorways and ranged from 0.46 by 0.64 m to 0.53 by 0.58 m. Given the similarities between the two hatchway remnants at Grasshopper and those at Canyon Creek (Haury 1934:Plate XXXI), it can be assumed that their size, location, and frequency were also similar.

The best-preserved example of a hatchway at Grasshopper comes from Room 40 in Room Block 1, where a stack of thin sandstone slabs was found sitting on the roof fall layer (Figure 3.31). The stack of slabs was probably set

FIGURE 3.31. Rooms 40 and 41 being bailed out after a monsoon rain. Collapsed hatchway remnant is visible in foreground. Photograph by R. Gwinn Vivian, 1969. Courtesy of the Arizona State Museum, University of Arizona; neg. no. 22830.

on top of the final wooden covering layer. Clay was then piled around it and other slabs that framed the entryway to prevent the earthen material from falling into the room below. The other example comes from Room 104, where two large flat slabs were found in association with other collapsed roof material. One of these slabs was notched on one side, and it could have fit onto a secondary beam or some other wooden element. Again, the vertical slab likely kept the roof's covering material from falling into the room. Both examples are similar to hatchway construction techniques described at Canyon Creek (Haury 1934:43–44).

Roofing methods in the outliers and their implications for the Pueblo III period. Similarities in roof construction methods in the outliers with sites of the Pueblo III period reveal parallels suggesting a decreased commitment to construction activities. When comparing the main pueblo to the outliers, the prevalence of roof features in the main pueblo presents further evidence in support of the wall height data discussed above, which indicates that the outliers did not possess usable roof surfaces. With the exception of Room Blocks 5 and 7, which are known to have been full-standing masonry room blocks, not a single roof feature was found in the low-walled outliers. The excavation of 77 out of 314 (25 percent) rooms in the core room blocks, however, produced 26 rooms (34 percent) with one or more roof features. Haury's discussion of Canyon Creek, where hearths and other features were found on most roof and second-story surfaces further reinforces this point in a well-preserved context. In contrast to Canyon Creek and the site core of Grasshopper, no roof features or possible roof features were recovered from Grasshopper's outliers or from the Pueblo III period sites of Chodistaas and Grasshopper Spring.

Projecting the observations concerning standing wall height and roof feature distributions back to the Pueblo III sites of Chodistaas and Grasshopper Spring further strengthens the argument for insubstantial roofs at these earlier pueblos. If Grasshopper Spring and Chodistaas Pueblos had full-standing masonry walls and the accompanying usable roof surfaces typical of pueblos throughout the Southwest (Adams 1983; Cameron 1999a:18, 1996; Creamer 1993:26; Dohm 1996; Haury 1934; Lekson 1984; Mindeleff 1891), we would expect some evidence for features on these surfaces. In the excavation of 17 of Chodistaas's 18 rooms (94 percent), not a single roof feature was recorded. At Grasshopper Spring, where 8 of 9 rooms (89 percent) were excavated, the same is true. No roof features were recovered in the extensive excavation of two Pueblo III period sites, whereas 39 features in roof contexts have been noted in a 25 percent sample of the core room blocks at Grasshopper (Room Blocks 1, 2, 3, 5, and 7). When the 14 features in second-story contexts are added to this number, an extensive use of roof surfaces is indicated. This pattern does not appear for Grasshopper's late outliers or during the Pueblo III period.

The absence of usable roof surfaces in the outliers suggests that these structures were less substantial than rooms in the site core and marked a return to seasonal use of the Grasshopper locale, much like that of the preceding Pueblo III period, as exemplified by Chodistaas Pueblo. Using Chodistaas as an architectural analogue for the construction and use of Grasshopper's outliers not only provides an understanding of the use of the outliers but also highlights comparative data that helps to bolster interpretations of construction practices at Chodistaas.

Roof construction in the low-walled outliers is less well understood than that in the core room blocks and at Canyon Creek. One problem with discerning outlier roof structure is that few outlier rooms burned and preservation of wooden elements was uncommon. Another problem is that few postholes were found in outlier rooms, making it difficult to reconstruct roof support systems. To understand how Grasshopper's outliers were roofed, it is necessary to look to the Pueblo III period and Chodistaas Pueblo, which burned sometime in the A.D. 1290s, preserving some limited evidence for roof construction techniques.

Data from Chodistaas Pueblo (Crown 1981; Montgomery 1992; Zedeño 1994) and from Grasshopper Spring, both within a mile and a half of Grasshopper Pueblo (Figure 2.1), suggest that earlier communities in the region were characterized by an impermanent style of architecture that manifested itself in several ways, including room size, wall construction characteristics, the partitioning of activities, and the use of exterior space (Reid 1989:77–78; Reid and Riggs 1995). In contrast to the site core, where masonry rooms of one and two stories were constructed, which housed rooms that reflect more rigidly partitioned activities, walls at Chodistaas and Grasshopper's outliers consisted of dressed low-walled masonry, atop which was constructed a pole frame.

In her doctoral dissertation on Chodistaas ceramics, Crown (1981) assumed that the walls of Chodistaas were full-standing, load-bearing masonry walls. She interpreted pots as resting on the remains of burned roof fall, having collapsed from what were ostensibly roof activity areas. Montgomery's dissertation targeted the formation processes of the archaeological record at Chodistaas and discussed the evidence for low-walled masonry rooms with *jacal* superstructures, such as those in the outliers (Montgomery 1992:148–149). Montgomery suggests that Chodistaas's roofs were either brush ramada-like structures exposed to the elements from the top of the masonry to the roof or were constructed of *jacal* from the masonry portion to the roof. Unfortunately, the excavations at Chodistaas did not reveal the mode of support for these less substantial roofs. Few postholes were found at Chodistaas, and Montgomery (personal communication 1997) hypothesizes that the posts may have been set atop the low masonry walls.

No large primary beams were found at Chodistaas, where the largest beams ranged from 0.06 to 0.16 m in diameter with a mean size of 0.09 m (Montgomery 1992:213). This size range is comparable to secondary beam size from the multiregional sample provided in the following section and suggests that roofs at Chodistaas were not structurally capable of supporting great weights.

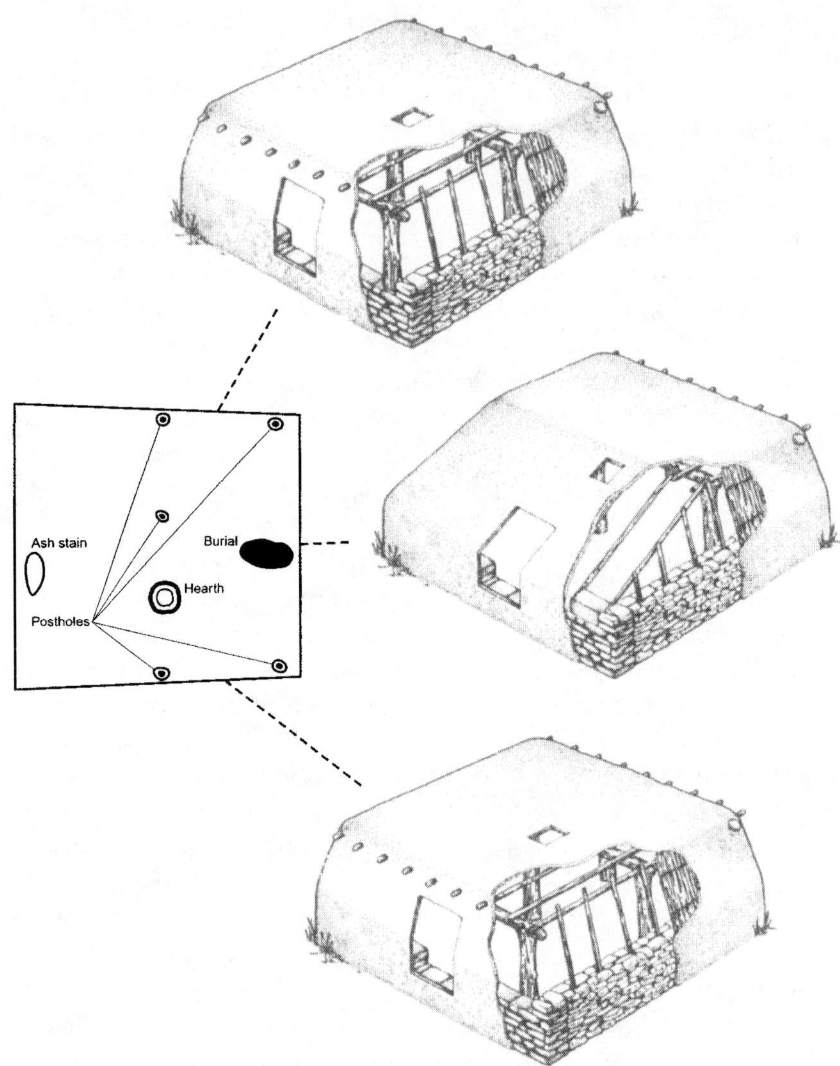

FIGURE 3.32. Three possible roof reconstructions for Room 411 in Room Block 12.

Furthermore, these small diameter beams spanned the long axis of some large rooms (ranging from 4 to 9 m) (Montgomery 1992:214). All of these factors would have compromised the structural stability of the roofs.

Room 411 in Room Block 12 at Grasshopper Pueblo produced the only information about roof support in the outliers. The lower floor of Room 411 produced five postholes or chinked postholes, forming two parallel rows in the east half of the room, all measuring approximately 0.10 m in diameter (Figure 3.32). An additional posthole may have been obscured by an underlying burial (Burial 655). Roof support in the western part of the room was either achieved through a third row of postholes along the western wall, which were not preserved in the clay soil, or by means of posts set on or into the west wall.

As at Chodistaas, long beams approximately 0.10 m in diameter could have been set on top of these posts, spanning the north-south axis of the room in two or three parallel rows. From here, the roof was finished in a manner similar to that discussed above; it was either covered with brush to form a ramada or constructed more formally through the use of *jacal*. Because the wall was low, a doorway could have been left in any of the *jacal* walls, with the masonry portion of the wall acting as a sill. Three examples of possible roof construction in Room 411 are provided in Figure 3.32. These have been rendered as if Room 411 were an isolated room; however, the presence of adjacent rooms only simplified the roof construction depicted here by providing additional structural members on which to anchor the roof.

Room 411 provides the only substantial evidence of roofing techniques in the outliers. The remaining outliers did not yield any additional data. Either postholes were missed during excavation, or as Montgomery suggests, posts were set on the low masonry wall tops. Regardless, the data on outlier wall height undeniably confirms that masonry walls were not carried to the same height as walls in the site core. These impermanent looking rooms are an interesting but poorly understood architectural type in the region. They seem to combine characteristics of subterranean pit houses, like decreased construction costs and insubstantial roof structures (McGuire and Schiffer 1983), with aboveground masonry architecture. Structures like these appear to be adaptable architectural forms, indicating a certain degree of population mobility (Reid and Riggs 1995).

Although it could be suggested that Chodistaas and Grasshopper's outliers were stone robbed, this interpretation is questionable in the face of the available evidence. The excavated rooms in the outliers exhibit the same low walls as those noted at the earlier Pueblo III sites. Because the region was abandoned after the construction of these outliers (Reid 1989:85), and no large later sites were constructed, we know that the outliers could not have been stone robbed. As for the Pueblo III period sites, the availability of limestone and sandstone around the Grasshopper locality today (Scarborough and Shimada 1974) and the evidence provided above, namely the absence of roof features at Pueblo III sites, defies the hypothesis that the builders of Grasshopper's main pueblo stone robbed the Pueblo III rooms. The most parsimonious explanation, given the large body of architectural data available, is that the outliers and the Pueblo III period sites were low-walled masonry structures with insubstantial roofs associated with a seasonal or part-time occupation of the region (Reid 1989:85).

Second-Story Floors

As noted early on by Mindeleff (1891:148–149), there was no difference between roof and floor construction techniques, except that one separated upper-story and lower-story rooms and the other separated a room from the elements, requiring more regular maintenance. The same features found in roof construction at Grasshopper were common on second-story floors, although only one second-story mealing bin was recorded. This duplication of features between roofs and second-story floors explains in part why it is so difficult to identify two-story rooms.

In all, only nine of the rooms thought to have had two stories have produced evidence of second-story floors in the form of features. Fourteen features were recorded from the nine rooms with two-story floor feature assemblages. The majority of these features were rectangular slab-lined hearths (Table A.22). In general, floor/second-story floor/roof features tended to be complementary rather than redundant. For example, rooms with second-story hearths usually did not have ground-floor hearths and rooms with mealing features on the first floor tended not to have mealing features on the second story (Ciolek-Torrello 1978:155–158). Four of the nine rooms with second-story floor features also contained second-story roof features (Table A.21; cf. Table A.22; see also Ciolek-Torrello 1978:159–161). The distribution of second-story floor features corroborates the interpretation that only the three room blocks of the main pueblo contained two-story rooms.

Estimating two-story rooms. One feature of second-story room construction partially explains the difficulty in estimating two-story rooms. As in all pueblos, two-story rooms were constructed as stacked one-story rooms (cf. Graves 1983:296), and the deterioration of the wooden elements within the second-story floor may have caused more damage than if the wall had been built as a single, continuous vertical masonry unit. Given that the roof beams were set into the wall, the deterioration of the upper floor created a weak point that caused the second-story wall to buckle and fall. Thus, much of the upper-story wall may have collapsed into the room below as the ceiling collapsed. Given this, the amount of rubble removed from the room fill, combined with standing wall height, is the best evidence for the original height of the walls in a room. Unfortunately, these data were not collected until late in the history of the field school, after the excavation of two-story rooms had ceased. The limited experimental work with wall weight in the outliers (Rooms 309 and 312) was discussed above and provides an estimate of the amount of rock needed to construct a two-story room.

Several lines of evidence have been used to identify room spaces with a second story. The previous discussion addressed the first two: the standing wall height of excavated rooms and the presence of features in second-story contexts. In addition to these data, the individual room excavation records note the number of stories within a given room, providing a means of verifying the interpretations based on wall height and upper-story feature data. Not only do these groups of information provide a list of excavated second-story rooms (Table 3.21); the distribution of wall height within the rooms was also used to estimate the number of stories of adjacent, unexcavated rooms. Visits to the site and impressions of the rubble mound were used to predict likely locations of second-story rooms and constitute another class of data.[5]

TABLE 3.21.
Characteristics of Likely Two-Story Rooms

Room	Room Block	Standing Wall Height (m)				2d-Story Features	Roof Features	Wall Features
		East	North	South	West			
47	1	3.55	2.75	3	3.1	—	1	5
62	1	2.8	2.12	2.85	2.34	5	1	2
68	1	1.8	2.15	2.4	2.42	—	1	4
69	1	1.7	1.5	2.55	2.34	1	2	3
70	1	2.5	2.5	2.8	2.68	1	—	3
19	2	2.15	2.2	2	1.5	1	—	3
21	2	2.36	2.2	2.14	3.15	—	—	2
146	2	2.0	3.0	1.0	2.14	1	1	5
164	2	2.5	3.19	2.15	2	—	—	5
231	3	2.1	2.21	2.23	2.08	—	2	4
246	3	2.5	2.5	1.83	1.65	2	2	6
269	3	2.16	2.33	2.42	2.57	1	—	10
270	3	2.56	3.05	2.8	3.05	1	—	4
274	3	2.07	2.2	2.45	2.54	1	—	3

The original wall height of single-story rooms is key to estimating which rooms were two stories. Using this measurement, we can more accurately classify as two-story any room with a preserved height greater than the one-story maximum. The first factor to be considered is the height of the roof above the floor. The preceding analysis of beam sockets determined that roof beams were likely to be located between 1.52 and 2.12 m above the room floor. This provides a height estimate for the bottom of the roof, or the room ceiling.

The previous discussion of roof construction demonstrated that roofs in pueblo sites like Grasshopper were composed of several layers of construction material. Several accounts of pueblo roofs were consulted to arrive at an estimate of the potential thickness of roofs at Grasshopper (Table 3.22). These data yielded a mean of 0.55 m with a standard deviation of 0.13 m (1 sigma) and a roof thickness range of 0.42 to 0.68 m. Combining these data with the

TABLE 3.22.
Estimated Roof Thickness Based on a Multisite Sample

Site	Primary Beams	Secondary Beams	Shakes or Planks	Earth	Total
Zuñi	0.18	0.09	0.03	0.19[a]	0.49
Canyon Creek	0.30	0.10	0.03	0.30	0.73
Mug House	0.23[a]	0.09	0.03[a]	0.08	0.43
Montezuma Castle	0.22	0.10	0.03[a]	0.19[a]	0.54
Mean	0.23	0.10	0.03	0.19	0.55
SD	0.05	0.01	0.00	0.09	0.13

Sources: Zuñi (Mindeleff 1891); Canyon Creek (Haury 1934); Mug House (Rohn 1971); Montezuma Castle (Wells and Anderson 1988).

[a]Numbers not provided by author. Values are averages from other sites in the sample.

beam seat data indicates that walls for one-story rooms could have been anywhere from 1.94 to 2.8 m high. This number does not account for the added wall height created by copings around the roofs, which served to contain the earthen covering material (Mindeleff 1891:151–152).

From this point it would be tempting to simply generate a list of those walls exceeding 2.8 m in height and to classify the associated rooms as two-story rooms. Several factors compromise the accuracy of this approach, however. First, many one-story rooms in the main pueblo shared one or more walls with adjacent two-story rooms. This raised certain walls to heights inconsistent with a one-story room, potentially biasing results toward more two-story rooms. Another factor responsible for differential wall height within a room is its location with respect to the underlying topography. This is especially marked in Room Block 3, where the underlying ground surface slopes upward from the southeast to the northwest. Rooms located downslope tended to have higher walls on the upward side to compensate for the increased downslope wall height in the adjacent, upslope, room.

The extent of wall collapse, determined by numerous factors such as quality of construction, the use of perishable materials like wooden doorway lintels, the presence of underlying burials, or (most important) the location of the room relative to the exterior walls of the room block, must also be considered. The walls of rooms adjacent to extramural or plaza areas were more prone to collapse because they were not as well supported by the surrounding masonry as the interior walls. This is especially true for rooms located along the old channel of Salt River Draw, where past bank erosion has caused a serious collapse of many nearby walls. This factor contributes to an underestimation of wall height.

The location of the room relative to areas of rapid sedimentation and refuse disposal is another factor. As discussed previously, this location resulted in walls with deeply buried foundations abutted by new rooms with shorter walls. The final factor related to this phenomenon concerns the way in which a wall was recorded in the field. Most walls were measured from floor to top, but many were measured from the base of the wall. For some walls it was not possible to determine which measure was recorded. These walls, when located in areas where sediments accumulated rapidly, are another source of potential misinterpretation.

Accounting for all possible sources of error and combining wall height data, beam seat and roof thickness data, excavated second-story floor features, and the characteristics of the present Grasshopper mound, I estimate that 68 rooms consisted of two stories, bringing the total number of rooms to 515. This number fits well with past estimates of 500 rooms (Longacre and Graves 1982:1; Longacre and Reid 1974:12; Reid 1989:81), although it is substantially smaller than the 597 rooms estimated by Ciolek-Torrello (1978:Table 3). Of these two-story rooms, 14 were excavated, yielding a 21 percent sample of the two-story rooms. Figure 3.33 shows the excavated and estimated two-story rooms. The

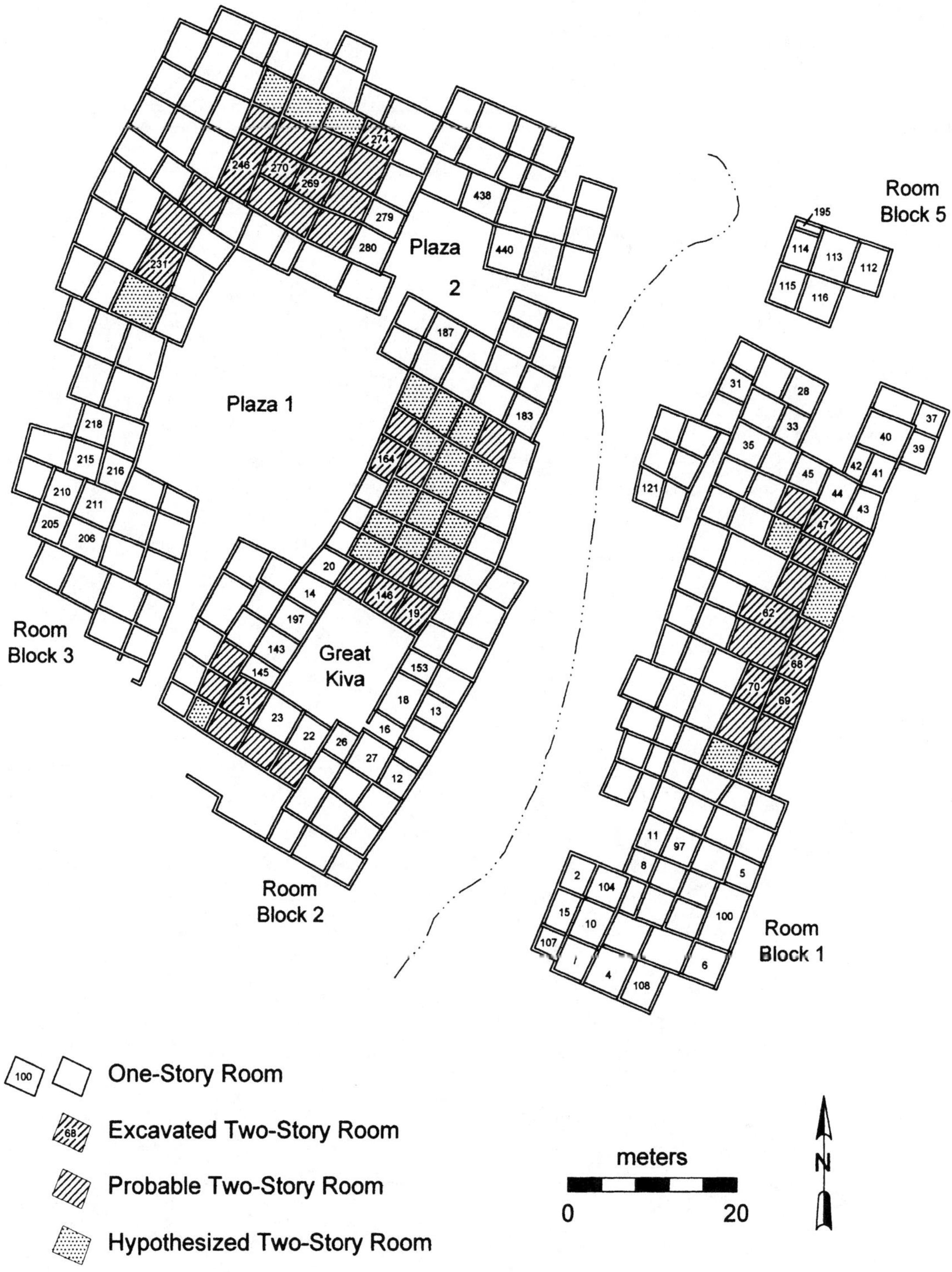

FIGURE 3.33.
Two-story rooms.

unexcavated two-story rooms are divided into two classes. Probable two-story rooms ($n = 29$) were adjacent to one or more excavated rooms, for which there is a higher confidence in the assessment of a second story. The hypothesized second-story rooms ($n = 25$) are based on the presence of surrounding one- and two-story rooms and on the height of the rubble mound in the areas containing the rooms. Room Block 2 has the largest number of two-story rooms ($n = 31$), making it the largest room block, with 123 total rooms. Room Blocks 1 and 3 have fewer two-story rooms, with 18 in Room Block 1 and 19 in Room Block 3, bringing the total room counts to 112 and 120 rooms respectively for these room blocks.

Finally, the extensive excavation of rooms, areas adjacent to exterior rooms, and room cornering has not generated evidence for a three-story room at Grasshopper. Again, Canyon Creek and Red Rock House serve as parallels in that neither of these well-preserved cliff dwellings extended above two stories (Chapter 3; Graves 1982, 1983; Haury 1934; Reynolds 1981). In spite of some claims to the contrary (e.g., Cummings 1940:20; Upham 1982:170), there are few examples of buildings in the Southwest with more than two stories. Exceptions include the sites of Chaco Canyon (Lekson 1983, 1984) and several of its outliers (Fowler et al. 1987; Marshall et al. 1979:57–72), a few examples from Mesa Verde (Fewkes 1909, 1911), and some of the modern Pueblos (Adams 1983; Cameron 1996, 1999a; Mindeleff 1891).

Ground Floors

Floor surfaces were never plastered and most often consisted of packed earth in which the floor features were set. In rooms with multiple floor remodelings, the different floor surfaces were often separated by layers of refuse or by one or more layers of laminated silt, suggesting that rooms were used for refuse disposal and were also periodically inundated by water before and after abandonment. Flagstone floors or partial flagstone floors have been noted in addition to the common earthen floors. Room 9 in Room Block 4 and Room 274 in Room Block 3 had complete flagstone floors, and Room 183 in Room Block 2 had a partial flagstone floor in its southeast corner (Figure 3.34). Rooms 9 and 274 are interpreted to have been ceremonial rooms, based on the presence of flagstone floors and ash pits or ash boxes. Flagstone floors in these rooms are consistent with evidence from other nearby late pueblos such as the Pinedale Ruin in the Silver Creek area or Table Rock and Hooper Ranch Pueblos in the Upper Little Colorado River area, where rooms with ceremonial functions also had flagstone floors (Haury and Hargrave 1931:19, 49–50, Figure 12; Martin et al. 1961:48; Martin and Rinaldo 1960:161). The partial flagstone floor in Room 183 may have been part of a storage bin, or it may have been a remnant from the room's previous use.

The majority of rooms (59 percent) contained only one recorded floor, and a significant number of rooms (27 percent) contained two floors (Table A.24).

FIGURE 3.34. Room 274 in Room Block 3, with flagstone floor. Floor features are visible as breaks in the flagstones. Photograph by Susan E. Luebbermann, 1972. Courtesy of the Arizona State Museum, University of Arizona; neg. no. 31686.

Single floors were especially common outside of the core room blocks. As many as six floor surfaces have been recorded (Room 187 in Room Block 2) in the main pueblo, where rooms were constructed earlier and were occupied for a longer period. Rooms with four or five floor surfaces also occurred in small numbers. Only two rooms lacked features or clear surface indications, and no floor was recorded for them. Room 17 in Room Block 4 was not completely excavated, and trenching of the walls did not expose a floor surface, although one surely existed. The other room that lacked a floor was Room 153 in Room Block 2, which contained some artifacts but no prepared surface or features indicative of a floor. The room did not appear to have been early abandoned, and its proximity to the great kiva and Room 18 to the south (Room 18 is a kiva) implies that Room 153 may have had a limited ceremonial function.

Floor Features: The Semifixed Feature Elements

Numerous floor features were recorded (Table 3.23). The rectangular slab-lined hearth was by far the most ubiquitous (39 percent). These hearths were commonly associated with domestic activities such as food preparation and are often used as a primary indicator of room function (Ciolek-Torrello 1978; Hill 1970a, 1970b; Lowell 1991). Rectangular hearths occurred in all of the 13 room blocks and were found in many of the unaffiliated rooms (Table A.8). Another prevalent class of features consisted of mealing bins (Table A.9) and double mealing bins (Table A.10), which made up 15 percent of the sample of feature

TABLE 3.23.
Number and Percentage of Floor Features by Type

Feature Type	*n*	%
Rectangular slab-lined hearth	118	38.7
Circular hearth	19	6.2
Fire pit	21	6.9
Masonry storage box	15	4.9
Mealing bin	37	12.1
Double mealing bin	8	2.6
Pit	17	5.6
Posthole	26	8.5
Ash box	9	3.0
Bench	7	2.3
Storage bin	5	1.6
Room partitions	3	1.0
Other	20	6.6
Total	305	100.0

types. As with rectangular hearths, these features were found in all room blocks and suggest domestic, food-processing activities. As discussed above, rectangular hearths and mealing bins were relatively common on roofs and second-story floors and were the only classes of features to be preserved in these contexts.

Circular hearths were also common and tend to be indicators of rooms with ceremonial functions (Table A.11). These typically co-occurred with ash boxes and benches (Tables A.12 and A.13; Reid and Whittlesey 1982:693). Fire pits were more informal thermal features than hearths and were somewhat common on floors. They were most often associated with rooms with limited activity and probably provided light and warmth rather than serving a cooking function (Table A.14). The final classes of regularly occurring features were slab-lined storage boxes, subfloor pits, and postholes (Tables A.15, A.16, A.17). Postholes occurred either in isolation or in sets, serving to anchor support timbers in the outliers or acting as components of other room features including *jacal* storage bins and room partitions (Tables A.18 and A.19). Several other features such as vertical slabs, stone platforms, and foot drums occurred in low frequency (Table A.20).

Apart from the patterns just described, there are no correlations between the location of various features within a room and that room's inclusion in a particular room block, nor is there a correlation between the way a feature was oriented and a given room block. The actual placement of features within rooms appears to have been random outside of some general parameters. For example, hearths were usually placed in the center of a room, whereas fire pits usually were constructed closer to walls. Mealing bins were usually placed in a room corner or adjacent to a wall but did not face a standard direction. Storage boxes and ash bins were typically off center in the room but not necessarily near a wall; storage bins were always in or near a corner; benches always lined an entire wall, although they were not located along a specific room wall.

Only one type of feature appears to exhibit a spatially significant distribution. Double mealing bins occurred with a high frequency in Room Blocks 1 and 5, the room blocks constituting the East Village. Two other examples come from later outliers (Room Blocks 6, 8, and 9). The fact that these features occurred only in Room Blocks 1 and 5 in the site core supports the architectural evidence suggesting social differentiation among the community's inhabitants (Chapter 5).

Storage bins and partitions. This class of features occurred intermittently. Storage bins and partitions are discussed in more detail than other floor features because, although not strictly architectural, these features used construction techniques usually associated with architecture. In addition, bins and partitions functioned, like architecture, to partition space. These features are discussed in reference to similar features at Canyon Creek Pueblo in order to provide a more complete picture.

Three types of storage bins occur at Canyon Creek, two of which have direct analogues at Grasshopper. The first type was constructed of masonry. Haury recorded two contiguous masonry storage bins on the roof of Room 27B. Each of these was approximately 1.5 m long by 0.91 m wide and was constructed to a height of 0.91 m. The presence of numerous corncobs in the east bin suggested to Haury (1934:49) that these features were used for corn storage. At Grasshopper an almost identical set of masonry bins was discovered in the north end of Room 352 in Room Block 7. These bins, given room numbers (Rooms 338 and 360), were slightly larger than those at Canyon Creek, measuring 1.43 by 1.4 m (338) and 1.56 by 1.14 m (360) with a maximum height of 1.20 m and 1.12 m respectively (Figure 3.35). Although the material contents were not assessed for this analysis, an absence of floor features in both supports a storage function similar to those at Canyon Creek.[6] Another possible masonry storage bin occurred in Room 216 in Room Block 2, but this feature may simply have been the remnant of a stone partition wall.

Haury's second type of storage bin is of *jacal* construction. These bins measured approximately 1.22 m^2 (4 square feet) and were constructed with a series of vertical posts spaced approximately 0.30 m (1 foot) apart. Smaller branches were then lashed to these posts with bear grass, and the entire structure was covered with clay. One of these features had a flagstone floor (Haury 1934:49). Four, or possibly five, examples of these were found at Grasshopper. One was located on the first story of Room 270 in Room Block 3 (Figure 3.36), and another was located in Room 145 in Room Block 2. Both of these features were constructed in or near the southwest corner of the room and consisted of perpendicular alignments of postholes in the room floor, forming a box in the room corner. The bin in Room 145 was slightly different; it seems to have been lined along the bottom with vertical slabs set into the room floor. The third

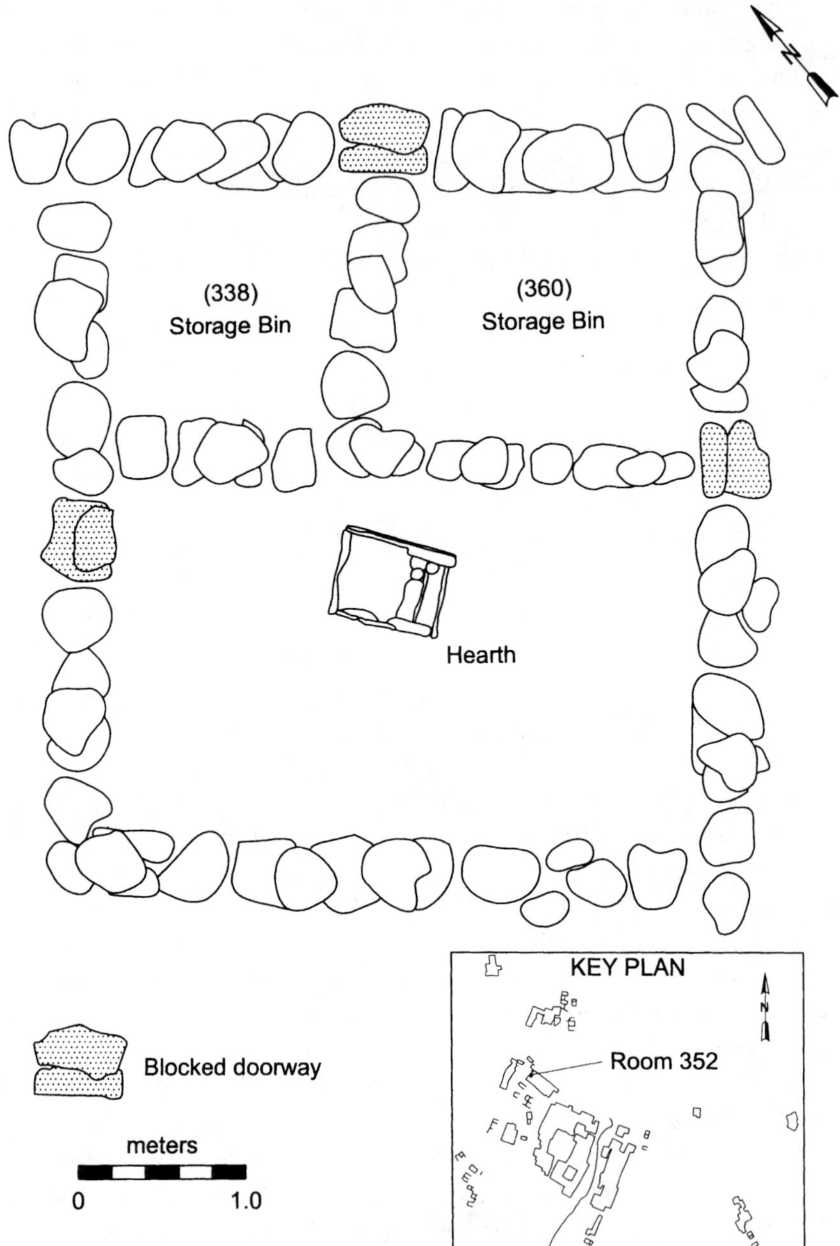

FIGURE 3.35. Masonry storage bins in Room 352 in Room Block 7.

example of a *jacal* storage bin came from Room 27 in Room Block 2. This feature consisted of a series of stone-lined postholes; however, because there was only one line of postholes, it may have been a *jacal* partition wall rather than a storage bin. It was located in the southwest corner of the room like the previous two examples. The fourth *jacal* bin was found in Room 183 in Room Block 2. It consisted of four postholes in a square arrangement less than 1 m

FIGURE 3.36. West wall of Room 270 in Room Block 3, showing the remnant of a *jacal* storage bin in the southwest room corner. Photograph by Susan E. Luebbermann, 1971. Courtesy of the Arizona State Museum, University of Arizona; neg. no. 31192.

apart in the northeast corner of the room. Apart from the postholes, however, no other evidence of a feature was reported. Finally, a stone platform in the southwest corner of Room 143 may be the remnant of a fifth example of these *jacal* bins. Although there was no associated posthole pattern, the platform was similar to the *jacal* bin with the flagstone floor at Canyon Creek (Haury 1934:49).

Haury's third type of storage bin consists of a clay-lined coiled basket, which he found in Room 16B at Canyon Creek (Haury 1934:49). At Grasshopper, however, the poor preservation and the high clay content of the soil composing the room fill would have made identifying this type of feature extremely difficult. Location of these features on a second-story room floor, as in the example given by Haury, would further hinder any identification.

Similar features called granaries were common in the Tonto Basin to the west of Grasshopper, where they were encountered as circular platforms constructed of flat stones or cobbles (e.g., Craig and Clark 1994:103; Elson 1994:236; Jacobs 1997a:83, 1997b:127; Lindauer 1995:141, 1996:128; Vanderpot 1994:154). Many of these features supported the preserved remains of burned, clay-lined basketry or basketry impressions in clay (Craig and Clark 1994:103; Lindauer 1996:845–846). Although it was rectangular, the stone platform from Room 143 at Grasshopper could have been a similar feature. At least one example of a rectangular granary pedestal was documented at the Griffin Wash site in the Tonto Basin (Swartz and Randolph 1994:381).

Preroom Surfaces

Prior to aggregation in the fourteenth century, the Grasshopper locale was the site of a Pueblo III occupation that was probably similar to nearby Chodistaas and Grasshopper Spring Pueblos (Chapter 2). Evidence in the form of ceramics and wall segments found beneath some of the Pueblo IV period rooms attests to an earlier occupation between A.D. 1275 and 1300 (Reid 1989:83). The only definite examples of pre–fourteenth-century architecture recorded in the excavation notes come from the southeast corner of Plaza 1 and from Room 14 in the same general area (Figure 3.9). In Room 14 a subfloor wall segment was recorded south of, and running parallel to, the north wall of the room.

Later excavations in the southeast corner of Plaza 1 (Plaza Section 501) recorded an additional wall segment located approximately 0.50 m to the west of, and roughly parallel to, the west wall of Room 20. The excavators described this wall as "dismantled to its foundations." This wall segment and the one recorded under Room 14 probably represented the west and south walls of a room predating the fourteenth-century aggregation. A failure to locate the remainder of these walls could reflect their partial location under existing walls, and either incomplete subflooring in Room 20 or a total dismantling of the underlying wall by Room 20's builders, which is more likely. The pre–fourteenth-century walls were undoubtedly exploited for building materials as they were leveled for construction of later rooms. The location of this single room is consistent with the hypothesis that locals constructed Room Block 2 (Chapter 5), and additional wall segments probably underlie the unexcavated rooms to the northeast of this area.

In addition to the data from the corner of Plaza 1, a pit house found beneath the floor of Room 113 in Room Block 5 suggests a possible earlier use of the Grasshopper locality (Figure 3.37). A second possible pit house was located near the wall segment in the southeast corner of Plaza 1 (Graves et al. 1982:110). It was not completely excavated. Apart from providing evidence for a possibly long-term use of this portion of the site, these two houses contribute little to our understanding of pre–fourteenth-century occupation.[7]

Although an earlier occupation of the locale produced a proportion of the preroom features, most of them resulted from the use of extramural areas contemporary with the fourteenth-century occupation. As discussed in Chapter 4, the main pueblo grew by accretion from eight core construction units. The exterior spaces around these early units were used intensively and were riddled with numerous features, especially hearths and pits. These extramural areas were also used as cemeteries. Through time, rooms were built over extramural activity areas and cemeteries, creating the abundance of subfloor features and adult burials found during subfloor excavations in the rooms (Reid et al. 1989:806). Although most predated room construction, burials are not always clear markers of preroom habitation surfaces because infants were often interred in late-abandoned room floors, and some adults were buried in early

FIGURE 3.37.
Room 113 in Room Block 5 with a pit house below. A T-shaped doorway is visible in the north wall. Photograph by Barbara K. Montgomery, 1981. Courtesy of the Arizona State Museum, University of Arizona; neg. no. GFS 81–11.

abandoned rooms. In addition, bird and other animal burials were also not counted as features because they, too, were likely interred into room floors. For example, subfloor excavations in Room 246 in Room Block 3 yielded several bird burials, including hawks and macaws.

Figure 3.38 shows the distribution of known preroom features in relation to core architecture (Chapter 4). As this figure shows, no features suggesting use surfaces were recorded beneath core architecture. The only exceptions are Room 345 in Room Block 8, all of the core rooms of Room Block 5, and Room 6 in Room Block 1. In the former case, however, Room 345 was once an extramural space in the open end of a three-walled carport. Because this room was separated from Room 353 by the addition of two partition walls and no bounding walls, it is, by necessity, classified as core architecture. In Room Block 5 there was significant evidence for preroom-block use of the area, including a pit house. Preroom features here were constructed as part of the use of the pit house or were associated with the activities of the early occupants of Room Block 1. The features under Room 6 suggest that it was constructed later than other core architectural units (Chapter 4).

Several areas of the site exhibit intensive use of extramural space. This is especially true of the area around the Great Kiva, once Plaza 3. The rooms around the Great Kiva were literally filled with subfloor hearths, pits, and other features (including burials) suggesting intensive preroom use of Plaza 3 before it became the Great Kiva. The same is true for the northern end of Room Block 1. Overall, the distribution of subfloor features is useful for identifying

FIGURE 3.38. Distribution of nonburial subfloor features in relation to core construction units (room block locations not to scale).

areas of intense extramural activity; however, lack of excavation in many of the core architectural units limits the usefulness of subfloor features as indicators of core versus noncore construction, a topic explored using other lines of architectural data in Chapter 4.

COMMUNAL SPACES

Plazas and Extramural Areas

Grasshopper's three plazas were architecturally unremarkable. They lacked a single prepared surface but were focal points for activity, evident in the number of features and burials contained within them (Whittlesey et al. 1982:29–30). They were not laid out and constructed as planned units but rather were left as open areas as the site grew around them. Growth patterns suggest that the plazas were always central to the community and that early site construction was directed toward demarcating public areas (Chapter 4; Riggs 1994a:81).

The large central plaza, Plaza 1, measured 750 m², Plaza 2 was 152 m², and Plaza 3/Great Kiva measured 185 m² (Table 3.24). All of these measurements

TABLE 3.24.
Metric Characteristics of Formal Communal Spaces

	Length	Width	Area[a]	Area[b]
Plaza 1	27.13	25.63	695.34	750.37
Plaza 2	16.10[c] (15.17)	10.14[c] (11.97)	163.25[c] (181.58)	152.25
Plaza 3/Great Kiva	14.88	12.22	181.83	185.16

[a]Length × width.

[b]Polygon measured by AutoCAD®

[c]Because of the irregular shape of the space, maximum continuous wall length is used and mean dimensions are shown in parentheses.

exclude the three corridors: the southern corridor into Plaza 1, the corridor connecting Plazas 1 and 2, and the eastern corridor into Plaza 2. Except for Plaza 3, which was converted into the Great Kiva, rooms were constructed inside these large spaces relatively late in the occupation (i.e., Room 438 was built in Plaza 2 between 1331 and 1340; see Graves 1991; Riggs 1994a). As is evident from this late infilling, the seemingly static spaces portrayed on the final site plan can be misleading in communities like Grasshopper, where rapid population influx continually altered the form of exterior space (Chapter 4), making the open spaces in which many of Grasshopper's inhabitants interacted look different at any given point in time from those portrayed on the modern site plan.

The Great Kiva

The size and the form of Grasshopper's Great Kiva are comparable to similar structures at other large, late-aggregated sites in the central mountains (Table 3.25). Rectangular great kivas have been excavated at three other large mountain pueblos. These include Turkey Creek Pueblo and Point of Pines Pueblo in the Point of Pines region (Figure 2.1; Gerald 1957; Haury 1989; Johnson 1965) and Kinishba Pueblo, southeast of Grasshopper near Fort Apache (Figure 2.1; Baldwin 1934, 1938; Cummings 1940; Haury 1950).[8] The Great Kiva at Grass-

TABLE 3.25.
Comparison of Metric Characteristics from Excavated, Rectangular Great Kivas in the Arizona Mountains

Site Name	Site Number (ASM)	Number of Rooms	Length	Width	Area	Entry
Grasshopper	AZ P:14:1	500+	14.88	12.22	181.83	East
Kinishba	AZ V:4:1	800	18.80	17.60	330.88	South
Point of Pines	AZ W:10:50	800+	15.50	13.80	213.90	East
Turkey Creek	AZ W:9:123	335	16.00	12.00	192.00	East

Sources: Grasshopper (this study); Kinishba (Cummings 1940; Haury 1950); Point of Pines (Gerald 1957; Haury 1989); Turkey Creek (Johnson 1965; Lowell 1991).

hopper was the smallest of those listed in Table 3.25, but aside from Turkey Creek, Grasshopper was also the smallest site. The great kiva at Turkey Creek was only slightly larger than Grasshopper's Great Kiva and, given the differences in settlement history, it may have served a different function (Riggs 1994b; Chapter 5).

All great kivas of this type were rectangular rather than square, and all were entered through a break in the eastern wall (except Kinishba, which is entered through the south). All of these structures contained a fire pit and a foot drum (although it is not clear whether Kinishba contained a foot drum), and all were presumably roofed. Only Kinishba's great kiva contained a bench, suggesting that benches were not common features in these late Mogollon great kivas. These structures were all incorporated into the enclosing room blocks and in most cases appear to have been converted into a ceremonial structure after the area had served as a plaza space. It is unclear whether these were formal plaza areas, but based on data from Grasshopper, these areas were probably intensively used prior to construction of the Great Kiva.

Grasshopper's Great Kiva was confined entirely by Room Block 2. It measured approximately 15 m north-south by 12 m east-west and enclosed 182 m^2. An open doorway connecting Room 16 (located at the southeast corner of the structure) to the Great Kiva may have been used to gain entry into the space (Figure 3.39). Room 16 was small and completely featureless, suggesting that it may have functioned as a vestibule (Thompson and Longacre 1966:263). It is also possible, based on modern Hopi kivas, that there was a roof entry into the structure, although this cannot be confirmed based on available evidence.

The floor of Grasshopper's Great Kiva contained twelve postholes arranged in two north-south oriented rows with an average post-to-post spacing of just under 3 m (Figure 3.40). The two rows of postholes were an average of 4.5 m apart, and the two end posts on either row rested almost against the north and south walls (Figure 3.39). The postholes on the structure floor attest to the fact that it was roofed; however, the manner of roof construction was not evident from materials recovered during the excavation of the structure. Much of the fill of the Great Kiva was removed by backhoe (Thompson and Longacre 1966:261–262), and, as a result, many subtle details of roof construction were missed. The proposed roof reconstruction, although somewhat conjectural, is the most logical, accounting for the location of the postholes, length of spans, and the presence of existing and new architecture at the time the Great Kiva was roofed.

The interpretation offered here is that the Great Kiva's primary beams were run across the short axis of the structure and were anchored to the masonry walls on the east and west sides as shown in Figure 3.41. Secondary beams were set on top of and at right angles to the primary beams (Figure 3.41). This solution allowed the primary beams to be anchored to the masonry walls on either side of the structure while minimizing the span of the secondary beams.

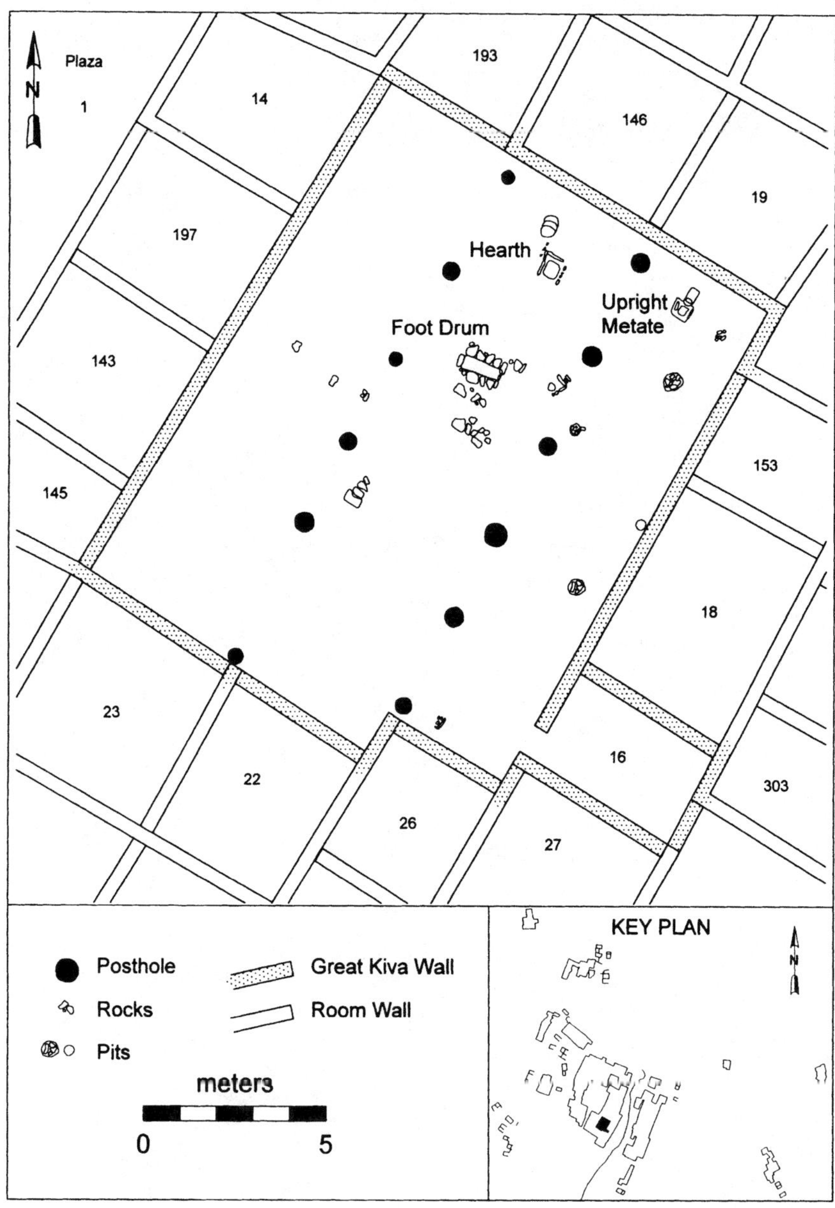

FIGURE 3.39. Plan view of the Great Kiva.

Considering the construction sequence of Room Block 2, this interpretation also explains the support posts adjacent to the north and south walls. These posts were necessary because the rooms to the north and south of the Great Kiva were existing structures, which prohibited the anchoring of beams to the walls (without significant remodeling). Because beams could not be anchored on the existing north and south walls, additional lines of auxiliary primary beams were necessary to support the ends of the secondary beams.

FIGURE 3.40. The Great Kiva after excavation in 1964 with field school students standing at each of the postholes. Photograph by Marion L. Parker. Courtesy of the Arizona State Museum, University of Arizona; neg. no. 10523.

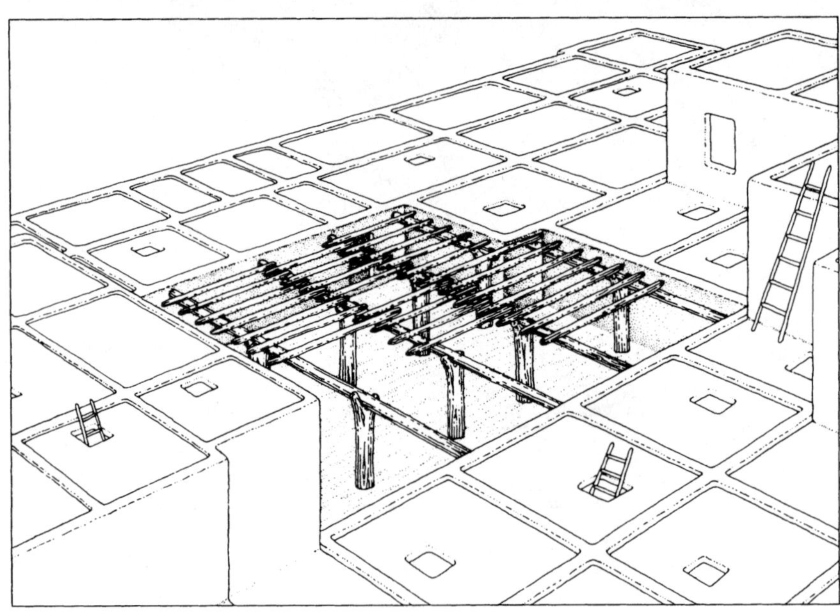

FIGURE 3.41. Artist rendering of Great Kiva roof construction (by Cynthia Elsner Hayward).

If the primary beams had been oriented along the long axis, they would not have been anchored into the masonry walls of the structure. The short axis orientation proposed here supports the ends of the beams on top of walls that were constructed at the same time that the Great Kiva was converted from Plaza 3 (Figure 3.41). This reconstruction is supported by the fact that rooms on either side of the structure were part of two approximately contemporaneous construction units (Riggs 1994a:64, Table 6). In this interpretation of the Great Kiva's roof construction, the span of individual primary beams was held at approximately 4 m (the same as the average Grasshopper room) and the smaller secondary beams were kept to a length of about 3 m. This provided a more stable and well-supported roof structure than if the orientation of the beams was switched and the secondary beams spanned 4 or more meters.

Dating the conversion of Plaza 3 into the Great Kiva has been a point of debate among Grasshopper researchers in the past (Graves 1991:108; cf. Reid 1989:83). The roofing plan advanced herein supports an earlier conversion date by proposing construction contemporary with rooms that enclosed it to the east and west. The roof structure had to have been anchored to these walls, and it seems unlikely that beam sockets were punched into existing walls on the east and west and not on the north and south, where posts adjacent to the walls suggest that a more efficient method of roof support was used. A conversion date after A.D. 1340, as proposed by Graves, would have required reconstruction of almost 30 linear meters of wall, whereas the earlier date dictates a more efficient and constructive scenario: that Grasshopper Pueblo's Great Kiva was demarcated and roofed as a single construction event in the late A.D. 1320s or early A.D. 1330s (Chapter 5).

4

Pueblo Growth and Intrasite Chronology

Time travels in divers paces with divers persons.
—William Shakespeare, *As You Like It*

Pueblo architecture is not a static artifact but one that is constantly being shaped by its users, while at the same time influencing the interactions of its users. This is obvious in the growth sequence developed for Grasshopper Pueblo, which achieved its final form through the construction of blocks of rooms of various size in close proximity to one another. Early on, arriving immigrants built these room suites, settling in close proximity to people with whom they had prior relationships, perhaps related kin groups or relocated small villages. The maintained separation of social groups and the arrival of immigrants throughout the occupation provide independent evidence for the presence of different groups of builders with culturally determined construction techniques and structure use patterns. A reconstruction of pueblo growth provides a dynamic map of the activities of the different builders who assembled Grasshopper Pueblo.

Growth has always been a central theme of Grasshopper research. Room excavation data and data collected by the Cornering and Growth Projects have been used in the past to reconstruct the occupational history of the community (Reid 1973; Reid and Shimada 1982). Reid's community growth model is predicated on a construction phase model for the main pueblo that relies on these data (see below; Reid 1973; Reid and Shimada 1982). In the following pages revised construction-date estimates provided by Graves (1991) are applied to Reid's construction phases to refine the growth sequence and intrasite chronology. Although this refining does not significantly alter Reid's original periodization scheme, it does provide greater temporal resolution for several events in the development of the community.

Community growth at Grasshopper also highlights the relationship between people and their dwellings by demonstrating clear, spatially defined links between individual groups of builders and their houses. The three room blocks constituting the main pueblo were not always the structures portrayed on the final site map. This study suggests that the social groups that made up the Grasshopper community were localized in discrete room blocks that, through time and with the addition of new households and new immigrant groups, coalesced into the larger structures known as Room Blocks 1, 2, and 3. Despite some evidence for homogenization of these groups, the continued separation between room blocks implies that social or ethnic differences were maintained throughout the occupation. Moving beyond chronology and growth, the following discussion provides a model for community settlement that highlights the complex nature of pueblo architecture and portrays the activities of different social or ethnic groups.

CONSTRUCTION DATA AND CONCEPTS

This reconstruction is based not only on room excavation data but also on the work of the Cornering and Growth Projects, which generated the bond-abut and wall face data necessary to reconstruct the sequence of architectural additions to the main pueblo (Reid 1973; Reid and Shimada 1982) and the growth of the outliers. The placement of individual rooms into either the aggregation or dispersion period benefits from relatively good dating of several events in Grasshopper's construction history, whereas assignments of many of the rooms to each period are based on construction unit size and location within the pueblo. Despite the problems in dating some of the architecture, the intrasite chronology provides relatively high resolution in spite of a total absence of cutting dates for construction wood. This chronology is a testament to the effort that went into room cornering and room excavation and the analytical power of the construction unit and construction phase concepts.

Cornering Project: 1967–1971

The year 1967 marked the beginning of a long-term project that ultimately generated a substantial portion of the data used in this study. Initially, opposing room corners were excavated in rooms from the main pueblo for mapping purposes. Data on wall corner relationships were collected, and in subsequent years these cornering operations became known as the "Cornering Project" (Longacre and Reid 1974:20; Wilcox 1982:19–20). Contemporary work in other parts of the Southwest greatly influenced the theoretical basis of the Cornering Project. Once it became clear that rooms were added to the main pueblo in sets, the goals of the Cornering Project were expanded to include the collection of data related to social groups that had been defined elsewhere in the Southwest (Dean 1969, 1970; Hill 1970b; Longacre 1970a; Rohn 1971). Sets of rooms sharing continuously bonded walls were labeled "construction units" and were thought to be the domain of domestic groups (Wilcox 1982:24). The data were used to generate a relative construction sequence for the main pueblo and to reconstruct a developmental history for the community.

Growth Project: 1971–1976

The Cornering Project spawned the Growth Project, implemented in 1971 (Longacre and Reid 1974:22; Reid and Shimada 1982:12). The room blocks of the main pueblo were divided into "construction phases" as a means of ordering contiguous construction units from earliest (core construction units) to latest. Tree-ring dates for the founding of the community were obtained through excavations in the earliest construction units. At the same time, cornering operations were expanded to the outliers, and rooms were excavated in each outlying room block to determine their chronological and social relationship to the main pueblo (Longacre and Reid 1974:22–26; Reid and Shimada 1982:12–14). Relative construction data from the Cornering Project and tree-ring dates from the excavation of rooms were combined to reconstruct a developmental history for the Grasshopper community (Reid 1973:124–134). The following discussion is devoted entirely to the issue of community growth. It combines all of the architectural data (some of which were collected after Reid's formulation of the model) with Reid's construction phase model and with Graves's reassessment of the tree-ring dates to provide a fuller description of community growth.

Reid originally (1973:133–134) modeled community growth using Fortes's (1971) developmental cycle model for the domestic group. The application of this model resulted in four periods, which were stated as follows:

> *Establishment Phase* A.D. 1275–1300
>
> Initial settlement may have begun around A.D. 1275. It certainly had been achieved by A.D. 1300 according to the interpretation of the tree-ring dates.
>
> *Expansion or Aggregation Phase* A.D. 1300–1330
>
> Maximum construction occurred during this period. Expansion in RB 2 and RB 3 was toward the south, forming the roofed corridor around A.D. 1320. Growth toward the north probably formed Plaza II soon after A.D. 1320. Some evidence exists to suggest immigration during the early half of this period was followed by normal population growth. It is hypothesized that the Great Kiva was constructed toward the end of the expansion phase, although stronger tree-ring evidence indicates roofing of this kiva at around A.D. 1350.
>
> *Dispersion Phase* A.D. 1340–?
>
> A dispersion phase is posited on the plausibility that such sites as Red Rock House and Canyon Creek were established initially for seasonal occupation and then for perennial habitation by people from Grasshopper.
>
> *Abandonment Phase* ?–A.D. 1400
>
> The beginning of abandonment would necessarily merge with a dispersion phase negating any neat division. There seems to have been only limited

construction after A.D. 1350. A gradual process of abandonment is suggested and this process was probably completed by A.D. 1400, although there is insufficient evidence to posit when activities finally ceased.

Reid's community growth model has provided the chronological basis for most subsequent analyses of Grasshopper materials and has not required substantive alterations since it was first proposed, although subsequent excavations and refinements in dating have added more detail to the individual growth periods (Graves 1991; Reid 1989; Riggs 1994a). The phases (now called "periods" [Reid and Whittlesey 1999]) identified in Reid's model can now be summarized in light of these refinements.

Little is known about the establishment period because the remains of this occupation underlie the Pueblo IV room blocks of the main pueblo. Excavations at the contemporary Pueblo III sites of Grasshopper Spring and Chodistaas since the original formulation of the community growth model have provided useful analogues for this period (Reid 1989:83). The founding of the main pueblo and most of the site's growth occurred during the subsequent aggregation period. This period culminated with the roofing of the southern corridor into Plaza 1 between A.D. 1323 and 1325 (Riggs 1994a) and with the construction of the Great Kiva in Plaza 3 around A.D. 1330 (Chapter 3; see below). The dispersion and abandonment periods represent a continuum in which at least a portion of the population began moving out of Grasshopper into satellite communities and began to use the area seasonally. Dispersion is represented by the outliers, which mark a return to a pattern of residential mobility just prior to the final abandonment of the region (Chapter 5; Reid 1989:85). The following study of intrasite growth and chronology supports this hypothesis by incorporating data from the outliers and examining their growth relative to that of the main pueblo and to roughly contemporaneous satellite communities, namely Canyon Creek Pueblo. Issues of community change raised by Reid's growth model, such as the nature of community dispersion, the establishment of the community, and the roofing of the Great Kiva, are addressed in more detail.

BOND-ABUT AND WALL FACE ANALYSIS

One of the early goals of the Cornering Project was to obtain bond-abut data to develop a construction sequence (Longacre and Reid 1974:18; Wilcox 1982:19). The analysis of bond-abut patterns has long served as the principal means for building construction sequences in the Southwest (Dean 1969; Graves 1982, 1983; Haury 1934; Lekson 1984; Prudden 1914:50; Rinaldo 1964; Rohn 1971; Wilcox 1975, 1982). Bond-abut analysis is based on the observation that two walls joined in a bonded corner represent a single construction event, whereas an abutted corner indicates either a later or a contemporaneous wall addition (Figure

FIGURE 4.1. Southwest corner of Room 37 in Room Block 1, showing a three-way corner abutment. Photograph by James E. Ayres, 1967. Courtesy of the Arizona State Museum, University of Arizona; neg. no. 15363.

4.1). Bond-abut maps for all 13 room blocks are provided in Chapter 3 (Figures 3.9 and 3.10).

Because walls are subject to a wide range of cultural and natural formation processes (Schiffer 1987), bond-abut relationships alone are not sufficient to build an accurate construction sequence. Remodeling can have dramatic effects on original corner relationships (Wilcox 1982:22). Walls are often remodeled, rebuilt, and replastered; in some cases these processes can be quite extensive (Ferguson et al. 1990). In addition to the complex human activities that alter walls, processes of natural decay can further obscure corner relationships.

Figure 4.2. North wall of Room 210 in Room Block 3, with Rooms 215 and 216 under excavation beyond. Note the number of wall relationships that are visible. Photograph by Susan E. Luebbermann, 1972. Courtesy of the Arizona State Museum, University of Arizona; neg. no. 31682.

In response to the ambiguities inherent in wall corner relationships, wall face analysis was used to further clarify the relationships between different architectural units. Wall face analysis assumes that walls were constructed from the outside of a structure rather than from the inside (Chapter 3). Given that rooms were added to the exterior of existing architecture through time, a smooth-faced wall within a room was almost certainly once exterior, and the space enclosing it was added later (Figure 4.2).[1] As with bond-abut analysis, remodeling and wall decay impact the ability to recognize smooth and rough wall faces. Unless a wall completely collapsed or was entirely reconstructed, however, these processes do not affect wall face analysis to the extent that they influence corner relationships. The wall face data are provided in Chapter 3 (Figures 3.6 and 3.7).

THE MAIN PUEBLO AND THE CONSTRUCTION PHASE MODEL

Analysis of bond-abut and wall face relationships in the main pueblo identified 127 construction units and core construction units (Reid, personal communication 1994). A construction unit is defined as a set of room spaces, built as a single construction episode, that share a continuously bonded wall (Reid 1973:106; Reid and Shimada 1982:13–14; Wilcox 1975:134–135, 1982:21–22). By extension, an individual room space is a subset of the construction unit (Reid 1973:106). Thus, a date assigned to a room contained within a given construction unit provides a construction date for all rooms in that unit.

A core construction unit (synonymous with Wilcox's [1975:133] "core structure") stands alone, independent of any other architecture, and acts as a focal point for subsequent additions (referred to as "aggregation units" by Wilcox [1975:133]). A room block has a specific definition at Grasshopper. It is a set of contiguous construction units *spatially separated* from other architectural units (Reid 1973:106). Although thirteen room blocks are recognized, Reid's construction phase model addressed only the main pueblo; as a result, the bulk of this discussion focuses on the growth of this portion of the site.

To track community growth, Reid organized the construction units in the main pueblo into 14 construction phases (Reid 1973; Riggs 1994a). The sequence of construction units by construction phase is based on dependency relationships among construction units. All units of a given construction phase depend directly on units of the immediately preceding phase. A single construction phase incorporates all of the construction units added at the same point in the relative sequence, regardless of their location in different room blocks (Reid and Shimada 1982:14). For example, all core construction units are assigned to Construction Phase 1; all construction units added to the core units are assigned to Construction Phase 2, and so on (Figure 4.3). Because this is a relative ordering, the relationship among construction units of a given phase is only a classificatory one (Dean 1969:198). The absolute date of a particular construction unit's addition is independent of its construction phase designation.

The major events in the construction history of the main pueblo are summarized briefly with reference to the 14 relative construction phases. During this discussion, absolute contemporaneity is assumed for each construction phase. Then, the tree-ring dates are incorporated to build a chronology for the main pueblo.[2] After reviewing main pueblo growth, the discussion turns to the outliers and incorporates data not used in the original study of pueblo growth (Riggs 1994a).

Relative Growth

Construction Phase 1 represents the founding of the Pueblo IV period component. In this phase the main pueblo was composed of eight spatially distinct core construction units. Four of these units acted as nodes for architectural additions in subsequent early growth. Construction units in these earliest phases were generally large and expanded outward from the four construction loci in trajectories incorporating the central open areas that later became the plazas (Figure 4.3). In contrast to these active construction loci, the four remaining core units remained inactive throughout the early construction phases. The inactive units were either not contemporaneous with, or were not socially linked to, the four active construction loci. By Construction Phase 4, one of the inactive units was incorporated into what became Room Block 3, signifying either new construction or perhaps a change in social relationships

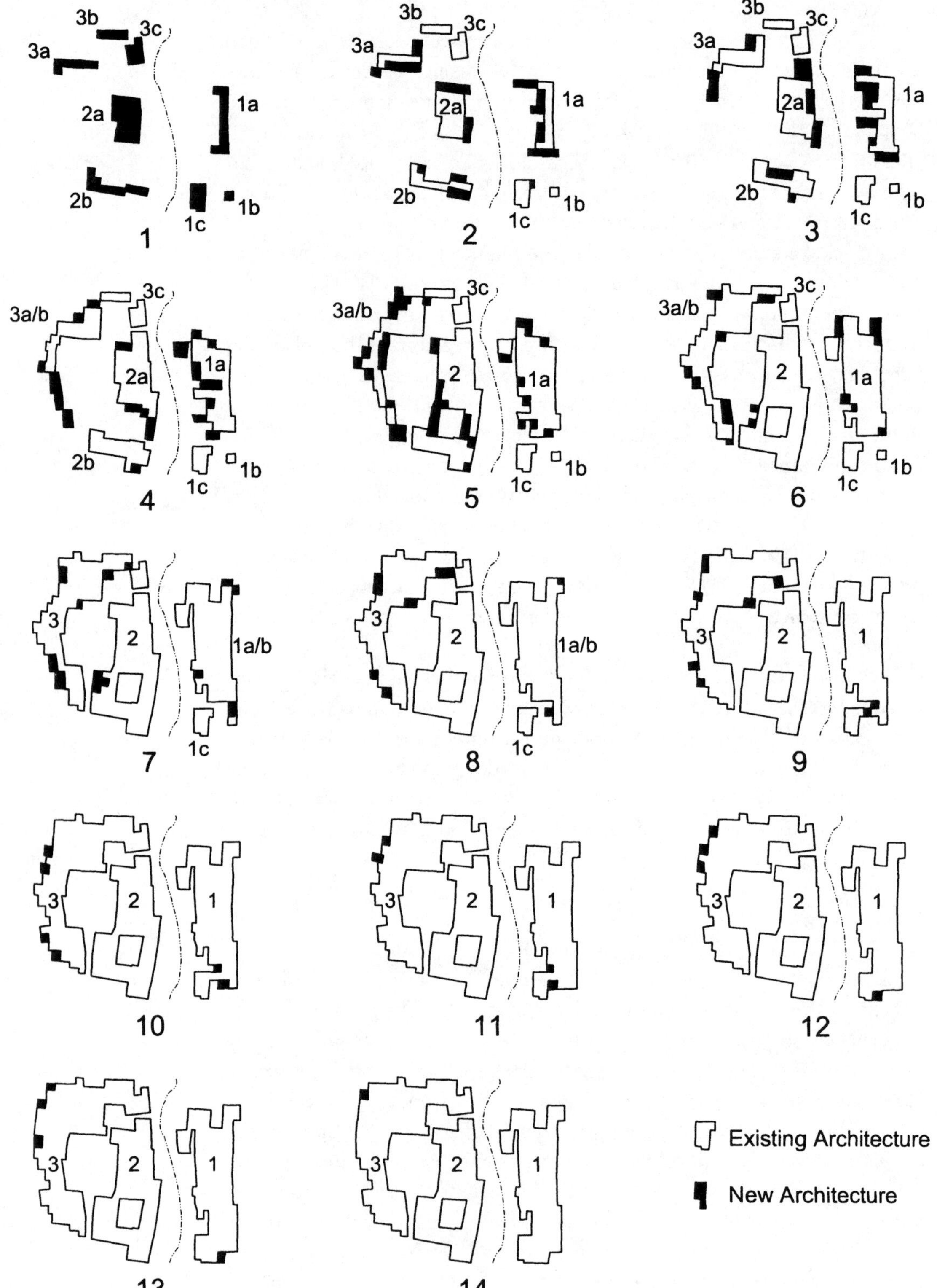

FIGURE 4.3. Construction phases in the main pueblo.

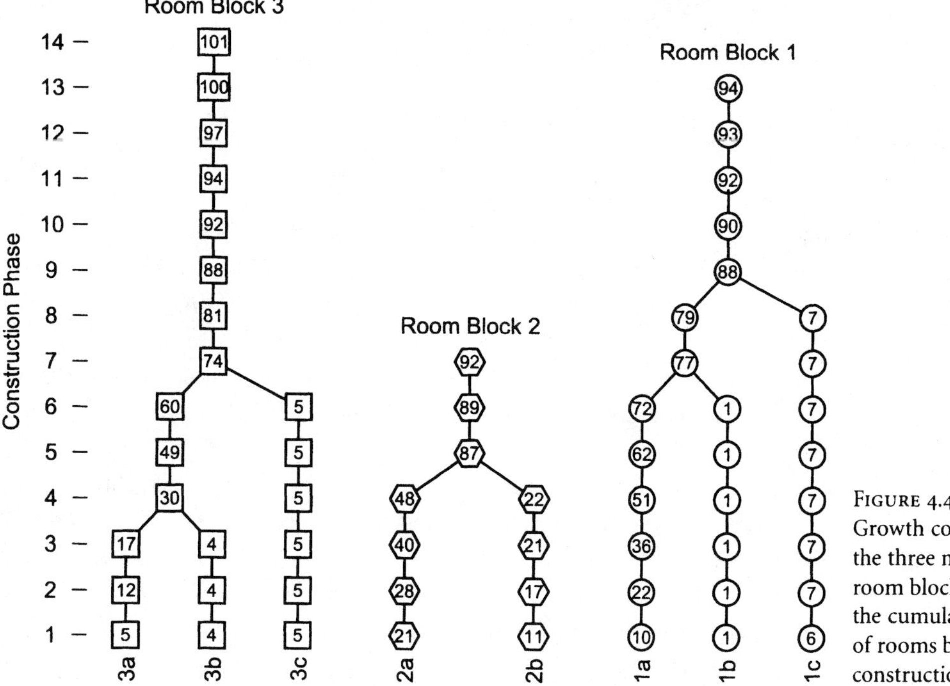

FIGURE 4.4. Growth comparison of the three main pueblo room blocks, showing the cumulative number of rooms by construction phase.

among the inhabitants of the existing architectural units. Single-room additions also became more prevalent at this point in the construction sequence. By Construction Phase 5, Room Block 3 had elongated to bound Plaza 1, and Room Block 2 was fully consolidated with the linkage of its two active construction loci (Figure 4.3).

Construction phases 6 and 7 are marked by a sudden decline in the number of added rooms. Growth was complete in Room Block 2 by Construction Phase 7, and further consolidation occurred in Room Blocks 1 and 3, leaving only four room blocks in the main pueblo (Figure 4.3). By this point in the relative sequence, single-room additions were as common as multiple-room construction units, and much of the new construction was restricted to the outer margins of the room blocks and to the plaza areas. The final consolidation of Room Block 1 occurred in Construction Phase 9, and all subsequent growth took the form of single-room additions in Room Blocks 1 and 3.

Several trends in the sequence are evident when relative growth is represented graphically (Figure 4.4). The main pueblo began as eight core construction units or room blocks and eventually coalesced into the three room blocks seen on the ground today. Room Blocks 1 and 3 each began as three room blocks (1a, 1b, 1c and 3a, 3b, 3c), and Room Block 2 initially consisted of two room blocks (2a, 2b). Room Block 2 also contrasts with Room Blocks 1 and 3 in that new rooms were added to both core units early in the relative sequence, and the entire room block had reached its final form by Construction Phase 7. Room Blocks 1 and 3, on the other hand, began as three individual core construction units, but subsequent early growth proceeded from a single construction unit while the remaining two units were initially inactive.

This inactivity points to two possible social processes. Either these Construction Phase 1 units were added later, or they were built early and no rooms were added to them until they were incorporated by construction of surrounding units. As examples of the first process, Room Block 3b could have been built as late as Construction Phase 3, and Room Block 1c could have been added as late as Construction Phase 8 (Figure 4.4). Room Block 5, located north of Room Block 1 (Figure 2.4), serves as a model for the latter possibility. It appears to have been built early and never incorporated into Room Block 1. In these cases no absolute dates were obtained that would confirm either interpretation.

The lack of additions to these early construction units is probably a combination of both processes listed above. Room Block 3b was probably not built at the same time as Room Block 3a, as implied if classificatory contemporaneity is assumed for construction units. Rooms were not added to Room Block 3b until Construction Phase 4, when it was joined to Room Block 3a. Room Block 3b probably represents the arrival of a new social group at the pueblo soon after the initial founding of the community. Subsequently, as resident households expanded, and as intracommunity relationships were formed, it was incorporated into Room Block 3. A similar process was probably working in Room Blocks 1c and 3c. In fact, Room Block 1c was probably constructed relatively early in the sequence and may have stood alone for an unknown length of time. This early unit was excavated in its entirety, and no subfloor features suggestive of preroom activities were found beneath its rooms. This situation mirrors Room Block 5's continued isolation despite its seemingly early construction (see below).

Room Block 1b, on the other hand, because of its size, was probably not constructed until relatively late. It probably represents the expansion of a resident household that built a single room (Room 6) and immediately joined it to Room Block 1 through the construction of Room 100 in Construction Phase 7 (Figure 4.3). The fact that the remains of three masonry ovens were found below the floor of this unit is further evidence that the area beneath it acted as an outdoor activity surface for an unknown length of time before the construction of Room Block 1b (Room 6).

The situation in Room Block 2 is relatively clear-cut. Residents built both of the core construction units early, defining a plaza space between them (Plaza 3), and added onto these units relatively quickly. The residents of Room Blocks 2a and 2b were locals, possibly representing large extended family groups. The size of the core units in Room Block 2 provides further evidence that the builders did not come from far away. Because the founding groups in Room Block 2 were large, subsequent household expansion quickly resulted in a single room block.

An additional phenomenon is evident in the relative construction sequence when comparing construction in the East Village (Room Block 1) with that in the West Village (Room Blocks 2 and 3). Although the pattern of growth in both areas can be described as agglomerative, the addition of new construction units in the West Village seems to have been directed to outline public spaces, whereas that in the East Village appears more random, consisting of large blocks of rooms joined to the western side of the room block. In the West Village, Room Block 3 was expanded rapidly to incorporate the space that later became Plaza 1. This suggests that a cooperative effort toward the construction of Plaza 1 may have affected the placement of newly arrived households. In fact, dates from these rooms suggest that most of this construction took place within a two-year span from A.D. 1323 to 1325 (see below).

This rapid early growth indicates another pattern. Throughout the construction sequence there was a dichotomy in the size of construction units between small, single-room additions, and large units composed of three or more rooms. From the beginning to the end of the relative sequence, the number of large units decreased as the frequency of smaller units increased (Figure 4.3). Long-standing models of aggregation at Grasshopper attribute early community growth to immigration and later construction to the budding off of households as part of the domestic cycle (Ciolek-Torrello 1978; Longacre 1975, 1976; Reid 1973; Reid and Shimada 1982; Tuggle 1970). The decrease in the average size of construction units supports this interpretation. Even without this support, however, it is beyond refute that five-room construction units result from activities of social groups that differ in size from groups that construct single-room units. The extent to which the spatial and temporal trends described above can be attributed to this particular phenomenon warrants further investigation, but these data suggest a demographic shift as one reason for the intricacies in the construction sequence.

This treatment of the relative construction data leads to three important conclusions regarding the social dynamics of the founding and growth of Grasshopper Pueblo in the early fourteenth century. First, the fact that the main pueblo grew from eight spatially distinct room blocks into three large room blocks suggests the presence of different social or ethnic groups in the founding population of the community. Direct parallels can be drawn with reference to Hopi ethnography, as discussed by Mindeleff (1900:648): "Related clans commonly built together, the newcomers seeking and usually obtaining permission to build with their kindred; thus clusters of rooms were formed, each inhabited by a clan or phraytry. As occupancy continued over long periods, these clusters became more or less joined together, and the lines of division on the ground became more or less obliterated in cases, but the actual division of the people remained the same."

Although it is not possible to suggest that early room blocks represent clans or phraytrys, Mindeleff's discussion closely parallels the situation at Grasshopper. Individual social groups of some form moved into the community and built their dwellings next to people with whom they shared some affinity. As growth continued, the lines between these groups became blurred. Conversely, room blocks that were initially isolated, such as Room Block 1c or some of the outliers, probably represent the constructions of people who were allowed to settle in the community without sharing preexisting social bonds with its inhabitants. Once again, Mindeleff (1900:649) provides a parallel from Hopi ethnography: "Detached rooms, such as those shown on these plans, *always* indicate a family or person not connected directly with the rest of the inhabitants, perhaps the representative of some other clan or people. A stranger coming into the village and wishing to build *would be required to erect his house on such a separate site*" (emphases added).

The second conclusion regarding social dynamics and community growth, the placement of construction units through time, especially in the West Village, suggests a strong cooperative element between residents of the community and newly arriving immigrants. The seemingly deliberate construction of rooms around what became Plaza 1 implies that new arrivals were instructed to build in a certain location, one that would serve to formalize public space in the community, probably as an attempt to spatially and symbolically segregate the inhabitants of the community from those outside it (cf. Rapoport 1982:169).

Finally, the overall change in the size of newly added construction units through time acts to separate the period of early immigration from a period during which the expansion of resident households was the primary contributor to main pueblo growth. In Room Blocks 1 and 3 the early large units indicate the arrival of new groups in the community. By contrast, the early additions to Room Block 2 are probably best viewed as the expansion of an already large group of people, who had been living at Grasshopper before the arrival of new groups from the region and from areas farther away. The final additions to the main pueblo in Room Blocks 1 and 3 clearly represent the slow expansion of households in these room blocks at a time when people may have been living at Grasshopper on a more seasonal basis. Adding absolute dates to this construction sequence further enhances the picture of the different social groups' activities by placing them in time.

Tree-Ring Dates

Alone, the relative ordering of wall construction provides no way of estimating the temporal hiatus between existing architecture and subsequently added rooms. For example, how much time elapsed between the arrival of one group and the arrival of the group that built rooms next to it? Assigning absolute dates to the construction sequence just described provides an understanding of the temporal relationships not only between these aggregation units but also, perhaps more important, among the spatially discrete construction loci. Fortunately, because the construction of wooden roofs is a typical component of pueblo rooms, the application of dendrochronology provides absolute construction dates (Dean 1978; Haury 1935). In open-air sites like Grasshopper, however, construction timbers are almost always inaccessible without excavation and, even then, are seldom preserved unless the structure's roof was burned.

Ceramics firmly place the major occupation of Grasshopper in the fourteenth century; however, the poor preservation of wood remains has hampered efforts to assign precise dates to most construction events. In spite of the fact that more than 2000 dendrochronological samples were collected, only 164 of these provided dates. Of these, only one sample represents a cutting date (Dean and Robinson 1982:Table 8.1). Unfortunately, the occurrence of this sample in Oven 2 increases the probability that it represents "old wood" (Schiffer 1986). Regardless, its nonarchitectural context renders this sample useless for dating room construction.

Because of the lack of cutting dates and the poor quality of samples in general, Dean and Robinson's analysis of the tree-ring material assigned construction dates to only two events. Based on the date distribution, including date clustering, the earliest event they could date was the roofing of the southern corridor into Plaza 1, which occurred at A.D. 1320 or slightly later (Dean and Robinson 1982:47). Conversion of Plaza 3 into the Great Kiva was the last event that they could place in time. Dean and Robinson (1982:47) could speculate only that this occurred sometime late in the sequence.

The vast majority of Grasshopper's tree-ring dates are "vv" dates, indicating that the outer ring on the specimen is an undetermined distance from the original outer ring (Dean and Robinson 1982:Table 8.1) and that the date is a noncutting date. Figure 4.5 is a stem-and-leaf plot (Ahlstrom 1985:62–63) of the raw tree-ring dates and includes the 164 dates provided by Dean and Robinson (1982:Table 8.1) as well as the 15 tentative dates included in Graves's ring-loss analysis (Graves 1991:104). Figure 4.5 confirms Dean and Robinson's (1982) assessment of the tree-ring sequence. Applying the principles of date clustering (Ahlstrom 1985; Bannister 1962) dates the majority of construction at the pueblo to post A.D. 1300. The peak in the first decade of the fourteenth century is best interpreted as founding and early population movement into the community. Dates earlier than this reflect either reuse activities, sample deterioration, stockpiling, or the use of old wood (Ahlstrom 1985:67). The small cluster of dates in the 1270s may represent reuse of beams from the earlier occupation of the locale, although the deterioration of samples cannot be discounted as a possible source of this anomaly. As mentioned above, the single underlined cutting date comes from a nonarchitectural context in one of the masonry ovens east of Room Block 1 and probably reflects the use of old wood for fuel. Dates later than the large cluster in the early 1300s reflect continued construction and repair activities until the site's abandonment sometime prior to A.D. 1400.

Following Ciolek-Torrello (1978:80), I have plotted the tree-ring dates as a cumulative density histogram and fit a curve to this plot. As noted by other researchers, the tree-ring dates approximate a logistical growth curve (Ciolek-

A.D.		
	138	5
	137	135
	136	6
1350	135	3
	134	236777
	133	00012222336
	132	000013356899
	131	00011111222233345567888888888899999
1300	130	011111222233334455555556678888999999
	129	113344788
	128	012246778
	127	123344478899
	126	1<u>3</u>57789
1250	125	233
	124	0022378
	123	12478
	122	56899
	121	
1200	120	045689
	119	004489
	118	14
	117	
	116	
1150	115	
	114	
	113	
	112	9
	111	
1100	110	1
	109	0

"_" = cutting date

N = 178; min. = 1090, max. = 1385, median = 1304, lower hinge = 1271, upper hinge = 1318, range = 295

Quartile Ranges

1st	2d	3d	4th
181 years	33 years	14 years	67 years

FIGURE 4.5. Stem-and-leaf plot of tree-ring dates from all recovery contexts.

Torrello 1978:80; Reid 1989:83) suggesting nonuniform, density-dependent growth processes (Eighmy 1979). A similar plot was created for the addition of construction units through time as an initial step in determining the fit between the tree-ring dates and the main pueblo construction sequence. Once again, a curve was fit to the cumulative growth histogram, and these data portray a logistical, or nonuniform, growth trajectory (although somewhat truncated at the establishment end). Figure 4.6 provides a side-by-side comparison of the relative room addition curve and the tree-ring curve and demonstrates that the two ways of estimating growth are similar, suggesting a good fit between the relative sequence and the tree-ring dates. The shape of the relative curve corresponds well with the tree-ring growth curve. Apart from size differences, the two curves could be overlaid if Construction Phase 1 on the relative curve were placed between A.D. 1290 and 1300, when logistic growth began (Ciolek-Torrello 1978:80). Given the apparent closeness of fit, how do individual tree-ring dates compare to the growth sequence described above and what can the combination of these two data sets say about the intrasite chronology?

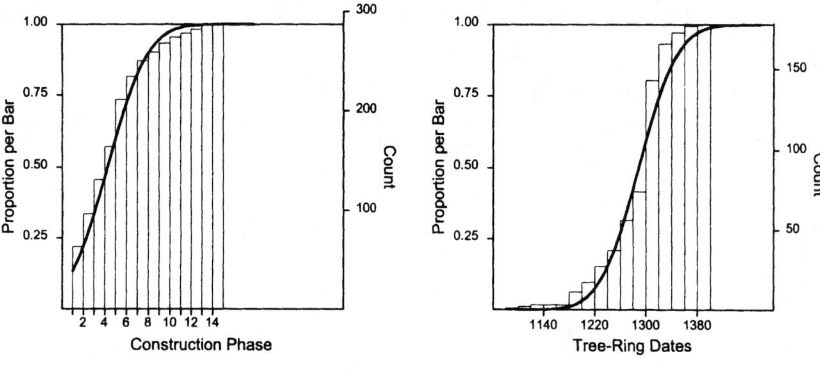

FIGURE 4.6. Comparison of relative growth vs. tree-ring date distribution.

Corrected tree-ring dates and construction date estimates. In an attempt to refine the Grasshopper chronology, Graves undertook a reanalysis of Grasshopper's tree-ring dates (Graves 1991). Graves's method for estimating ring loss from dendrochronological samples provides a probable construction-date range for several rooms. Graves's intent was to provide a means of estimating the gap between the dated event (the last preserved ring) and the reference event (the death of the tree) (Graves 1991:85; Dean 1978). Ultimately Graves sought to relate the last dated ring to the target event (room construction). Graves's method refined Plog's (1977, 1980) technique for estimating ring loss. To account for the shortcomings of Plog's method, Graves separated the tree-ring samples by species and used only samples from the same general region and time period (Graves 1991:89). These samples consisted of material from several Pueblo period sites in the mountains of east-central Arizona, including Grasshopper.

Through comparison with the estimator group of 38 sites, Graves determined that, with the exception of Douglas fir, the Grasshopper series is typical in the mean number of rings present as well as in patterns of wood use (Graves 1991:101–112). Combining his technique for estimating ring loss with the traditional methods of tree-ring analysis of date clustering and date overlap (Bannister 1962; Douglas 1935; Haury 1935), Graves generated ranges of possible construction dates for each room containing dated tree-ring specimens (Graves 1991:Table IX). The following discussion provides a construction chronology for the main pueblo by summarizing an earlier analysis that merged Reid's construction phase model with Graves's construction-date estimates (Riggs 1994a).

METHOD FOR DATING CONSTRUCTION UNITS

Although Graves's date estimates improve the resolution of construction dates, individual construction events can never be assigned a single calendar date. Only time placement (Smiley 1955:20) is possible for the construction of an individual room or construction unit.

Given that a construction unit is a set of rooms that are absolutely contemporaneous (Reid 1973:106; Reid and Shimada 1982:13–14; Wilcox 1975:134–135, 1982:21–22), a single dated room provides the construction date for the entire construction unit. Thus, Graves's construction-date estimates apply not only to individual rooms but also to the construction units containing those rooms. Further, because construction events are assigned temporal intervals rather than absolute dates, each construction unit has an initial construction date (the earliest possible date that the construction unit could have been built) and a terminal construction date (the latest possible construction date). As all architectural additions were dependent on a few core construction units, the spatial relationships among construction units are essential to assigning time placement to undated, and even unexcavated, rooms in the main pueblo.

A terminal date of a dated dependent unit provides a terminal construction date for all of the units on which it depends (see Riggs 1994a:65–82 for an in-depth discussion of the methods and application to Grasshopper construction). Following this logic, all architecture dependent on a single dated unit assumes the initial date of that unit as its initial construction date (cf. Wilcox 1975:133–139).[3] As noted above, architecture added independently of prior and subsequently dated construction units presents significant problems for dating construction. For example, all construction units added to Room Block 1 were independent of those added to Room Block 2 and, as such, have no bearing on the construction of Room Block 2 (cf. Rohn 1971:40).

Of the 127 construction units in the main pueblo, only 23 are directly dated by Graves's date estimates (Figure 4.7). Employing the principles above in an analysis of dependency relationships among construction units allows time placement for an additional 34 construction units, yielding 178 terminally dated rooms in 57 construction units. The absence of dates from rooms at the end of the relative construction sequence in all three main pueblo room blocks limits the dating to some extent. Because of this limitation, arbitrary terminal construction dates had to be assigned to rooms from the outer margins of all three room blocks.

Drawing on the observation that construction-unit size changed through the relative sequence (see above), two different terminal dates were assigned to construction units depending on their size. A two-room-construction-unit-size cutoff was used because, beyond this threshold, and given the possibility of two-room households (Ciolek-Torrello 1978), factors other than household expansion were most likely responsible for construction of larger room sets. Using only construction units dated within a 30-year range or less produced a date of A.D. 1345 for all construction units comprising more than two rooms. The A.D. 1345 date comes from a six-room construction unit in Room Block 2, which is directly abutted by dated architecture terminally dated at A.D. 1344. This date is relatively late in the construction sequence and is probably a conservative estimate of a point in time at which large construction units were *no* longer being added (see below for a less conservative estimate).

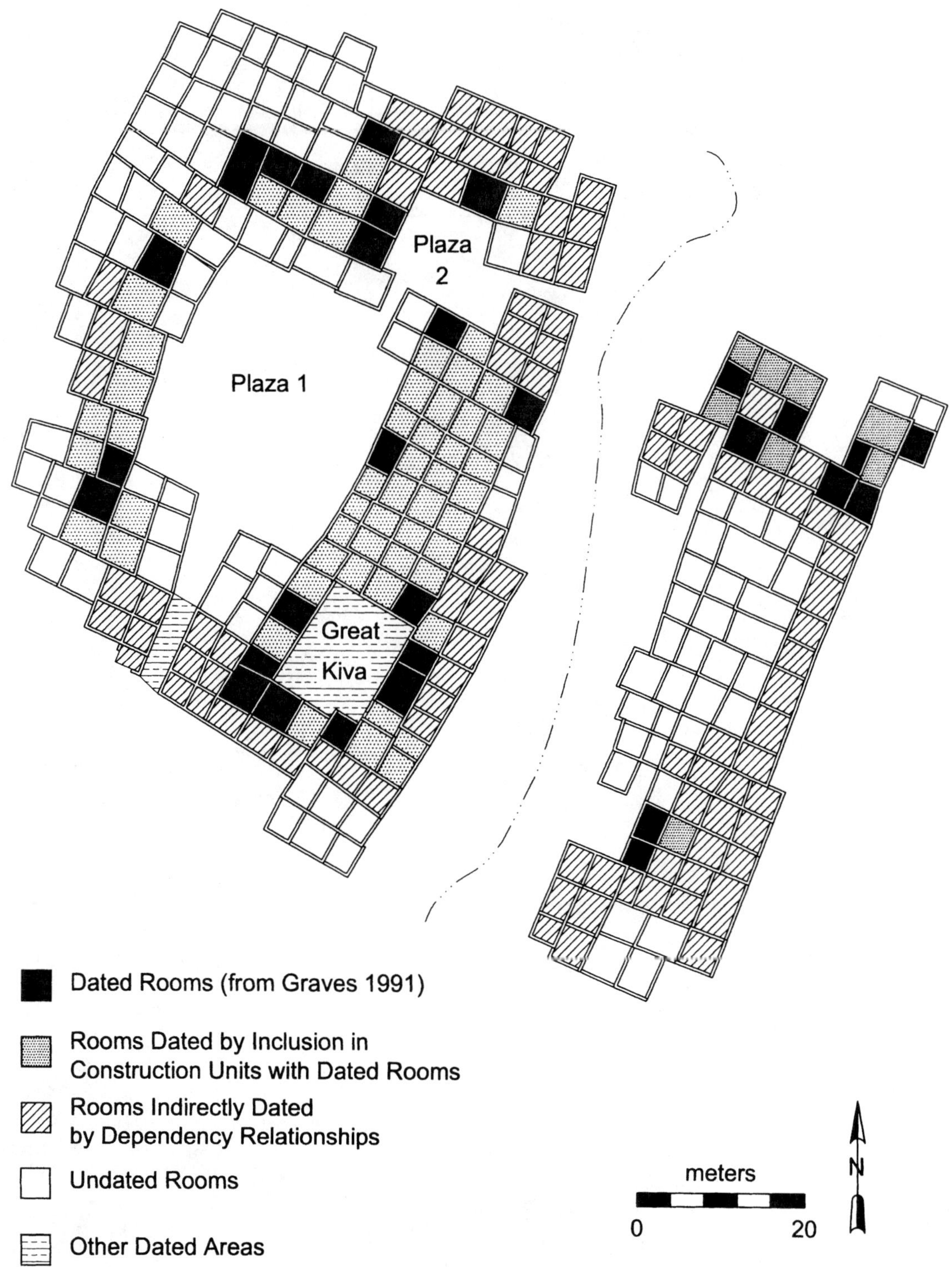

FIGURE 4.7.
Dated rooms and other dated areas in the main pueblo.

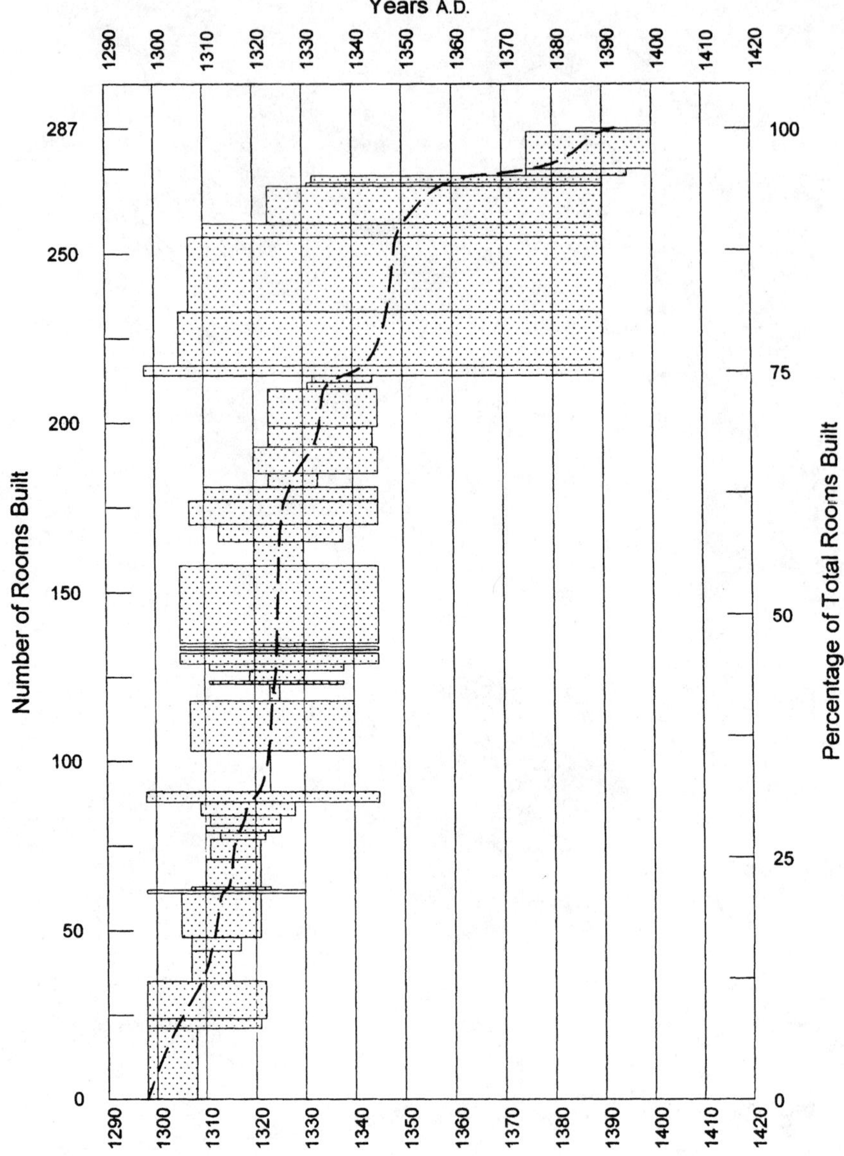

FIGURE 4.8.
Mean construction dates and construction date ranges for all 287 main pueblo rooms.

For smaller one- and two-room construction units an arbitrary terminal date of A.D. 1390 was assigned to all undated units based on Graves's latest construction-date estimate. This date is from Room 8 in the south end of Room Block 1 and again is probably conservative in terms of how late it assigns an end to construction of most rooms at Grasshopper. Small units that were abutted by large units all assumed a terminal date of A.D. 1345 rather than an A.D. 1390 date because of the principles of dependency discussed above. Applying these date estimates to the remaining undated architecture allows for the time placement of all 287 room spaces of the main pueblo (Figure 4.8).

To summarize the results, 26 percent of the rooms in the main pueblo have construction-date ranges of 10 years or less, 34 percent have date ranges of 11 to 30 years, and the remaining 40 percent of the rooms have construction-date ranges of greater than 30 years. Bias in the location of the dated rooms limits the ability of this method to provide higher resolution dates for many rooms in the main pueblo (yielding the large bars at the top of Figure 4.8). These limitations aside, it is still possible to assign date ranges to several important events in the construction history of the main pueblo.

DATING CONSTRUCTION EVENTS

Apart from the general chronological concerns just discussed, the combination of Reid's construction phases with Graves's construction-date estimates allows time placement of numerous construction events. The following discussion highlights some of these events and addresses some of the intricacies of main pueblo growth.[4]

Room Block 1

Room Block 1 is the least adequately dated of the three main pueblo room blocks, despite its containing the largest sample of excavated rooms. This is partially an artifact of tree-ring preservation but is also a result of the spatial clustering of the excavations, which were biased toward the northern and southern ends of the room block. The northern portion of Room Block 1 is well dated and construction there occurs relatively early in the sequence. The southern end of the room block also produced some dates but not for the core architectural unit (which was 100 percent excavated). The rooms in the southern end produced the latest tree-ring dates at the site, including the outliers (Graves 1991:Table IX). The middle portion of the room block, outside of the earliest units, was not sampled, and growth in this area can only be confidently assessed with respect to relative time.

Establishment of Room Block 1 occurred sometime prior to A.D. 1321, based on a Construction Phase 3 addition dependent on the north end of the large central core (Figure 4.3). The core construction unit did not produce any dates; however, elsewhere I have assigned a founding date of A.D. 1305 to 1321 to Room Block 1, based on the above evidence and on comparison with founding dates in Room Blocks 2 and 3 (Riggs 1994a:73).

After the room block was established, growth proceeded to the west and north of the core construction unit at a rapid rate, as is demonstrated by terminal construction dates of A.D. 1321 and A.D. 1325 for Rooms 44 and 39, respectively. These rooms were Construction Phase 5 and 7 additions in the far northern portion of the room block. Growth of the room block to the south of the Phase 2 addition to the core probably proceeded along a similar trajectory; the construction units were all relatively large (Figure 4.3). The absence of dated rooms from the central portion of the room block, however, does not allow an assessment of this observation. Growth at the southern end of Room Block 1 differed vastly in character from other areas of the site. The inability to date the southern core unit limits an understanding of the exact processes of growth in this area.

The fact that the six-room unit in the southern end is a core construction unit implies that it was early. This is further bolstered by the fact that subfloor excavations in this unit recovered no preroom activity areas (Figure 3.37). Two facets of growth in this southern area make it stand out. First, after Construction Phase 3, rooms were added only to the architecture associated with the northern core unit and only occurred in one-or two-room units (most units are single room additions). This pattern differs from growth in the rest of the site or even in the remainder of Room Block 1. This growth was achieved by means of an infilling process by which the southern core unit was eventually incorporated into Room Block 1. The other unusual aspect of growth in this area is that the two dated rooms yielded late construction dates. Room 11 was added to architecture dependent on the northern core in Construction Phase 4 and is dated by Graves at A.D. 1375–1395. Room 8 is a Construction Phase 11 room added to architecture dependent on both core units and is dated A.D. 1385–1400. These late dates, combined with the apparently slow filling of the space between core units, suggest late construction, perhaps associated with household expansion in this part of Room Block 1. It is also possible that the wood from these rooms represents repair timbers, later reoccupation, or, because both dates are from Graves's list of "tentative dates," they could be inaccurate. One final piece of evidence in support of the late construction date comes from Room 100, where Dean and Robinson (1982:47) note that the unidentifiable assemblage of wood remains is unique to the site. This finding fits the anomalous growth pattern and late dating of the surrounding rooms and may suggest that the area around Grasshopper Pueblo was either becoming deforested or depauperate in trees of sufficient size for construction, causing builders to incorporate nontraditional species as roof timbers (Dean and Robinson 1982:47).

Room Block 2 and the Great Kiva

The founding of Room Block 2 occurred earlier than either of the other two room blocks of the main pueblo (Riggs 1994a:75). Establishment of the large 21-room core construction unit is dated A.D. 1298–1308, based on a single date from Room 164 (Figure 4.3). This early date is supported by the dating of a Construction Phase 4 unit added to the southern end of the core with a date range of A.D. 1311–1321. The southern core unit yielded no tree-ring dates and was not directly dated, although a Construction Phase 2 unit added to the north between A.D. 1313 and 1322 provides a terminal construction date. A pre-1325 date for the southern core unit is further supported by dates for the roofing of the southern corridor into Plaza 1. This roof was anchored to rooms in the southern core of Room Block 2 and was constructed between A.D. 1323 and 1325 (Figure 4.9; Riggs 1994a:80).

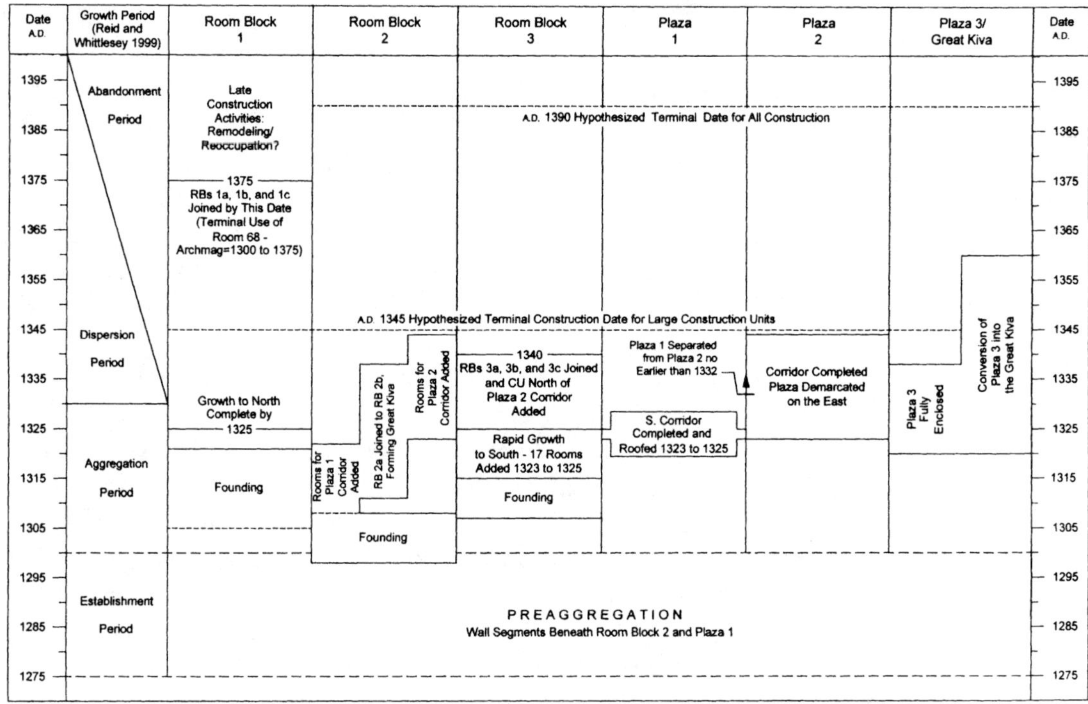

FIGURE 4.9. Growth chronology for the main pueblo.

FIGURE 4.10. Subfloor excavations in the Great Kiva. Note the continuous, Type 2 east wall of the construction unit containing Rooms 16, 18, and 153 beyond. Photograph by James E. Ayres, 1966. Courtesy of the Arizona State Museum, University of Arizona; neg. no. 12428.

From the two core units, growth in Room Block 2 rapidly progressed to outline Plaza 3 and to form the eastern and western walls of the Great Kiva. The discussion of Great Kiva construction in Chapter 3 suggests that the rooms on either side of the structure were built within a short time of one another and were designed to provide anchor points for the Great Kiva's primary beams (Figure 4.10). This chronology implies that the construction of the Great Kiva was coincident with the addition of the two construction units on either side of it. Both are Construction Phase 5 additions (Figure 4.3). The eastern one was probably in place first, dating between A.D. 1313 and 1338, whereas the western one was added to complete the structure sometime between A.D. 1320 and 1330. Combined, these dates suggest that the Great Kiva was constructed sometime between A.D. 1320 and 1338, most likely in the period from 1320 to 1330. This dating is consistent with the construction phase data but is counter to the date interpretations provided by Dean and Robinson (1982:47) and by Graves, who suggest that the Great Kiva was constructed in Plaza 3 relatively late, between A.D. 1347 and 1360+ (Graves 1991:105, Table IX). These assessments are based on four dates from the Great Kiva and from a single date from Room 197. Elsewhere I have suggested that these dates represent a remodeling episode (Riggs 1994a:78). Room 197 has five recorded floor surfaces and was apparently remodeled more than once during its occupation. Its final use was apparently as a ceremonial room (Chapter 5). Great kiva construction is based on 20 "vv" tree-ring specimens, six of which date to the fourteenth century. Of these six, four date late in the occupation: one at A.D. 1336, two at A.D. 1347, and one at A.D. 1355. One of the problems with these dates is that their context within the structure is not reported, and they could easily represent a single remodeling event or could be firewood. The other, related problem with the tree-ring material from the Great Kiva is that the structure fill was removed by backhoe to just above the floor (Longacre and Reid 1974:15; Thompson and Longacre 1966:261–262), and the context of individual samples could not have been well controlled. Although the later date cannot be totally discounted, an earlier date in the late 1320s or early 1330s is more consistent with the architectural evidence.

Overall, Room Block 2's growth rate is similar to that described in the north end of Room Block 1. Most of the construction units were large, and, in this case, many yielded terminal dates, making Room Block 2 the most thoroughly dated of the three main room blocks. In addition, the sequence in Room Block 2 was shorter than in the other room blocks, suggesting that it was completed more rapidly; however, second-story rooms were probably added for a longer period than the ground-floor rooms. The main limitations in assessing the completion of Room Block 2 are related to the lack of dates from rooms added to the south and for the Construction Phase 7 rooms added in Plaza 1, north of the corridor. The latest dates (apart from those just discussed) for Room Block 2 come from a Construction Phase 4 unit added to the northwestern part of the room block dated between A.D. 1332 and 1344. The addition of two more rooms in Construction Phase 5 to this unit demarcated the corridor between Plazas 1 and 2 and implies that these two areas were not physically separated until after A.D. 1332 (Figure 4.9).

Room Block 3 and the Southern Corridor

The central core unit of Room Block 3 (3a) contains the largest number of dated rooms of any construction unit in the main pueblo (Figure 4.3). Four of

FIGURE 4.11.
Southern corridor into Plaza 1 after excavation, looking south. Photograph by R. Gwinn Vivian, 1969. Courtesy of the Arizona State Museum, University of Arizona; neg. no. 22897.

its five rooms were excavated and produced 18 tree-ring dates yielding a construction-date range of A.D. 1307 to 1315. This sets the founding date of Room Block 3. Additions to this core unit, dated A.D. 1309 to 1328 (Construction Phase 2) and A.D. 1307 to 1315 (Construction Phase 3), further strengthen these dates and suggest rapid construction to the north and south of the core unit. Subsequent additions to the north, east, and west cannot be assigned tight temporal placement because of an absence of dated dependent rooms in these areas before Construction Phase 8. This addition consisted of a two-room unit adjacent to the far eastern core unit. It was dependent on all three of the Room Block 3 core construction units and assigns a late terminal date range of A.D. 1331 to 1340 to the eastern (3c) and northern (3b) core construction units. This suggests that Plaza 2 was not completely outlined until at least A.D. 1330 (Figure 4.9).

In contrast to the dating in the northern portion of Room Block 3, the southern end produced the tightest range of dates for any construction event. Critical to this is the dating of roof construction over the southern corridor into Plaza 1 (Figure 4.11). This event, as mentioned above, is terminally dated at A.D. 1325 (Graves 1991:105) and sets a temporal and spatial limit on the southward expansion of Room Block 3. The construction unit to which the corridor roof was anchored (Figure 4.3) was a Construction Phase 5 addition to a construction unit (Construction Phase 4) dating from A.D. 1323 to 1333. Because the dependent (Construction Phase 5) unit was not added any later than 1325, based on the dating of the corridor, the construction-date range of the previous unit (Construction Phase 4) is compressed to A.D. 1323 to 1325. A series of construction episodes (Construction Phases 5 through 7) added to this unit is assigned a construction range of A.D. 1313 to 1323. These construction units, however, were dependent on a unit that was not in place until A.D. 1323 to 1325, so they could not have been built before A.D. 1323, a date that corresponds to the terminal date for these units. Finally, because the Construction Phase 4 (A.D. 1323 to 1325) unit on which they were dependent could not have been built after the terminal date of these units, it too is assigned an initial and terminal date of A.D. 1323. In this way 12 rooms are assigned a single-year construction date of A.D. 1323, and another five rooms and the roof over the southern corridor into Plaza 1 appear to have been constructed between A.D. 1323 and 1325.

As for the remainder of Room Block 3, no definitive statements can be made about growth. No rooms were excavated in the northwest portion of the room block, where several single-room construction units could have been placed in time by the recovery of a date from one of the outer rooms. As mentioned, the core units bounding Plaza 2 have no initial dates, but were incorporated by A.D. 1331, or earlier, and no later than A.D. 1340. As with the core unit in the southern end of Room Block 1, the core units in this area may or may not have been contemporaneous with the founding core unit of Room Block 3. It is interesting to note that they were not built onto until Construction Phase 4, in the northern unit, and until Construction Phase 7, in the eastern core unit (Figure 4.3). In comparison with the trajectory of growth from the central core construction unit, this absence of activity implies that they could have been constructed later. On the other hand, Room Block 5 may offer an interesting analogy in that it is close to Room Block 1 and seems to have been built relatively early (see below) but maintained physical separation from the larger room block throughout its occupation. Finally, rooms added to Room Block 3 in Plaza 1 cannot be dated but are generally late in the relative sequence in the north and earlier in the south.

Construction Rates and Main Pueblo Growth

Although the absence of cutting dates limits dating resolution, it is still possible to arrive at some approximate construction rates for the main pueblo. Seventy-four (26 percent) of the room spaces in the main pueblo yielded construction-date ranges of 10 years or less (Figure 4.8). This provides a construction rate of between seven and eight (7.4) rooms per year. Because the majority of the well-dated rooms are from the earlier construction phases, this estimate applies primarily to rooms built during the aggregation period. Using A.D. 1330 as the end of the aggregation period (Reid 1973:133, 1989:83) suggests that between 210 and 240 rooms were constructed in the main pueblo by A.D. 1330.

This number is probably low because it includes no rooms from Room Block 1, where the dating resolution is poor and where no rooms can be assigned a date range of 10 years or less. The contention that Room Block 2 was built by locals is reinforced by the fact that 46 percent of its rooms yielded date ranges of less than 10 years, and a room construction rate of 4.2 rooms per year is derived, suggesting that 126 rooms could have been built before A.D. 1330. This number is much higher than the number of room spaces in Room Block 2 (92), but if second-story rooms are included, it approximates the 123-room estimate provided in Chapter 3. This estimate suggests that all or most of the rooms in Room Block 2 were built by A.D. 1330, which is in line with the small number of large construction units documented by the construction phase model, where the average construction-unit size was four rooms. This number is almost identical to the estimate provided here of 4.2 rooms per year.

Room Block 3's construction also conforms well to the construction phase model, which suggests a longer construction sequence. Thirty-two percent of the rooms in Room Block 3 were dated to within a 10-year range. This yields a construction rate of 3.2 rooms per year and suggests that 96 rooms could have been constructed in Room Block 3 by A.D. 1330. This figure is only five short of the total number of room spaces in Room Block 3, but if there were 120 rooms in Room Block 3, as suggested by the discussion of two-story rooms in Chapter 3, then approximately 80 percent of the rooms in Room Block 3 were constructed by A.D. 1330. The construction rate in Room Block 1 was probably similar to that in Room Block 3, which had similar construction patterns based on the construction phase model.

The estimated construction rates for the main pueblo fit well with the construction phase model in all respects. The rate of room construction is consistent with a model whereby aggregation occurred relatively rapidly at first, through the immigration of household and extended family units, who constructed large room suites between A.D. 1300 and 1330. Subsequently, this rate of construction dropped as immigration rates slowed, and subsequent growth in the main pueblo was through residential household expansion. We revisit this discussion of construction rates after a brief look at room construction patterns and dating in the outliers.

GROWTH AND DATING OF THE OUTLIERS

The founding dates and subsequent growth sequences of many of the outliers are not as easily reconstructed as those in the main pueblo. Few tree-ring dates exist for the outliers (Graves 1991:Table IX), and because of the low-walled construction of most, it was often difficult to identify corner relationships and

TABLE 4.1.
Summary of Growth for the Outliers

Room Block	Rooms	Construction Units (CU)	Construction Phases (CP)	Rooms/CP	CU/CP	Rooms/CU
4	6	5	3	2	1.7	1.2
5	6	2	2	3	1	3
6	13	9	5	2.6	1.8	3
7	21	14	9	2.3	1.6	1.5
8	10	8	4	2.5	2	1.3
9	26	17	7	3.7	2.4	1.54
10	11	9	5	2.2	1.8	1.2
12	17	9	3	5.7	3	1.9
13	4	2	2	2	1	2

wall faces. The principles of the construction phase model can also be applied to the growth of the outliers. As with the main pueblo, there is no necessary temporal relationship between the construction phase of individual room blocks. In fact, the timing of the founding and growth of an individual outlier probably had little, if anything, to do with the happenings in nearby room blocks. Although portrayed as if all of the outliers were constructed simultaneously, construction phases defined for the outliers (Figure 4.12) are measured relative only to the architectural additions within a given room block. Given the paucity of available dates for the outliers, an in-depth discussion of the growth of each adds no information that cannot be gained from inspection of the relative, internal growth sequences provided in Table 4.1 and Figures 4.12 and 4.13. Only three room blocks, Room Blocks 5, 7, and 10, benefit from absolute dating, and these are discussed in more detail. Room Block 11 is the only outlier for which construction-phase data are not available. Although most of its rooms were cornered and one was completely excavated, the room block's location made it an ideal position for the field camp's water tank, and most of the central portion of the room block was obscured by this structure (Figure 2.4).

Tree-Ring–Dated Outliers

Rooms 114 and 195 in Room Block 5 produced tree-ring dates. These rooms were initially added as a single room to the west of Room 113 (Figure 4.13) sometime between A.D. 1301 and 1320 (Graves 1991:Table IX). Subsequently, a partition wall was erected, separating Rooms 114 and 195. The roofing of Room 195 occurred sometime between A.D. 1313 and 1332 (Graves 1991:Table IX).

Room 114's construction date dictates that all of the rooms in Room Block 5 (with the exception of Room 195) were constructed prior to A.D. 1320. This early date is supported by archaeomagnetic dates from preroom features underlying Room 113 (Table 4.2). These dates apply to the last use of a preroom

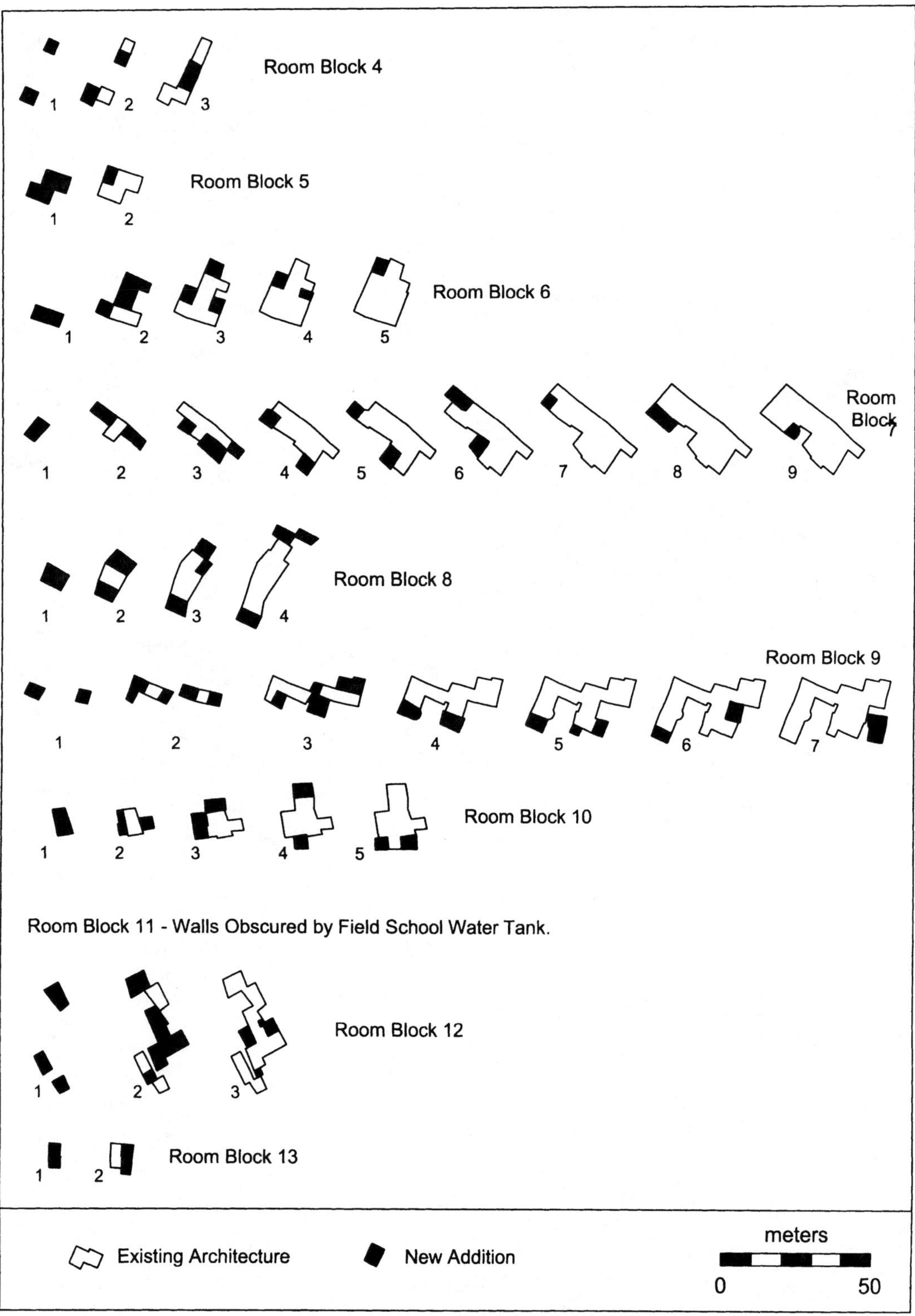

FIGURE 4.12.
Outlier growth by construction phase.

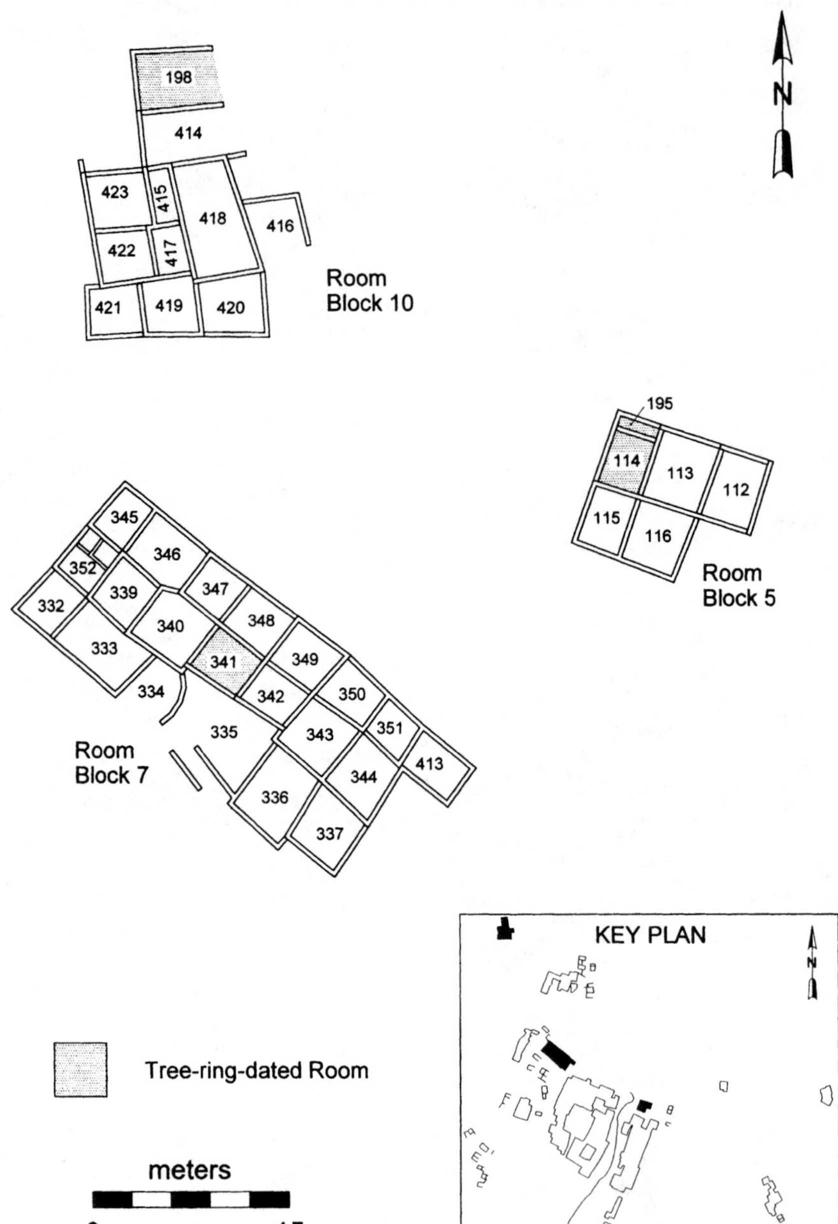

FIGURE 4.13. Tree-ring–dated outliers; Room Blocks 5, 7, and 10 (locations not to scale).

fire pit and range from A.D. 1300 to 1325, suggesting that Room 113 was constructed sometime after this last use but sometime before Room 114 was added. This early date is consistent with the other architectural characteristics of Room Block 5, indicating that it was more closely associated with the occupation of the main pueblo than with the other outliers.

Only one room in Room Block 7 produced a tree-ring date. Graves dated construction of Room 341 between A.D. 1308 and 1317 (Graves 1991:105, Table

TABLE 4.2.
Archaeomagnetic Dates from Grasshopper Pueblo, after Eighmy and Sternberg 1990:Table A-1

Room Block	Room	Feature	Context	Date Range (Years A.D.)
5	113	7	Preroom fire pit	1300–1325
5	113	?	?	1300–1325
5	113	12	Preroom fire pit	1300–1325
5	115	11	Preroom fire pit	1300–1350
1	68	2	Hearth on room floor	1300–1375
2	Oven 2	—	Nonroom	1350–1375
0	25	1	Hearth on room floor	1350–1400
0	25	5	Hearth on room floor	1350–1400
0	309	2	Hearth on room floor	1350–1400
0	312	2	Hearth on room floor	1350–1400

IX). This room is assigned to Construction Phase 3 (Figures 4.12 and 4.13), and its construction date provides an early founding date for Room Block 7 of no later than A.D. 1317 and perhaps as early as A.D. 1300. Like Room Block 5, an early date for this outlier is not counter to expectations because Room Block 7 may have been connected to Room Block 3 (Chapter 3). This date estimate, however, is based on a single specimen and Graves's construction-date estimate does not benefit from date clustering to assign the range. The possibility of a reused timber from the main pueblo or the use of old wood cannot be discounted.

Room Block 10 is the only true outlier to produce a tree-ring–dated room. The addition of Room 198 in Construction Phase 4 (Figures 4.12 and 4.13) dates the founding and northern growth of Room Block 10. Graves estimates Room 198's construction to have occurred between A.D. 1318 and 1337. This date suggests that the room block was founded and grew to at least five rooms before A.D. 1337. Of course, given the principles of room dependency, the dating of Room 198 and the north half of Room Block 10 has no bearing on the rate of construction to the south, west, and east of the core construction unit.

Unaffiliated Outlier Rooms and Archaeomagnetic Dates

The remaining isolated and small outlier units do not add much to the picture of chronology and growth. These rooms were typically not cornered although several were excavated (Table A.1; Figure 2.6). From the excavated rooms bond-abut data are available but in many cases are of limited utility because they are from isolated rooms or two-room units. Further, no tree-ring dates are available for the unaffiliated outliers, although three rooms provide archaeomagnetic dates (Table 4.2). These latter rooms (Rooms 25, 309, and 312) serve to date the final abandonment of the community, all yielding archaeomagnetic date ranges of A.D. 1350 to 1400. The large time span bracketed by this range makes these dates of limited utility.

OUTLIER GROWTH AND COMMUNITY DYNAMICS

It is difficult to compare growth among the various outlying room blocks because of the variability in the number of rooms and in their growth patterns. Furthermore, because they are so spatially separated and, where dates do exist, seem to have been founded at different times, absolute correlations between them are difficult. In general, there were two types of outliers (Table 4.1). One is the small, four- to six-room unit, like Room Blocks 4, 5, and 13, and the other is the larger unit, including Room Blocks 6, 7, 8, 9, 10, 11, and 12 (Figure 4.12). In the former case growth proceeded rapidly and was complete in no more than three construction phases; each of these phases consisted of from two to four room units. These smaller room blocks likely represent the dwellings of small social groups such as single households or perhaps larger family groups. Their small size implies that the room blocks were either constructed just before the abandonment of the area or that they remained socially isolated, small corporate groups throughout the occupation (e.g., Room Block 5).

The larger room blocks are consistent with a more prolonged arrival of immigrants and subsequent household expansion (Graves 1983; Reid 1973, 1989; see below). Their growth rates are consistent with this type of population model. Most of the larger outliers began as single core construction units and expanded from there, suggesting the construction activities of a single social group. By contrast, Room Blocks 9 and 12 exhibit a growth pattern similar to the main pueblo room blocks, and expanded from two construction loci to form a single room block. As discussed in relation to the main pueblo, this construction process may represent the activities of different social groups, such as extended families or other kin groups. Figure 4.14 compares the growth patterns of the nine room blocks discussed above. Because so few dates are available from the outliers, however, not much can be said comparing the relative timing of founding and subsequent expansion of the various room blocks.

Because few absolute dates are available for the outliers, inferences about their rate of growth must be derived primarily from their relative growth sequences. Assuming classificatory contemporaneity (Dean 1969:198) for the construction phases defined in the various outliers allows the construction phase data from the outliers to be plotted as a cumulative density histogram (Figure 4.15), similar to the one used for the main pueblo above (Figure 4.6). Inspection of Figure 4.15 reveals that relative growth, as in the main pueblo, can be described by a logistical, or density-dependent, growth curve (Eighmy 1979:218). Unlike the main pueblo, the growth curve for the outliers is significantly less steep (Figure 4.15; cf. Figure 4.6). The difference in the magnitude

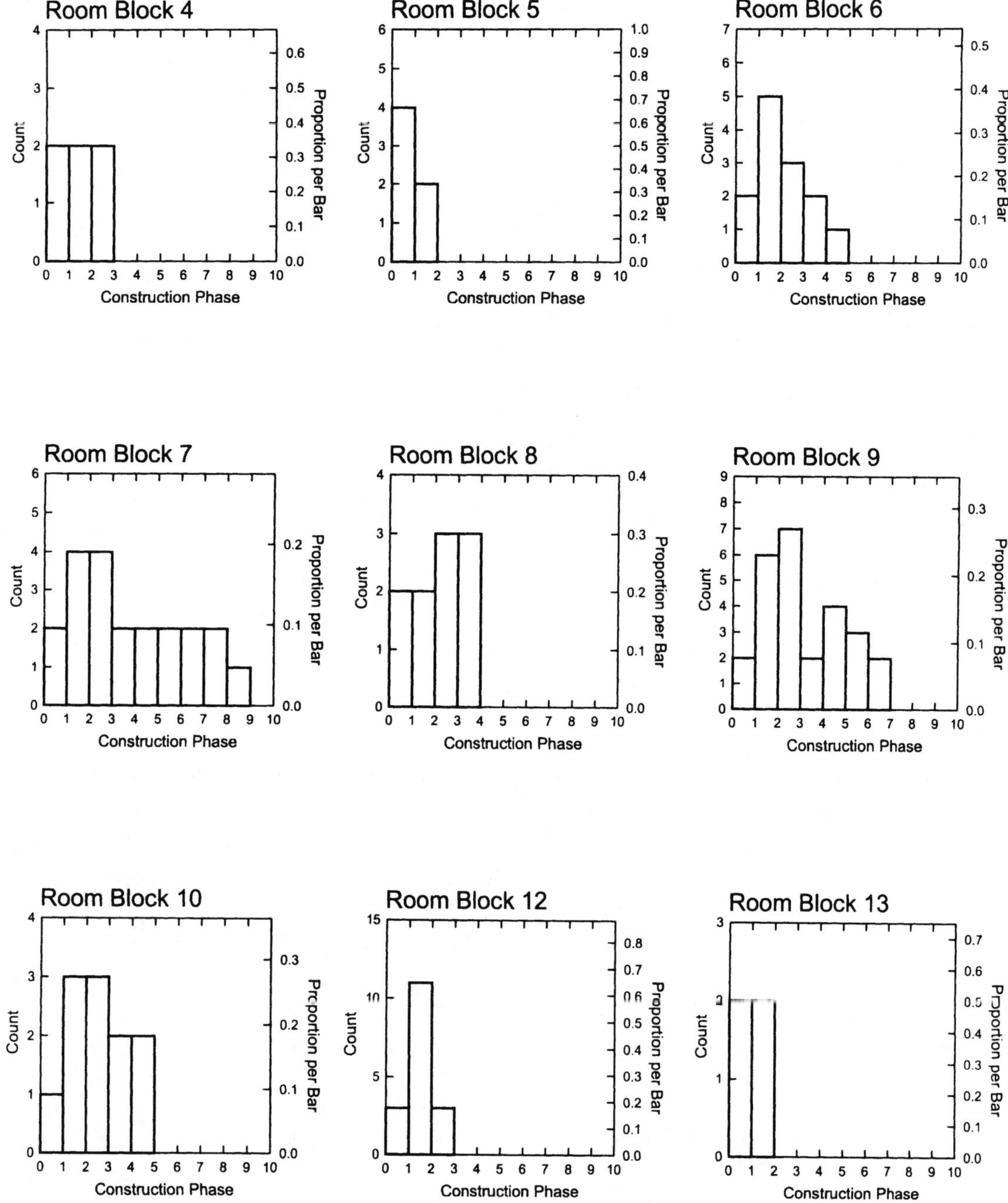

FIGURE 4.14.
Comparison of growth among the outliers.

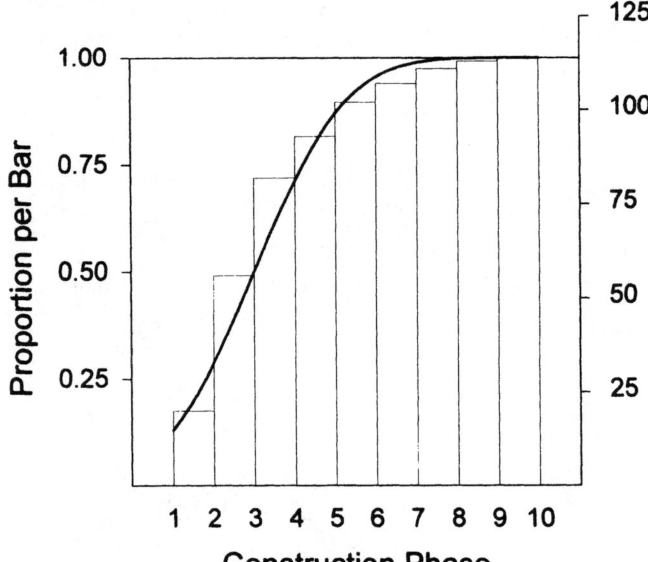

FIGURE 4.15. Composite relative growth curve for the outliers.

of these two curves suggests that different social processes from those portrayed in the early occupation were at work during the occupation of the later outliers (Reid 1989:85).

Construction of Canyon Creek Pueblo and of Red Rock House, slightly later, has been seen as evidence that Grasshopper residents moved into satellite communities because of community dispersion (Reid 1989:82). The timing of the founding and growth of these communities is consistent with this interpretation. The founding of Canyon Creek in A.D. 1327, preceded by the stockpiling of timber for secondary beams (Graves 1983:293), coincided with the end of the period of rapid expansion at Grasshopper (Reid 1989:85). Graves (1983) has suggested that several individual households constructed Canyon Creek Pueblo over a period of approximately 20 years and that stockpiling of timbers before the actual construction of Canyon Creek demonstrates that the founding households anticipated their eventual relocation. Many of these households might have previously been established in the already large and highly nucleated Grasshopper Pueblo (Reid 1989:82), or they might have selected Canyon Creek as an alternative (Graves 1983:305). The subsequent founding of Red Rock House prior to A.D. 1343 (Reynolds 1981:160) provides evidence for a continuation of the dispersion process. The link between Grasshopper and these satellite communities provides a model for understanding the demographic processes that resulted in the occupation of the outliers.

Graves's discussion of the growth and population dynamics at Canyon Creek Pueblo is illustrative of these processes (Graves 1982, 1983; Chapter 3). As at Canyon Creek, immigration was at least partially responsible for the establishment of new outliers. This observation is reinforced by the work of Ezzo and colleagues, who note that some individuals buried in the outliers exhibit nonlocal dietary signatures (Ezzo et al. 1997:461). As Graves notes, immigration and natural population increase can account for the type of architectural growth seen at Canyon Creek (Graves 1983:305). In the type of community growth posited by Graves the rate of immigration lessened through time as the natural population growth rate increased, a consequence of movement into a new locality (Graves 1983:305). This process is remarkably similar to the growth pattern observed in the outliers. A comparison of the shape of the growth curves from the main pueblo (Figure 4.6), Canyon Creek Pueblo (Graves 1983:Figure 9), and the Grasshopper outliers (Figure 4.15) demonstrates that outlier growth is more similar to Canyon Creek in its magnitude than it is to the growth of the main pueblo, where exceedingly high immigration rates masked local population growth rates (Graves 1983:307; Longacre 1976). This interpretation of outlier growth is bolstered by the fact that many of the rooms were probably more closely related in time to the expansion of Canyon Creek than they were to the growth of the main pueblo at Grasshopper (Reid 1989:89).

The source of the population responsible for the construction of the outliers is an important consideration in the foregoing discussion. Several processes may have been acting to account for the outliers. Immigration from outside of the Grasshopper region is one possibility. For example, there is compelling skeletal and material culture evidence suggesting that Room Block 5 represents an enclave with an Anasazi tradition (Reid and Whittlesey 1999:118; Triadan 1989:45–47, 74). At the same time, some room blocks outside of the main pueblo and satellite communities like Canyon Creek and Red Rock House may represent the establishment of new households by residents of Grasshopper (Reid 1973:133, 1989:85). The occupation of the outliers marks the onset of the dispersion period, a change in residential mobility patterns resulting from a new strategy of coping with local social and environmental conditions (cf. Reynolds 1981:269).

THE GROWTH MODEL REVISITED

The foregoing discussion of pueblo growth and chronology provides time placement for numerous events in the construction history of the community and supports the existing community growth model (Reid 1973; Reid and Shimada 1982). It is not possible to refine the dating for the establishment period, which consisted of earlier rooms underlying the fourteenth-century pueblo (Reid 1989:83; Chapter 3). Refinement of the dating for the subsequent expansion or aggregation period was also not necessary, even with the addition of new construction-date estimates. This period dated from just before A.D. 1300 to around A.D. 1330 and was bracketed by the founding of the fourteenth-century room blocks on the early end and by the construction of the Great Kiva around A.D. 1330 (Figure 4.16). The dispersion period remains

FIGURE 4.16.
Aggregation- vs. dispersion-phase construction.

poorly dated, with only a few one- and two-room additions to the core of the pueblo and to the outliers dating after A.D. 1330–1340.

This discussion of community growth examines the main pueblo and the outliers separately for the purposes of addressing community development. In many ways this is an accurate reflection of the actual sequence of events. Several rooms in the main pueblo, however, were added after A.D. 1330 and reflect the dispersion of the community into satellite settlements and into a more mobile adaptation to the region (Reid 1989). On the other hand, not all of the outliers date to the dispersion period. Once again, Room Blocks 5 and 7 stand out as being earlier than other outliers, suggesting that they represent aggregation-period construction. The archaeomagnetic and tree-ring dates from Room Block 5 suggest that it was completed before A.D. 1332 and perhaps as early as A.D. 1320. Room Block 7 also exhibits early tree-ring dates that place the founding and early growth before A.D. 1317. Additions to the room block after the construction of Room 341 may date to either the aggregation or the dispersion period. Thus, as in other categories of architectural information, Room Blocks 5 and 7 appear to be more closely linked to the main pueblo than to the remainder of the outliers.

Most of the remaining outliers did not yield chronometric information, and those that did appear to have been constructed late in the occupation. In addition to these late outliers, dispersion-period rooms were found in the main pueblo; these include the rooms built to consolidate the southern end of Room Block 1, those constructed in Plazas 1 and 2, and the additions to the northwestern portion of Room Block 3 (Figure 4.16).

If the estimated A.D. 1345 terminal date for large construction units used above is adjusted to conform to the end of the aggregation period (A.D. 1330), construction of all the rooms at Grasshopper can be assigned to either the aggregation or the dispersion period. In all, 260 ground-floor rooms were constructed from A.D. 1300 to 1330 (aggregation period). This growth was entirely restricted to the room blocks of the site core (Room Blocks 1, 2, 3, 5, and 7) and closely approximates the estimate of 240 rooms determined by the examination of well-dated rooms above, especially when the 27 rooms (21 of which are estimated to have been constructed before A.D. 1330) of Room Blocks 5 and 7 are considered. Most aggregation-period construction took place in the main pueblo, where 239 of the 287 (92 percent) ground-floor rooms were built. The subsequent dispersion period, from A.D. 1330 to 1390, saw the construction of only 187 ground-floor rooms. In contrast to the aggregation period, most of this construction took place in the outliers, where 139 (74 percent) of the dispersion-period rooms were built.

The 68 second-story rooms added to the main pueblo cannot be dated but could have been built in either the aggregation period or the dispersion period. By analogy with Canyon Creek Pueblo, we infer that they were subsequent to, rather than in tandem with, existing ground-floor rooms and could have been constructed anywhere from moments to years after the completion of the ground-floor room. These second-story rooms likely do not indicate the arrival of immigrants but rather the expansion of existing households that had been circumscribed by later architecture. Estimated room construction rates provided above, however, closely predict the number of second-story rooms as generated by the analysis of construction and roofing methods in Chapter 3.

5

Architecture and Grasshopper Society

> Ask the old grey standing stones who show the sun his way to bed.
> Question all as to their ways, and learn the secrets that they hold.
> —Ian Anderson, "Cup of Wonder"

GRASSHOPPER PUEBLO, LIKE ALL EXAMPLES OF PREINDUSTRIAL VERNACULAR architecture, not only influenced the activities of its inhabitants but also was shaped by its occupants' actions. At Grasshopper these occupants were local inhabitants of the region and immigrants from places such as the Colorado Plateau, the Mogollon Highlands, and the Tonto Basin. Pueblo growth at Grasshopper was spawned by the forces of immigration and intracommunity relationships that were important demographic forces throughout the pueblo Southwest at the beginning of the fourteenth century. The architecture of aggregation demonstrates that there were different builders at work not only in the beginning of the fourteenth century but throughout the occupation of Grasshopper Pueblo. Room block divisions imposed on the community appear to have reflected real social groups that had distinct construction practices. The most significant division noted was between the East and West villages. Architectural and mortuary data support this division and indicate that the West Village was constructed primarily by locals with some indications of the activities of nonlocals in Room Block 3. By contrast, Room Block 1 appears to have been the home of the nonlocal population. As these immigrants came into Grasshopper and previously established resident households expanded, space became increasingly restricted, causing concomitant changes in the organization of household space. The most obvious expression of this pattern was in second-story room construction in the oldest part of the pueblo.

As these diverse builders assembled their rooms, they imprinted the architecture with their own technological styles. Room form and wall elements in each of the three room blocks of the main pueblo differ from one another in several ways that indicate subtle differences in culturally determined construction practices. Through time, room floors were remodeled as the systems of activities in the daily lives of Grasshopper's inhabitants were conducted in changing settings. Households expanded, requiring new rooms, and second stories were added, necessitating changes in the activities conducted in the lower stories and adjacent rooms. Fortunately, few if any walls were rebuilt, and the imprints of the original builders are still present within the walls, despite this loose fit between architecture and activities.

Grasshopper Pueblo continued to grow while rooms decayed and were remodeled or abandoned entirely and used for refuse dumps. At some point in the growth process, people began to use the Grasshopper site less intensively. The construction of the Great Kiva in Plaza 3 around A.D. 1330 is linked to this process. This important structure continued to act as a center for the community's residents, who were now constructing less substantial rooms similar to those that preceded the full-standing masonry rooms of the fourteenth century. Throughout the dispersion period nonlocal people continued to come into the region, as the continued spatial separation between room blocks in the outliers suggests. This immigration, however, is masked archaeologically by changes in settlement patterns occurring around A.D. 1330, when satellite sites like Canyon Creek pueblo were first established, providing an alternative to immigration to Grasshopper and a place for Grasshopper Pueblo's inhabitants to resettle. At this time Grasshopper remained an important community center by providing a place for participation in rituals and other social gatherings. This latter role for Grasshopper was not a long-term solution, however, and the community eventually drifted away from the region, becoming immigrants at other growing pueblo sites as the puebloan occupation of the Southwest became increasingly localized in areas inhabited by modern pueblo peoples.

In recent years migration, community organization, and, to some extent, abandonment have become popular topics within southwestern archaeology (Adler 1996; Cameron 1993, 1995; Clark 2001; Spielmann 1998), and the Pueblo IV period, during which Grasshopper was occupied, has been central to many of these discussions. Important evidence in the form of differing technical variants in room construction practices emerge from this analysis. This reinforces the notion that the separateness of the main pueblo room blocks consciously marked the boundaries between different social groups. A delineation of the groups in residence during the fourteenth century provides insight into the processes of migration that shaped the Grasshopper community. Room function and its correlation to various lines of architectural evidence define patterns of community organization and evolution, such as the expansion of resident households, spurred by a continuing influx of people into the region. An examination of the architectural evidence for community dispersion describes the means used to reorganize the community as people began to leave the area and the process that ultimately led to the abandonment of the Grasshopper region.

The architectural data, supported by mortuary evidence, provide a reasonably strong argument for the activities of groups of builders with differing conventions of room form, wall construction, and structure use. Given the rapid construction of the main pueblo, it is not surprising to find that different social groups were responsible for the construction of Grasshopper Pueblo. The notion that Grasshopper was a community of immigrants and locals living in close proximity is not new (Reid 1989). By focusing on technological style, as reflected in architectural elements, this analysis confirms the pattern of cohabitation suggested by the spatial divisions between room blocks. This is especially apparent in the division of the community into East and West villages created by construction on either side of Salt River Draw. The following look at the early occupation of the community provides strong evidence that an immigrant group living in Room Block 1 coresided with locals and perhaps nonlocals of different origin, whose residences were in the West Village, on the other side of Salt River Draw. Given the number of convergent lines of architectural and other material evidence, I suggest that Grasshopper, like the Maverick Mountain phase occupation of Point of Pines, is a strong case for evaluating the process of migration in a prehistoric community. Unlike Point of Pines, however, there is no evidence for a site unit intrusion. Instead, subtle patterns in the use of various architectural features and materials are combined in the following pages to build a case for different groups of builders at the pueblo. Given the rarity of the site unit intrusion (Cordell 1995; Reed 1958) in situations of ethnic coresidence in the Southwest, this study makes an important contribution to our attempts to identify different social and ethnic groups in prehistory.

SOCIAL GROUP DYNAMICS: THE ARCHITECTURE OF AGGREGATION

Architecture is intrinsically linked to human action (Hillier and Hanson 1984; Lawrence and Low 1990; Rapoport 1969, 1982), and unlike other classes of material culture, it is nonportable. Therefore, it is a powerful and reliable indicator of group identity and is relatively resistant to many of the processes that affect the distribution of portable artifacts. Apart from mortuary analysis, architecture provides the best approximation for the location of individuals in the archaeological record. Architecture, like mortuary data, is not subject to the same processes as portable artifacts and can more accurately provide data to locate an individual's daily domestic activities than mortuary evidence. Numerous independent lines of archaeological evidence have established that immigrant groups coexisted at Grasshopper in the fourteenth century (Birkby 1973, 1982; Ezzo 1993; Ezzo et al. 1997; Graves et al. 1982; Longacre 1975, 1976; Longacre and Graves 1982; Reid 1973, 1989, 1998; Triadan 1997; Zedeño 1994; Chapter 2). The actual locations of the resident groups in the pueblo, however, have not been as well established (although see Reid and Whittlesey 1982, 1999; Ezzo et al. 1997; Triadan 1989:74). Architectural data provide numerous independent lines of evidence indicating that there were clearly defined social enclaves throughout the occupation. Although similar processes seem to have occurred during the dispersion period(see below), the architecture of the aggregation period contains the clearest and most compelling evidence for spatially discrete construction, suggesting the activities of local and immigrant builders, each with different subtly marked construction techniques.

Aggregation consisted of groups of immigrants building rooms next to one another in contiguous blocks, called construction units in the previous chapter (Chapter 4; Reid and Shimada 1982; Riggs 1994a, 1999a, 1999b; Wilcox 1982). The formal characteristics of these discrete additions to the pueblo would have been internally homogeneous, with more variability between two-room-set additions (or spatially discrete room blocks) than within them. Other examples from the Southwest suggest that this type of pattern appears where coresidence of different ethnic or social groups has been documented (Clark 2001; Haury 1958; Lindsay 1987). Grasshopper's inherent spatial divisions—main pueblo, outliers, core room blocks, East Village, West Village—permit this hypothesis to be tested, and the delineation of construction units within the main pueblo allows testing at yet finer scales of analysis.

A number of architectural characteristics suggest that the main pueblo was built by socially distinct groups of builders. These characteristics include differences in the layouts and growth patterns of the core room blocks, the size and orientation of rooms, the distribution and physical characteristics of various wall features, the use of different types of building materials, and the types of various floor features constructed (see below). Reid and Whittlesey (1999:63–66) have posited that Room Block 2 was founded by the local inhabitants of the Grasshopper locality, Room Block 1 by people from Grasshopper Spring Pueblo, and Room Block 3 by people from Chodistaas Pueblo. The various lines of architectural data discussed below support these observations and help to build a strong case for ethnic coresidence.

Room Block 1, isolated on the east side of Salt River Draw, was most likely constructed by a nonlocal group. This social separation is further indicated by an absence of adjacent, formal public space. The timing of its founding, the rate of room block growth, and the low incidence of higher quality local building stone provide further evidence for construction by nonlocals. Furthermore, the large core unit in Room Block 1 was built through ladder-type construction in which long linear walls were subdivided into several rooms. Some researchers have suggested that ladder-type construction was a plateau phenomenon (Cameron 1999b:226) and that linear room blocks, like the central core unit of Room Block 1, indicate the presence of different groups of builders in settings where block construction is the local pattern (Mills 1998:72).

In direct contrast, Room Block 2 looks to be local for a number of reasons. It was the first to be founded, was established as a large block of rooms rather than as a linear, ladder-type block, grew rapidly, and was the largest when two-story rooms are taken into account, implying that the founding population came from nearby. Pueblo III period walls were found exclusively beneath Room Block 2, one more indication that its builders were local people. Finally, Room Block 2, which was connected to all three of the public spaces and enclosed the Great Kiva, was also central to the community and contained the greatest amount of high-quality local building stone (Area 4 sandstones).

In many ways the general architectural characteristics of Room Block 3 appear to be a blend of those in Room Blocks 1 and 2. Room Block 3 forms part of the West Village because it is physically linked to Room Block 2 through roofed corridors into Plazas 1 and 2. Room Block 3's growth sequence is more similar to Room Block 1's in that it appears to have grown at a much slower rate (Chapter 4). These general observations and the other data presented below suggest that Room Block 3 was probably constructed by builders with highly variable construction practices, perhaps people of local and nonlocal origins.

The settlement model just described is confirmed by analyzing spatial variability in numerous categories of architectural data. Incorporation of other lines of architectural data will further test this general model for the early settlement of Grasshopper Pueblo. First, room form is examined for all 287 room spaces within the main pueblo, followed by an abbreviated discussion of room form in the outliers. Next is a spatial analysis of architectural data from the 68 excavated rooms in the main pueblo, but a similar discussion of the outliers is not possible given their shortage of wall features.

Room Form

There was clear variability in room size, shape, and orientation among the three large main pueblo room blocks (Table 5.1). If each room block was constructed by small groups of related or unrelated builders, some of whom potentially came from well outside the Grasshopper region, we would expect the

TABLE 5.1.
Summary of Room Form Measures by Room Block

Size[a]	Small		Large		Total	
	n	%	*n*	%	*n*	%
Room Block 1	46	49	48	51	94	100
Room Block 2	66	72	26	28	92	100
Room Block 3	41	41	60	59	101	100
Total	153	53	134	47	287	100
Shape	**Square**		**Rectangular**		**Total**	
	n	%	*n*	%	*n*	%
Room Block 1	55	59	39	41	94	100
Room Block 2	58	63	34	37	92	100
Room Block 3	49	49	52	51	101	100
Total	162	56	125	44	287	100
Orientation	**North-South**		**East-West**		**Total**	
	n	%	*n*	%	*n*	%
Room Block 1	57	61	37	39	94	100
Room Block 2	41	45	51	55	92	100
Room Block 3	57	56	44	44	101	100
Total	155	54	132	46	287	100

[a]Large vs. small rooms are based on the site median of 15.53.

main pueblo room blocks to demonstrate internal variability in construction, in addition to the variability expressed among them as a collective.

Room size is perhaps the most significant of these three variables for understanding differences in construction practices, although all three provide complementary data. Baldwin (1987), in a proxemics approach to room size variability between McElmo and Bonito Phase sites, suggests that the patterns in room size between these two roughly contemporaneous phases express different, subconscious proxemics systems between two culturally distinct groups. A similar assertion can be made regarding the differences in room size and form between the three main pueblo room blocks.

Internally patterned variability in room form within each room block of the main pueblo was explored using spatial autocorrelation analysis.[1] Spatial autocorrelation measures the influence of a given variable on values of the same variable in adjacent areas (Odland 1988). Clustered results indicate that the value in one region causes similar values in adjacent regions. Conversely, in a dispersed distribution, the value in one cell creates divergent values in adjacent cells. In a random pattern the value in a given location has no influence on adjacent regions (Odland 1988; Thomas and Hugget 1980). Rooms constructed in sets with similar physical characteristics should result in a clustered distribution; these clusters would be expected among sets of rooms (construction units) built by groups with different construction traditions.

Founding and immigration: Room variability and the construction of the main pueblo. The spatial autocorrelation analysis indicates that the three room blocks in the main pueblo were constructed by different groups of builders (Table 5.2). At this scale of analysis none of the three room blocks showed significant results for the room shape variable, suggesting a random distribution for the location of square and rectangular rooms (Table 5.1). By contrast, Room Blocks 1 and 3 exhibit significant clustering based on room size, indicating that large rooms were located next to other large rooms and that small rooms occurred

TABLE 5.2.
Results of Spatial Autocorrelation Analysis

Variable	Room Block	Expected Value	Moran's I	z statistic
Size	1	−0.01	0.19	3.32[a]
	2	−0.01	0.08	1.44
	3	−0.01	0.23	4.00[a]
Shape	1	−0.01	−0.02	−0.09
	2	−0.01	−0.04	0.54
	3	−0.01	0.03	0.72
Orientation	1	−0.01	0.08	1.62
	2	−0.01	−0.06	−0.075
	3	−0.01	0.27	4.76[a]

[a]Significant at a 0.05 level with a critical value of 1.64, one-tail distribution.

TABLE 5.3.
Kruskal-Wallis Tests of Room Form Variables Grouped by Room Block

	Variable	Construction Units	Rooms	Kruskal-Wallis Statistic	Probability
Room Block 1		6	33		
	Size			10.817	0.055
	Shape			9.597	0.088
	Orientation			22.154	0.095
Room Block 2		7	59		
	Size			3.387	0.759
	Shape			6.585	0.361
	Orientation			10.388	0.109
Room Block 3		9	42		
	Size			23.554	0.003
	Shape			13.409	0.099
	Orientation			18.833	0.016

together. Room Block 2 is slightly clustered, but room size distribution could not be distinguished from a random pattern.

Room orientation results are similar. Room Block 3 exhibits significant clustering; Room Block 1 is highly clustered but not significantly (given a 0.05 significance level [Table 5.2]). Room orientation in Room Block 2 is slightly dispersed but cannot be differentiated from a random distribution (Table 5.2). Again, these results suggest that rooms of similar orientation were constructed in contiguous sets in Room Block 3 and perhaps in Room Block 1. In Room Block 2 room orientation was randomly distributed.

Construction in the main pueblo is divided into 14 construction phases (Chapter 4), each composed of several construction units. A sample of construction units was selected from each room block to test whether rooms constructed as internally similar sets caused the intraroom-block variability seen in the main pueblo. The two selection criteria were a pre-A.D. 1330 construction date and four or more rooms in the unit. This strategy allowed the isolation of those units representing early construction in the main pueblo, when immigration is thought to have played a critical role in site growth. The four-room-size threshold insured higher confidence in statistical results.

The results indicate that the trends in room size and orientation just described were indeed a function of the construction in internally similar blocks. An analysis of variance demonstrates that construction units in Room Blocks 1 and 3 show substantial variability in room size, whereas those in Room Block 2 do not (Table 5.3; Figure 5.1). Although rooms in Room Block 2 were, in general, smaller than in the remainder of the main pueblo (Table 5.1), they sort into a single size class when grouped in this manner (Figure 5.1). On the other hand, Room Blocks 1 and 3 were characterized by distinct size separation (however, results for Room Block 1

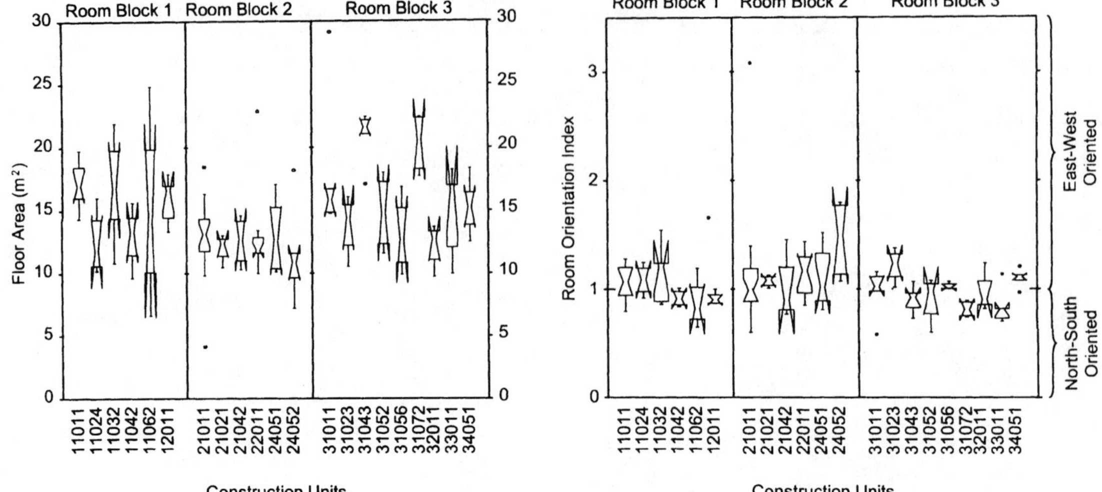

FIGURE 5.1.
Notched box plots comparing area and orientation among large, early-construction units in the main pueblo.

indicate a 0.055 significance level but are supported in the spatial autocorrelation analysis [Tables 5.2 and 5.3]).

Kruskal-Wallis analysis of variance for room orientation also reinforces the spatial autocorrelation analysis (Table 5.3). Room Block 3 and Room Block 1 exhibit separation of room orientation by construction unit and tend to divide into groups, with north-south and east-west oriented construction units, although the variability in Room Block 1 is not significant at the 0.05 level (Figure 5.1; Table 5.3). As expected, Room Block 2 also shows no patterning of room orientation by construction unit, but, in contrast to Room Block 1, most of its rooms were east-west oriented. Compared to Room Blocks 1 and 3, Room Block 2 stands out for the regularity in the size and orientation of rooms in the early construction units (Figure 5.1). This implies that Room Block 2's builders, as a group, had more uniform construction practices than their counterparts in Room Blocks 1 and 3. Following a discussion of room form in the outliers, other architectural data derived from room excavations are examined to provide additional support for these results.

Continued immigration and dispersion: Room variability in the outliers. The division between the aggregation and dispersion periods around A.D. 1330 is revealed in a change in the rate of construction (Chapter 4). At this time the construction of large units that resulted from the rapid influx of immigrants ceased, and subsequent growth consisted of reduced immigration rates, the natural budding off of already resident households, and a shift in local residential mobility patterns. This division impacted the rate of community growth and the architectural makeup and location of subsequent room construction;

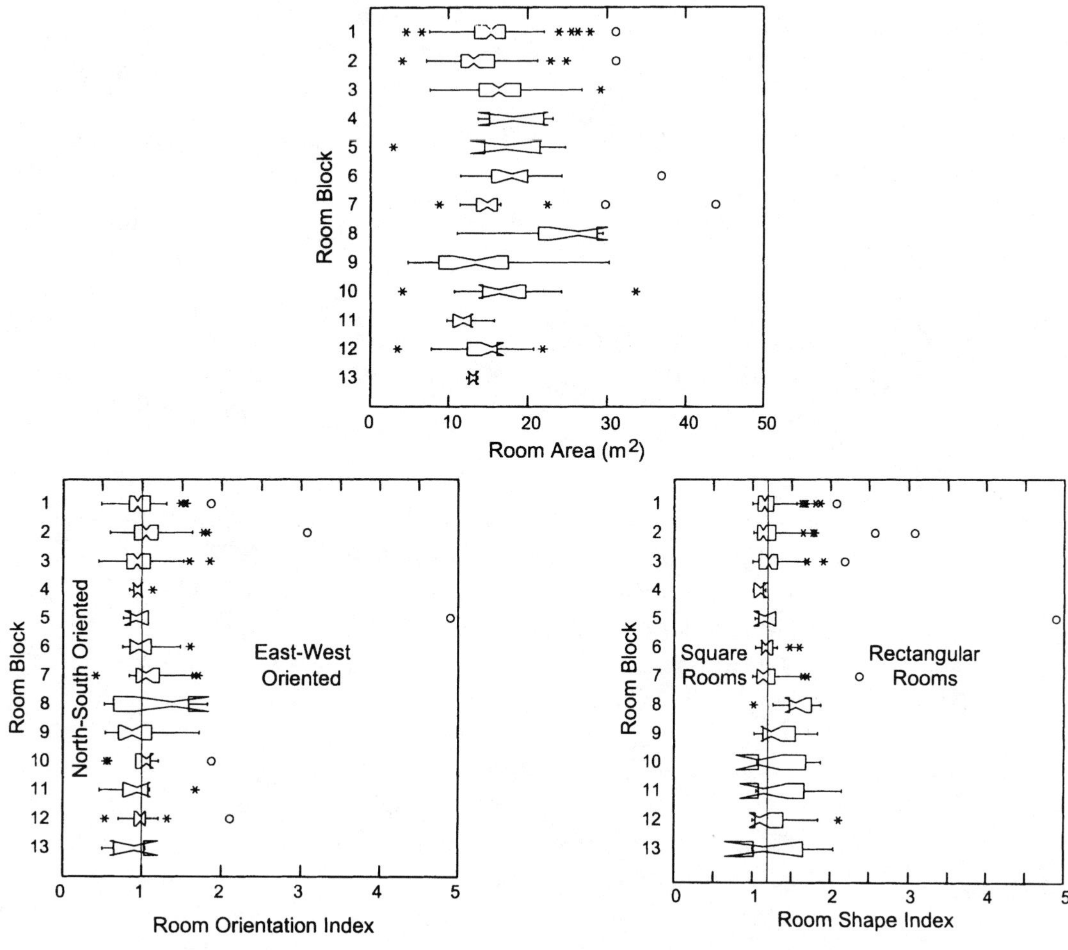

FIGURE 5.2.
Notched box plots comparing room area, shape, and orientation in all 13 room blocks.

the emergence of the outlier rooms and room blocks is the most obvious consequence of this shift in the local settlement pattern.

Variability in the architecture of these later rooms is a logical expectation given the spatial dispersion of the outliers compared to the more compact occupation of the main pueblo. In general, the rooms in the main pueblo were similar to one another in various ways, and, accordingly, the outliers exhibit internal similarities. Although the main pueblo itself was internally heterogeneous, the magnitude of the differences between outliers and the main pueblo represent fundamental changes in construction practices between the aggregation and dispersion periods.

An examination of room area reveals several community-scale patterns. As previously discussed, mean room size was greater but also more variable for the outliers when compared to the main pueblo (Table A.2; Figure 5.2). When rooms are grouped by room block, the data suggest that individual room blocks

TABLE 5.4.
Kruskal-Wallis Tests of Room Form Variables Grouped by Room Block

Variable	Room Blocks	Rooms	Kruskal-Wallis Statistic	Probability
Size	10	123	30.016	0.000
Shape	10	123	16.644	0.055
Orientation	10	123	6.187	0.721

were characterized by significant room size parameters (Table 5.4; Figure 5.2). For example, contrasting Room Blocks 8 and 11 suggests that each room block was constructed by a different group of builders with slightly different room size standards.

Room orientations in a given room block also point to some differences in construction techniques (Figure 5.2), although results are not statistically significant (Table 5.3). Of note are Room Blocks 7 and 8, which contained large numbers of east-west oriented rooms. Other room blocks like 4, 5, and 13 contained significant numbers of north-south oriented rooms.

Turning to room shape, the outlier rooms as a whole were more rectangular than rooms in the main pueblo (Figure 5.2). The distribution of room shape also appears to pattern when rooms are sorted by room block, although results are not statistically significant (Table 5.3). As Figure 5.2 illustrates, several of the outliers were composed largely of square rooms, whereas others consisted of rectangular rooms. In general, the outliers closer to the main pueblo contained more square rooms with less overall variability in room shape (Figures 2.4 and 5.2).

Considering all measures of room form used in this analysis, the outliers were not as clearly separated as the main pueblo room blocks. They are striking for the range of variability expressed within single room blocks and between room blocks, however, implying different conventions of size and space. The number of outliers and this range of variability have the effect of randomizing the results in statistical tests. This reflects a more informal utilization of walled space than that expressed by the main pueblo and reinforces the notion that the outlier room blocks signify a change in the utilization of the Grasshopper locality after the period of rapid aggregation.

Socially Determined Variability in Other Architectural Data

The room form data, which include the excavated rooms and rooms measured by the Cornering Project (Chapter 4), support the hypothesis of local and nonlocal construction traditions in the main pueblo. Wall feature and other data support the preceding analysis of room form by providing additional data on the technical choices made by the builders of the three room blocks. These span the full range of the manufacturing and use process, from the selection of building stone and wood species, to the number and size of the wall features, to the types of floor features used. An in-depth look at these technical choices further strengthens the case for the presence of immigrant groups and provides additional confirmation of the representativeness of the cornering data, as measured by room size, shape, and orientation.

Wall feature associations and distribution patterns. Spatial patterning in the distribution of wall features produced by different construction traditions is supported by the preceding discussion of room form. Some fascinating patterns in the location and dimensions of crawlways, doorways, vents, and niches emerge from an analysis of wall openings in the three room blocks of the main pueblo. Overall, Room Block 1 contains the fewest wall feature types per room (Table 5.5), although it contains the largest sample of excavated rooms, suggesting differences in the traditions related to wall construction and room use. Although the data from other aggregation-period room blocks are scant, Room Block 5 is more similar to Room Block 1 than to Room Block 2 in terms of the number of wall features per excavated room, indicating a closer affiliation with Room Block 1 than with the West Village. Room Block 2 demonstrates the most homogeneity, although it shared some feature characteristics with Room Block 3. Room Block 3 was aligned with either Room Block 1 or 2, depending on the variable examined.

The distribution of crawlways reveals obvious distinctions among the room blocks. Although few were found, only rooms in Room Blocks 2, 3, 6, and 7 contained crawlways (Figure 3.21; Table 5.5). Notably, these room blocks are all

TABLE 5.5.
Distribution of Wall Features by Room Block and by Number of Excavated Rooms per Room Block

Room Block	Doors		Crawlways		Vents		Niches	
	n	*n*/Excav Rooms	*n*	*n*/Excav Rooms	*n*	*n*/Excav Rooms	*n*	*n*/Excav Rooms
1	56	1.75	0	0.00	17	0.53	27	0.84
2	43	2.15	2	0.10	18	0.90	23	1.15
3	35	2.18	7	0.43	11	0.68	20	1.25
4	1	0.33	0	0.00	0	0.00	0	0.00
5	9	1.50	0	0.00	2	0.33	4	0.66
6	0	0.00	1	1.00	0	0.00	0	0.00
7	4	1.33	1	0.33	2	0.66	1	0.33
8	8	2.00	0	0.00	0	0.00	0	0.00
9	0	0.00	0	0.00	0	0.00	0	0.00
10	1	0.33	0	0.00	0	0.00	0	0.00
11	1	1.00	0	0.00	0	0.00	0	0.00
12	0	0.00	0	0.00	0	0.00	0	0.00
13	0	0.00	0	0.00	0	0.00	0	0.00
0	2	0.33	0	0.00	0	0.00	0	0.00

TABLE 5.6.
Kruskal-Wallis Tests on Door Metrics Grouped by Core Room Blocks

Door (n = 94)	Count	Rank Sum	Kruskal-Wallis Statistic	*df*	Probability
Height			14.513	4	0.006
RB 1	24	748.5	—	—	—
RB 2	31	1598.5	—	—	—
RB 3	29	1696.0	—	—	—
RB 5	6	237.0	—	—	—
RB 7	4	185.0	—	—	—
Width			1.460	4	0.834
RB 1	23	1062.5	—	—	—
RB 2	32	1638.5	—	—	—
RB 3	29	1257.0	—	—	—
RB 5	6	303.0	—	—	—
RB 7	4	204.0	—	—	—

west of Salt River Draw. The most conspicuous absence of crawlways is in Room Blocks 1 and 5, which were intensively sampled (Room Block 5 was completely excavated). The absence of these features in the East Village, despite the intensity of excavation there, suggests that its residents may have had more formal rules regarding the manipulation of standing walls than did residents of the West Village.

Analysis of variance performed on fully preserved doorways (i.e., the tops did not collapse during wall collapse) indicates notable variability in door size within room blocks (Table 5.6). The analysis demonstrates statistically significant variability in door height, whereas door width does not pattern. When the distribution of door metric data is grouped by room block, the doorways in Room Block 1 stand out as significantly shorter than those in Room Blocks 2 and 3, which were similar to one another (Figure 5.3). It is noteworthy that Room Block 5, although exhibiting a tight range of variability, overlaps (i.e., overlapping confidence intervals) in height with Room Blocks 1 and 3 but not with Room Block 2. This trend is completely reversed when considering door width, where the range in Room Block 5 overlaps with all other rooms at the site.

Similar patterns are evident in vents and niches, which were present in all five of the site core room blocks. The same Kruskal-Wallis test was run on vent and niche height and width to test for spatially patterned variability in size (Table 5.7). Neither set of tests produced statistically significant results, although some subtle patterning is apparent. Vents in Room Block 1 exhibit a greater median height and width than those in the West Village. Vent height in Room Block 2 is less variable than in the other two room blocks, and Room Block 2's niches have a tighter range of variability than those in Room Blocks 1 and 3. In fact, the width of Room Block 2's niches stands out from Room Block 1 as a discrete population based on nonoverlapping confidence intervals. Room Block 3 exhibits the most variability in vent width and shows the most variability in the height and width

FIGURE 5.3. Doorway in the west wall of Room 69 in Room Block 1, with Room 70 beyond. Doorway was originally blocked but was opened during excavation. Note its diminished height. Photographer unknown, 1977.

of its niches. At the same time, however, the median size of wall niches in Room Block 3 is much closer to Room Block 2 than to Room Block 1.

This variability in wall feature size and distribution indicates room block–specific patterns of wall manipulation in the main pueblo. As with room form, wall feature size and placement strongly suggest that the groups who built the three main room blocks acted from different social realities concerning size and shape conventions when constructing wall openings.

TABLE 5.7.
Kruskal-Wallis Tests on Vent and Niche Metrics Grouped by Core Room Blocks

	Count	Rank Sum	Kruskal-Wallis Statistic	*df*	Probability
Vent height (*n* = 41)			5.999	4	0.199
RB 1	12	261.5	—	—	—
RB 2	16	269.0	—	—	—
RB 3	10	247.0	—	—	—
RB 5	1	14.0	—	—	—
RB 7	2	69.5	—	—	—
Vent width (*n* = 43)			6.505	4	0.164
RB 1	13	328.5	—	—	—
RB 2	16	271.0	—	—	—
RB 3	10	227.0	—	—	—
RB 5	2	45.0	—	—	—
RB 7	2	74.5	—	—	—
Niche height (*n* = 55)			6.002	4	0.199
RB 1	21	666.0	—	—	—
RB 2	16	343.5	—	—	—
RB 3	14	439.5	—	—	—
RB 5	3	83.0	—	—	—
RB 7	1	3.0	—	—	—
Niche width (*n* = 58)			5.166	4	0.271
RB 1	21	680.0	—	—	—
RB 2	19	498.0	—	—	—
RB 3	14	413.0	—	—	—
RB 5	3	118.5	—	—	—
RB 7	1	1.5	—	—	—

Spatial and formal patterns in the distribution of two-story rooms. The relationship between the number of stories and room size also seems to indicate different construction practices. The builders of the East and West villages seem to have had slightly different conceptions of appropriate size parameters for construction of second-story rooms. Viewing the main pueblo as a whole, there is not a statistically significant difference in room size between upper-story and single-story rooms (Table 5.8). Two-story room spaces were only slightly smaller on average than one-story spaces. This is a logical relationship: walls shorter in length were probably more resistant to collapse and as a result could probably be carried to greater heights. Different patterns of structure use appear once again, however, when focusing on individual room blocks. Two-story rooms in nonlocal Room Block 1 were slightly larger than one-story rooms, whereas in Room Blocks 2 and 3 the opposite was true. On the other hand, the distribution of room size in Room Blocks 2 and 3 cannot be differentiated from a random pattern when the data are organized by the number of stories. Table 5.8 demonstrates that although Room Block 2 cannot be distinguished from a random pattern (at a 0.05 significance level), the difference

TABLE 5.8.
Mann-Whitney Tests on Room Size Grouped by Number of Stories

	n	Mean	*SD*	Rank Sum	*U* Statistic	Probability
Main Pueblo					7993.00	0.36
1 Story	219	15.23	4.18	32083.00		
2 Story	68	15.09	4.02	9245.00		
Room Block 1					429.00	0.01
1 Story	76	15.21	4.18	3355.00		
2 Story	18	17.36	3.18	1110.00		
Room Block 2					1125.00	0.14
1 Story	61	14.44	4.31	3016.00		
2 Story	31	12.85	2.78	1262.00		
Room Block 3					849.50	0.54
1 Story	82	16.62	3.88	4252.00		
2 Story	19	16.60	4.63	899.00		

in mean room sizes between one-story and two-story room spaces reflects a trend opposite to that in Room Block 1. Once again, three main room blocks exhibit subtle differences in the overall organization of room space. One final piece of evidence further strengthens the hypothesis that distinct social groups were responsible for constructing the three large main pueblo room blocks.

Wood-use practices. As Lemonnier (1986:154) suggests, raw material selection is an important component of the technical process. Like all other technical variants, the use of particular raw materials can signal different socially determined conventions. As noted above, there are spatially patterned distributions in the use of various types of building stone within the main pueblo (Chapter 3). Wood-use practices within the main pueblo also appear to exhibit socially determined variability. In their analysis of the tree-ring material, Dean and Robinson (1982:49) found that juniper was the predominant species used in late rooms. The majority of these dated juniper samples came from the northern end of Room Block 1, which, counter to Dean and Robinson's initial assessment, dates solidly to the aggregation period (Chapter 4). The lack of juniper in contemporaneous rooms in Room Blocks 2 and 3 indicates that other species were not in short supply at this time and that deforestation was probably not a factor. In another study Sullivan (1974) examined wood-use and construction practices to demonstrate original room function and noted that storage rooms were roofed with juniper more often than were other room types. A reexamination of Sullivan's study confirmed his results and discovered another pattern of juniper use in construction.

A comparison of species use by room block indicates a marked preference for juniper and piñon as construction materials by the builders of the East Village (Room Blocks 1 and 5) relative to the builders of the West Village (Table 5.9). The East Village contained 71 percent of all dated juniper and piñon. By

TABLE 5.9.
Distribution of Construction Wood Species by Village (Expected Values Shown in Parentheses)

	Ponderosa/Douglas fir	Piñon/Juniper	Total
East Village	11 (20.90)	15 (5.10)	26
West Village	75 (65.10)	6 (15.90)	81
Total	86	21	107

Note: $\chi^2 = 31.55$; $df = 1$; $p = 0.000$; $\phi = -0.543$; Yule's Q = – 0.889

contrast, only 13 percent of the sample of Douglas fir and ponderosa pine came from the East Village. Thus, not only were juniper and piñon present in a higher frequency in the East Village, but other wood species appear to have been used less frequently than in the West Village. This suggests that the East Village's builders either preferred juniper for construction or perhaps were restricted in their access to the longer and straighter types of construction wood. If the inhabitants of the East Village came from the Colorado Plateau, as hypothesized, where piñon and juniper are the predominant materials available for construction, they may have preferred these more familiar species for the construction of roofs. It is interesting to note that, although piñon does not occur as frequently as other types of wood, three of the five dated samples came from Room Block 5 in the East Village.

Social Groups and the Founding and Early Growth of the Grasshopper Community

The internal regularity of Room Block 2 seems to reflect the activities of a single group, with similar rules for putting rooms together. As noted, convergent lines of architectural and other material evidence suggest that Room Block 2 was constructed by groups of local builders (Table 5.10). The analysis is supported by bone chemistry and other skeletal analyses indicating that individuals in Room Blocks 2 and 3 enjoyed better overall health and could acquire more agricultural products, implying differential access to local resources (Ezzo 1993:83; Hinkes 1983:156).

Room Block 3 seems to represent the construction activities of local and nonlocal groups. Although the majority of architectural data align Room Block 3 more closely to Room Block 2, strontium isotope data from the skeletal remains suggest that Room Block 3 was at least partially settled by a nonlocal population (Ezzo et al. 1997:456–457) and that its residents continued to rely more heavily on agricultural products than did the residents of Room Block 2, who had the most transitional diets, relying on wild gathered plants, meat, and agricultural products (Ezzo 1993:56, 83). Architecturally, Room Block 3 conforms to expectations of local and nonlocal construction by exhibiting

TABLE 5.10.
Comparison of Architectural Traits within the Main Pueblo

Room Block 1	Room Block 2	Room Block 3
Larger Rooms	Small, homogeneous rooms	Larger, variable size rooms
North-south oriented rooms	East-west oriented rooms	Variably (randomly) oriented rooms
No crawlways	Crawlways	Crawlways
Smaller (shorter) doors	Larger doors	Larger doors
Fewer wall features (per excavated room)	—	—
Smaller wall features	—	—
Two-story rooms larger than one-story	Two-story rooms smaller than one-story	No relationship between room size and no. of stories
More juniper relative to other species of wood	Less juniper relative to other wood species	Less juniper relative to other wood species
No large storage bins	Large storage bins	Large storage bins
Double mealing bins	No double mealing bins	No double mealing bins
Low frequency of Area 4 sandstones	High frequency of Area 4 sandstones	?
No kivas, only ceremonial rooms	Kivas and ceremonial rooms	Kivas and ceremonial rooms
Spatial isolation—East of Salt R. Draw	Connected to RB 3 by corridor roof	Connected to RB 2 by corridor roof
No formal plaza	Great Kiva, Plaza 1, Plaza 2	Plaza 1, Plaza 2
Last founded—slow growth (13 construction phases)	First founded—rapid growth (7 construction phases)	slow growth (14 construction phases)
Ladder-type, linear core construction	Block-type core construction	Linear core construction
?	Overlies Pueblo III architecture	?

some characteristics that are distinct from those of Room Block 2 and some that are similar (Table 5.10). The connection of Room Block 3 to Room Block 2 by means of roof corridors into Plazas 1 and 2 implies a social connection, whereas many of the architectural details described above suggest similarities to Room Block 1. Yet construction in both West Village room blocks closed the corridor into Plaza 1 by A.D. 1325 (Riggs 1994a; Chapter 4), suggesting cooperation and close social ties between the two room blocks that may not have existed with Room Block 1. Finally, the combined dietary data from Room Blocks 2 and 3 indicate a closer tie to each other than either do to Room Block 1. The early residents of Room Block 1 relied much more heavily on wild plant resources than did the inhabitants of Room Blocks 2 and 3, who seem to have had more access to agricultural products (Ezzo 1993:83).

This analysis finds Room Block 1 more internally homogeneous than Room

Block 3 and less so than Room Block 2. Yet it differed from Room Block 2 in all regards (Table 5.10). Room Block 1's dissimilarities from Room Block 2 reinforce the assertion that it was built by nonlocals. Once again, skeletal data strengthen this claim. Nutritional analyses of the burials associated with Room Block 1 have found indications of limited access to agricultural products (Ezzo 1993:83) and increased dietary stress (Hinkes 1983:156), suggesting a resource base different from that available to the inhabitants of Room Blocks 2 and 3. Finally, additional bone chemistry data suggest that the inhabitants of Room Block 1 exhibited a nonlocal dietary signature (Ezzo et al. 1997:461).

ROOM FUNCTION AND CHANGING SYSTEMS OF SETTINGS

Room function analysis has been widely used to understand social and community organization in the Southwest (Ciolek-Torrello 1978; Dean 1969, 1970; Hill 1970a, 1970b); however, it was recognized early on at Grasshopper that room function did not correlate well with architectural data—namely room size. As indicated in Chapter 1, this lack of fit is predictable because of architecture's loose relationship to activities (Rapoport 1982, 1990). The main reason for this disjunction is that function is often, but not always (e.g., Dean 1969), determined by the activities that took place in a given room rather than by architectural characteristics of the space enclosing the activities. Although some have used nonarchitectural data exclusively (Ciolek-Torrello 1978, 1984, 1985), many analyses of southwestern pueblos rely heavily on room form and construction features to predict the function of a given architectural space (Creamer 1993; Dean 1969, 1970; Hill 1970a, 1970b; Lekson 1984; Lowell 1991), suggesting that there is a relationship between architecture and room function. I suggest that this relationship may only be preserved at sites not subject to a great deal of floor remodeling. Remodeling of room floors at Grasshopper significantly obscured the relationship between a room's original function and its function at abandonment (Ciolek-Torrello 1978; Sullivan 1974), and Grasshopper researchers have addressed room function from an activity organization perspective (Ciolek-Torrello 1978, 1984, 1985; Reid and Whittlesey 1982; Rock 1974; Sullivan 1974). Using Rapoport's (1982:89–101) terminology, this perspective has focused primarily on the semifixed (floor features) and nonfixed (artifacts) feature elements.

This having been said, however, the significance of architectural characteristics and their exclusive relevance to room function have never been systematically studied. An examination of the relationship between fixed architectural characteristics—room size and wall feature data—not only reinforces the notion that systems of activities were performed in fluid settings over time but also strengthens the previous discussion of different social groups by eliminating the possibility that the room size and wall feature characteristics were a result of room function. Overall, this brief treatment of room function and remodeling demonstrates the complexity of the relationship between architectural variables and room function in a community where the resident population was constantly in a state of flux.

Community Organization and the Role of Room Function

Room function at Grasshopper can only be determined for rooms with sets of de facto refuse on the floor because of extensive room floor remodeling and because a room's function is defined primarily by the activities that took place in it over time. Rooms lacking sets of de facto refuse on their floors were those abandoned during the occupation, which then served as refuse disposal areas. In order to eliminate these trash-filled rooms from the sample, Reid (1973:114–115) developed the relative room abandonment measure as a means of identifying rooms abandoned while Grasshopper was still occupied. "Rooms abandoned while Grasshopper was still occupied contain little or no de facto refuse, defined as tools, facilities, and materials that, although still usable, were abandoned at an activity area on the last utilized floor. These rooms do contain in the room fill, however, a high density of secondary refuse, defined as trash discarded away from its location of use" (Reid and Shimada 1982:14–15).

In his analysis of activity organization, Ciolek-Torrello (1978) applied the relative room abandonment measure to eliminate rooms that were not occupied at the time of community abandonment, which did not contain floor assemblages indicating room use activities (Ciolek-Torrello 1978, 1984, 1985). Principal components and cluster analyses were then applied to develop a room function typology using features and artifacts discovered on late-abandoned floors (Ciolek-Torrello 1978). This study strayed from traditional room function analyses that relied heavily on room size and other architectural features (cf. Dean 1969; Hill 1970a; Rohn 1971). Ciolek-Torrello identified six functional types based on the co-occurrence of various floor features and artifact categories (Ciolek-Torrello 1984:144). These six functional classes are as follows:

Type 1—Limited Activity Rooms
Type 2—Habitation Rooms
Type 3—Domestic Storage Rooms
Type 4—Multifunctional Habitation Rooms
Type 5—Manufacturing Rooms
Type 6—Storage/Manufacturing Rooms

Reid and Whittlesey (1982) expanded Ciolek-Torrello's typology (Table 5.11) by incorporating some fixed and semifixed architectural elements to break up Ciolek-Torrello's limited activity and storage types.[2] Reid and Whittlesey identified kivas and ceremonial rooms based on the presence or absence of salient features, such as benches, ash boxes, and circular hearths, and used features

TABLE 5.11.
Room Function for All Late-Abandoned Excavated Rooms

Room Number	Room Block	Room Function (after Ciolek-Torrello 1978)	Room Function (after Reid and Whittlesey 1982)
2	1	Limited activity	Limited activity, food processing
3	4	Multifunctional habitation	Generalized habitation
4	1	Habitation	Specialized habitation
5	1	Habitation	Specialized habitation
6	1	Habitation	Specialized habitation
7	1	Habitation	Specialized habitation
8	1	Habitation	Specialized habitation
9	4	Domestic storage	Ceremonial
11	1	Multifunctional habitation	Generalized habitation
12	2	Limited activity	Limited activity, food processing
13	2	Storage, Manufacturing	Storage, Manufacturing
15	1	Limited activity	Limited activity, food processing
18	2	Limited activity	Kiva
19	2	Domestic storage	Storage
21	2	Storage, manufacturing	Storage, manufacturing
22	2	Manufacturing	Manufacturing
24	0	Habitation	Specialized habitation
25	0	Multifunctional habitation	Generalized habitation
26	2	Limited activity	Limited activity, manufacturing
27	2	Habitation	Specialized habitation
33	1	Limited activity	Ceremonial
35	1	Domestic storage	Storage
37	1	Limited activity	Limited activity, food processing
39	1	Storage, manufacturing	Storage, manufacturing
40	1	Limited activity	Limited activity, manufacturing
42	1	Limited activity	Limited activity, manufacturing
43	1	Storage, manufacturing	Storage, manufacturing
44	1	Storage, manufacturing	Storage, manufacturing
45	1	Domestic storage	Storage
68	1	Multifunctional habitation	Generalized habitation
69	1	Manufacturing	Manufacturing
70	1	Manufacturing	Manufacturing
97	1	Multifunctional habitation	Generalized habitation
100	1	Habitation	Specialized habitation
104	1	Habitation	Specialized habitation
107	1	Limited activity	Ceremonial
108	1	Manufacturing	Manufacturing
112	5	Manufacturing	Manufacturing
113	5	Storage, manufacturing	Storage, manufacturing
114	5	Habitation	Specialized habitation
115	5	Multifunctional habitation	Generalized habitation
116	5	Multifunctional habitation	Generalized habitation
121	1	Limited activity	Limited activity, manufacturing
143	2	Habitation	Specialized habitation
145	2	Manufacturing	Manufacturing
153	2	Limited activity	Limited activity, manufacturing
183	2	Domestic storage	Storage
187	2	Manufacturing	Manufacturing
195	5	Limited activity	Limited activity, food processing

TABLE 5.11. *(continued)*

Room Number	Room Block	Room Function (after Ciolek-Torrello 1978)	Room Function (after Reid and Whittlesey 1982)
197	2	Limited activity	Ceremonial
198	10	Domestic storage	Limited activity, manufacturing
205	3	Multifunctional habitation	Generalized habitation
206	3	Limited activity	Kiva
210	3	Domestic storage	Ceremonial
211	3	Habitation	Specialized habitation
215	3	Domestic storage	Storage
216	3	Multifunctional habitation	Generalized habitation
218	3	Habitation	Specialized habitation
231	3	Manufacturing	Manufacturing
246	3	Storage, manufacturing	Storage, manufacturing
269	3	Manufacturing	Manufacturing
274	3	Limited activity	Ceremonial
279	3	Manufacturing	Manufacturing
280	3	Limited activity	Limited activity, manufacturing
309	0	Multifunctional habitation	Generalized habitation
312	0	Multifunctional habitation	Generalized habitation
319	6	Multifunctional habitation	Generalized habitation
341	7	Limited activity	Kiva
349	7	Storage, manufacturing	Storage, manufacturing
352	7	Limited activity	Limited activity, food processing
353	8	Habitation	Specialized habitation
354	8	Multifunctional habitation	Generalized habitation
355	8	Multifunctional habitation	Generalized habitation
356	8	Limited activity	Limited activity, food processing
359	0	Multifunctional habitation	Generalized habitation
371	9	Multifunctional habitation	Generalized habitation
376	9	Domestic storage	Ceremonial
395	12	Manufacturing	Manufacturing
397	12	Habitation	Specialized habitation
398	12	Habitation	Specialized habitation
404	12	Limited activity	Limited activity, manufacturing
411	12	Multifunctional habitation	Generalized habitation
414	10	Limited activity	Ceremonial
420	10	Multifunctional habitation	Generalized habitation
425	11	Limited activity	Limited activity, food processing
434	13	Limited activity	Ceremonial
438	3	Manufacturing	Manufacturing

and implements recovered from floors to separate nonceremonial limited activity rooms into food processing and manufacturing rooms (Reid and Whittlesey 1982:693). Reid and Whittlesey's types are as follows:

Specialized Habitation Rooms
Generalized Habitation Rooms
Storage Rooms
Storage-Manufacturing Rooms

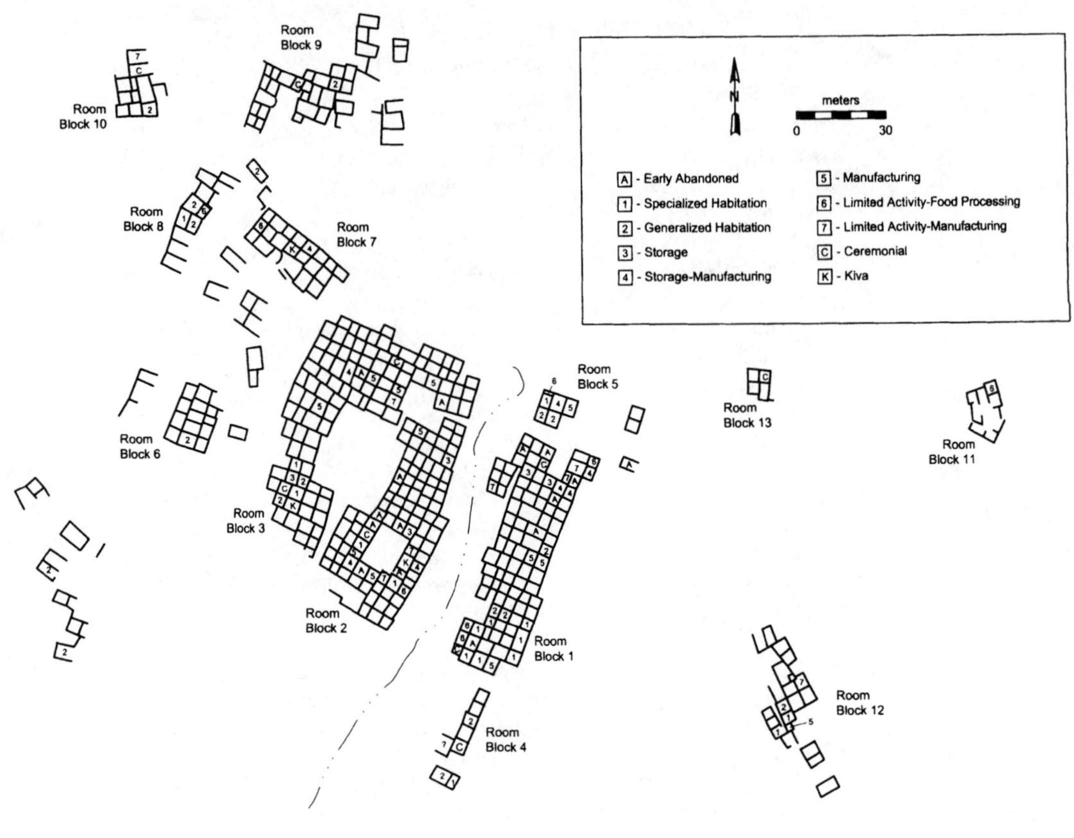

FIGURE 5.4. Distribution of Reid and Whittlesey's (1982) room types (room block locations not to scale).

Manufacturing Rooms
Limited Activity–Food Processing Rooms
Limited Activity–Manufacturing Rooms
Ceremonial Rooms
Kivas

As shown in Figure 5.4, which illustrates the distribution of Reid and Whittlesey's room types, habitation rooms (Types 1 and 2) predominate among the rooms excavated. Specialized habitation rooms were more common in the main pueblo than in the outliers, suggesting a higher diversification of activity areas in the main pueblo (Reid 1989:85). A ceremonial room or kiva was excavated in most room blocks, although there is a noticeable absence of kivas in Room Block 1, despite the number of excavated rooms (however, two ceremonial rooms were excavated). The complete absence of storage rooms in the outliers is also significant. This absence supports the idea that the outliers were used by a more mobile population and that long-term storage may not have been important in the later occupation (Reid 1989:86; Reid and Whittlesey 1982:694). Aside from these general observations, there is no significant relationship between room location (i.e., room block) and room function.

TABLE 5.12.
Reid and Whittlesey's Room Function and the Reduced Typology

This Study	Reid and Whittlesey (1982)
1—Habitation	1—Specialized habitation
	2—Generalized habitation
2—Storage Rooms	3—Storage
	4—Storage, manufacturing
3—Ceremonial	8—Ceremonial Room
	9—Kiva
4—Other	5—Manufacturing
	6—Limited activity, food processing
	7—Limited activity, manufacturing

Both typologies were updated for this analysis to include rooms excavated since the two original studies were reported (Table 5.11). Only a modified version of Reid and Whittlesey's classification was used in this analysis because their study recognizes rooms with ceremonial functions. Although the nine-class typology is useful for subdividing activity areas, it is overly specific for the types of statistical analyses used here. The number of classes is unwieldy and creates categories of rooms that occur too infrequently to allow confidence in analytical results. A four-class reduced typology that combines similar types of rooms into fewer categories was used for this analysis primarily to insure higher confidence in the statistical tests used below (Table 5.12).

Formal, Functional, and Spatial Correlations

Because room function was determined largely without considering the formal properties of the architecture—walls, roofs, wall features—the relationship between room function and some of the architectural features described in Chapter 3 remains to be examined. The following discussion also serves a second, and perhaps more important, purpose. Demonstrating that the architectural patterns at Grasshopper are not related to room function strengthens the previous discussion of social group identity by eliminating room function as a possible source of variability in the size of rooms and in the size and distribution of wall features. Furthermore, this analysis indicates that several assumptions about the relationships between architectural characteristics and room function at plateau pueblo sites are not supported in sites with even a moderate amount of room floor remodeling, justifying the notion that architecture contains activities only loosely.

On the other hand, some of these findings are consistent with modern pueblo room-use practices. Habitation rooms and ceremonial rooms at Grasshopper were located either on the second story of a two-story room suite or were single-story rooms. Rooms with more limited functions, such as storage rooms or manufacturing rooms, tended to be located on the lower story of two-story room suites. Almost without exception the construction of a second story atop an existing habitation or ceremonial room required a change in first-story room function.

Finally, drawing on parallels with Turkey Creek Pueblo, a Tularosa phase pueblo in the Point of Pines region (Figure 2.1; Johnson 1965; Lowell 1991), this analysis indicates that a set of rooms with specialized functions surrounded Grasshopper's Great Kiva. This lends additional support to the construction sequence data for the Great Kiva, suggesting that many of the surrounding rooms were constructed specifically to outline, or were remodeled to reflect a new role associated with, this important space.

Room size and function. Room size has been one important indicator of room function in the Southwest. In general, rooms with a primary habitation function are large, whereas those used for storage tend to be smaller (Adams 1983; Hill 1970a; Johnson 1965; Lowell 1991; Martin et al 1961:53). Contrary to this normative statement, however, several studies suggest that size and function do not always correlate well (Dean 1969:29; Sullivan 1974:95). At Grasshopper, where room size and function are not correlated, it has long been recognized that room size cannot be used to predict room function (Ciolek-Torrello 1978:100). The data used in this analysis reveal a relationship between room function and room size only when the entire community is considered and the four-function typology is used (Table 5.13). Habitation rooms tend to be slightly larger, in keeping with the results of other room function analyses. When the focus shifts to the main pueblo, where room remodeling was more common and room function more rigidly defined, the relationship between room size and function is not significant (Table 5.13). This results from two processes: (1) the practice of floor remodeling in the longer occupied rooms of

TABLE 5.13.
Kruskal-Wallis Tests on Room Area Grouped by Room Function

Late-Abandoned Excavated Rooms	Count	Rank Sum	Kruskal-Wallis Statistic	Probability
All ($n = 86$)			14.25	0.003
Habitation	33	1770.00	—	—
Storage	13	657.00	—	—
Ceremonial	12	445.50	—	—
Other	28	868.50	—	—
Main Pueblo ($n = 54$)			6.689	0.082
Habitation	16	541.00	—	—
Storage	11	342.00	—	—
Ceremonial	7	183.50	—	—
Other	20	418.50	—	—

TABLE 5.14.
Cross-Tabulation of Wall Features and Room Function at Various Spatial Scales (Expected Values Shown in Parentheses)

Late-Abandoned Rooms[a]	Doors/Crawlways	Vents	Niches	Totals
All				
Habitation	53 (44.38)	12 (11.88)	10 (18.75)	75
Storage	27 (31.55)	6 (8.39)	20 (13.25)	53
Ceremonial	16 (13.61)	4 (3.64)	3 (5.75)	23
Other	46 (52.66)	16 (14.09)	27 (22.25)	89
Total	142	38	60	240
In site core[b]				
Habitation	43 (36.94)	12 (10.88)	10 (17.18)	65
Storage	27 (30.12)	6 (8.72)	20 (14.01)	53
Ceremonial	16 (13.07)	4 (3.85)	3 (6.08)	23
Other	43 (48.72)	16 (14.40)	27 (22.73)	86
Total	129	38	60	227
In main pueblo[c]				
Habitation	37 (32.01)	10 (9.55)	10 (15.44)	57
Storage	24 (25.27)	5 (7.54)	16 (12.19)	45
Ceremonial	14 (11.23)	3 (3.35)	3 (5.42)	20
Other	39 (45.49)	16 (13.57)	26 (21.95)	81
Total	114	34	55	203

[a] $\chi^2 = 14.372$; $df = 6$; $p = 0.026$; $\phi = 0.24$; Cramer's V = 0.17

[b] $\chi^2 = 11.834$; $df = 6$; $p = 0.066$; $\phi = 0.22$; Cramer's V = 0.16

[c] $\chi^2 = 8.735$; $df = 6$; $p = 0.189$; $\phi = 0.20$; Cramer's V = 0.15

the main pueblo and (2) the homogenization of activities in the larger outlier rooms, reflected in more generalized room use.

Nevertheless, main pueblo habitation rooms had the highest median room size but also the greatest range of variability in size, whereas the metric characteristics of the other room types were relatively similar to one another. Thus, this analysis finds that room size is only marginally related to room function. It appears that there may have been a lower size threshold for habitation rooms, below which a room space was not suitable for certain domestic activities. Beyond this, room size is not a predictor of room function.

Room function and wall features. A correspondence between the presence of wall features and room function has been found in previous studies of southwestern pueblo architecture (Haury 1934:52; Hill 1970b:23). To test for a similar correspondence at Grasshopper, the distribution of each wall feature type was compared to room function using the four-class typology. Because the scale of analysis has been critical to all treatments of the architectural data thus far, several spatial scales were also examined here (Table 5.14). When the entire Grasshopper site is examined, the distribution of features does vary significantly from a random pattern, although the strength of the relationship is weak (Cramer's V = 0.17). When the focus narrows, the pattern of association becomes more random, and the relationships among cells continue to be weak (Table 5.14).

In the main pueblo the distribution of features by room function cannot be distinguished from a random pattern, indicating that many of the expectations derived from other pueblo communities are not supported. For example, in his study of Broken K Pueblo, Hill noted that wall niches were associated with ceremonial rooms (Hill 1970a:53) and that vents most often indicated a habitation room (Hill 1970b:29). At Grasshopper, rooms with a ceremonial function, which would be expected to contain more niches than a random distribution (such as at Broken K Pueblo), contained fewer of these features at all spatial scales. Other associations also defy expectations. For example, the associations between vents and ceremonial rooms and vents and habitation rooms do not deviate significantly from random distributions.

In light of data from other sites, the association between doorways and storage rooms also did not pattern in predictable ways. At the Hopi pueblo of Walpi, doorways were found to occur less frequently in storage rooms than other room types and were almost never found on exterior walls (Adams 1983:53–54). In room suites owned by a household, however, doorways often connect the granaries and storage rooms (Adams 1983:54). As Table 5.14 demonstrates, doorways were found associated with storage rooms in a frequency similar to that expected for a random distribution. This suggests that, once again, remodeling of room floors may have obscured the original function of rooms resulting in a disjunction between the placement of doorways and the use of the rooms in question. Despite the lack of support for Adams's findings at Walpi, the association between room use and the few doors that were not sealed suggests other patterns of room use (Table 5.15).

Apart from the open doorway that connected Room 16 to the Great Kiva (Figure 5.5), only two open doorways were recorded between excavated rooms. These two examples connected a limited-activity manufacturing room to an early-abandoned room (Rooms 41 and 42 in Room Block 1), and a manufacturing room to a limited-activity manufacturing room (Rooms 279 and 280 in Room Block 3). Half of the open doorways were definitely associated with early-abandoned rooms. Three of these (60 percent) opened into unexcavated rooms, suggesting that many of the remaining doorways opening to unexcavated rooms from later abandoned spaces could have opened into abandoned rooms as well. One open doorway was associated with a storage room, whereas the majority of open doorways and crawlways were associated with rooms with manufacturing functions (6 doorways).

Overall, these data support the suggestion in Chapter 3 that open doorways connected rooms with limited-activity functions to early-abandoned rooms, perhaps for easy disposal of manufacturing debris. Conversion of the lower story into storage rooms and other limited activity rooms with the addition of a new second-story habitation room probably partially explains the higher

TABLE 5.15.
Relationship between Open Doorways and Crawlways and Room Function

	Room	Wall	Wall Type	Room Function	Connected Room/Space	Connected Function
Doors						
	146	North	Existing bounding	Early abandoned	149	Unexcavated
	153	North	Existing bounding	Limited activity, manufacturing	152	Unexcavated
	16	West	New bounding	Vestibule/entry	Great Kiva	Great Kiva
	183	North	New bounding	Domestic storage	190	Unexcavated
	23	South	Existing bounding	Early abandoned	135	Unexcavated
	359	South	New bounding	Early abandoned	Extramural	Extramural
	41	West	Partition	Early abandoned	42	Limited activity, manufacturing
	42	East	Partition	Limited activity, manufacturing	41	Early abandoned
	4	North	Existing bounding	Specialized habitation	106	Unexcavated
	62	East	Existing bounding	Early abandoned	61	Unexcavated
	279	South	New bounding	manufacturing	280	Limited activity, manufacturing
	280	North	Existing bounding	Limited activity, manufacturing	279	Manufacturing
Crawlways						
	269	South	New bounding	Manufacturing	248	Unexcavated
	274	East	New bounding	Ceremonial	267	Unexcavated

occurrence of doorways in storage rooms than that noted at Walpi. It is also possible that storage rooms at Grasshopper had open doors at one time that were sealed to protect their contents, although the multiple issues of equifinality related to doorway placement and blocked doorways discussed in Chapter 3 render this discussion highly speculative.

This examination of the relationship between room function and architectural characteristics at Grasshopper supports the long-held idea that final room function was not necessarily related to a room's function as conceived during construction (Ciolek-Torrello 1978:100; Sullivan 1974:94–95). It is not surprising, therefore, that the spatial distribution of wall features and wall feature size is not related to final room function in predictable ways.

FIGURE 5.5. Room 16, looking west. Note the open doorway to the Great Kiva. Photograph by Marion L. Parker, 1964. Courtesy of the Arizona State Museum, University of Arizona; neg. no. 10506.

Quantifying room remodeling activities. The lack of correlation between specific architectural characteristics and room function arises from the effects of room floor remodeling. These effects can significantly obscure original room function. A comparison of the floor features on each room floor partially reveals how remodeling affects the relationship between architectural characteristics and room function. Based on the number of floors recorded for each excavated room, 41 (40 percent) of the 103 excavated rooms were remodeled. Of these, 35 were late abandoned (Table 5.16), and 13 (37 percent) appear to have retained their original function, although 14 rooms (40 percent) probably changed function, and eight rooms (23 percent) did not have enough floor feature data to determine if room function changed.

Six early-abandoned rooms also had multiple floors. Unfortunately, there were insufficient floor feature data to determine if any of these underwent a change in function. In most instances it is also impossible to predict how room function changed because the occupants removed the associated artifacts (nonfixed elements) and many of the floor features (semifixed elements) when they remodeled the room floor. The estimations based on the remaining floor features are presented in Table 5.16.

In the core room blocks (1, 2, 3, 5, and 7), where rooms were occupied for longer periods, the incidence of remodeling was slightly higher (43 percent); 33 of the 77 excavated rooms contained more than one recorded floor. Of these rooms, 29 were late abandoned. Of the late-abandoned rooms, 10 (34 percent) retained their function, 13 (45 percent) changed function, and 6 (21 percent) could not be assessed with respect to changes in room function. Again, the six

TABLE 5.16.
Assessment of Floor Remodeling for All Late-Abandoned Rooms with Multiple Floors ($n = 34$)

Room Block	Room	Floors	Stories	Change	Final Room Function (Reid and Whittlesey 1982)	Estimated Prior Function(s)
1	2	3	1	?	Limited activity, food processing	Indeterminate
	5	2	1	No	Specialized habitation	Habitation
	6	2	1	No	Specialized habitation	Habitation
	11	2	1	No	Generalized habitation	Habitation
	15	2	1	No?	Limited activity, food processing	Limited activity, food processing (habitation?)
	37	2	1	Yes	Limited activity, food processing	Habitation
	68	2	2	Yes	Generalized habitation	Ceremonial?
	69	2	2	?	Manufacturing	Indeterminate
	70	2	2	?	Manufacturing	Indeterminate
	104	2	1	No	Specialized habitation	Habitation
	121	3	1	?	Limited activity, manufacturing	Indeterminate
2	13	2	1	Yes	Storage, manufacturing	Habitation?
	18	2	1	No	Kiva	Kiva
	19	2	2	Yes	Storage	Habitation?
	21	3	2	Yes	Storage, manufacturing	Habitation?
	22	2	1	Yes	Manufacturing	Habitation?
	143	4	1	No	Specialized habitation	Habitation
	145	2	1	Yes	Manufacturing	Habitation?
	187	6	1	No?	Manufacturing	Manufacturing?
	197	5	1	Yes	Ceremonial	Habitation?
3	216	2	1	No	Generalized habitation	Habitation
	246	3	2	Yes	Storage, manufacturing	Ceremonial
	269	4	2	Yes	Manufacturing	Ceremonial
	274	2	2	Yes	Ceremonial	Habitation
	279	5	1	?	Manufacturing	Indeterminate
	438	2	1	?	Manufacturing	Indeterminate
5	114	3	1	Yes	Specialized habitation	Kiva
6	319	2	1	No	Generalized habitation	Habitation
7	341	2	1	No	Kiva	Kiva

TABLE 5.16. *(continued)*

Room Block	Room	Floors	Stories	Change	Final Room Function (Reid and Whittlesey 1982)	Estimated Prior Function(s)
8	356	4	1	?	Limited activity, food processing	Indeterminate
10	198	2	1	?	Limited activity, manufacturing	Indeterminate
12	411	2	1	No	Generalized habitation	Habitation
13	13	2	1	Yes	Ceremonial	Habitation
0	24	2	1	No	Specialized habitation	Habitation

early-abandoned rooms did not have sufficient data to assess a change in room function.

These data suggest a moderately high incidence of room remodeling during the occupation of Grasshopper and support the pattern of community development discussed in Chapter 4. Almost half of all excavated rooms underwent one or more floor remodelings, and more than a third of these showed definite evidence of modified function. If this figure is applied to the entire site (assuming that the excavated sample is representative, as argued in Chapter 2), then potentially 179 of the 447 recorded rooms, most in the main pueblo, underwent one or more floor remodelings. Factoring in the rooms that did not have subfloor excavations (Table A.1) would increase this number. And, as previously discussed, the frequency of room floor remodeling obscured the relationship between architectural characteristics and room function. Clearly, changing intrasite relationships among the constant stream of immigrants and the effects of natural population increase on existing household size profoundly shaped the use of space.

The strong link between the number of room stories and ground-floor remodeling also needs to be addressed. As Table 5.16 demonstrates, all of the remodeled rooms in two-story room spaces except for Rooms 69 and 70 underwent a change in room function after remodeling. This trend, supported by the following points, probably resulted from the addition of a second-story habitation room and a concomitant change in the use of the lower story (see below). First, all of the remodeled lower-story rooms changed from either habitation or ceremonial rooms to limited function rooms such as storage or manufacturing rooms with the exception of Rooms 68 and 274, which changed from ceremonial to habitation and from habitation to ceremonial, respectively. Second, many of the two-story rooms with adequate data contained second-story features suggestive of habitation rooms (Table A.22). This pattern of two-story-room remodeling conforms to expectations arising from the pueblo room-use model, where lower story rooms were typically used for storage or for other limited functions.

TABLE 5.17.
Relationship between Room Function and Number of Stories ($n = 68$)

	One-Story Room Spaces	Two-Story Room Spaces	Total
Early abandoned	9	5	14
Specialized habitation	11	0	11
Generalized habitation	4	1	5
Storage	4	1	5
Storage/Manufacturing	4	2	6
Manufacturing	6	4	10
Limited activity, food processing	4	0	4
Limited activity, manufacturing	6	0	6
Ceremonial	4	1[a]	5
Kiva	2	0	2
Total	54	14	68

[a]Room 274 ceremonial function is not based on the last floor but an earlier floor that may predate the second-story addition.

TABLE 5.18.
Room Function by Number of Stories

	Habitation	Storage	Manufacturing/ Limited Activity	Ceremonial	Total
1 Story	15	8	16	6	45
2 Stories	1	3	4	1	9
Total	16	11	20	7	54

$\chi^2 = 2.329$; $df = 3$; $p = 0.507$; $\phi = 0.20$; Cramer's V = 0.20

Room function and two-story rooms. Among the historic pueblos, a room's function is often related to its first- or second-story position. Storage rooms were typically located on the ground floor, whereas habitation rooms were usually located in the upper stories (Adams 1983:52–53; Cameron 1999a:63; Kidder 1958:122–123; Mindeleff 1891:103, 223). If this were the case at Grasshopper, one would expect the lower story of room spaces estimated to have had two stories to have been primarily storage rooms or rooms of other limited function. After early abandoned rooms are eliminated, only nine two-story rooms remain (Table 5.17). This small sample is dwarfed by the 45 excavated one-story rooms in the main pueblo, making results of statistical tests suspect and generating a weak association between cells in the cross tabulation (Table 5.18). The high prevalence of early-abandoned rooms associated with two-story room spaces, however, does suggest that the lower story may have functioned as a refuse disposal area in some cases (cf. Kidder 1958:122–123).

Only one habitation room (Room 68) and one ceremonial room (Room 274) can be considered two-story rooms. In the former case the room is a generalized habitation room, which means it had a storage component. In the latter case a ceremonial function is based on an earlier room floor, not the final room floor, which could not be assigned a function because of a lack of

TABLE 5.19.
Kruskal-Wallis Test on Standing-Wall Height Grouped by Room Function

Room Function	Count	Rank Sum	Kruskal-Wallis Statistic	Probability
Specialized habitation	11	174.00	20.734	0.008
Generalized habitation	5	123.50		
Storage	4	138.00		
Storage, manufacturing	6	226.50		
Manufacturing	10	379.50		
Limited activity, food processing	4	45.00		
Limited activity, manufacturing	6	185.00		
Ceremonial	5	131.50		
Kiva	2	28.00		

floor data. This lack of floor data for the upper floor surface is consistent with a limited room function, and the earlier ceremonial room probably predated the addition of the second-story room, which supports the idea that construction of a second story necessitated a change in room function (see Table 5.16).

Looking at the data another way provides support for the relationship between room function and upper-story position noted at Walpi. Table 5.19 reveals that a relationship exists between preserved height of individual walls and the final function of a room space (Figure 5.6). Habitation and ceremonial rooms exhibit a lower median wall height than do storage, manufactur-

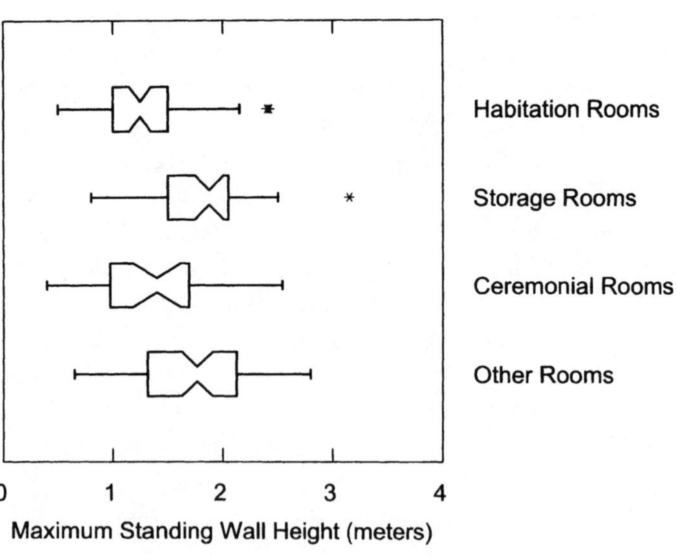

FIGURE 5.6. Notched box plots comparing standing wall height grouped by room function.

ing, and limited-activity rooms, suggesting that the latter spaces were typically associated with the ground floor in two-story rooms (Ciolek-Torrello 1978:158).

Overall, the relationship between room function and number of stories suggests some parallels in room use between Grasshopper Pueblo and the modern pueblos. Because the second story was rarely well preserved, it is difficult to reconstruct the nature of the upper-story occupation of the main pueblo. If Grasshopper were truly analogous to Hopi and other modern pueblos, one would expect to find habitation rooms on the second story, with doorways opening onto roofed space and hatchway entries opening into lower-story rooms (Adams 1983:52–53; Mindeleff 1891:103). The evidence from intact second-story floor assemblages supports this expectation and suggests that second-story rooms often had a habitation function (Ciolek-Torrello 1978:167).

Rooms around the Great Kiva. One of the most striking, and perhaps the most socially important, features at Grasshopper Pueblo was the Great Kiva (Chapter 3). Chapter 3 provides an assessment of its construction; its role in community organization is addressed below. This discussion focuses on the Great Kiva's adjacent rooms, whose characteristics deviate significantly from other rooms in the main pueblo, suggesting that they, like the Great Kiva, had a special role in the community.

When rectangular great kivas are found in large prehistoric pueblo villages, they are centrally located within one or more of the enclosing room blocks (Cummings 1940; Gerald 1957; Haury 1985, 1989; Lowell 1991). At Turkey Creek Lowell noted that the two room groups linked to the great kiva were similar to one another but were also unlike other room groups. Some of the distinguishing characteristics include more rooms with circular hearths (nonhabitation rooms), fewer rooms with rectangular hearths (habitation rooms), a high percentage of rooms with only a single coat of wall plaster, and a high frequency of rooms with multiple floors (Lowell 1991:53). Lowell's analysis raises the possibility that the rooms surrounding a great kiva could signify special, ceremonial use.

In general, the distribution of room types around the Great Kiva at Grasshopper was similar to the overall distribution of room types throughout the main pueblo (Table 5.20). Late occupied habitation rooms and food-processing rooms as a group, however, were present in low frequency, implying that customary domestic activities were not carried out in these rooms (Figure 5.4). It is also notable that five of the associated rooms housed manufacturing activities (Types 4, 5, and 7), and, as at Turkey Creek, habitation rooms were underrepresented around the Great Kiva (Table 5.21). Of the three types of manufacturing rooms found in the main pueblo, 23 percent were located adjacent to the Great Kiva. In addition, a ceremonial room and a kiva shared a wall with the Great Kiva and were located directly across from one another (Figure 5.4; Table 5.21). Finally, it is also noteworthy that 31 percent of all early-abandoned rooms in the main pueblo occurred in this set of rooms.

TABLE 5.20.
Comparison of Room Function between the Great Kiva Rooms and Other Main Pueblo Rooms

Room Function	Great Kiva Rooms (n = 14)		Main Pueblo (n = 67)	
	n	%	*n*	%
Early abandoned	4	28.6	13	19.4
Specialized habitation	2	14.3	11	16.4
Generalized habitation	0	0.0	5	7.4
Storage	1	7.1	5	7.4
Storage, manufacturing	1	7.1	6	9.0
Manufacturing	2	14.3	10	14.9
Limited activity, food processing	0	0.0	4	6.0
Limited activity, manufacturing	2	14.3	6	9.0
Ceremonial room	1	7.1	5	7.4
Kiva	1	7.1	2	3.0
Totals	14	100.0	67	100.0

TABLE 5.21.
Function of Rooms Bordering the Great Kiva (n = 17)

Room	Area	Description
14	16.52	*Early abandoned*
16	9.6	Great Kiva entry/vestibule
18	18.2	Kiva
19	14.61	Storage
20	11.51	*Early Abandoned*
21	18.26	Storage, manufacturing
22	18.46	Manufacturing
23	17.68	*Early Abandoned*
26	9.92	Limited activity, manufacturing
27	21.25	Specialized habitation
143	14.53	Specialized habitation
145	10.3	Manufacturing
146	10.16	*Early Abandoned*
152	11.7	*Unexcavated*
153	10.88	Limited activity, manufacturing
193	11.7	*Unexcavated*
197	17.01	Ceremonial

The two habitation rooms adjacent to the Great Kiva differed from typical habitation rooms in that they contained infrequently recorded features. A stone platform was found in the southwest corner of Room 143, as was a small limestone storage box. The function of this platform is not known, but it may have been the foundation for a large storage bin (Chapter 3). The other habitation room, Room 27, had a posthole pattern in its southwest corner that was probably the remnant of a *jacal* storage bin, and an additional *jacal* storage bin with a footing of vertical slabs was found along the west wall of Room 145, in both the northwest and southwest quadrants. Three of the four *jacal* storage bins or possible bins in the main pueblo were found next to the Great Kiva, and it is compelling that these bins were located in or near the southwest corner of their respective rooms.

Overall, the architectural evidence indicates that there was a ceremonial section surrounding the Great Kiva. The infrequently occurring features in the habitation rooms, the presence of large storage bins in the southwest corners of three rooms, and the presence of a kiva and a ceremonial room attest to the distinctive nature of this subset of rooms. In addition, a slight increase in the number of room floors and the lower occurrence of habitation rooms are directly analogous to Turkey Creek Pueblo. The rooms around Grasshopper's Great Kiva had a slightly higher number of floors per room (1.87) than rooms in the remainder of the main pueblo (1.72). This suggests that these rooms may have been important structures that were remodeled more often than other rooms. These stand in stark contrast to the large number of early-abandoned rooms around the Great Kiva that may have been used to dispose of refuse related to ceremonies conducted within the large communal structure.

The frequency of manufacturing rooms and late-abandoned spaces is suggestive of specialized activities having been carried out in the rooms surrounding the Great Kiva. The manufacturing rooms may have been used to prepare materials for ceremonial use, and the abundance of trash-filled rooms may indicate that they were receptacles for ceremonial refuse (e.g., Walker 1995). The large storage bins in three of the rooms may have housed religious paraphernalia, food for ceremonies, or firewood to be used in the Great Kiva. Whatever the specific uses of these rooms or the features within them, their unusual characteristics are in accord with their position adjacent to the Great Kiva.

The exact impetus to build the Great Kiva cannot be explained. The timing of its construction, however, coincides with a time of changing community organization. Furthermore, the structuring of activities in the rooms around the Great Kiva indicates that it was a singular and important religious structure for the community. Not only was it demarcated and roofed as a single event, but the enclosing rooms were modified to serve the needs of the Great Kiva. This structure's importance to the community was probably its role in integrating a dispersing population.

Community integration and the continuing role of the Great Kiva. Although there are two interpretations for the timing of the conversion of Plaza 3 into the Great Kiva, and therefore two initial construction dates, it is obvious that the structure was in use during the dispersion period. The earlier date estimate (furnished by this analysis) put construction of the Great Kiva between A.D. 1320 and 1330, and Graves's later-date estimate suggests that the Great Kiva was built as late as A.D. 1360 (Graves 1991:105). The earlier date makes more sense architecturally, given the construction sequence and the nature of its roof construction. Initially, the Great Kiva might have played a role in integrating Grasshopper's resident population during the aggregation period. Subsequently, however, the Great Kiva may have served as a focal point for the integration of regionally dispersed populations, much like the large plaza at Chodistaas, for previous inhabitants of the region, or, like the great kivas of the Point of Pines region, for people in that area. A brief discussion of the role of great kivas in other areas of the Mogollon heartland reinforces this interpretation.

Rectangular great kivas and focal communities in the Mogollon area. In much of the Mogollon culture area there is a well-documented sequence of community development in which great kivas figure prominently (Anyon 1984; Anyon and LeBlanc 1980). From the earliest occupations, large structures are interpreted to have been great kivas based on their size and atypical characteristics (Anyon 1984; Breternitz 1959; Haury 1985; Wheat 1954). Through time these structures became more formal and more closely integrated into the village architecture. In the Mimbres area, unwalled plazas developed in the Classic period and served to integrate large villages, functions once served by great kivas (Anyon and LeBlanc 1980:266). In other areas, like Point of Pines, great kivas became larger, whereas their associated villages remained approximately the same size. This phenomenon has suggested to some that great kivas acted to integrate several dispersed but related villages (Breternitz 1959:72). In the Grasshopper region the arrangement of rooms around a plaza suggests that Chodistaas may have served an integrative function similar to the great kivas in the Point of Pines area during the Pueblo III period (Reid 1989; Riggs 1994b). Chodistaas may have been a ritual focal point for several surrounding villages that reflect a part-time, seasonal use of the region and in which focal communities were important social organizational mechanisms (Reid 1989:77; Reid and Riggs 1995; Reid et al. 1996).

The apex of the great kiva's role in the Point of Pines region occurred at Turkey Creek Pueblo, where it served as a focal point around which the community aggregated (Riggs 1994b). Lowell's (1991:43) division of the Turkey Creek community into several groups of rooms indicates that it was composed of numerous small, previously autonomous villages similar to those of the preceding Reserve Phase in the region (e.g., Olson 1959). At Turkey Creek Pueblo the great kiva acted as a focal point in a physical and a social sense (Riggs 1994b:11).

At Grasshopper the process of aggregation was somewhat different. Plaza space was certainly important during aggregation, as discussed in Chapter 4. The Great Kiva, as a later addition to the community, did not act as a focal point for aggregation as did the great kiva at Turkey Creek. Instead, Grasshopper's Great Kiva may have been constructed to integrate the diverse immigrant population. As the community dispersed, and reverted to a less sedentary pattern of land use, the Great Kiva probably still served as the focus for ceremonies and social gatherings for the now-scattered population.

As in the eastern mountains, the Great Kiva made Grasshopper Pueblo the focal community for several villages, including Grasshopper and its outliers and villages like Red Rock House and Canyon Creek Pueblo. It is interesting that no formal kivas of the type found in the core room blocks (Room Blocks 1, 2, 3, 5, and 7) were found at Red Rock House or Canyon Creek Pueblo (Haury 1934), nor were they found in Grasshopper's outliers. The ceremonial rooms in the outliers were similar to ceremonial rooms in the core room blocks, and one of them (Room 414), reminiscent of ceremonial rooms at Chodistaas (Montgomery 1992:242), occurred in a three-wall structure open to the east. The absence of formal kivas in the outliers and the satellite communities underscores the special function of the Great Kiva at Grasshopper Pueblo—it acted to integrate a dispersing population rather than serving as a focal point around which aggregation occurred.

ARCHITECTURAL VARIABILITY AND COMMUNITY ORGANIZATION PATTERNS

The variability in room size, shape, and orientation suggests that different room blocks continued to be built by people with differing construction programs, even after the process of community dispersion began. It has already been noted that the outliers represented a different adaptation to the area than did the main pueblo (Chapter 2; Reid 1989:85). The occurrence of increased residential mobility and community dispersion is responsible for much of the variability in room form. The ever-present immigrants who interacted with local people throughout the occupation, building and remodeling rooms, are another factor.

Chapter 4 identifies several rooms in the core room blocks (1, 2, 3, 5, and 7) that were assigned to the dispersion period despite their location within the site. As Grasshopper's inhabitants began to use the area on a more seasonal basis and as rules for structuring the use of domestic spaces became less formal during the dispersion period, room floor area became greater. The dichotomy in room size between the main pueblo and the outliers is the most obvious confirmation of this pattern. There was also a slight increase in room size for dispersion-period rooms in the site core (Table 5.22), where room size not only increased but became more variable. In fact, dispersion-period rooms in the main pueblo and in the outliers exhibited this same general trend. This pattern was much more pronounced in the outliers, where average room size increased by over 3 m^2. In the main pueblo, room size also increased in the dispersion period but not substantially (Table 5.22).

Wall height during the dispersion period also reflects this trend. Mean wall height for first-story aggregation-period rooms is 1.47 m and only 0.84 m for the dispersion-period rooms (Table 5.23). In the main pueblo, dispersion-period rooms had a significantly lower overall mean wall height (Table 5.23). Although

TABLE 5.22.
Mann-Whitney Tests Comparing Aggregation-Period and Dispersion-Period Room Size.

Room and Phase	*n*	Mean	*SD*	Rank Sum	*U* Statistic	Probability
All Rooms	447				19583.00	0.00
Aggregation	260	15.25	4.00	53513.00		
Dispersion	187	17.68	7.09	46615.00		
Core Rooms	252				6126.50	0.14
Aggregation	260	15.25	4.00	40056.50		
Dispersion	54	16.84	6.28	9398.50		
Main Pueblo	287				5111.50	0.23
Aggregation	239	15.27	4.00	33791.50		
Dispersion	48	16.17	4.76	7536.50		
Outliers, including Room Blocks 5 and 7	160				1122.00	0.09
Aggregation	21	15.03	4.06	1353.00		
Dispersion	139	18.20	7.68	11527.00		

TABLE 5.23.
Mann-Whitney Tests Comparing Standing Wall Height in the Aggregation and Dispersion Periods

Excavated Single-Story Rooms	No. of Walls	Mean	*SD*	Rank Sum	*U* Statistic	Probability
All	351				25522.00	0.00
Aggregation	204	1.47	0.43	46432.00		
Dispersion	147	0.84	0.42	15344.00		
In the Main Pueblo	216				5404.00	0.00
Aggregation	168	1.51	0.46	19600.00		
Dispersion	48	1.28	0.32	3836.00		
In the Outliers	135				3449.00	0.00
Aggregation	36	1.30	0.22	4115.00		
Dispersion	99	0.63	0.28	5065.00		
Total Aggregation-Period Rooms	204				2028.50	0.00
Main Pueblo	168	1.51	0.48	18215.50		
Outliers	36	1.30	0.22	2694.50		
Total Dispersion-Period Rooms	147				264.00	0.00
Main Pueblo	48	1.28	0.32	5664.00		
Outliers	99	0.63	0.28	5214.00		

aggregation- and dispersion-period rooms in the main pueblo are characterized by statistically significant differences in mean wall height, these do not reflect differences in wall construction methods (e.g., low-walled vs. full-standing). The difference in means in the main pueblo is likely a result of walls shared with two-story rooms and the differential depth of walls in some of the rooms. Comparing dispersion-period wall height in the main pueblo with wall height in the outliers underscores the point that the late main pueblo rooms continued to be built with full-standing masonry walls, indicated by a difference in means of 0.65 m between the two areas.

Differences in room size and standing wall height resulting from the dispersion of the community indicate that the construction and residence patterns of the late period occupation differed significantly from those of the earlier period. In contrast to the architecture of community aggregation, the sample of rooms from the outliers, although not small, is spread over 13 spatially discrete room blocks ranging in size from 4 to 26 rooms, prohibiting statistically meaningful analyses of dispersion-period architectural features. In addition to this spatial limitation, it is also true that few wall features occur outside of the core room blocks, further strengthening the inference that the later rooms were architecturally distinct. Given these considerations, it is more fruitful to examine the architecture of the dispersion period for what it says about community settlement patterns and part-time use of the area.

SIGNATURES OF MOBILITY AND SEDENTISM: THE ARCHITECTURE OF DISPERSION

The identification of the Great Kiva as a focal structure serving to integrate an increasingly dispersed population is one indicator of a shift in settlement patterns late in the occupation of Grasshopper Pueblo. The Great Kiva's role underscores an important aspect of the dispersion period—its architecture reveals more about changes in the use of the Grasshopper locality after A.D. 1330 than it does about the activities of social groups. The architecture of the outliers is different from that of the main pueblo, which reflects the change in settlement patterns between the earlier aggregation period and the later dispersion period. The small size of many of the outliers limits their usefulness for applying statistical techniques, yet by analogy with the earlier aggregation period we can attribute the spatial division between the various room blocks to the activities of socially distinct groups of builders. The spatial distinctiveness of the various room blocks suggests that ethnic groups (at least social groups) remained distinct throughout the occupation.

Decreasing room construction rates and the establishment of satellite communities like Canyon Creek Pueblo and Red Rock House indicate a decline in population growth during this late period (Figure 5.7). The larger, low-walled, impermanently constructed outlier rooms, which were similar to Pueblo III

FIGURE 5.7. Canyon Creek Pueblo. Photographer unknown, 1970.

period rooms at sites like Chodistaas Pueblo, point to a return to a less intensive occupation of the locale by at least some of the population that may have looked much like the Pueblo III period occupation of the region (Chapter 2). Thus, the architecture of the outliers is important to understand not only for its information about the processes of regional abandonment in the fourteenth century but also for how it contributes to our understanding of construction practices in the previous Pueblo III period.

Archaeological treatments of the transition from pit house to pueblo (Gilman 1987; McGuire and Schiffer 1983) suggest a correlation between the level of sedentism and architectural form and serve as an analog for the processes at work at Grasshopper just before the abandonment of the region. The transition from in-ground pit houses to aboveground masonry architecture can be evaluated in many ways, including a cost-benefit analysis (Gilman 1987; McGuire and Schiffer 1983), or in light of the divisibility of form related to higher differentiation of activities (Flannery 1972; Hunter-Anderson 1977). One essential factor behind the decision to construct pueblos, however, seems to be a decrease in mobility patterns. The low-walled architecture of the outliers and of the preceding Pueblo III period offers a structural form that combined many of the advantages of pit houses and pueblos.

Their insubstantial roof and upper walls (analogous to pit houses) offered the inhabitants minimal initial construction costs (McGuire and Schiffer 1983). Low-walled and composed of ephemeral, nonweight-bearing roofs, these structures would not have required the felling of large trees. Low-walled structures also required less procurement and shaping of wall rocks than did full-standing masonry rooms. For people who did not intend to use the structures on a

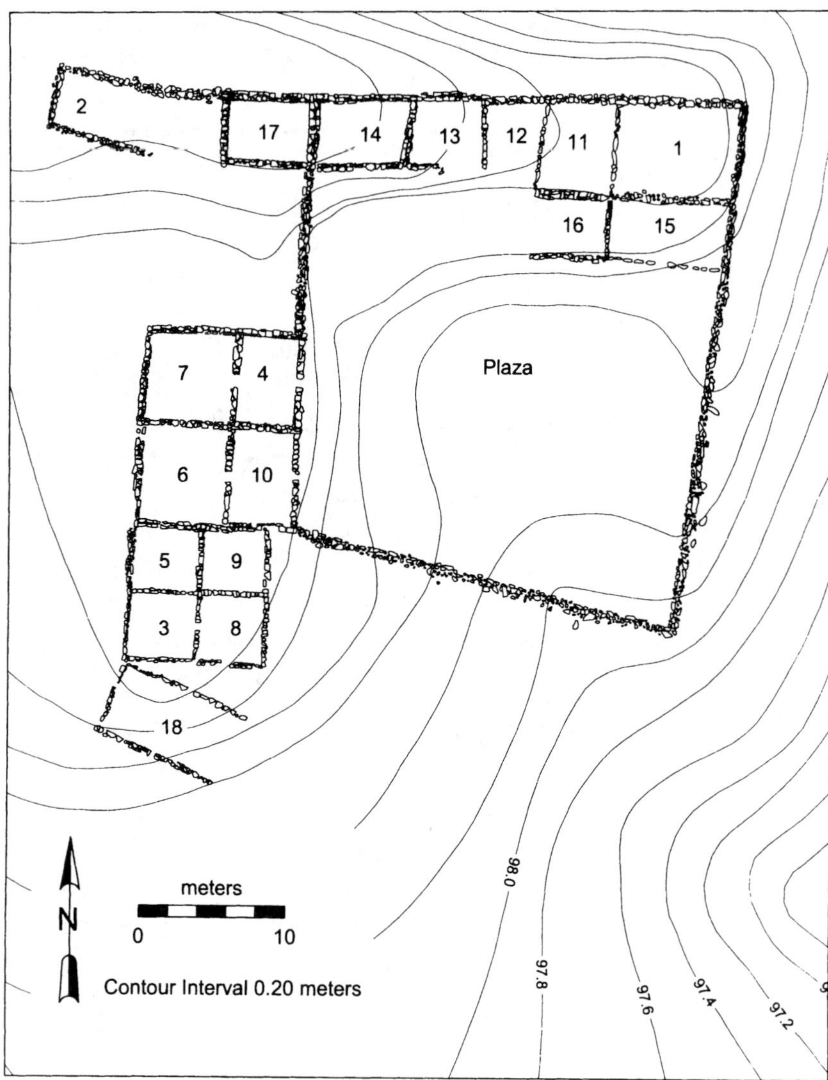

FIGURE 5.8.
Chodistaas Pueblo, AZ P:14:24 (ASM).

year-round basis, a low initial construction cost may have been perceived as important. In contrast to the constructions of the aggregation period, when occupation of Grasshopper was year-round, the potentially higher maintenance costs of the outliers may not have been an issue because they were not used as intensively. One disadvantage of this form was that it did not provide the thermal properties of a pueblo room or a pit structure. If the outliers were occupied primarily during the summer, however, thermal efficiency would not have been a deciding factor.

The architectural building block in the outliers was the "carport"—the low-walled structure often consisting of only three walls open to the east. This structure was also the primary architectural element at Chodistaas during the Pueblo III period. As Figure 5.8 shows, several rooms at Chodistaas were initially constructed with three masonry walls, and the space was subsequently closed off (Rooms 13, 14, 17) or was enclosed and further subdivided into two spaces (Rooms 4, 6, 7, and 10). Carports, found throughout the central mountains of Arizona, were associated with populations that were at least seasonally mobile (Chenhall 1972; Klie et al. 1982; Redman 1993; Tuggle 1982; Whittlesey 1982). They were important components of the Pueblo III period adaptation to the Grasshopper region and became a significant type in the outliers at Grasshopper Pueblo after the demographic processes of the early Pueblo IV period had run their course (Reid 1989).

The versatile, low-walled structures characteristic of the dispersion period provided their inhabitants all the advantages of aboveground, rectilinear masonry architecture, but the real advantage of these low-walled structures for mobile people (with perhaps the intention of eventual sedentism) was that they could be easily modified. The structures were easy to subdivide for the partitioning of activity areas or storage spaces (Hunter-Anderson 1977). The rectangular shape facilitated addition of rooms built to accommodate arriving immigrants or new members of the domestic group. Because they were above ground they did not require the effort of excavation, which would have entailed digging into bedrock in places like Chodistaas or the low hills around Grasshopper Pueblo.

The carport was an ideal form for people following a seasonal occupation round; the open end could have been closed with *jacal* walls (e.g., see Dean 1969:25) or more substantial masonry walls. This structure could then be further subdivided as household needs changed. The walls could be carried to a full standing height, and a usable roof could be added if the inhabitants intended to stay at the locale for longer periods. There is evidence for this at Chodistaas, as demonstrated by the addition of four storage rooms in the mid-A.D. 1280s (Reid 1989:77). These rooms appear to have been true pueblo rooms with full-standing walls suggesting a shift to a full-time occupation (Reid 1989:77).

At Grasshopper this trend toward settlement intensification was the reverse of that noted at Chodistaas; the earliest outliers (Room Blocks 5 and 7) exhibit the same type of wall construction as the main pueblo, whereas the later outliers exhibit the low-walled characteristics of the Pueblo III period sites. Some of the most insubstantially constructed rooms are the late, unaffiliated outliers, such as Rooms 309 and 312 in the southwest portion of the site. This reversal in structure use supports the notion that the later outliers represented a return to a more mobile occupation of the Grasshopper region in the middle and late fourteenth century.

Like sites of the Pueblo III period, rooms in the outliers at fourteenth-century Grasshopper Pueblo were relatively large, reflecting a higher diversity of activities associated with the room spaces (Figure 5.9). Nevertheless, the rooms were not as large as the habitation rooms at Chodistaas (18 m^2 vs. 29 m^2), and there is no evidence that two households shared rooms at Grasshopper as data

FIGURE 5.9.
Rooms 355 and 356 in Room Block 8. These rooms are typical of the later outliers. Note the low height of the walls and the density of floor features and artifacts. Photograph by Barbara K. Montgomery, 1985. Courtesy of the Arizona State Museum, University of Arizona; neg. no. GFS 85-30.

from Chodistaas suggest (Montgomery 1992:247). Thus, the resurgence of the low-walled architectural form does seem to reflect a similar adaptation to the region as that seen in the Pueblo III period, one with higher levels of mobility and a more seasonally based adaptation. The remaining differences in room use, however, suggest that aggregation did have lasting effects on the domestic organization of the inhabitants of the Grasshopper region.

6

Summary and Conclusions

> Better the rudest work that tells a story or records a fact, than the richest without meaning.
>
> —John Ruskin, *The Seven Lamps of Architecture*

THE ARCHITECTURE OF GRASSHOPPER PUEBLO IS AN IMPORTANT CONTRIBUTION to the archaeology of architecture. It has implications for architectural research in the pueblo Southwest as well as in other settings where people live in densely packed communities. It is also important for what it reveals about life at Grasshopper Pueblo during the fourteenth century. Given these two important contributions, it is useful to revisit both the larger implications of Grasshopper architectural research and the architectural perspective this study provides on the settlement history of Grasshopper Pueblo.

IMPLICATIONS OF GRASSHOPPER ARCHITECTURAL RESEARCH

Grasshopper's architectural record is an important data set in several ways and will serve not only future Grasshopper scholars but also anyone interested in the architecture of a large compact village or in issues of migration and community organization. This analysis of Grasshopper Pueblo's architecture provides an invaluable model for the study of prehistoric architecture by contributing to our understanding in the several ways that are listed as follows and are elaborated below:

1. the importance of a large representative excavated sample for making well-founded archaeological inferences
2. the utility of comparative data and ethnographic information to a successful architectural analysis
3. the significance of socially determined intrasite architectural divisions
4. the utility of a well-understood intrasite chronology and pueblo growth reconstruction that will serve not only future Grasshopper researchers but will also provide a body of techniques for others attempting to build intrasite growth sequences

5. the importance of understanding room function and its relationship to architectural variability and, by extension, the importance of understanding room floor remodeling

6. a larger understanding of the influence of individual immigrant groups on the architecture of a pueblo community and the power of architectural details for delimiting these groups

7. architecture's role in reflecting patterns of community organization

First, this analysis underscores the absolute necessity of representative excavation data for making inferences about ruined architecture. The complexity of architecture as a material class is indicated in many ways, such as in the variability in construction elements (e.g., wall features), the extent of floor remodeling, and in the nature of community growth described in Chapter 4. Only through a large and representative sample was this complexity simplified and the activities responsible for the architectural variability uncovered during excavations understood.

Second, comparative data and ethnographic information were critical to solving several of Grasshopper's architectural puzzles. The preserved roofs of cliff dwellings in various parts of the Southwest, especially nearby Canyon Creek Pueblo, filled in the details concerning missing architectural information related to roof construction and allowed for an assessment of the number of two-story rooms. The estimation of two-story rooms, even in well-excavated contexts, was a difficult endeavor. Problems of room adjacency, underlying topography, wall collapse, and original roof height all combined to make estimates of two-story rooms relatively complicated. Perhaps the most important contribution of the discussion of two-story rooms at Grasshopper is that it provides a cautionary tale to those who would suggest that accurate counts of second-story rooms can be made without excavation data. Further, the difficulties in predicting the number of stories, even for excavated, well-documented rooms, makes a stronger case for cautious estimates of community size.

Third, this study highlights the relationship between spatial divisions and architectural variability and emphasizes that researchers cannot ignore the spatial separation imposed by the builders of any given pueblo community. At Grasshopper the most striking spatial separation, that between the East and West villages, is also the most socially significant. When other architectural data and nonarchitectural data are examined at East and West villages they reflect significant variability. This is not to say that every room block excavated within a community will reflect these same differences. Based on this research, however, these types of divisions can never be ignored by scholars interested in reconstructing prehistoric societies.

Fourth, this analysis offers to future Grasshopper research a more refined intrasite chronology than has been available in the past (although see Riggs 1994a). One possible use for these data is in analyses of mortuary items from burials beneath room floors. The settlement chronology and growth sequences described in Chapter 4 provide tighter temporal control for the construction of rooms over burial areas and will allow more precise dating of given burials. The same is true for material found on room floors. In a related topic the identification of architecturally distinct "ethnic precincts" at Grasshopper will provide a basis for assessing room floor assemblages across social boundaries within the community.

The Grasshopper architectural data described above also provide a strong comparative record for research on early aggregated pueblo communities in the Southwest. Although the dynamics of community growth at Grasshopper may not precisely parallel those in other areas of the Southwest, this study provides a baseline for comparison and a body of data and techniques useful for reconstructing patterns of pueblo growth and architectural details. Here I specifically refer to the techniques of chronology building described in Chapter 4 and some of the brief comparative analyses contained in Chapter 3.

Fifth, this study suggests that room function and architecture are not necessarily correlated. Assessments of room function rely on architecture's role as a container of artifacts and activities. This study finds a disjunction between the use of a room floor and the architectural characteristics of its enclosing space. Through floor remodeling, the final use of a room often has very little to do with its originally planned function. This fact should caution archaeologists to proceed carefully when assigning functional categories to rooms based entirely on architectural remains (although see Dean 1969). The implications of this go beyond remodeling's effect on the identification of room function to its impact on our ability to accurately reconstruct population densities and household groups.

Sixth, this study impacts our understanding of immigration patterns within a large pueblo site. Grasshopper researchers have always stressed the role of migration in the development of the Grasshopper community (Graves et al. 1982; Longacre 1975, 1976; Reid 1973, 1989, 1998). The architectural data in this study strongly suggest that patterns of construction and use within the site indicate ethnically determined construction practices. When combined with the ceramic evidence and mortuary data, the architectural data described above make a strong case for evaluating migration as a social process and for going beyond a simple cultural-historical treatment of migration.

Unlike some recent treatments of migration that eschew site-level approaches because they lack the appropriate data (e.g., Cordell 1995; Duff 1998), this analysis highlights the power of a site-level approach. Reminiscent of the Maverick Mountain occupation of Point of Pines Pueblo (Haury 1958; Lindsay 1987), Grasshopper's extensive excavation record and large sample make the site a strong case for evaluating migration and community organization in a community. Unlike Point of Pines, however, a strong case for an immigrant presence was made in the absence of a site-unit intrusion. This study contributes to migration and community organization by providing a well-excavated and well-controlled sample of a community known to have been founded by locals and immigrants. The large sample of rooms and burials supports studies of these groups' location in the pueblo and their interactions. The data here will allow us to advance beyond culture history, to examine migration as a process with real demographic consequences. Using biological data and ceramics, future work focused on migration at Grasshopper should be able to identify the origin of the various immigrant groups. Ceramic evidence already suggests that many may have come from the Mogollon Rim area (Triadan 1997), and ongoing bone chemistry analysis by Ezzo (personal communication 2001) should help to pinpoint the places of origin of Grasshopper's immigrants.

The seventh and final major contribution of this study is that it is a critical step in our attempts to understand community organization. By focusing on the technical choices made during construction, this study documents the domestic areas used by the diverse inhabitants by demonstrating a relationship between spatially discrete constructions and individual groups of builders. The data presented here also confirm other community patterns identified by past Grasshopper researchers, including the disjunction of room function from the architecture through floor remodeling, the distinctive pattern of room construction between the main pueblo and the later outliers, the rapid construction of the main pueblo, and several other patterns of structure use and room location.

Evidence for continual arrival of immigrants implies that the Grasshopper community was probably only loosely organized and that a hierarchical political organization, such as that espoused by Upham (1982) and others (Cordell and Plog 1979; Upham and Plog 1986) could not have functioned. A better interpretation, one that fits the architectural and mortuary data, is that Grasshopper was organized heterarchically (Crumley 1995) into a series of social groups, probably determined along different ethnic lines (Ezzo 1999; Riggs 1998). Participation in sodalities and other ceremonial societies helped to integrate these diverse populations and allowed for the decision making that was necessary to build communal structures like the Great Kiva. Village expansion around central public spaces, despite the haphazard construction displayed in the growth of the pueblo, further suggests a level of cooperation among the different immigrant groups that was facilitated by participation in larger socioreligious groups that cut across ethnic lines.

AN ARCHITECTURAL PERSPECTIVE ON THE GRASSHOPPER COMMUNITY

Despite a rich history of study in the Southwest and around the world, architecture is a difficult class of material culture to study systematically because of its formal and behavioral complexities, combined with various related sampling issues. Although many approaches have been used to examine architecture and how it reflects and structures human activities, no single approach fully explains the significant variability in decision making apparent in architectural forms. Space syntax studies, cosmological approaches, studies of construction materials, activity area studies, and symbolic approaches address specific characteristics of architectural spaces, but not one can fully account for the variability encountered in any given architectural entity.

Nevertheless, the challenges of analyzing architecture as a material class should not obscure architecture's relationship to human behavior. By viewing pueblo architecture as a complex artifact, constantly in a state of flux, and by focusing on the details of construction or the "technical choices" (Lemonnier 1986) of the builders, this analysis extracted a great deal of information from Grasshopper's architectural record. This information includes low-level inferences about the nature of roof construction and use and the number and location of two-story rooms, as well as higher-level inferences like the construction habits and intrasite localization of different immigrant groups or the use of the Great Kiva as an integrative structure. This analysis benefits from the influence of various architectural perspectives, from ethnographic data, and from construction details from several other pueblo sites, which provided missing architectural information that did not survive the passage of time at Grasshopper. The strength of this analysis, however, lies in the solid body of data documenting the physical manifestations of human activity buried in the rubble mound that is Grasshopper Pueblo today. This analysis has attempted to reconstruct the pueblo in its many incarnations, piecing together architectural patterns and correlating them with past human activity throughout the life history of the Grasshopper community.

By focusing on construction techniques, this analysis demonstrated that groups with different social identities were involved in the construction and use of Grasshopper Pueblo, which was the product of unprecedented demographic changes throughout the Pueblo area in the late thirteenth and early fourteenth centuries. Through time, as the settings that contained systems of activities were modified, the semifixed and nonfixed feature elements left on the room floors had less to do with the original function of individual rooms as conceived by their builders. The fixed feature elements, namely the walls, however, continued to bear the stamp of their original builders, allowing us to see the subtle signs of different ways of viewing architectural spaces and shedding light on the marked disjunction between fixed feature architectural characteristics and the final function of rooms when the community was abandoned.

The period during which Grasshopper was occupied was characterized by large-scale population movements, resulting in the founding of large pueblos throughout the Mogollon Rim area. In the Grasshopper region several large pueblo sites of over 35 rooms were constructed after A.D. 1300, whereas before this time the two largest sites in the region consisted of less than 20 rooms (Reid 1989; Reid and Whittlesey 1990). A marked change in the number of constructed rooms and the size of settlements in the area assuredly had consequences for intraregional and intrasite social relationships. This was likely the case at other large sites around Grasshopper and has been noted in other parts of the Southwest where populations immigrated into new areas (Clark 2001; Haury 1958; Lindsay 1987).

Establishment of the Grasshopper community occurred in the late Pueblo III period (A.D. 1275–1300). The nature and extent of this occupation, however, is not well understood because the earlier remains lie buried beneath the Pueblo IV period constructions. The only definitive evidence of this occupation consists of wall segments underlying Plaza 1 and Room 14 in Room Block 2. In addition, certain areas of the site, especially around the Great Kiva and in the northern end of Room Block 1, were intensively used extramural areas before expansion of Grasshopper Pueblo. Although most of these areas were used during fourteenth-century occupation of the locale, some of the preroom features found in them could have been associated with the Pueblo III period habitations. A pit house discovered under Room Block 5 and another possible one under Room Block 2 are evidence for perhaps an even earlier use of the site. Contemporary occupations at Chodistaas and Grasshopper Spring pueblos are the best analog for the Pueblo III period occupation of Grasshopper Pueblo.

Immigration and the Founding of the Grasshopper Community

The aggregation period at Grasshopper began around A.D. 1300 and was initiated by the inhabitants of Room Block 2, who built the large 21-room construction unit north of what later became the Great Kiva. Room Blocks 1 and 3 were founded subsequent to, or perhaps coincident with, the founding of Room Block 2. After this point the pueblo, as depicted in Reid's construction phase model, grew rapidly. Throughout the aggregation period (A.D. 1300–1330) different immigrant groups settled at the site and constructed new rooms in spatial proximity to people with whom they shared social ties.

The architectural evidence, backed by biological data, suggests that Room Block 2 housed a local population, whereas nonlocal immigrant groups, perhaps from the Colorado Plateau, built Room Blocks 1 and 5. Room Block 3 seems to have been constructed by either a mix of locals and nonlocals or a group local to the Grasshopper Region, perhaps even from Chodistaas (Reid and Whittlesey 1999). The technical choices of the builders, specifically room form, wall feature size and placement, construction material use, and elements of community layout combined make a strong case for the presence of different groups of builders at the Grasshopper community during the aggregation period.

This analysis demonstrates that at least two different social groups founded the Grasshopper community and that these groups resided in spatially discrete room blocks. These data are reinforced by skeletal analyses, which have found that two biologically distinct populations inhabited Grasshopper (Birkby 1973; Shipman 1982). In addition, several large public areas, including a great kiva, are central to the pueblo. These spaces hosted secular and ceremonial communal activities, which served to integrate the various groups residing at Grasshopper. This integration also surfaces in the mortuary record, which contains evidence for the existence of several sodalities identified by distinct offerings placed in the grave as part of the burial ritual (Reid 1989; Reid and Whittlesey 1982).

When all of the architectural variables are considered, Room Block 1's architecture stands in marked contrast to Room Block 2. The large size of Room Block 2's initial core construction unit (21 rooms), the homogeneity of its architecture, and its location at the center of the community suggests construction by local builders. By contrast, Room Block 1's differing architectural characteristics and its isolated location to the east of Salt River Draw imply that immigrants with distinct technological styles, probably from the Colorado Plateau, constructed Room Block 1. The diversity of architectural characteristics within Room Block 3 strongly indicates that it was built by at least two distinctive groups of builders, and its proximity to Room Block 2 implies a closer local tie.

The spatial segregation of Room Block 1 on the east side of Salt River Draw may indicate the arrival of immigrants later in the settlement history. In Hopi tradition (although perhaps somewhat of a historical rationalization on the part of the Hopi), land ownership is determined along clan lines, and the primary clans are those who were first on the scene. Newly arriving groups settle away from the community (Mindeleff 1900:649) and earn land-use rights in exchange for ceremonial sponsorship (Titiev 1992:63). This practice might be reflected archaeologically in technical choices like spatially separate architecture and differential use of local construction materials (building stone and tree species) or in the biological data by physical characteristics arising from differential access to food resources.

In the Grasshopper example the compiled evidence for Room Block 1 parallels Hopi tradition. The founding of Room Block 1 is the least well documented but could have occurred anywhere from 2 years before to 14 years after Room Block 3 and from 7 to 23 years after Room Block 2 (Riggs 1994a). In either case it was probably the last room block to be established. In a rapidly aggregating community such as Grasshopper, a difference of even five years could have had implications for access to local resources. Undoubtedly local people and early immigrants had already claimed local farmland and resource territory, creating a situation in which nonlocal latecomers experienced restricted access to the best local resources. A high prevalence of dietary stress markers in burials associated with Room Block 1 indicates limited access to certain key nutrients (Hinkes 1983), whereas bone chemistry data suggest that the inhabitants of Room Block 1 were deprived of cultigens and depended greatly on wild foods (Ezzo 1993). Additionally, the apparent isolation of Room

Block 1 mirrors the Hopi practice of segregating newly arriving clans from the village until they are able to be incorporated into the community (Mindeleff 1900:649). Yet through time, and with participation in sodalities and ceremonial societies, social boundaries probably became less marked as inhabitants of Room Block 1 became incorporated into the Grasshopper community (cf. Mindeleff 1900:648).

Remodeling room floors was one way of accommodating the needs of growing or changing households. Changing the semifixed feature elements in rooms through floor remodeling to accommodate different activities through time was a critical component of room use at Grasshopper. Of the excavated rooms at Grasshopper, 40 percent exhibited evidence of floor remodeling, and about the same percentage of these changed in function. In the main pueblo, where remodeling was more prevalent, a space's function changed once a second-story room space was constructed above it. In the end this remodeling obscured the original relationship between a room's planned function and its final function, making it impossible to use architecture as a predictor of room function. Apart from the patterning in room function around the Great Kiva and the correlation between the number of stories and room function, no other patterns of room use emerged from the analysis of architecture and room function. Despite its influence on the relationship between room function and architecture, room remodeling was found to be a significant variable for analyzing the rate of immigration and resultant changes in household composition. The construction of the Great Kiva was itself an important remodeling event that marked the end of the aggregation period, which had been a time of substantial population influx and significant negotiation of space within the main pueblo.

The aggregation period at Grasshopper culminated in the construction of the roofed entry into Plaza 1 between A.D. 1323 and 1325 and the subsequent construction of the Great Kiva by A.D. 1330. The plaza spaces were not created as discrete architectural features but rather as by-products of community growth, a seemingly directed process that retained open areas as important communal spaces. The Great Kiva, by contrast, was a planned communal structure, with many of the same elements found in rooms but on a significantly larger scale. Based on an examination of the layout of postholes and the timing of room additions around it, the construction of the Great Kiva in Plaza 3 was a single event. The Great Kiva was formalized through the construction of several surrounding rooms, which may have had special, ceremonial functions.

The Outliers: Immigration, Emigration, and the Dispersion of the Community

Construction of the Great Kiva between A.D. 1320 and 1330 signaled the onset of the dispersion period, when people began to use Grasshopper in a different way than they had during the aggregation period. Although the activities of different social groups probably continued to contribute to the architectural variability after rapid aggregation had slowed, the architecture of the dispersion period is much more informative for the data it yields regarding the shift in regional settlement patterns. The growth curve for the outliers is similar to that of Canyon Creek Pueblo. This finding was expected based on past Grasshopper research suggesting that the occupation of the outliers and of satellite communities was contemporary and part of the same demographic process. The later architecture of the outliers was an adaptable form of structure that combined some of the roofing techniques of pit houses with masonry pueblos and was well suited to groups with higher levels of mobility than those seen in the early occupation of Grasshopper Pueblo. The return of the low-walled structure marked a return to a settlement pattern that more closely resembled that of the preceding Pueblo III period, such as that at Chodistaas. During the dispersion period, the Great Kiva's role mirrored that of earlier great kivas in the eastern mountains, where large communal structures acted as focal points for a dispersed population living in small settlements (Reid 1989). The dispersion process at Grasshopper, as seen in the architecture, can be thought of as the reverse of the aggregation process at Turkey Creek Pueblo, where several small communities, previously linked by a great kiva, came together in one locale (Lowell 1991). At Grasshopper the Great Kiva acted to integrate dispersed populations who were moving out of large aggregated villages and probably served the immediate Grasshopper community as well as sites like Canyon Creek Pueblo and Red Rock House.

Artifacts left on room floors as de facto refuse and archaeomagnetic dates for the outliers indicate late occupation. As mentioned, most of the outliers were composed of low-walled masonry rooms with *jacal* superstructures, an architectural form born of a diminished commitment to construction activities. At the same time, a few of the outlying room blocks, such as 5 and 7 (and possibly 13), were composed of rooms with full-standing masonry walls. Undoubtedly, these differences represent divergent processes. Room Blocks 5 and 7 were constructed prior to community dispersion and were probably built by nonlocals and later arriving immigrant groups, reminiscent of the interpretation offered above for Room Block 1.

The remainder of the outliers, especially those southwest of the main pueblo not associated with named room blocks (Figure 4.1), exhibit informal characteristics similar to Chodistaas Pueblo, the largest community in the region prior to aggregation (Crown 1981; Montgomery 1992; Zedeño 1994). This informality is reflected in the low masonry walls, the large size and rectangularity of the rooms, and the number of three-walled rooms open to the east. These architectural characteristics imply a return to residential mobility similar to that which characterized the Grasshopper region before A.D. 1300 (Reid 1989).

The data offered here suggest that, as the Grasshopper community dispersed and people began to live at the Grasshopper locale on a more seasonal basis, some differences in construction styles may have been maintained. The variability in room form exhibited by the outliers when compared to the main pueblo, however, is as likely a result of the informality of the architecture as it is a result of any socially determined construction practices. The rooms were neither as spatially restricted nor as internally partitioned and lacked usable roof space, which was compensated for by a larger floor area. At the same time, however, the spatial separation between the various outliers indicates the social separation evident throughout the brief occupation of the Grasshopper community.

Social cohesion during the dispersion of the community, represented by the later outliers, was cemented by activities associated with the Great Kiva and the two plazas. This type of adaptation has direct parallels in other regions of the mountains, where dispersed populations living in small pueblos were socially united by the cooperative use of a focal community with a large ceremonial structure. In the Grasshopper region during the Pueblo III period, this community was probably Chodistaas Pueblo with its large plaza. During the dispersion period, Grasshopper Pueblo, with its Great Kiva and large plazas, probably acted as the focal community for several other smaller pueblos.

Because this analysis focuses on architecture, which is by definition a constructive process, it offers no new information concerning the abandonment of Grasshopper Pueblo. A couple of late tree-ring dates from the southern end of Room Block 1 suggest that some wood cutting was occurring as late as A.D. 1395, but this particular date was described by Graves as "tentative" (Graves 1991:104–105). Archaeomagnetic dates from some of the very late outliers produced ranges ending after A.D. 1400; however, the poor resolution of these dates does not add much to our understanding of final community abandonment.

CONCLUDING THOUGHTS

However unremarkable the final stages of the occupation might have been, Grasshopper Pueblo represents an almost unprecedented case in southwestern archaeology. It is well sampled and well recorded, and the majority of rooms produced collections of de facto refuse. It is also a rare circumstance that 30 years of active fieldwork could be devoted, in large part, toward the excavation of a site the size of Grasshopper. An effort of this magnitude will, in all likelihood, not be undertaken at a large pueblo any time in the near future, especially at a site with the wealth of room floor and other accompanying data recovered from Grasshopper.

For these reasons the analysis of the architecture of Grasshopper Pueblo is a contribution not only to Grasshopper and prehistoric puebloan research, as suggested above, but it is also a synthesis of heretofore unavailable data and, it is hoped, a body of procedures that subsequent scholars will find useful for examining architectural data. Thus, this study is, and will remain, a significant contribution not only to southwestern archaeology but to the immense body of method and theory that have been applied to the analysis of architecture and use of space in prehistoric settings on a worldwide scale.

Appendix

Architectural Data Tables

Table A.1.

Excavated Rooms and Excavation Dates by Room Block (n = 103)

	Room	Began	Completed	Subfloored
Room Block 1	2	1963	1963	1963
	4	1963	1963	1963
	5	1964	1964	1964
	6	1963	1963	1963
	7	1963	1963	1963
	8	1963	1963	1963
	10	1964	1964	1964
	11	1964	1964	1964
	15	1964	1964	1964
	28	1967	1968	1968
	31	1967	1967	1968
	33	1969	1969	1969
	35	1969	1969	1969
	37	1967	1967	1967
	39	1969	1969	1970
	40	1969	1969	1970
	41	1969	1969	1970
	42	1967	1967	1968
	43	1969	1969	1969
	44	1969	1969	1971
	45	1969	1969	1971
	47	1971	1971	1971
	62	1973	1973	1973
	68	1977	1977	1977
	69	1977	1977	1977
	70	1977	1977	1977
	97	1992	1992	—
	100	1967	1967	1968
	104	1992	1992	—
	107	1992	1992	—
	108	1967	1967	1968
	121	1967	1967	1968
Room Block 2	12	1964	1964	1964
	13	1964	1964	1964
	14	1964	1964	1964
	16	1964	1964	1967
	18	1965	1965	1965
	19	1965	1965	1966
	20	1965	1965	1965
	21	1965	1965	1966
	22	1965	1965	1966
	23	1966	1966	1967
	26	1967	1967	1967
	27	1967	1967	1968
	143	1969	1969	1970
	145	1973	1973	1973
	146	1970	1970	1971
	153	1968	1968	1970
	164	1971	1971	1972
	183	1972	1972	1973
	187	1972	1972	1973

TABLE A.1. *(continued)*

	Room	Began	Completed	Subfloored
	197	1969	1969	1970
Room Block 3	205	1970	1970	1971
	206	1971	1971	1971
	210	1971	1971	1972
	211	1970	1971	1971
	215	1970	1971	1972
	216	1972	1972	1972
	218	1971	1971	1972
	231	1972	1972	1973
	246	1974	1975	1975
	269	1974	1974	1975
	270	1971	1971	1972
	274	1972	1972	1973
	279	1974	1974	1975
	280	1974	1974	1975
	438	1974	1974	1975
	440	1974	1974	1975
Room Block 4	3	1963	1963	1963
	9	1964	1964	1964
	17	1964	1964	—
Room Block 5	112	1981	1981	1981
	113	1980	1981	1981
	114	1968	1968	1968
	115	1980	1980	1980
	116	1969	1969	1969
	195	1969	1969	—
Room Block 6	319	1972	1972	1973
Room Block 7	341	1972	1972	1972
	349	1973	1973	1973
	352	1973	1973	1973
Room Block 8	353	1985	1985	1987
	354	1986	1986	1987
	355	1985	1985	1987
	356	1985	1985	1985
Room Block 9	371	1973	1973	1973
	376	1973	1973	1973
Room Block 10	198	1968	1968	1968
	414	1991	1991	1991
	420	1991	1991	1991
Room Block 11	425	1973	1973	1973
Room Block 12	395	1976	1976	1976
	397	1976	1976	1976
	398	1973	1973	1973
	404	1972	1972	—
	411	1976	1976	1976
Room Block 13	434	1973	1973	1973
Unaffiliated	1	1963	1963	—
	24	1966	1966	1966
	25	1980	1980	1980
	309	1980	1980	1980
	312	1980	1980	1980
	359	1972	1972	1972

TABLE A.2.
Room Block Characteristics

Room Block Number	Number of Rooms	Room Block Area (m^2)	Mean Room Area (m^2)	Distance to Plaza 1 (m)[a]	Distance to Plaza 2 (m)[a]	Distance to Plaza 3 (m)[a]
Unaffiliated	33	—	—	—	—	—
1	94	1468.79	15.63	61.48	56.52	45.54
2	92	1281.01	13.92	24.63	37.59	11.60
3	101	1678.21	16.62	15.80	22.91	47.88
4	6	110.18	18.36	93.71	103.69	62.01
5	6	99.33	16.56	66.47	43.56	73.50
6	13	244.3	18.79	56.92	76.75	76.91
7	21	345.01	16.43	69.41	65.72	101.53
8	10	238.76	23.88	95.20	98.11	125.71
9	26	353.03	13.59	141.07	130.37	173.09
10	11	173.40	15.76	>204.04	>198.51	>235.99
11	9	110.12	12.24	254.73	232.59	251.97
12	17	244.94	14.41	209.55	196.82	192.85
13	4	51.97	12.99	150.68	126.96	153.59

[a]Distances are between the spatial means of room blocks and plazas.

TABLE A.3.
Summary Data for All 447 Ground-Floor Room Spaces

Room Number	Room Block	Wall Lengths North	South	East	West	Room Form Length	Width	Area	Shape	Orient.[a]
1	0	4.45	4.20	—	4.00	4.33	4	17.32	Square	E-W
2	1	3.75	3.80	4.30	4.40	4.35	3.78	16.44	Square	N-S
3	4	4.35	4.25	4.30	4.35	4.33	4.3	18.62	Square	N-S
4	1	4.05	4.00	5.15	5.05	5.1	4.03	20.55	Rect.	N-S
5	1	3.60	3.50	3.80	3.90	3.85	3.55	13.67	Square	N-S
6	1	3.60	3.60	4.40	4.40	4.4	3.6	15.84	Rect.	N-S
7	1	4.25	4.20	4.30	4.15	4.23	4.23	17.89	Square	—
8	1	4.00	4.15	3.10	3.15	4.08	3.13	12.77	Rect.	E-W
9	4	4.20	4.10	3.70	3.60	4.15	3.65	15.15	Square	E-W
10	1	3.75	4.06	4.55	4.12	4.34	3.91	16.97	Square	N-S
11	1	2.90	3.00	4.25	4.30	4.28	2.95	12.63	Rect.	N-S
12	2	3.50	3.55	3.40	3.30	3.53	3.35	11.83	Square	E-W
13	2	4.35	4.20	3.60	3.50	4.28	3.55	15.19	Rect.	E-W
14	2	3.85	4.10	4.15	4.15	4.15	3.98	16.52	Square	N-S
15	1	3.80	3.30	3.85	3.65	3.75	3.55	13.31	Square	N-S
16	2	4.12	4.12	2.28	2.38	4.12	2.33	9.6	Rect.	E-W
17	4	4.80	4.75	4.85	—	4.85	4.78	23.18	Square	N-S
18	2	4.60	4.50	4.30	3.70	4.55	4	18.2	Square	E-W
19	2	3.47	3.57	4.15	4.15	4.15	3.52	14.61	Square	N-S
20	2	3.40	3.62	3.41	3.14	3.51	3.28	11.51	Square	E-W
21	2	4.30	4.00	4.50	4.30	4.4	4.15	18.26	Square	N-S
22	2	4.25	3.98	4.30	4.65	4.48	4.12	18.46	Square	N-S
23	2	4.34	4.13	4.20	4.13	4.24	4.17	17.68	Square	E-W
24	0	2.70	2.75	2.25	2.25	2.73	2.25	6.14	Rect.	E-W
25	0	5.75	5.88	4.42	4.32	5.82	4.37	25.43	Rect.	E-W
26	2	3.01	2.92	3.30	3.38	3.34	2.97	9.92	Square	N-S
27	2	4.68	4.50	4.63	4.62	4.63	4.59	21.25	Square	N-S
28	1	4.18	4.30	4.00	4.30	4.24	4.15	17.6	Square	E-W
29	1	4.29	4.07	4.78	4.82	4.8	4.18	20.06	Square	N-S
30	1	4.37	4.55	3.82	4.30	4.46	4.06	18.11	Square	E-W
31	1	3.97	4.45	3.40	3.23	4.21	3.32	13.98	Rect.	E-W
32	1	4.47	4.37	3.93	3.94	4.42	3.94	17.41	Square	E-W
33	1	3.34	3.64	3.76	3.74	3.75	3.49	13.09	Square	E-W
34	1	3.85	3.91	4.22	4.46	4.34	3.88	16.84	Square	N-S
35	1	4.32	4.21	3.85	3.93	4.27	3.89	16.61	Square	E-W
36	1	3.65	3.86	3.70	3.89	3.8	3.75	14.25	Square	N-S
37	1	3.50	3.51	3.55	3.50	3.53	3.51	12.39	Square	N-S
38	1	5.45	5.49	2.89	2.95	5.47	2.92	15.97	Rect.	E-W
39	1	3.74	3.76	4.15	4.12	4.14	3.75	15.53	Square	N-S
40	1	5.40	5.50	4.47	4.65	5.45	4.56	24.85	Rect.	E-W
41	1	3.11	3.47	4.15	4.10	4.13	3.29	13.59	Rect.	N-S
42	1	2.05	2.10	3.22	3.15	3.19	2.08	6.64	Rect.	N-S
43	1	3.29	3.78	4.21	4.20	4.21	3.54	14.9	Square	N-S
44	1	3.80	3.84	4.67	5.12	4.9	3.82	18.72	Rect.	N-S
45	1	3.75	3.45	3.85	3.57	3.71	3.6	13.36	Square	N-S
46	1	3.76	4.20	3.81	3.84	3.98	3.82	15.2	Square	E-W
47	1	4.32	4.21	3.85	3.93	4.27	3.89	16.61	Square	E-W
48	1	3.77	3.70	3.92	3.78	3.85	3.73	14.36	Square	N-S
49	1	3.59	3.66	3.43	3.33	3.62	3.38	12.24	Square	E-W

TABLE A.3. *(continued)*

Room	Room	*Wall Lengths*				*Room Form*				
Number	Block	North	South	East	West	Length	Width	Area	Shape	Orient.[a]
50	1	4.57	4.36	3.88	3.78	4.47	3.83	17.12	Square	E-W
51	3	3.20	3.50	3.00	3.20	3.35	3.1	10.39	Square	E-W
52	1	4.49	4.43	3.57	3.60	4.46	3.58	15.97	Rect.	E-W
53	1	4.07	4.26	4.01	4.03	4.16	4.02	16.72	Square	E-W
54	1	3.76	3.41	4.03	4.00	4.02	3.59	14.43	Square	N-S
55	1	4.88	5.04	4.04	3.94	4.96	3.99	19.79	Rect.	E-W
56	1	3.07	3.04	3.47	3.59	3.53	3.05	10.77	Square	N-S
57	1	3.69	3.69	4.65	4.51	4.58	3.69	16.9	Rect.	N-S
58	1	6.03	5.63	3.69	3.83	5.83	3.76	21.92	Rect.	E-W
59	1	3.52	3.73	4.57	4.66	4.62	3.62	16.72	Rect.	N-S
60	1	3.74	3.65	4.61	4.70	4.66	3.69	17.2	Rect.	N-S
61	1	4.04	3.96	3.58	3.58	4	3.58	14.32	Square	E-W
62	**1**	**6.20**	**6.10**	**4.10**	**4.20**	**6.15**	**4.15**	**25.52**	**Rect.**	**E-W**
63	1	4.41	4.56	3.58	3.85	4.49	3.72	16.7	Rect.	E-W
64	1	4.34	4.02	4.03	4.17	4.18	4.1	17.14	Square	E-W
65	1	4.23	3.86	4.82	4.69	4.76	4.04	19.23	Square	N-S
66	1	4.07	4.24	4.17	3.91	4.15	4.04	16.77	Square	E-W
67	1	6.17	6.00	3.86	4.01	6.08	3.94	23.96	Rect.	E-W
68	**1**	**4.15**	**4.20**	**4.40**	**4.45**	**4.43**	**4.18**	**18.52**	**Square**	**N-S**
69	**1**	**4.04**	**4.10**	**3.86**	**4.04**	**4.07**	**3.95**	**16.08**	**Square**	**E-W**
70	**1**	**3.23**	**3.48**	**4.00**	**4.02**	**4.01**	**3.36**	**13.47**	**Rect.**	**N-S**
71	1	4.00	3.83	4.20	4.18	4.19	3.92	16.42	Square	N-S
72	1	3.05	3.01	4.55	4.71	4.63	3.03	14.03	Rect.	N-S
73	1	3.10	2.73	4.48	4.69	4.59	2.92	13.4	Rect.	N-S
74	1	4.11	4.31	4.43	4.52	4.47	4.21	18.82	Square	N-S
75	1	3.48	3.83	4.56	4.64	4.6	3.66	16.84	Rect.	N-S
76	1	3.33	3.05	3.95	4.02	3.98	3.19	12.7	Rect.	N-S
77	1	3.93	4.08	5.59	5.47	5.53	4	22.12	Rect.	N-S
78	1	3.89	—	4.14	—	4.14	3.89	16.1	Square	N-S
79	1	4.24	4.35	3.44	3.41	4.29	3.43	14.71	Rect.	E-W
80	1	—	3.55	4.20	—	4.2	3.55	14.91	Square	N-S
81	1	3.40	3.29	3.37	3.34	3.36	3.35	11.26	Square	—
82	1	4.59	4.73	3.90	3.84	4.66	3.87	18.03	Rect.	E-W
83	1	4.96	5.09	3.97	3.90	5.02	3.93	19.73	Rect.	E-W
84	1	4.31	4.21	3.74	3.76	4.26	3.75	15.98	Square	E-W
85	1	2.90	3.90	3.66	3.75	3.7	3.4	12.58	Square	N-S
86	1	3.99	3.44	2.95	2.98	3.71	2.96	10.98	Rect.	E-W
87	1	3.31	3.21	3.09	3.18	3.26	3.14	10.24	Square	E-W
88	1	1.60	—	3.33	—	3.33	1.6	5.33	Rect.	N-S
89	1	4.13	3.07	3.19	3.48	3.6	3.33	11.99	Square	E-W
90	1	3.28	3.34	4.34	4.37	4.35	3.31	14.4	Rect.	N-S
92	1	2.95	2.82	3.81	3.71	3.76	2.88	10.83	Rect.	N-S
93	1	3.48	3.48	4.07	4.12	4.1	3.48	14.27	Square	N-S
94	1	4.06	4.36	4.50	4.45	4.47	4.21	18.82	Square	N-S
95	1	3.79	3.67	4.09	4.07	4.08	3.73	15.22	Square	N-S
96	1	4.28	4.54	3.87	4.09	4.41	3.98	17.55	Square	E-W
97	**1**	**3.57**	**3.54**	**3.90**	**4.09**	**4**	**3.55**	**14.2**	**Square**	**N-S**
98	1	2.39	2.40	3.16	3.18	3.17	2.4	7.61	Rect.	N-S
99	1	3.51	3.64	3.28	3.21	3.57	3.24	11.57	Square	E-W
100	**1**	**4.19**	**3.64**	**7.13**	**7.08**	**7.11**	**3.92**	**27.87**	**Rect.**	**N-S**

TABLE A.3. *(continued)*

Room	Room	*Wall Lengths*				*Room Form*				
Number	Block	North	South	East	West	Length	Width	Area	Shape	Orient.[a]
101	1	4.20	4.32	4.14	4.33	4.26	4.24	18.06	Square	E-W
102	1	2.40	2.40	3.98	—	3.98	2.4	9.55	Rect.	N-S
103	1	—	2.90	—	4.00	4	2.9	11.6	Rect.	N-S
104	**1**	**4.00**	**3.70**	**4.25**	**4.67**	**4.46**	**3.85**	**17.17**	**Square**	**N-S**
105	1	6.16	6.31	5.00	4.98	6.23	4.99	31.09	Rect.	E-W
106	1	3.30	3.33	3.65	3.52	3.58	3.31	11.85	Square	N-S
107	**1**	**3.62**	**3.47**	**4.10**	**4.04**	**4.07**	**3.55**	**14.45**	**Square**	**N-S**
108	**1**	**3.48**	**3.60**	**3.35**	**5.11**	**4.23**	**3.54**	**14.97**	**Square**	**N-S**
109	4	3.74	4.02	4.50	4.57	4.54	3.88	17.62	Square	N-S
110	4	3.48	3.53	4.01	3.80	3.9	3.51	13.69	Square	N-S
111	4	4.32	4.63	4.86	4.99	4.92	4.47	21.99	Square	N-S
112	**5**	**4.66**	**4.50**	**4.28**	**5.12**	**4.7**	**4.58**	**21.53**	**Square**	**N-S**
113	**5**	**4.34**	**4.40**	**5.42**	**5.91**	**5.67**	**4.37**	**24.78**	**Rect.**	**N-S**
114	**5**	**3.68**	**3.46**	**4.10**	**4.04**	**4.07**	**3.57**	**14.53**	**Square**	**N-S**
115	**5**	**4.46**	**3.91**	**4.40**	**4.09**	**4.25**	**4.19**	**17.81**	**Square**	**N-S**
116	**5**	**3.45**	**4.10**	**4.30**	**4.50**	**4.4**	**3.78**	**16.63**	**Square**	**N-S**
118	1	4.25	3.70	4.07	3.78	3.98	3.93	15.64	Square	E-W
119	1	3.61	3.08	4.04	3.91	3.97	3.34	13.26	Square	N-S
120	1	3.40	3.03	4.07	4.38	4.23	3.22	13.62	Rect.	N-S
121	**1**	**3.50**	**2.65**	**4.60**	**4.80**	**4.7**	**3.08**	**14.48**	**Rect.**	**N-S**
122	1	2.93	2.90	3.37	3.23	3.3	2.91	9.6	Square	N-S
123	1	3.59	3.53	3.87	3.62	3.74	3.56	13.31	Square	N-S
125	2	2.62	—	—	4.00	4	2.62	10.48	Square	E-W
126	2	3.37	—	—	4.27	4.27	3.37	14.39	Rect.	N-S
127	2	4.47	—	—	4.25	4.47	4.25	19	Square	E-W
128	2	—	3.50	—	4.83	4.83	3.5	16.91	Rect.	N-S
129	2	—	3.82	4.10	4.30	4.2	3.82	16.04	Square	E-W
130	2	—	3.22	—	4.10	4.1	3.22	13.2	Rect.	N-S
131	2	4.00	4.00	3.50	3.20	4	3.35	13.4	Square	E-W
132	2	—	3.37	3.51	—	3.51	3.37	11.83	Square	N-S
133	2	—	3.40	3.56	—	3.56	3.4	12.1	Square	N-S
134	2	—	3.97	2.91	—	3.97	2.91	11.55	Rect.	E-W
135	2	—	3.50	2.85	—	3.5	2.85	9.98	Rect.	E-W
136	2	4.10	4.10	2.85	2.85	4.1	2.85	11.69	Rect.	E-W
137	2	—	4.10	2.85	—	4.1	2.85	11.69	Rect.	E-W
138	2	3.55	—	3.65	—	3.65	3.55	12.96	Square	N-S
139	2	—	3.85	—	3.30	3.85	3.3	12.71	Square	E-W
140	2	3.30	—	3.15	—	3.3	3.15	10.4	Square	E-W
141	2	—	3.60	4.00	—	4	3.6	14.4	Square	N-S
142	2	4.40	—	5.20	—	5.2	4.4	22.88	Square	N-S
143	**2**	**4.05**	**4.25**	**3.50**	**3.50**	**4.15**	**3.5**	**14.53**	**Square**	**E-W**
144	2	—	3.50	—	3.00	3.5	3	10.5	Square	E-W
145	**2**	**4.00**	**3.80**	**2.23**	**3.05**	**3.9**	**2.64**	**10.3**	**Rect.**	**E-W**
146	**2**	**3.90**	**3.80**	**2.23**	**3.05**	**3.85**	**2.64**	**10.16**	**Rect.**	**E-W**
147	2	—	3.92	2.58	—	3.92	2.58	10.11	Rect.	E-W
148	2	4.20	4.20	3.20	3.20	4.2	3.2	13.44	Rect.	E-W
149	2	3.80	3.80	3.20	3.20	3.8	3.2	12.16	Square	E-W
150	2	4.00	4.20	3.20	3.20	4.1	3.2	13.12	Rect.	E-W
151	2	3.20	3.00	5.00	5.20	5.1	3.1	15.81	Rect.	N-S
152	2	2.80	3.20	4.00	3.80	3.9	3	11.7	Rect.	N-S

TABLE A.3. *(continued)*

Room Number	Room Block	*Wall Lengths* North	South	East	West	*Room Form* Length	Width	Area	Shape	Orient.[a]
153	**2**	**4.05**	**4.00**	**2.70**	**2.69**	**4.03**	**2.7**	**10.88**	**Rect.**	**E-W**
154	2	4.20	4.20	3.50	3.00	4.2	3.25	13.65	Rect.	E-W
155	2	4.50	—	—	4.30	4.5	4.3	19.35	Square	E-W
156	2	—	4.80	4.75	—	4.8	4.75	22.8	Square	E-W
157	2	—	4.28	—	4.10	4.28	4.1	17.55	Square	E-W
158	2	4.00	3.20	3.80	3.50	3.65	3.6	13.14	Square	N-S
159	2	—	3.32	—	4.32	4.32	3.32	14.34	Rect.	N-S
160	2	3.32	—	—	3.50	3.5	3.32	11.62	Square	N-S
161	2	3.90	4.20	3.00	2.80	4.05	2.9	11.75	Rect.	E-W
162	2	2.93	—	3.54	—	3.54	2.93	10.37	Rect.	N-S
163	2	3.32	—	—	4.12	4.12	3.32	13.68	Rect.	N-S
164	**2**	**3.30**	**3.30**	**4.10**	**4.30**	**4.2**	**3.3**	**13.86**	**Rect.**	**N-S**
165	2	3.68	—	4.34	—	4.34	3.68	15.97	Square	N-S
166	2	3.67	—	—	3.45	3.45	3.67	12.66	Square	E-W
167	2	—	3.53	—	3.85	3.85	3.53	13.59	Square	N-S
168	2	—	3.74	—	4.20	4.2	3.74	15.71	Square	N-S
169	2	3.21	—	—	3.06	3.21	3.06	9.82	Square	E-W
170	2	3.13	—	—	5.21	5.21	3.13	16.31	Rect.	N-S
171	2	4.16	—	—	3.85	4.16	3.85	16.02	Square	E-W
172	2	—	3.45	—	4.05	4.05	3.45	13.97	Square	N-S
173	2	3.30	—	—	3.69	3.69	3.3	12.18	Square	N-S
174	2	3.12	—	—	3.19	3.19	3.12	9.95	Square	N-S
175	2	—	3.57	—	1.16	3.57	1.16	4.14	Rect.	E-W
176	2	3.35	—	—	3.52	3.52	3.35	11.79	Square	N-S
177	2	—	3.81	—	3.39	3.81	3.39	12.92	Square	E-W
178	2	3.35	—	3.79	—	3.79	3.35	12.7	Square	N-S
179	2	—	3.71	—	2.72	3.71	2.72	10.09	Rect.	E-W
180	2	3.79	—	—	4.04	4.04	3.79	15.31	Square	N-S
181	2	4.49	—	—	4.11	4.49	4.11	18.45	Square	E-W
182	2	3.25	3.30	4.18	4.45	3.27	3.28	10.73	Rect.	E-W
183	**2**	**4.00**	**4.39**	**3.71**	**3.71**	**4.2**	**3.71**	**15.58**	**Square**	**E-W**
184	2	—	3.70	—	3.36	3.7	3.36	12.43	Square	E-W
185	2	3.72	—	—	3.50	3.72	3.5	13.02	Square	E-W
186	2	3.39	3.12	3.29	3.13	3.26	3.21	10.46	Square	E-W
187	**2**	**3.65**	**3.62**	**3.31**	**3.47**	**3.64**	**3.39**	**12.34**	**Square**	**E-W**
188	2	3.71	—	—	3.52	3.71	3.52	13.06	Square	E-W
189	2	4.70	—	—	3.20	4.7	3.2	15.04	Rect.	E-W
190	2	3.10	—	3.43	—	3.43	3.1	10.63	Square	N-S
191	2	4.30	—	—	3.79	4.3	3.79	16.3	Square	E-W
192	2	3.94	—	3.41	—	3.94	3.41	13.44	Square	E-W
193	2	3.60	3.60	3.80	3.80	3.8	3.6	13.68	Square	N-S
195	**5**	**3.80**	**3.80**	**0.80**	**0.75**	**3.8**	**0.78**	**2.96**	**Rect.**	**E-W**
197	**2**	**4.05**	**4.05**	**4.05**	**4.35**	**4.2**	**4.05**	**17.01**	**Square**	**N-S**
198	**10**	**4.60**	**4.80**	**3.90**	**4.40**	**4.7**	**4.15**	**19.51**	**Square**	**E-W**
199	0	4.20	4.20	4.00	4.00	4.2	4	16.8	Square	E-W
200	0	4.20	4.20	4.00	4.00	4.2	4	16.8	Square	E-W
201	3	3.82	—	—	4.48	4.48	3.82	17.11	Square	N-S
202	3	4.20	—	4.57	—	4.57	4.2	19.19	Square	N-S
203	3	—	4.10	—	4.10	4.1	4.1	16.81	Square	—
204	3	—	3.18	—	3.11	3.18	3.11	9.89	Square	E-W

TABLE A.3. *(continued)*

Room Number	Room Block	*Wall Lengths* North	South	East	West	*Room Form* Length	Width	Area	Shape	Orient.[a]
205	**3**	**3.50**	**3.50**	**5.50**	**5.00**	**5.25**	**3.5**	**18.38**	**Rect.**	**N-S**
206	**3**	**4.07**	**4.16**	**4.55**	**4.63**	**4.59**	**4.12**	**18.91**	**Square**	**N-S**
207	3	—	4.75	—	4.43	4.75	4.43	21.04	Square	E-W
208	3	—	4.95	4.81	—	4.95	4.81	23.81	Square	E-W
209	3	3.96	—	4.97	—	4.97	3.96	19.68	Rect.	N-S
210	**3**	**3.14**	**3.34**	**4.62**	**4.47**	**4.55**	**3.24**	**14.74**	**Rect.**	**N-S**
211	**3**	**4.07**	**4.15**	**5.38**	**5.43**	**5.41**	**4.11**	**22.24**	**Rect.**	**N-S**
212	3	4.45	4.70	5.10	4.70	4.9	4.58	22.44	Square	N-S
213	3	5.30	5.20	5.01	5.20	5.25	5.11	26.83	Square	E-W
214	3	—	5.28	4.57	—	5.28	4.57	24.13	Square	E-W
215	**3**	**3.87**	**3.92**	**4.40**	**4.67**	**4.54**	**3.9**	**17.71**	**Square**	**N-S**
216	**3**	**3.80**	**3.70**	**4.60**	**4.50**	**4.55**	**3.75**	**17.06**	**Rect.**	**N-S**
217	3	3.94	—	—	4.45	4.45	3.94	17.53	Square	N-S
218	**3**	**3.90**	**4.25**	**5.35**	**5.65**	**5.5**	**4.08**	**22.44**	**Rect.**	**N-S**
219	3	3.93	—	5.36	—	5.36	3.93	21.06	Rect.	N-S
220	3	4.24	—	5.19	—	5.19	4.24	22.01	Rect.	N-S
221	3	4.52	—	4.89	—	4.89	4.52	22.1	Square	N-S
222	3	3.86	3.78	5.13	5.52	5.33	3.82	20.36	Rect.	N-S
223	3	3.79	—	4.60	—	4.6	3.79	17.43	Rect.	N-S
224	3	4.61	—	—	4.81	4.81	4.61	22.17	Square	N-S
225	3	—	3.90	5.13	5.17	5.15	3.9	20.09	Rect.	N-S
226	3	—	2.80	5.34	—	5.34	2.8	14.95	Rect.	N-S
227	3	—	4.80	4.85	—	4.85	4.8	23.28	Square	N-S
228	3	—	4.28	4.20	—	4.28	4.2	17.98	Square	E-W
229	3	—	4.04	4.11	4.97	4.54	4.04	18.34	Square	N-S
230	3	2.89	—	4.68	—	4.68	2.89	13.53	Rect.	N-S
231	**3**	**4.28**	**4.50**	**4.30**	**4.70**	**4.5**	**4.39**	**19.76**	**Square**	**N-S**
232	3	2.75	—	—	4.87	4.87	2.75	13.39	Rect.	N-S
233	3	3.53	—	—	4.86	4.86	3.53	17.16	Rect.	N-S
234	3	5.43	—	—	4.33	5.43	4.33	23.51	Rect.	E-W
235	3	4.20	—	—	3.90	4.2	3.9	16.38	Square	E-W
236	3	4.57	4.49	4.22	4.30	4.53	4.26	19.3	Square	E-W
237	3	3.63	3.61	4.06	4.11	4.09	3.62	14.81	Square	N-S
238	3	4.90	4.99	3.77	4.17	4.95	3.97	19.65	Rect.	E-W
239	3	2.63	—	4.40	—	4.4	2.63	11.57	Rect.	N-S
240	3	4.21	—	4.48	4.59	4.54	4.21	19.11	Square	N-S
241	3	2.18	—	4.96	4.58	4.77	2.18	10.4	Rect.	N-S
242	3	4.52	—	3.53	—	4.52	3.53	15.96	Rect.	E-W
243	3	3.52	—	4.48	—	4.48	3.52	15.77	Rect.	N-S
244	3	—	3.55	—	4.65	4.65	3.55	16.51	Rect.	N-S
245	3	3.63	—	4.95	4.31	4.63	3.63	16.81	Rect.	N-S
246	**3**	**4.12**	**4.15**	**7.30**	**6.80**	**7.05**	**4.14**	**29.19**	**Rect.**	**N-S**
247	3	—	3.75	—	2.96	3.75	2.96	11.1	Rect.	E-W
248	3	4.00	4.23	3.38	3.38	4.12	3.38	13.93	Rect.	E-W
249	3	3.93	3.83	4.18	3.45	3.88	3.82	14.82	Square	E-W
250	3	3.57	3.77	4.52	4.49	4.51	3.67	16.55	Rect.	N-S
251	3	—	3.73	4.45	—	4.45	3.73	16.6	Square	N-S
252	3	3.13	—	4.74	—	4.74	3.13	14.84	Rect.	N-S
253	3	—	3.83	—	3.15	3.83	3.15	12.06	Rect.	E-W
254	3	3.87	3.87	3.57	3.57	3.87	3.57	13.82	Square	E-W

TABLE A.3. *(continued)*

Room Number	Room Block	*Wall Lengths* North	South	East	West	*Room Form* Length	Width	Area	Shape	Orient.[a]
255	3	—	3.50	4.32	—	4.32	3.5	15.12	Rect.	N-S
256	3	—	3.96	—	4.40	4.4	3.96	17.42	Square	N-S
257	3	—	3.04	4.29	—	4.29	3.04	13.04	Rect.	N-S
258	3	—	3.45	4.11	—	4.11	3.45	14.18	Square	N-S
259	3	4.70	—	3.90	—	4.7	3.9	18.33	Rect.	E-W
260	3	3.50	—	3.74	—	3.74	3.5	13.09	Square	N-S
261	3	—	4.44	2.79	—	4.44	2.79	12.39	Rect.	E-W
262	3	2.39	—	3.20	—	3.2	2.39	7.65	Rect.	N-S
263	3	3.42	—	4.11	—	4.11	3.42	14.06	Rect.	N-S
264	3	3.14	—	—	4.44	4.44	3.14	13.94	Rect.	N-S
265	3	—	4.27	3.78	—	4.27	3.78	16.14	Square	E-W
266	3	3.98	—	4.11	—	4.11	3.98	16.36	Square	N-S
267	3	3.71	—	3.37	—	3.71	3.37	12.5	Square	E-W
268	3	4.41	4.41	3.57	3.57	4.41	3.57	15.74	Rect.	E-W
269	**3**	**3.65**	**3.96**	**3.77**	**3.97**	**3.87**	**3.81**	**14.74**	**Square**	**N-S**
270	**3**	**3.90**	**3.90**	**3.87**	**3.73**	**3.9**	**3.8**	**14.82**	**Square**	**E-W**
271	3	4.00	—	—	3.57	4	3.57	14.28	Square	E-W
272	3	5.87	—	3.22	—	5.87	3.22	18.9	Rect.	E-W
273	3	3.45	—	3.41	—	3.45	3.41	11.76	Square	E-W
274	**3**	**3.75**	**4.01**	**3.62**	**3.60**	**3.88**	**3.61**	**14.01**	**Square**	**E-W**
275	3	—	4.55	3.00	—	4.55	3	13.65	Rect.	E-W
276	3	4.32	—	3.28	—	4.32	3.28	14.17	Rect.	E-W
277	3	—	4.13	3.92	—	4.13	3.92	16.19	Square	E-W
278	3	4.55	4.00	3.49	3.89	4.28	3.69	15.79	Square	E-W
279	**3**	**4.72**	**3.90**	**3.90**	**3.83**	**4.31**	**3.87**	**16.68**	**Square**	**E-W**
280	**3**	**4.70**	**4.70**	**3.40**	**3.42**	**4.7**	**3.41**	**16.03**	**Rect.**	**E-W**
281	3	—	3.34	3.72	—	3.72	3.34	12.42	Square	N-S
282	3	—	4.01	—	3.23	4.01	3.23	12.95	Rect.	E-W
283	3	—	3.36	—	4.08	4.08	3.36	13.71	Rect.	N-S
284	3	—	2.97	—	3.27	3.27	2.97	9.71	Square	N-S
285	3	3.44	—	—	3.60	3.6	3.44	12.38	Square	N-S
286	3	3.82	—	—	3.60	3.82	3.6	13.75	Square	E-W
287	3	3.93	—	3.19	—	3.93	3.19	12.54	Rect.	E-W
288	3	2.84	—	3.50	—	3.5	2.84	9.94	Rect.	N-S
289	3	—	3.80	—	3.55	3.8	3.55	13.49	Square	E-W
290	3	4.19	4.19	3.78	—	4.19	3.78	15.84	Square	E-W
291	3	—	5.70	4.60	—	5.7	4.6	26.22	Rect.	E-W
292	3	—	3.52	4.81	—	4.81	3.52	16.93	Rect.	N-S
293	3	—	3.71	—	3.25	3.71	3.25	12.06	Square	E-W
294	3	3.35	4.00	4.10	4.87	4.49	3.68	16.52	Rect.	N-S
295	3	3.57	—	—	5.10	5.1	3.57	18.21	Rect.	N-S
297	3	—	6.12	—	3.30	6.12	3.3	20.2	Rect.	E-W
298	3	5.20	5.20	4.17	3.65	5.2	3.91	20.33	Rect.	E-W
299	2	—	4.50	3.35	—	4.5	3.35	15.08	Rect.	E-W
300	2	—	3.31	3.35	—	3.35	3.31	11.09	Square	N-S
301	2	—	4.49	—	2.75	4.49	2.75	12.35	Rect.	E-W
302	2	—	3.03	—	2.42	3.03	2.42	7.33	Rect.	E-W
303	2	3.80	3.60	4.20	4.20	4.2	3.7	15.54	Square	N-S
304	2	3.60	3.60	2.00	2.00	3.6	2	7.2	Rect.	E-W
305	2	—	5.10	6.00	6.20	6.1	5.1	31.11	Rect.	N-S

TABLE A.3. *(continued)*

Room	Room	*Wall Lengths*				*Room Form*				
Number	Block	North	South	East	West	Length	Width	Area	Shape	Orient.[a]
306	2	—	3.90	4.20	6.00	5.1	3.9	19.89	Rect.	N-S
307	2	5.10	4.55	5.70	4.60	5.15	4.83	24.87	Square	N-S
308	2	3.70	3.80	4.50	3.90	4.2	3.75	15.75	Square	N-S
309	**0**	**6.80**	**6.75**	**—**	**4.75**	**6.78**	**4.75**	**32.21**	**Rect.**	**E-W**
310	0	4.10	4.03	4.31	4.15	4.23	4.06	17.17	Square	N-S
311	0	4.87	5.16	3.70	4.17	5.02	3.93	19.73	Rect.	E-W
312	**0**	**7.00**	**6.35**	**1.20**	**3.50**	**6.68**	**3.5**	**23.38**	**Rect.**	**E-W**
313	0	6.80	6.47	4.40	4.10	6.63	4.25	28.18	Rect.	E-W
314	0	8.70	8.60	4.56	5.19	8.65	4.87	42.13	Rect.	E-W
315	0	5.31	6.50	5.40	4.02	5.9	4.71	27.79	Rect.	E-W
316	0	4.33	4.08	4.19	4.21	4.21	4.2	17.68	Square	—
317	8	6.42	7.00	—	4.28	6.71	4.39	29.46	Rect.	E-W
318	6	4.40	—	—	4.59	4.59	4.4	20.2	Square	N-S
319	**6**	**5.10**	**5.32**	**4.62**	**4.72**	**5.21**	**4.67**	**24.33**	**Square**	**E-W**
320	6	—	3.50	4.40	—	4.4	3.5	15.4	Rect.	N-S
321	6	4.03	—	—	4.52	4.52	4.03	18.22	Square	N-S
322	6	5.29	—	—	3.30	5.29	3.3	17.46	Rect.	E-W
323	6	—	3.98	—	3.65	3.98	3.65	14.53	Square	E-W
324	6	—	4.10	—	4.87	4.87	4.1	19.97	Square	N-S
325	6	—	5.28	6.99	—	6.99	5.28	36.91	Rect.	N-S
326	6	3.86	—	3.13	—	3.86	3.13	12.08	Rect.	E-W
327	6	3.82	—	—	4.47	4.47	3.82	17.08	Square	N-S
328	6	—	4.56	4.10	—	4.56	4.1	18.7	Square	E-W
329	8	7.10	6.81	—	3.81	6.96	3.81	26.52	Rect.	E-W
330	8	6.04	7.10	—	4.43	6.57	4.43	29.11	Rect.	E-W
331	8	7.43	6.04	—	4.25	6.74	4.25	28.65	Rect.	E-W
332	7	3.41	—	4.05	—	4.05	3.41	13.81	Square	N-S
333	7	6.95	6.50	4.57	4.26	6.73	4.42	29.75	Rect.	E-W
334	7	1.92	—	—	4.57	4.57	1.92	8.77	Rect.	N-S
335	7	8.43	—	5.20	—	8.43	5.2	43.84	Rect.	E-W
336	7	—	4.55	—	4.94	4.94	4.55	22.48	Square	N-S
337	7	3.56	—	4.13	—	4.13	3.56	14.7	Square	N-S
339	7	—	3.76	3.78	—	3.78	3.76	14.21	Square	N-S
340	7	4.35	—	—	3.81	4.35	3.81	16.57	Square	E-W
341	**7**	**4.09**	**4.06**	**3.03**	**3.09**	**4.08**	**3.06**	**12.48**	**Rect.**	**E-W**
342	7	4.17	3.94	3.02	3.45	4.06	3.24	13.15	Rect.	E-W
343	7	—	4.07	3.83	—	4.07	3.83	15.59	Square	E-W
344	7	3.59	—	—	4.14	4.14	3.59	14.86	Square	N-S
345	7	3.18	—	—	3.60	3.6	3.18	11.45	Square	N-S
346	7	4.13	—	3.61	—	4.13	3.61	14.91	Square	E-W
347	7	3.86	3.84	—	3.60	3.85	3.6	13.86	Square	E-W
348	7	3.97	—	3.88	—	3.97	3.88	15.4	Square	E-W
349	**7**	**4.19**	**3.84**	**4.15**	**3.86**	**4.02**	**4.01**	**16.12**	**Square**	**—**
350	7	3.55	4.59	3.76	4.17	4.07	3.97	16.16	Square	E-W
351	7	3.73	—	—	3.55	3.73	3.55	13.24	Square	E-W
352	**7**	**3.45**	**3.52**	**3.91**	**3.81**	**3.86**	**3.49**	**13.47**	**Square**	**N-S**
353	8	3.92	3.65	5.77	5.88	5.83	3.79	22.1	Rect.	N-S
354	8	3.25	2.85	5.40	5.55	5.48	3.05	16.71	Rect.	N-S
355	8	5.06	5.30	4.75	5.37	5.18	5.06	26.21	Square	E-W
356	**8**	**2.35**	**2.50**	**4.37**	**4.75**	**4.56**	**2.43**	**11.08**	**Rect.**	**N-S**

TABLE A.3. *(continued)*

Room Number	Room Block	*Wall Lengths* North	South	East	West	*Room Form* Length	Width	Area	Shape	Orient.[a]
357	8	6.60	5.46	4.75	4.77	6.03	4.76	28.7	Rect.	E-W
358	8	6.20	6.00	3.80	3.20	6.1	3.5	21.35	Rect.	E-W
359	**0**	**7.00**	**7.00**	**3.67**	**3.74**	**7**	**3.71**	**25.97**	**Rect.**	**E-W**
361	9	—	2.40	—	3.00	3	2.4	7.2	Rect.	N-S
362	9	—	3.10	3.15	—	3.15	3.1	9.77	Square	N-S
363	9	—	3.40	—	4.20	4.2	3.4	14.28	Rect.	N-S
364	9	7.20	—	4.20	—	7.2	4.2	30.24	Rect.	E-W
365	9	—	2.20	2.50	—	2.5	2.2	5.5	Square	N-S
366	0	—	6.00	4.20	—	6	4.2	25.2	Rect.	E-W
367	9	—	4.60	5.40	—	5.4	4.6	24.84	Square	N-S
368	9	—	3.10	5.70	—	5.7	3.1	17.67	Rect.	N-S
369	9	—	2.80	2.60	—	2.8	2.6	7.28	Square	E-W
370	9	—	4.00	3.40	—	4	3.4	13.6	Square	E-W
371	**9**	**3.53**	**3.65**	**3.78**	**3.87**	**3.83**	**3.59**	**13.75**	**Square**	**N-S**
372	9	—	5.00	—	3.10	5	3.1	15.5	Rect.	E-W
373	9	2.30	—	—	2.10	2.3	2.1	4.83	Square	E-W
374	9	—	3.70	—	4.20	4.2	3.7	15.54	Square	N-S
375	9	—	4.20	—	3.50	4.2	3.5	14.7	Rect.	E-W
376	**9**	**2.80**	**2.75**	**4.34**	**4.34**	**4.34**	**2.78**	**12.07**	**Rect.**	**N-S**
377	9	—	4.50	3.90	—	4.5	3.9	17.55	Square	E-W
378	9	—	2.30	—	3.40	3.4	2.3	7.82	Rect.	N-S
379	9	—	2.20	3.40	—	3.4	2.2	7.48	Rect.	N-S
380	9	—	2.40	—	3.80	3.8	2.4	9.12	Rect.	N-S
381	9	—	3.40	—	3.80	3.8	3.4	12.92	Square	N-S
382	9	6.20	—	—	3.60	6.2	3.6	22.32	Rect.	E-W
384	9	2.60	3.75	4.23	4.00	4.12	3.18	13.1	Rect.	N-S
385	9	3.30	2.20	4.00	4.53	4.27	2.75	11.74	Rect.	N-S
386	9	2.20	2.90	3.00	3.84	3.42	2.55	8.72	Rect.	N-S
387	0	5.50	—	—	3.30	5.5	3.3	18.15	Rect.	E-W
388	0	5.60	5.60	4.00	4.00	5.6	4	22.4	Rect.	E-W
389	0	3.00	3.00	5.00	5.00	5	3	15	Rect.	N-S
390	0	4.80	5.00	7.00	7.20	7.1	4.9	34.79	Rect.	N-S
391	0	4.20	4.20	5.60	5.20	5.4	4.2	22.68	Rect.	N-S
392	0	7.00	5.50	—	4.00	6.25	4.8	30	Rect.	E-W
393	0	8.00	8.00	—	4.00	8	4	32	Rect.	E-W
394	12	—	3.80	6.00	6.00	6	3.65	21.9	Rect.	N-S
395	**12**	**1.83**	**1.91**	**1.93**	**1.80**	**1.87**	**1.87**	**3.5**	**Square**	—
396	12	3.64	—	—	4.00	4	3.64	14.56	Square	N-S
397	**12**	**3.70**	**4.00**	**3.70**	**4.60**	**4.15**	**3.85**	**15.98**	**Square**	**N-S**
398	**12**	**3.78**	**3.89**	**3.20**	**3.23**	**3.84**	**3.22**	**12.36**	**Square**	**E-W**
399	12	4.17	3.65	3.85	3.68	3.91	3.77	14.74	Square	E-W
400	6	4.11	4.14	2.79	2.79	4.13	2.79	11.52	Rect.	E-W
401	12	3.70	4.00	4.11	4.33	4.22	3.85	16.25	Square	N-S
402	12	4.02	3.90	4.00	—	4	3.96	15.84	Square	N-S
403	12	—	3.30	3.25	3.40	3.33	3.3	10.99	Square	N-S
404	**12**	**3.02**	**3.71**	**3.78**	**3.25**	**3.52**	**3.37**	**11.86**	**Square**	**N-S**
405	12	3.85	—	5.35	5.44	5.4	3.85	20.79	Rect.	N-S
406	12	4.52	3.80	—	3.55	4.16	3.55	14.77	Square	E-W
407	12	4.90	4.35	—	4.40	4.63	4.4	20.37	Square	E-W
408	12	2.95	—	—	5.45	5.45	2.95	16.08	Rect.	N-S

TABLE A.3. *(continued)*

Room	Room	*Wall Lengths*				*Room Form*				
Number	Block	North	South	East	West	Length	Width	Area	Shape	Orient.[a]
409	12	—	3.30	—	4.88	4.88	3.3	16.1	Rect.	N-S
411	**12**	**4.03**	**4.02**	**3.68**	**4.02**	**4.03**	**3.85**	**15.52**	**Square**	**E-W**
412	12	4.05	4.05	2.04	1.80	4.05	1.92	7.78	Rect.	E-W
413	7	5.00	5.20	3.00	3.20	5.1	3.1	15.81	Rect.	E-W
414	**10**	**6.80**	**6.70**	—	**3.60**	**6.75**	**3.6**	**24.3**	**Rect.**	**E-W**
415	10	1.65	1.45	2.60	2.75	2.68	1.55	4.15	Rect.	N-S
416	10	3.95	—	3.60	4.20	3.9	3.63	14.16	Square	N-S
417	10	2.40	2.70	4.45	3.95	4.2	2.55	10.71	Rect.	E-W
418	10	3.95	4.67	7.65	7.95	7.8	4.31	33.62	Rect.	N-S
419	10	4.34	4.00	4.25	3.60	4.17	3.93	16.39	Square	E-W
420	**10**	**4.30**	**4.30**	**5.10**	**4.20**	**4.65**	**4.3**	**20**	**Square**	**N-S**
421	10	3.70	4.20	3.60	3.70	3.95	3.65	14.42	Square	E-W
422	10	4.57	3.00	3.96	4.01	4.28	3.99	17.08	Square	E-W
423	10	4.00	4.00	3.50	3.90	4	3.7	14.8	Square	E-W
424	6	4.00	4.00	4.20	4.80	4.5	4	18	Square	N-S
425	**11**	**3.50**	**3.40**	**3.40**	**3.90**	**3.65**	**3.45**	**12.59**	**Square**	**N-S**
426	11	2.35	—	4.55	4.40	4.48	2.35	10.53	Rect.	N-S
427	11	3.25	3.30	3.15	2.80	3.28	2.98	9.77	Square	E-W
428	11	3.15	3.45	4.35	3.40	3.88	3.3	12.8	Square	N-S
429	11	2.35	—	—	5.05	5.05	2.35	11.87	Rect.	N-S
430	11	—	3.95	3.75	—	3.95	3.75	14.81	Square	E-W
431	11	3.95	3.15	3.10	3.50	3.55	3.3	11.72	Square	E-W
432	11	4.85	5.40	3.50	2.65	5.13	3.08	15.8	Rect.	E-W
433	11	2.64	3.37	3.45	3.44	3.45	3.01	10.38	Square	N-S
434	13	3.20	3.00	4.00	3.90	3.95	3.1	12.25	Rect.	N-S
435	13	3.80	3.70	3.50	3.80	3.75	3.65	13.69	Square	E-W
436	13	2.40	2.70	5.00	5.40	5.2	2.55	13.26	Rect.	N-S
437	13	4.00	3.20	3.70	3.50	3.6	3.6	12.96	Square	—
438	**3**	**4.40**	**4.30**	**4.22**	**4.00**	**4.35**	**4.11**	**17.88**	**Square**	**E-W**
439	3	3.80	4.50	5.00	4.50	4.75	4.15	19.71	Square	N-S
440	**3**	**3.35**	**2.96**	**4.87**	**5.03**	**4.95**	**3.16**	**15.64**	**Rect.**	**N-S**
441	0	6.90	7.50	—	4.65	7.2	4.65	33.48	Rect.	E-W
442	0	5.90	6.90	5.55	4.40	6.4	4.98	31.87	Rect.	E-W
443	0	5.60	4.80	—	3.50	5.2	3.5	18.2	Rect.	E-W
444	0	6.95	6.25	3.00	3.35	6.6	3.18	20.99	Rect.	E-W
445	0	4.10	3.25	4.20	4.45	4.33	3.68	15.93	Square	N-S
446	0	5.95	6.60	3.50	3.55	6.28	3.53	22.17	Rect.	E-W
447	0	4.40	3.75	4.65	4.55	4.6	4.08	18.77	Square	N-S
448	0	4.75	4.40	1.70	2.05	4.58	1.88	8.61	Rect.	E-W
449	0	5.50	6.25	—	4.60	5.88	4.6	27.05	Rect.	E-W
450	0	4.80	5.55	2.95	—	5.18	3.6	18.65	Rect.	E-W
451	0	3.35	3.85	—	4.15	4.28	3.75	16.05	Square	E-W
452	0	4.05	5.15	—	4.50	4.6	3.95	18.17	Square	E-W
453	0	6.45	6.45	—	3.00	6.45	3	19.35	Rect.	E-W
454	0	6.30	6.45	—	3.60	6.38	3.6	22.97	Rect.	E-W
455	0	8.15	7.65	3.75	4.95	7.9	4.35	34.37	Rect.	E-W
456	0	4.70	6.70	—	4.35	5.7	4.35	24.8	Rect.	E-W
457	0	4.15	3.50	4.00	3.90	3.95	3.83	15.13	Square	N-S

Note: Rooms in boldface denote excavated spaces.

[a]Empty cells in this column indicate rooms whose length and width are identical and whose orientation could not be calculated.

TABLE A.4.
Door Data (n = 163)

Room	Wall	Room Block	Height (m)	Width (m)	Area (m^2)	Distance to Floor (m)	Distance to Wall Base (m)	Horizontal Location
312	W	0	—	0.48	—	0	—	Right
359	S	0	—	0.41	—	0	—	Left
2	E	1	0.90	0.65	0.59	0.10	—	Center
2	S	1	—	—	—	—	—	Center
4	N	1	—	—	—	—	—	—
5	N	1	0.81	0.43	0.35	—	0.45	Center
5	S	1	—	—	—	—	—	—
5	W	1	0.77	0.54	0.42	—	0.38	Center
6	S	1	—	0.55	—	0.10	0.30	Center
6	W	1	0.50	0.55	0.28	0.40	0.60	Center
7	N	1	1.00	0.50	0.50	0.25	—	Center
7	W	1	0.55	0.50	0.28	—	—	Center
8	E	1	0.90	0.50	0.45	0.40	—	Center
10	E	1	0.68	0.53	0.36	0	—	Left
10	N	1	0.70	0.50	0.35	0.63	—	Left
10	S	1	0.65	0.60	0.39	0.33	—	Center
10	W	1	0.70	0.50	0.35	0	—	Right
15	E	1	—	0.66	—	0.69	1.00	Center
15	N	1	0.81	0.50	0.45	0	—	Center
28	S	1	—	0.55	—	0.23	—	Left
31	E	1	—	—	—	—	—	Right
31	W	1	—	0.41	—	0.50	—	Left
33	N	1	1.10	0.55	0.65	0	—	Left
35	E	1	0.78	0.55	0.43	0	—	Center
37	S	1	0.67	0.45	0.32	0.40	—	Center
39	N	1	0.45	0.36	0.16	—	—	Center
39	W	1	—	0.26	—	—	0.55	Left
40	E	1	—	—	—	—	—	Right
41	S	1	0.63	0.46	0.29	—	0.58	Center
41	W	1	0.65	0.68	0.44	—	—	Center
42	E	1	0.64	0.62	0.40	0.22	0.56	Center
42	S	1	0.84	0.44	0.37	—	0.44	Right
43	N	1	0.60	0.50	0.30	0.08	0.58	Right
44	N	1	0.84	0.76	0.64	—	0.45	Center
44	W	1	—	0.48	—	0	—	—
45	E	1	—	0.58	—	0	—	Center
45	W	1	—	0.40	—	0	—	Center
47	E	1	0.81	0.45	0.36	0	—	Center
47	W	1	1.10	0.60	0.66	0	—	Left
62	E	1	0.70	0.65	0.46	0	0.65	Left
68	E	1	1.00	0.55	0.55	0.20	0.50	Center
68	N	1	1.03	0.60	0.62	0	0.50	Center
68	W	1	1.03	0.60	0.62	0	0.18	Center
69	S	1	0.75	0.50	0.38	0	—	—
69	W	1	0.76	0.56	0.43	0	—	Center
70	E	1	0.61	—	—	0.25	—	—
70	S	1	—	0.60	—	1.80	—	Right
97	N	1	0.70	0.45	0.32	0.10	—	Left

TABLE A.4. *(continued)*

Room	Wall	Room Block	Height (m)	Width (m)	Area (m^2)	Distance to Floor (m)	Distance to Wall Base (m)	Horizontal Location
100	E	1	—	0.54	—	0.10	—	Center
100	N	1	0.61	0.60	0.37	0.30	—	Right
100	W	1	—	0.45	—	0.22	—	Left
100	W	1	—	0.49	—	0.22	—	Right
104	E	1	0.88	0.65	0.57	0	—	Right
104	S	1	0.84	0.60	0.54	0	—	Right
104	W	1	0.95	0.65	0.62	0	—	Left
107	E	1	0.85	0.60	0.51	0	—	Right
107	W	1	0.84	0.67	0.32	0	—	Center
121	E	1	—	0.52	—	0.43	—	Right
12	W	2	0.95	0.65	0.62	0	0.20	Right
13	S	2	—	0.50	—	0.44	—	Center
13	W	2	—	0.80	—	—	—	Right
14	S	2	1.74	0.91	1.58	0	—	Right
14	W	2	1.20	0.68	0.82	0	0.45	Center
16	W	2	—	—	—	—	—	Left
18	E	2	0.80	0.80	0.64	0	—	Left
18	N	2	0.70	0.60	0.42	0.30	1.05	Center
19	W	2	0.75	0.50	0.38	0.30	0.70	Right
20	N	2	1.13	0.94	1.62	0	—	—
20	W	2	0.75	1.00	0.75	0.63	—	—
21	E	2	—	—	—	—	—	—
21	N	2	0.90	0.58	0.52	—	—	—
22	N	2	1.00	0.70	0.70	—	—	—
22	S	2	0.60	0.50	0.30	0.15	0.40	—
22	W	2	0.88	0.53	0.47	0.16	0.46	Left
23	E	2	0.90	0.55	0.50	0	—	Center
23	S	2	0.55	0.55	0.33	0.40	—	Left
23	W	2	1.07	0.41	0.44	0	—	—
26	N	2	0.64	0.34	0.22	—	—	—
26	S	2	0.68	0.68	0.46	0.64	—	Left
27	E	2	—	0.55	—	—	—	Right
27	S	2	—	0.57	—	—	—	Left
143	N	2	—	0.80	—	0	0.30	Left
143	S	2	—	0.50	—	—	—	Left
145	S	2	0.90	0.58	0.52	—	0.35	Left
145	W	2	0.96	0.56	0.54	0	—	Left
145	N	2	—	0.50	—	—	0.40	Right
146	E	2	1.00	0.57	0.57	0.35	—	Left
146	N	2	1.10	0.65	0.72	0.10	—	Center
153	N	2	0.62	0.55	0.34	0.65	—	Right
153	S	2	0.65	0.63	0.50	0.90	—	Center
164	E	2	0.96	0.46	0.44	0.30	—	Left
164	N	2	1.01	0.60	0.66	0.23	—	Center
183	N	2	—	0.30	—	—	—	Right
183	S	2	0.85	0.44	0.37	0	—	Right
183	S	2	1.01	0.49	0.49	0	—	Left
183	W	2	1.00	0.50	0.50	0	—	Right
187	E	2	1.25	0.50	0.63	0.12	—	Center

TABLE A.4. *(continued)*

Room	Wall	Room Block	Height (m)	Width (m)	Area (m^2)	Distance to Floor (m)	Distance to Wall Base (m)	Horizontal Location
187	S	2	0.95	0.53	0.54	0	—	Center
197	E	2	—	1.16	—	—	—	—
197	N	2	1.41	0.89	1.25	—	0.22	—
197	S	2	1.15	0.78	0.90	0.10	—	—
205	N	3	1.17	0.71	0.84	0.61	—	Center
205	S	3	0.80	0.60	0.48	—	—	—
206	N	3	—	0.41	—	0.18	0.25	Center
206	S	3	—	0.57	—	0	0.20	Center
210	S	3	1.12	0.70	0.78	0	—	Center
211	N	3	0.94	0.41	0.39	—	—	Left
211	S	3	0.94	0.46	0.43	—	—	Center
215	N	3	0.89	0.43	0.38	—	—	—
215	S	3	0.80	0.4	0.32	0	0.13	Left
216	E	3	0.90	0.65	0.59	—	—	—
216	N	3	0.75	0.55	0.41	0.35	—	—
218	E	3	0.70	0.56	0.39	0	0.18	Left
218	N	3	1.12	0.50	0.56	0	0.32	Left
218	S	3	0.89	0.43	0.38	0	0.18	Left
231	E	3	1.35	0.75	1.13	0.70	—	Center
231	N	3	1.09	0.66	0.72	0.89	—	Left
231	S	3	1.10	0.70	0.77	0.35	—	Left
246	E	3	0.96	0.55	0.53	0	0.25	Left
246	E	3	1.18	0.47	0.55	0	0.25	Right
246	S	3	0.91	0.51	0.46	0	0.20	Right
269	E	3	0.75	0.54	0.45	0	—	Left
269	S	3	0.78	0.79	0.62	—	—	Center
269	W	3	1.10	0.50	0.55	—	—	—
270	E	3	0.90	0.47	0.42	–0.21	—	Center
270	S	3	0.81	0.57	0.46	0	—	Center
270	W	3	1.23	0.58	0.71	—	—	Left
274	N	3	1.02	0.57	0.58	0	0.30	Center
274	S	3	1.02	0.55	0.56	0	0.30	Left
279	S	3	1.00	0.58	0.58	—	—	Right
279	W	3	0.82	0.50	0.41	—	—	—
280	E	3	0.98	0.78	0.76	0	—	—
280	N	3	0.87	0.56	0.49	—	—	—
438	E	3	0.74	0.46	0.34	—	0.21	Center
438	N	3	0.84	0.48	0.43	0	0.51	Right
440	E	3	—	—	—	—	—	—
3	S	4	0.65	0.50	0.33	0	0.30	Center
113	S	5	0.85	0.75	0.64	0.48	0.55	Center
113	W	5	0.88	0.65	0.57	0.40	0.64	Left
114	N	5	—	0.40	—	—	—	—
114	E	5	—	0.65	—	—	—	Right
115	E	5	0.80	0.50	0.40	0.35	—	Right
115	W	5	0.85	0.43	0.37	0.10	—	Right
116	W	5	0.80	0.50	0.4	—	—	Left
116	N	5	0.85	0.75	0.64	—	0.48	Center
195	S	5	—	0.40	—	—	—	—

TABLE A.4. *(continued)*

Room	Wall	Room Block	Height (m)	Width (m)	Area (m^2)	Distance to Floor (m)	Distance to Wall Base (m)	Horizontal Location
341	N	7	0.80	0.54	0.43	0.30	—	Right
349	S	7	0.87	0.70	0.69	0	—	—
352	E	7	1.11	0.56	0.62	–0.09	0	Center
352	W	7	0.78	0.52	0.46	0.13	0.16	Center
352	N	7	0.76	0.55	0.42	0.60	–0.01	Center
353	E	8	—	0.65	—	0.15	—	Center
354	E	8	—	0.75	—	0	—	Center
354	N	8	—	0.60	—	0	—	Center
354	W	8	—	0.57	—	0	—	Center
355	N	8	—	0.50	—	—	—	Left
355	E	8	—	0.47	—	0	—	Left
356	S	8	—	—	—	0	—	Right
356	W	8	—	0.47	—	0	—	Right
420	E	10	—	0.60	—	0.45	—	Right
425	S	11	0.80	0.50	0.40	0	—	—

TABLE A.5.
Crawlway Data ($n = 11$)

Room	Wall	Room Block	Height (m)	Width (m)	Area (m^2)	Distance to Floor (m)	Distance to Wall Base (m)	Horizontal Location
19	N	2	0.45	0.36	0.16	0.15	0.55	Left
164	S	2	1.10	0.72	0.79	0	—	Center
211	N	3	0.42	0.61	0.26	0.05	—	Right
211	N	3	0.31	0.32	0.99	0.05	—	Right
215	E	3	0.52	0.65	0.34	0	0.36	
216	S	3	0.40	0.56	0.22	0.63	0.95	Center
216	W	3	0.52	0.65	0.34	—	—	
274	E	3	0.59	0.52	0.37	0	0.45	Center
269	S	3	1.00	0.80	0.80	0.40	—	Right
319	E	6	0.51	0.53	0.27	0.08	—	Right
341	E	7	0.50	0.34	0.17	—	—	Right

TABLE A.6.
Vent Data ($n = 50$)

Room	Wall	Room Block	Height (m)	Width (m)	Area (m^2)	Distance to Floor (m)	Distance to Wall Base (m)	Horizontal Location
4	S	1	0.20	0.32	0.64	0	—	Left
7	S	1	0.20	0.20	0.40	0.15	—	Center
10	N	1	0.20	0.15	0.30	1.13	—	Right
28	N	1	—	—	—	—	—	Center
33	N	1	0.24	0.24	0.58	0.68	—	Center
35	W	1	0.20	0.16	0.32	0	—	Center
39	E	1	0.20	0.30	0.6	—	0.50	Center
43	W	1	0.08	0.21	0.17	0.8	1.30	Right
43	W	1	0.09	0.13	0.12	0.73	1.23	Left
44	E	1	—	—	—	—	—	—
69	W	1	—	0.43	—	—	—	Center
70	E	1	—	—	—	1.96	—	—
70	N	1	0.26	0.20	0.52	2.28	—	Right
104	E	1	0.12	0.20	0.24	– 0.10	—	Right
104	E	1	0.15	0.29	0.44	0	—	Right
104	W	1	0.16	0.23	0.37	0	—	Left
108	S	1	—	—	—	—	—	—
16	E	2	0.10	0.25	0.25	0.10	—	Right
16	N	2	0.30	0.23	0.69	0	—	Center
16	W	2	0.19	0.26	0.49	0	—	Left
18	S	2	0.10	0.15	0.15	—	—	Center
20	W	2	—	—	—	1	—	—
22	W	2	0.16	0.23	0.37	—	—	Left
23	N	2	0.20	0.23	0.46	0.25	—	Right
23	S	2	0.15	0.15	0.23	0.20	—	Center
145	W	2	0.18	0.16	0.29	0	—	Left
146	N	2	0.18	0.20	0.36	0.10	—	Right
164	N	2	0.18	0.15	0.27	0.05	—	Center
164	W	2	0.20	0.22	0.44	—	—	Left
187	E	2	0.12	0.14	0.17	0.88	—	Left
187	E	2	—	—	—	—	—	Right
187	N	2	0.12	0.12	0.14	1.72	—	Right
187	N	2	0.11	0.15	0.17	1.75	—	Left
187	W	2	0.14	0.13	0.18	0.79	—	Right
187	W	2	0.10	0.12	0.12	0.71	—	Left
205	E	3	—	—	—	—	—	—
206	W	3	0.17	0.19	0.32	0	0.15	Center
216	S	3	0.17	0.19	0.32	– 0.12	0.20	Center
218	E	3	0.17	0.41	0.70	—	—	Left
218	N	3	0.24	0.23	0.55	1.08	1.23	Right
218	N	3	0.27	0.20	0.54	0.12	0.37	Right
231	N	3	0.30	0.30	0.90	—	—	Left
438	E	3	0.13	0.17	0.22	0.78	—	Left
438	E	3	0.14	0.13	0.18	0.67	—	Right
438	N	3	0.21	0.36	0.76	– 0.21	0.30	Right
440	E	3	0.17	0.13	0.22	—	—	Center
114	S	5	—	0.53	—	—	—	Right
115	W	5	0.15	0.12	0.18	0.10	—	Right
341	E	7	0.30	0.28	0.84	—	—	Left
349	E	7	0.20	0.41	0.82	0	—	—

TABLE A.7.
Niche Data ($n = 78$)

Room	Wall	Room Block	Height (m)	Width (m)	Area (m²)	Distance to Floor (m)	Distance to Wall Base (m)	Horizontal Location
2	E	1	—	—	—	0.10	—	Center
10	E	1	0.18	0.22	0.40	1.18	—	Left
10	E	1	0.15	0.23	0.35	0.19	—	Left
28	E	1	0.45	0.35	0.16	—	—	Left
33	S	1	0.11	0.14	0.15	0.37	—	Left
33	S	1	0.22	0.23	0.56	0.62	—	Right
35	E	1	0.17	0.16	0.27	1.11	—	Right
35	E	1	0.12	0.19	0.23	1.68	—	Left
35	S	1	0.22	0.20	0.44	0.45	—	Right
35	S	1	0.21	0.23	0.48	0.45	—	Left
37	W	1	0.23	0.32	0.74	0.26	—	Left
42	S	1	0.10	0.15	0.15	—	—	Center
44	S	1	—	—	—	—	—	—
45	N	1	—	—	—	—	—	—
45	S	1	—	—	—	—	—	Right
45	S	1	—	—	—	—	—	Center
45	S	1	0	0	—	0	0	Left
47	E	1	0.12	0.18	0.22	2.49	2.74	Left
47	W	1	0.25	0.13	0.33	—	—	Right
47	W	1	0.14	0.16	0.22	—	2.28	Center
62	N	1	0.24	0.24	0.58	—	—	Right
68	W	1	0.24	0.24	0.58	1.80	2.03	Right
97	E	1	0.25	0.15	0.38	0.45	—	Left
97	S	1	0.18	0.12	0.22	0.97	—	Right
104	E	1	0.16	0.24	0.38	1.05	—	Left
104	E	1	0.19	0.34	0.65	0.93	—	Right
121	N	1	0.24	0.24	0.58	0.875	—	Left
16	S	2	0.13	0.15	0.02	0.66	—	Left
18	N	2	0.10	0.15	0.15	0.7	1.45	Left
19	N	2	0.15	0.22	0.33	1.00	1.4	Right
22	E	2	0.16	0.15	0.24	0.98	1.33	Left
22	E	2	0.10	0.10	0.10	1.01	1.36	Center
22	E	2	0.13	0.18	0.23	0.53	0.88	Right
22	S	2	—	—	—	—	—	Left
22	S	2	—	—	—	—	—	Right
22	W	2	0.11	0.18	0.20	0.86	1.16	Right
22	W	2	0.18	0.22	0.40	0.98	1.28	Left
23	E	2	—	0.15	—	0.85	—	Left
23	E	2	—	0.17	—	1.05	—	Center
23	E	2	—	0.20	—	1.15	—	Right
23	S	2	0.17	0.18	0.36	1.30	—	Right
23	S	2	0.13	0.18	0.23	1.06	—	Left
23	S	2	—	—	—	2.05	—	Right
23	S	2	—	—	—	1.86	—	Left
26	W	2	0.30	0.30	0.90	—	—	Left
145	N	2	—	—	—	—	—	—
146	N	2	0.16	0.18	0.29	1.80	—	Left
146	N	2	0.15	0.17	0.26	1.80	—	Right

TABLE A.7. *(continued)*

Room	Wall	Room Block	Height (m)	Width (m)	Area (m^2)	Distance to Floor (m)	Distance to Wall Base (m)	Horizontal Location
153	E	2	0.13	0.22	0.29	1.20	—	Center
153	N	2	—	—	—	—	—	Left
183	N	2	0.15	0.20	0.30	0.87	—	Left
183	S	2	0.20	0.17	0.34	1.00	—	Left
183	W	2	0.19	0.2	0.38	1.10	—	Right
211	E	3	0.17	0.18	0.36	0.24	—	Center
216	N	3	—	—	—	—	—	—
216	N	3	—	—	—	—	—	—
216	S	3	0.23	0.12	0.28	0.21	0.53	Left
218	S	3	0.33	0.31	0.12	—	—	Left
246	N	3	0.30	0.38	0.11	0.95	1.2	Right
246	N	3	0.28	0.23	0.64	0.90	1.15	Center
246	N	3	0.25	0.33	0.83	1.03	1.28	Left
269	E	3	0.16	0.16	0.26	0.90	—	Left
269	E	3	0.17	0.15	0.26	1.00	—	Right
269	N	3	—	—	—	—	—	Left
269	N	3	—	—	—	—	—	Right
269	S	3	0.14	0.15	0.21	0.88	—	Left
269	W	3	—	—	—	—	—	Left
270	S	3	—	—	—	—	—	Center
279	E	3	0.13	0.30	0.39	—	—	Left
280	S	3	0.15	0.30	0.45	—	—	Right
438	W	3	0.17	0.13	0.22	1.25	—	Left
438	W	3	0.15	0.12	0.18	1.25	—	Center
438	W	3	0.13	0.18	0.23	1.25	—	Right
112	N	5	0.31	0.42	0.13	0.10	0.5	Right
113	E	5	0.16	0.33	0.53	0.29	0.63	Center
113	S	5	—	—	—	—	0	Left
113	W	5	0.11	0.13	0.14	—	—	Left
349	N	7	0.12	0.10	0.12	—	—	Right

Table A.8.
Distribution of Rectangular Slab-Lined Hearths ($n = 118$)

Room Block	Room	Location	Associated Floor
Unaffiliated Rooms	1	Center	1
	24	Center	1
	24	Center	2
	25	Center	1
	25	Center	1
	309	Center	1
	309	NE Quad	1
	309	SE Quad	1
	311	Center	1
	312	Center	1
	359	Center	1
Room Block 1	2	Center	1
	4	Center	1
	5	Center	1
	5	Center	2
	5	Center	Roof
	6	Center	1
	6	SE Quad	2
	7	Center	1
	8	Center	1
	11	Center	1
	11	Center	2
	11	Center	Roof
	15	Center	1
	15	Center	2
	28	Center	1
	28	Center	2
	28	Center	Roof
	31	Center	Roof
	37	Center	2
	39	Center	1
	40	SW Quad	Roof
	40	Center	Roof
	40	NW Quad	Roof
	41	Center	Roof
	44	Center	Roof
	45	Center	Roof
	47	Center	1
	62	Center	Roof
	62	Center	Second Story
	62	SE Quad	Second Story
	62	Center	Second Story
	62	SE Quad	Second Story
	62	SE Quad	Second Story
	68	NE Quad	1
	68	NE Quad	2
	68	NW Quad	Roof
	69	SE Quad	Roof
	69	Center	Second Story
	70	Center	Second Story

TABLE A.8. *(continued)*

Room Block	Room	Location	Associated Floor
	97	Center	1
	100	Center	1
	104	Center	1
	104	Center	2
	104	Center	Roof
	108	Center	1
	121	Center	1
Room Block 2	12	Center	1
	13	Center	2
	19	Center	2
	19	Center	Second Story
	21	Center	1
	22	Center	2
	23	Center	2
	23	Center	Roof
	27	Center	1
	143	Center	2
	145	Center	1
	146	Center	1
	146	Center	Roof
	146	Center	Second Story
	183	Center	Roof
	183	Center	Roof
	183	Center	Roof
	187	Center	Roof
	197	NW Quad	5
Room Block 3	216	Center	1
	216	SE Quad	2
	218	Center	1
	231	Center	1
	231	Center	Roof
	246	Center	Roof
	246	SW Quad	Second Story
	269	Center	3
	269	Center	Second Story
	270	Center	Second Story
	274	Center	3
	274	Center	4
	274	NE Quad	Second Story
	279	Center	Roof
	280	Center	1
	280	Center	Roof
Room Block 4	3	Center	1
	9	SE Quad	1
Room Block 5	112	SE Quad	1
	112	Center	Roof
	114	Center	2A
	115	Center	1
	115	NE Quad	Roof
	116	Center	1
	116	Center	1B
Room Block 6	319	Center	2

TABLE A.8. *(continued)*

Room Block	Room	Location	Associated Floor
Room Block 7	341	SE Quad	2
	341	SW Quad	Roof
	349	Center	1
	352	Center	1
	352	Center	Roof
Room Block 8	353	Center	1
	354	Center	1
	355	Center	1
	356	Center	1
Room Block 9	371	Center	1
Room Block 10	420	Center	1
Room Block 11	425	Center	1
Room Block 12	397	Center	1
	398	Center	1
	411	Center	2
Room Block 13	434	Center	2

TABLE A.9.
Distribution of Mealing Bins (n = 37)

Room Block	Room	Location	Mealing Bin Faces	Associated Floor
Unaffiliated	25	Center	—	2
	309	Center	—	1
	312	SE Quad	North	1
	359	SW Quad	North	1
Room Block 1	4	NE Quad	South	1
	6	—	West	1
	8	SW Quad	East	1
	31	NW Quad	South	1
	31	NE Quad	—	1
	37	NW Quad	South	1
	47	NW Quad	South	1
	47	NE Quad	South	Roof
	97	NE Quad	West	1
	104	NW Quad	East	1
	107	SE Quad	—	1
Room Block 2	27	SE Quad	East	1
	183	SE Quad	—	Roof
Room Block 3	205	NW Quad	East	1
	211	SW Quad	East	1
	216	NW Quad	East	1
	218	NW Quad	South	1
	231	SE Quad	—	Roof
	246	NE Quad	South	Roof
	246	SE Quad	—	Second Story
Room Block 4	3	NE Quad	South	1
Room Block 5	112	SE Quad	—	Roof
	113	NE Quad	—	Roof
	113	NW Quad	—	Roof
	195	NW Quad	East	1
Room Block 7	349	NE Quad	South	1
	352	—	—	Roof
Room Block 8	354	NW Quad	East	1
	354	SE Quad	—	1
Room Block 10	198	NE Quad		1
	414	NE Quad	South	1
	420	NE Quad	South	1
Room Block 12	398	SW Quad	North	1

TABLE A.10.
Distribution of Double Mealing Bins ($n = 8$)

Room Block	Room	Location	Mealing Bin Faces	Associated Floor
Room Block 1	5	SE Quad	West	1
	7	SE Quad	West	1
	11	NW Quad	South	1
Room Block 5	114	NE Quad	West	1
	116	SW Quad	East	1
Room Block 6	319	NW Quad	—	2
Room Block 8	355	SE Quad	West	1
Room Block 9	371	SE Quad	North	1

TABLE A.11.
Distribution of Circular Hearths ($n = 20$)

Room Block	Room	Location	Associated Floor
Room Block 1	107	Center	1
	31	Center	1
	33	Center	1
	40	Center	1
	43	Center	1
	68	Center	2
Room Block 2	18	Center	2
	197	Center	4
Room Block 3	206	Center	1
	210	Center	1
	246	NE Quad	2
	246	NE Quad	3
	246	NE Quad	4
	274	Center	2
	440	Center	1
Room Block 5	112	SW Quad	1
	114	Center	2A
Room Block 9	376	Center	1
Room Block 10	414	Center	1
Room Block 13	434	Center	1

TABLE A.12.
Distribution of Ash Boxes ($n = 9$)

Room Block	Room	Location	Associated Floor
Unaffiliated	25	Center	1
Room Block 1	33	NW Quad	1
	107	NE Quad	1
Room Block 2	18	SE Quad	2
	197	NW Quad	4
Room Block 3	269	Center	3
	269	Center	3
	440	SW Quad	1
Room Block 9	376	SE Quad	1

TABLE A.13.
Distribution of Benches (n = 8)

Room Block	Room	Location	Associated Floor
Unaffiliated	1	East Wall	1
Room Block 1	44	North Wall	1
Room Block 2	18	South Wall	2
Room Block 3	206	West Wall	1
Room Block 5	112	South Wall	1
	113	South Wall	1
	114	North Wall	2A
Room Block 7	341	East Wall	2

TABLE A.14.
Distribution of Fire Pits (n = 21)

Room Block	Room	Location	Associated Floor
Unaffiliated	312	SE Quad	1
Room Block 1	70	Center	2
	100	NE Quad	1
	100	NE Quad	1
	107	SE Quad	1
	107	SW Quad	1
Room Block 2	22	Center	1
	164	Center	1
	187	NE Quad	1
	197	SE Quad	1
	197	NW Quad	3
Room Block 3	246	NW Quad	2
	246	Center	2
	269	Center	3
	270	Center	2
	280	SE Quad	3
	280	NE Quad	3
	440	Center	1
Room Block 5	113	NE Quad	1
Room Block 8	353	SW Quad	1
Room Block 10	414	SE Quad	1

TABLE A.15.
Distribution of Slab-Lined Storage Boxes ($n = 15$)

Room Block	Room	Location	Associated Floor
Room Block 1	4	NE Quad	1
	5	SE Quad	1
	10	NE Quad	1
	39	NW Quad	1
	40	NW Quad	1
Room Block 2	12	SE Quad	1
	18	Center	1
	143	SE Quad	2
	164	NE Quad	1
	164	SE Quad	1
	197	NE Quad	4
Room Block 5	114	SW Quad	2A
	114	SW Quad	2A
Room Block 8	353	SE Quad	1
Room Block 9	371	SW Quad	1

TABLE A.16.
Distribution of Postholes ($n = 26$)

Room Block	Room	Location	Associated Floor
Unaffiliated	1	SE Quad	1
	1	Center	1
	1	Center	1
Room Block 1	10	SW Quad	2
	40	SW Quad	1
	40	SW Quad	1
	40	SW Quad	1
	40	SW Quad	1
	104	SW Quad	2
Room Block 2	12	Center	1
	27	SW Quad	1
	27	NW Quad	1
	27	SW Quad	1
	27	SW Quad	1
	164	NW Quad	1
	164	SW Quad	1
	164	NW Quad	1
Room Block 3	246	NE Quad	4
Room Block 4	3	Center	1
Room Block 12	411	NW Quad	1
	411	NE Quad	1
	411	NW Quad	2
	411	NW Quad	2
	411	NW Quad	2
	411	NW Quad	2
	411	NE Quad	2

Table A.17.
Distribution of Pits (n = 17)

Room Block	Room	Location	Associated Floor
Unaffiliated	309	SE Quad	1
	359	SE Quad	1
Room Block 2	12	SE Quad	1
	164	SE Quad	1
	164	NE Quad	1
	164	SE Quad	1
	187	NW Quad	3
	187	NE Quad	5
	187	NE Quad	6
Room Block 3	246	NE Quad	1
	246	NE Quad	1
	274	NE Quad	2
	274	NE Quad	2
	280	SE Quad	4
Room Block 4	9	SE Quad	1
Room Block 5	112	SE Quad	1
	115	NW Quad	1

Table A.18.
Distribution of Storage Bins (n = 5)

Room Block	Room	Location	Associated Floor
Room Block 2	145	SW Quad	1
Room Block 3	216	SE Quad	1
	270	SW Quad	1
Room Block 7	352	NW Quad	1
	352	NE Quad	1

Table A.19.
Distribution of Room Partitions (n = 3)

Room Block	Room	Location	Associated Floor
Unaffiliated	359	SE Quad	1
Room Block 1	45	NW Quad	1
Room Block 7	349	SW Quad	1

TABLE A.20.
Distribution of Infrequently Occurring Floor Features ($n = 20$)

Room Block	Room	Location	Associated Floor	Feature Description
Unaffiliated	1	NE Quad	1	Stone steps
Room Block 1	28	NE Quad	1	Deflector slab
	40	SE Quad	Roof	Hatchway remnant
	69	NW Quad	Roof	Cluster of roof pots with slabs
	104	Center	Roof	Hatchway remnant
Room Block 2	18	Center	2	Foot drum
	143	SW Quad	3	Stone platform
	145	NW Quad	1	Vertical slab (part of *jacal* storage bin)
	183	SE Quad	1	Partial flagstone floor
Room Block 3	206	SW Quad	1	Vent and deflector in bench
	246	NE Quad	2	Slab and mano cluster
	246	Center	2	Stone oven
	274	Entire room	1	Flagstone floor
	280	Center	3	Roasting pit (may predate room)
Room Block 4	9	Entire room	1	Flagstone floor
Room Block 5	113	SW Quad	1	Stone platform
	116	NE Quad	1	Partial slab floor (associated with a fire pit)
Room Block 7	341	NW Quad	2	Ventilator shaft
	341	SE Quad	2	Ventilator shaft
Room Block 13	434	NW Quad	2	Loom support (posthole?)

TABLE A.21.
Excavated Rooms with Roof Features ($n = 26$)

Room	Room Block	Description
5	1	Rectangular slab-lined hearth
11	1	Rectangular slab-lined hearth
23	2	Rectangular slab-lined hearth
28	1	Rectangular slab-lined hearth
31	1	Rectangular slab-lined hearth
40	1	3 Rectangular slab-lined hearths, collapsed roof hatch
41	1	Rectangular slab-lined hearth
44	1	Rectangular slab-lined hearth
45	1	Rectangular slab-lined hearth
47	1	Mealing bin
62	1	Rectangular slab-lined hearth
68	1	Rectangular slab-lined hearth
69	1	Rectangular slab-lined hearth, possible hearth
104	1	Rectangular slab-lined hearth, collapsed roof hatch
112	5	Rectangular slab-lined hearth, mealing bin
113	5	2 Mealing bins
115	5	Rectangular slab-lined hearth
146	2	Rectangular slab-lined hearth
183	2	3 Rectangular slab-lined hearths, mealing bin
187	2	Rectangular slab-lined hearth
231	3	Rectangular slab-lined hearth, mealing bin
246	3	Rectangular slab-lined hearth, mealing bin
279	3	Rectangular slab-lined hearth
280	3	Rectangular slab-lined hearth
341	7	Rectangular slab-lined hearth
352	7	Rectangular slab-lined hearth, mealing bin

TABLE A.22.
Excavated Rooms with Second-Story Features ($n = 9$)

Room	Room Block	Description
19	2	Rectangular slab-lined hearth
62	1	5 Rectangular slab-lined hearths
69	1	Rectangular slab-lined hearth
70	1	Rectangular slab-lined hearth
146	2	Rectangular slab-lined hearth
246	3	Rectangular slab-lined hearth, mealing bin
269	3	Rectangular slab-lined hearth
270	3	Rectangular slab-lined hearth
274	3	Rectangular slab-lined hearth

TABLE A.23.
Excavated Rooms with Preroom (Nonburial) Features ($n = 47$)

Room	Room Block	Room	Room Block
5	1	114	5
6	1	115	5
11	1	116	5
13	2	121	1
14	2	145	2
16	2	146	2
19	2	153	2
21	2	183	2
22	2	187	2
23	2	197	2
24	0	205	3
27	2	206	3
28	1	216	3
31	1	231	3
39	1	274	3
40	1	341	7
41	1	352	7
44	1	356	8
45	1	359	0
62	1	398	12
70	1	420	10
108	1	434	13
112	5	438	3
113	5		

TABLE A.24.
Number of Room Floors by Room Block

	No Floor		1 Floor		2 Floors		3 Floors		4+ Floors	
	n	%	*n*	%	*n*	%	*n*	%	*n*	%
Main Pueblo	1	1	35	34	22	21	5	5	5	5
Room Blocks 5 and 7	—	—	7	7	1	1	1	1	—	—
Outliers	1	1	19	18	5	5	—	—	1	1
Totals	2	2	61	59	28	27	6	6	6	6

Notes

CHAPTER 2

1. An examination of the Grasshopper field records yields an initial figure of 106 excavated rooms. Three spaces classified as rooms before excavation have been removed for this analysis. The corridor between Rooms 399/412 and Rooms 411/398 in Room Block 12 was designated as a "room" during excavation but is clearly not a room space. The two other deletions are found in Room Block 7. Rooms 338 and 360 were excavated as rooms; however, they are actually internal masonry storage facilities within Room 352 and have been included with Room 352 in this analysis. One possible deletion that was not removed from the room count is Room 395 in Room Block 12. This "room" is similar to Rooms 338 and 360 in its size and complete lack of floor features. It is defined, however, by four bounding walls and was not constructed within an existing room space, so it is retained as a room in this analysis. After these deletions 103 excavated rooms remain (Figure 2.6; Table A.1).

2. Kruskal-Wallis was used to assess the three measurement ranks discussed in the text. The Kruskal-Wallis statistic is a nonparametric test analogous to a one-way ANOVA. The test allows comparison of more than two groups of data by measuring how the sums of rankings (rankings are generated by Systat from ratio data) for each of the categories of data differ from expected results under the null hypothesis that samples are drawn from the same continuous population. The distribution of the Kruskal-Wallis statistic (expressed as H) approximates Chi-square when more than five cases occur in each class and critical values for H are derived from the Chi-square table (Blalock 1972:349–350).

CHAPTER 3

1. Following Cowgill (1977), all applications of Chi-square are accompanied by power statistics that measure the strength of the associations among the cells. Phi is used for all tables, Yule's Q is applied to all 2×2 tables, and Cramer's V is given for all $r \times c$ tables. The use of these measures is detailed in Blalock (1972:295–300).

2. It can be argued that even early abandoned rooms served a specific function. One of the defining characteristics of these rooms is the presence of a great deal of trash in the room fill. Thus, they functioned as refuse dumps.

3. Walls were not consistently measured from the floor or from the base of the wall. Most were measured from the floor, and in a small proportion of cases it is not always

clear from the room excavation records whether wall heights were measured from the floor or from the base of the wall.

4. A Jaccard (S3) correlation, which measures the proportion of pairs with both values present given that at least one is present, was used. This ensured that walls without a specific type of feature were not counted because walls lacking a feature biased the results (i.e., S3 does not measure coabsence). For example, the paucity of crawlways throughout the site could have caused high correlations in cases where both crawl spaces and other features were absent.

5. One source of data was not used because it does not accurately reflect the number of two-story rooms. Ciolek-Torrello (1978:75:Figure 3) provided a list of possible second-story rooms in his analysis of activity organization. A comparison of his map with observations about wall height in adjacent rooms (adjacent to Ciolek-Torrello's two-story rooms), however, suggests that Ciolek-Torrello overestimated the number of two-story rooms.

6. A similar feature was found in the northeast corner of Room 5 at the Bailey Ruin (Mills et al. 1999), and it also occurs with some frequency at Turkey Creek and Point of Pines pueblos in the Point of Pines region (Lowell 1991; Wendorf 1950) and at Q-Ranch Pueblo, to the west of Grasshopper.

7. At Point of Pines Pueblo immigrants are hypothesized to have lived in temporary pit structures before or during the construction of masonry rooms in the late A.D. 1200s (Lindsay 1987:193). A similar strategy could account for the pit structure under Room Block 5 at Grasshopper. The architectural characteristics of both Room Block 5 and nearby Room Block 1 are consistent with the activities of immigrants (Chapter 5).

8. One additional rectangular great kiva was recorded at Hooper Ranch Pueblo in the Upper Little Colorado area (Figure 1.1; Martin et al. 1961) but was never excavated.

CHAPTER 4

1. Although this assumption holds at Grasshopper, at sites in Tsegi Canyon masonry techniques and wall faces are determined by room function (Dean 1969:27–33).

2. These first two sections summarize an earlier study of pueblo growth. For a more in-depth account of community growth at Grasshopper, see Riggs 1994a.

3. Many of the principles applied here expand Wilcox's (1975) methods for delimiting social groups at the Joint Site, which are based on his previous work at Grasshopper (see Wilcox 1982).

4. This is by no means an exhaustive treatment of the subject, and the reader is referred to Riggs (1994a) for a more detailed account. Differences in interpretation between the original discussion of this material (Riggs 1994a) and the current treatment are related to the incorporation of architectural data that were not consulted at the time of the original analysis. Where discrepancies exist, the current interpretations are considered more reliable than the original analysis.

CHAPTER 5

1. For this analysis a king's case correlation matrix was used, and Moran's *I* was calculated (Odland 1988; Thomas and Hugget 1980). Values for Moran's *I* were com-

pared to expected values for a random distribution. Values higher than expected represent clustered distributions, whereas those lower than expected signify a dispersed distribution. Significance of results was determined using the z statistic and a 0.05 significance level. As used in this analysis, individual rooms were the "regions" being compared. Contiguity of any two rooms was determined by any shared portion of wall space, including corners (king's case).

2. Reid and Whittlesey (1982) incorporated elements such as hearth style, presence-absence of benches, ash boxes, and other features, and to some extent room size, to subdivide Ciolek-Torrello's (1978) broad category of limited activity rooms and, to a lesser extent, storage rooms into four additional categories, including ceremonial rooms, which Ciolek-Torrello had not taken into account.

References

Adams, E. Charles

1983 The Architectural Analogue to Hopi Social Organization and Room Use, and Implications for Prehistoric Northern Southwestern Culture. *American Antiquity* 48:44–61.

1998 Late Prehistory in the Little Colorado River Area: A Regional Perspective. In *Migration and Reorganization: The Pueblo IV Period in the American Southwest,* edited by Katherine A. Spielmann, pp. 53–64. Arizona State University Anthropological Research Papers No. 51. Arizona State University, Tempe.

Adler, Michael A. (editor)

1996 *The Prehistoric Pueblo World,* A.D. 1150–1350. University of Arizona Press, Tucson.

Ahlstrom, Richard V. N.

1985 The Interpretation of Archaeological Tree-Ring Dates. Unpublished Ph.D. dissertation, Department of Anthropology, University of Arizona.

Ahlstrom, Richard V. N., Jeffrey S. Dean, and William J. Robinson

1991 Evaluating Tree-Ring Interpretations at Walpi Pueblo, Arizona. *American Antiquity* 56:628–644.

Anderson, Keith M., Gloria J. Fenner, Don P. Morris, George A. Teague, and Charmion McKusick

1986 *The Archaeology of the Gila Cliff Dwellings.* Publications in Anthropology 36, Western Archaeological and Conservation Center, National Park Service, Department of the Interior, Tucson, Arizona.

Anyon, Roger

1984 Mogollon Settlement Patterns and Communal Architecture. Unpublished master's thesis, Department of Anthropology, University of New Mexico.

Anyon, Roger, and Steven LeBlanc

1980 The Architectural Evolution of Mogollon-Mimbres Communal Structures. *Kiva* 45:253–277.

Baldwin, Gordon C.

1934 The Prehistoric Pueblo of Kinishba. Unpublished master's thesis, University of Arizona, Tucson.

1938 Excavations at Kinishba Pueblo, Arizona. *American Antiquity* 4:11–21.

Baldwin, Stuart J.

1987 Roomsize Patterns: A Quantitative Method for Approaching Ethnic Identification in Architecture. In *Ethnicity and Culture: Proceedings of the 18th Annual Conference of the Archaeological Association of the University of Calgary,* edited by Réginald Auger, Margaret F. Glass, Scott MacEachern, and Peter H. McCartney, pp. 163–174. University of Calgary Archaeological Association, Calgary.

Bannister, Bryant

1962 The Interpretation of Tree-Ring Dates. *American Antiquity* 27:508–514.

Beaglehole, Ernest
1937 *Notes on Hopi Economic Life.* Yale University Publications in Anthropology 15. Yale University Press, New Haven.
Binford, Lewis R.
1962 Archaeology as Anthropology. *American Antiquity* 28:217–225.
Birkby, Walter H.
1973 Discontinuous Morphological Traits of the Skull as Population Markers in the Prehistoric Southwest. Unpublished Ph.D. dissertation, Department of Anthropology, University of Arizona, Tucson.
1982 Bio-Social Interpretations from Cranial Non-metric Traits of the Grasshopper Pueblo Skeletal Remains. *In Multidisciplinary Research at Grasshopper Pueblo, Arizona,* edited by W. A. Longacre, S. J. Holbrook, and M. W. Graves. Anthropological Papers of the University of Arizona 40:36–41. University of Arizona Press, Tucson.
Blalock, Hubert M., Jr.
1972 *Social Statistics.* McGraw-Hill, New York.
Blanton, Richard
1994 *Houses and Households: A Comparative Study.* Plenum, New York.
Bourdieu, Pierre
1973 The Berber House. In *Rules and Meaning,* edited by Mary Douglas, pp. 98–110. Penguin, Suffolk.
1977 *Outline of a Theory of Practice.* Translated by R. Nice. Cambridge University Press, Cambridge.
Branigan, Keith
1970 *The Foundations of Palatial Crete.* London.
Breternitz, David A.
1959 *Excavations at Nantack Village, Point of Pines, Arizona.* Anthropological Papers of the University of Arizona 1. University of Arizona Press, Tucson.
Brew, J. O.
1946 *Archaeology of Alkalai Ridge, Southeastern Utah.* Papers of the Peabody Museum of American Archaeology and Ethnology 21. Harvard University, Cambridge.
Cameron, Catherine M.
1995 Migration and the Movement of Southwestern Peoples. *Journal of Anthropological Archaeology* 14:104–124.
1996 Multistory Construction in Southwestern Pueblo Architecture. In *Interpreting Southwestern Diversity: Underlying Principles and Overarching Patterns,* edited by Paul R. Fish and J. Jefferson Reid, pp. 195–199. Anthropological Research Papers No. 48. Arizona State University, Tempe.
1998 Coursed Adobe Architecture, Style, and Social Boundaries in the American Southwest. In *The Archaeology of Social Boundaries,* edited by Miriam T. Stark, pp. 183–207. Smithsonian Institution Press, Washington.
1999a *Hopi Dwellings: Architecture at Orayvi.* University of Arizona Press, Tucson.
1999b Room Size, Organization of Construction, and Archaeological Interpretation in the Puebloan Southwest. *Journal of Anthropological Archaeology* 18:201–239.
Cameron, Catherine M. (editor)
1993 *Abandonment of Settlements and Regions.* Cambridge University Press, Cambridge.
Chenhall, Robert G.
1972 Random Sampling in an Archaeological Survey. Unpublished Ph.D. dissertation, Department of Anthropology, Arizona State University, Tempe.
Childs, S. T.
1991 Style, Technology, and Iron Smelting Furnaces in Bantu-Speaking Africa. *Journal of Anthropological Archaeology* 10:332–359.
Ciolek-Torrello, Richard S.
1978 A Statistical Analysis of Activity Organization: Grasshopper Pueblo, Arizona. Unpublished Ph.D. dissertation, Department of Anthropology, University of Arizona, Tucson.

1984 An Alternative Model of Room Function from Grasshopper Pueblo, Arizona. In *Intrasite Spatial Analysis in Archaeology,* edited by Harold J. Hietala, pp. 127–153. New York: Cambridge University Press.

1985 A Typology of Room Function at Grasshopper Pueblo, Arizona. *Journal of Field Archaeology* 12:41–63.

Clark, Jeffery J.

2001 *Tracking Prehistoric Migrations: Pueblo Settlers among the Tonto Basin Hohokam.* Anthropological Papers of the University of Arizona 65. University of Arizona Press, Tucson.

Clarke, David L.

1972 A Provisional Model of an Iron Age Society and Its Settlement System. In *Models in Archaeology,* edited by David L. Clarke, pp. 801–869. Methuen, London.

Cook, Sherburne F., and Robert F. Heizer

1968 Relationships among Houses, Settlement Areas, and Population in Aboriginal California. In *Settlement Archaeology,* edited by K. C. Chang, pp. 79–116. National Press Books, Palo Alto, California.

Cooper, Laurel

1995 Space Syntax Analysis of Chacoan Great Houses. Unpublished Ph.D. dissertation, Department of Anthropology, University of Arizona, Tucson.

Cordell, Linda S.

1995 Tracing Migration Pathways from the Receiving End. *Journal of Anthropological Archaeology* 14:203–211.

Cordell, Linda S., David E. Doyel, and Keith W. Kintigh

1994 Processes of Aggregation in the Prehistoric Southwest. In *Themes in Southwestern Prehistory,* edited by George J. Gumerman, pp. 109–133. School of American Research Press, Santa Fe.

Cordell, Linda, and Fred Plog

1979 Escaping the Confines of Normative Thought: A Reevaluation of Puebloan Prehistory. *American Antiquity* 44:405–429.

Cowgill, George L.

1977 The Trouble with Significance Tests and What We Can Do About It. *American Antiquity* 42:350–368.

Craig, Douglas B., and Jeffery J. Clark

1994 The Meddler Point Site: AZ V:5:4/26 (ASM/TNF). In *The Roosevelt Community Development Study. Volume 2: Meddler Point, Pyramid Point, and Griffin Wash Sites,* by Mark D. Elson, Deborah L. Swartz, Douglas B. Craig, and Jeffery J. Clark, pp. 1–198. Center for Desert Archaeology Anthropological Papers No. 13. Tucson.

Creamer, Winifred

1993 *The Architecture of Arroyo Hondo Pueblo, New Mexico.* Arroyo Hondo Archaeological Series Vol. 8. School of American Research Press, Santa Fe.

Crown, Patricia L.

1981 Variability in Ceramic Manufacture at the Chodistaas Site, East-Central Arizona. Unpublished Ph.D. dissertation, Department of Anthropology, University of Arizona, Tucson.

Crown, Patricia L., and Timothy A. Kohler

1994 Community Dynamics, Site Structure, and Aggregation in the Northern Rio Grande. In *The Ancient Southwestern Community: Models and Methods for the Study of Prehistoric Social Organization,* edited by W. H. Wills and Robert D. Leonard, pp. 103–117. University of New Mexico Press, Albuquerque.

Crumley, Carole L.

1995 Heterarchy and the Analysis of Complex Societies. In *Heterarchy and the Analysis of Complex Societies,* edited by Robert M. Ehrenreich, Carole L. Crumley, and Janet J. Levy, pp. 1–5. Archaeological Papers of the American Anthropological Association No. 6. American Anthropological Association, Arlington, Virginia.

Cummings, Byron

1940 *Kinishba: A Prehistoric Pueblo of the Great Pueblo Period.* Hohokam Museums Association and the University of Arizona, Tucson.

Cushing, Frank Hamilton

1896 *Outlines of Zuni Creation Myths.* 13th Annual Report of the Bureau of American Ethnology, pp. 325–447, U.S. Government Printing Office, Washington, D.C.

Dean, Jeffrey S.

1969 *Chronological Analysis of Tsegi Phase Sites in North-Eastern Arizona.* Papers of the Laboratory of Tree-Ring Research 3. University of Arizona Press, Tucson.

1970 Aspects of Tsegi Phase Social Organization. In *Reconstructing Prehistoric Pueblo Societies,* edited by W. A. Longacre, pp. 140–174. School of American Research, University of New Mexico Press, Albuquerque.

1978 Independent Dating in Archaeological Analysis. In *Advances in Archaeological Method and Theory* 1, edited by Michael B. Schiffer, pp. 223–255. Academic Press, New York.

1988a A Model of Anasazi Behavioral Adaptation. In *The Anasazi in a Changing Environment,* edited by G. J. Gumerman, pp. 25–44. School of American Research and Cambridge University Press, Cambridge.

1988b The View from the North: An Anasazi Perspective on the Mogollon. *Kiva* 53:197–199.

Dean, Jeffrey S., William H. Doelle, and Janet D. Orcutt

1994 Adaptive Stress, Environment, and Demography. In *Themes in Southwest Prehistory,* edited by George J. Gumerman, pp. 53–86. School of American Research Press, Santa Fe.

Dean, Jeffrey S., and John C. Ravesloot

1993 The Chronology of Cultural Interaction in the Gran Chichimeca. In *Culture and Contact: Charles C. Di Peso's Gran Chichimeca,* edited by Anne I. Woosley and John C. Ravesloot, pp. 83–104. Amerind Foundation Publication, University of New Mexico Press, Albuquerque.

Dean, Jeffrey S., and William J. Robinson

1982 Dendrochronology at Grasshopper Pueblo. In *Multidisciplinary Research at Grasshopper Pueblo, Arizona,* edited by W. A. Longacre, S. J. Holbrook, and M. W. Graves. Anthropological Papers of the University of Arizona 40:46–60. University of Arizona Press, Tucson.

Di Peso, Charles, John B. Rinaldo, and Gloria J. Fenner

1974 *Casas Grandes: A Fallen Trading Center of the Gran Chichimeca, Architecture and Dating Methods, Volume* 4. Amerind Foundation Series No. 9. Dragoon, Arizona.

Dohm, Karen

1996 Rooftop Zuni: Extending Household Territory Beyond Apartment Walls. In *People Who Lived in Big Houses: Archaeological Perspectives on Large Domestic Structures,* edited by Gary Coupland and E. B. Banning, pp. 89–106. Monographs in World Archaeology No. 27. Prehistory Press, Madison.

Donaldson, Thomas

1893 *Moqui Pueblo Indians of Arizona and Pueblo Indians of New Mexico.* 11th Census of the United States, Extra Census Bulletin. Washington, D.C.

Donley-Reid, Linda W.

1990 A Structuring Structure: The Swahili House. In *Domestic Architecture and the Use of Space,* edited by S. Kent, pp. 114–126. Cambridge University Press, Cambridge.

Douglas, A. E.

1935 *Dating Pueblo Bonito and Other Ruins of the Southwest.* National Geographic Society Contributed Technical Papers, 1. Washington, D.C.

Duff, Andrew I.

1998 The Process of Migration in the Late Prehistoric Southwest. In *Migration and Reorganization: The Pueblo IV Period in the American Southwest,* edited by Katherine A. Spielmann, pp. 31–52. Arizona State University Anthropological Research Papers No. 51. Arizona State University, Tempe.

Eighmy, Jeffrey L.

1979 Logistic Trends in Southwest Population Growth. In *Transformations: Mathematical Approaches to Culture Change*, edited by C. Renfrew and K. L. Cooke, pp. 205–220. Academic Press, New York.

Eighmy, Jeffrey L., and Robert S. Sternberg (editors)

1990 *Archaeomagnetic Dating*. University of Arizona Press, Albuquerque.

Elson, Mark D.

1994 The Pyramid Point Site: AZ V:5:1/25 (ASM/TNF). In *The Roosevelt Community Development Study. Volume 2: Meddler Point, Pyramid Point, and Griffin Wash Sites*, by Mark D. Elson, Deborah L. Swartz, Douglas B. Craig, and Jeffery J. Clark, pp. 199–296. Center for Desert Archaeology Anthropological Papers No. 13. Tucson.

Ezzo, Joseph A.

1993 *Human Adaptation at Grasshopper, Arizona: Social and Ecological Perspectives*. International Monographs in Prehistory, Archaeological Series 4. Ann Arbor, Michigan.

1999 A Heterarchical Perspective on Aggregated Pueblo Social Organization: A Case Study from Grasshopper Pueblo. In *Sixty Years of Mogollon Archaeology: Papers of the Ninth Mogollon Conference, Silver City, New Mexico* 1996, edited by Stephanie M. Whittlesey, pp. 31–37. SRI Press, Tucson.

Ezzo, Joseph A., Clark M. Johnson, and T. Douglas Price

1997 Analytical Perspectives on Migration: A Case Study from East-Central Arizona. *Journal of Archaeological Science* 24:447–466.

Ferguson, T. J.

1996 *Historic Zuni Architecture and Society: An Archaeological Application of Space Syntax*. Anthropological Papers of the University of Arizona 60. University of Arizona Press, Tucson.

Ferguson, T. J., and Barbara J. Mills

1987 Settlement and Growth of Zuni Pueblo: An Architectural History. *Kiva* 52:243–266.

Ferguson, T. J., Barbara J. Mills, and Calbert Seciwa

1990 Contemporary Zuni Architecture and Society. In *Pueblo Style and Regional Architecture*, edited by Nicholas C. Markovich, Wolfgang F. E. Preiser, and Fred G. Strum, pp. 103–121. Van Nostrand Reinhold, New York.

Fewkes, Jesse W.

1900 *Tusayan Migration Traditions*. 19th Annual Report of the Bureau of American Ethnology, Pt. 2. U.S. Government Printing Office, Washington, D.C.

1909 *Antiquities of the Mesa Verde National Park: Spruce-Tree House*. Bureau of American Ethnology Bulletin 41. Government Printing Office, Washington, D.C.

1911 *Antiquities of Mesa Verde National Park: Cliff Palace*. Bureau of American Ethnology Bulletin 51. Smithsonian Institution, Washington, D.C.

Fish, Paul R., Suzanne K. Fish, George J. Gumerman, and J. Jefferson Reid

1994 Toward an Explanation of Southwestern "Abandonments." In *Themes in Southwest Prehistory*, edited by George J. Gumerman, pp. 135–163. School of American Research Advanced Seminar Series, School of American Research Press, Santa Fe.

Flannery, Kent V.

1972b The Origins of the Village as a Settlement Type in Mesoamerica and the Near East: A Comparative Study. In *Man, Settlement, and Urbanism*, edited by P. J. Ucko, R. Tringham, and G. W. Dimbleby, pp. 23–53. Schenkman, Cambridge.

Forde, C. Daryell

1931 Hopi Agriculture and Land Ownership. *Journal of the Royal Anthropological Institute of Great Britain and Ireland* 61:357–405.

Fortes, Meyer

1971 Introduction. In *The Developmental Cycle in Domestic Groups*, edited by Jack Goody, pp 1–14. Cambridge Papers in Social Anthropology 1. Cambridge University Press, Cambridge.

Fowler, Andrew P., John R. Stein, and Roger Anyon
1987 *An Archaeological Reconnaissance of West-Central New Mexico: The Anasazi Monuments Project.* Report Submitted to the Office of Cultural Affairs, Historic Preservation Division, State of New Mexico, Santa Fe.

Gerald, M. Virginia
1957 Two Great Kivas of Point of Pines Ruin. Unpublished master's thesis, University of Arizona, Tucson.

Giddens, Anthony
1979 *Central Problems in Social Theory: Action, Structure, and Contradiction in Social Analysis.* Macmillan, London.

Gifford, James C.
1980 *Archaeological Explorations in Caves of the Point of Pines Region, Arizona.* Anthropological Papers of the University of Arizona 36. University of Arizona Press, Tucson.

Gilman, Patricia A.
1987 Architecture as Artifact: Pit Structures and Pueblos in the American Southwest. *American Antiquity* 52:538–564.

Graves, Michael W.
1982 Anomalous Tree-Ring Dates and the Sequence of Room Construction at Canyon Creek Ruin, East-Central Arizona. *Kiva* 47:107–131.
1983 Growth and Aggregation at Canyon Creek Ruin: Implications for Evolutionary Change in East-Central Arizona. *American Antiquity* 48:290–315.
1986 *Room Construction Strategies and Dynamics at Grasshopper Pueblo and Other Late Prehistoric Sites in East Central Arizona.* Paper Presented at the 4th Mogollon Conference, Tucson, Arizona, October 1986.
1991 Estimating Ring Loss on Tree-Ring Specimens from East-Central Arizona: Implications for Prehistoric Pueblo Growth at the Grasshopper Ruin. *Journal of Quantitative Anthropology* 3:83–115.

Graves, Michael W., Sally J. Holbrook, and William A. Longacre
1982 Aggregation and Abandonment at Grasshopper Pueblo: Evolutionary Trends in the Late Prehistory of East-Central Arizona. In *Multidisciplinary Research at Grasshopper Pueblo, Arizona,* edited by W. A. Longacre, S. J. Holbrook, and M. W. Graves. Anthropological Papers of the University of Arizona 40:110–121. University of Arizona Press, Tucson.

Hall, Edward T.
1959 *The Silent Language.* Doubleday, Garden City, New Jersey.
1966 *The Hidden Dimension.* Doubleday, New York.
1968 Proxemics. *Current Anthropology* 9:83–103.

Haury, Emil W.
1928 The Succession of House Types in the Pueblo Area. Unpublished masters thesis, University of Arizona, Tucson.
1934 *The Canyon Creek Ruin and the Cliff Dwellings of the Sierra Ancha.* Medallion Papers 14. Globe, Arizona: Gila Pueblo.
1935 Tree Rings: The Archaeologist's Time-Piece. *American Antiquity* 1:98–108.
1936 *The Mogollon Culture of Southwestern New Mexico.* Medallion Papers 20. Globe, Arizona: Gila Pueblo.
1950 A Sequence of Great Kivas in the Forestdale Valley, Arizona. In *For the Dean: Essays in Honor of Byron Cummings on His Eighty-Ninth Birthday, September* 20, 1950, edited by Erik K. Reed and Dale S. King, pp. 29–39. Hohokam Museums Association and the Southwestern Monuments Association, Santa Fe.
1958 Evidence at Point of Pines for a Prehistoric Migration from Northern Arizona. In *Migrations in New World Culture History,* edited by R. Thompson, pp. 1–6. University of Arizona Bulletin 27. University of Arizona Press, Tucson.
1985 *Mogollon Culture in the Forestdale Valley, East-Central Arizona.* University of Arizona Press, Tucson.

1989 *Point of Pines, Arizona: A History of the University of Arizona Archaeological Field School.* Anthropological Papers of the University of Arizona 50. University of Arizona Press, Tucson.

Haury, Emil W., and Lyndon L. Hargrave

1931 *Recently Dated Pueblo Ruins in Arizona.* Smithsonian Miscellaneous Collections 82(11). Smithsonian Institution, Washington, D.C.

Hawley, Florence M.

1938 The Family Tree of Chaco Canyon Masonry. *American Antiquity* 3:247–255.

Herr, Sarah A., and Jeffery J. Clark

1997 Patterns in the Pathways: Early Historic Migrations in the Rio Grande Pueblos. *Kiva* 62:365–390.

Hewett, Edgar L.

1993 *Ancient Communities in the American Desert.* Archaeological Society of New Mexico Monograph Series 1. (English translation of the 1908 document *Les Communautés Anciennes dans le Désert Américain,* Geneva).

Hieb, Louis A.

1979 Hopi World View. In *Southwest,* edited by Alfonso Ortiz, pp. 577–580. Handbook of North American Indians, vol. 9. Smithsonian Institution, Washington, D.C.

1990 The Metaphors of Hopi Architectural Experience in Comparative Perspective. In *Pueblo Style and Regional Perspective,* edited by N. C. Markovich, W. F. E. Preiser, and F. G. Strum, pp. 122–132. Van Nostrand Reinhold, New York.

Hill, James N.

1970a *Broken K Pueblo: Prehistoric Social Organization in the American Southwest.* Anthropological Papers of the University of Arizona 18. University of Arizona Press, Tucson.

1970b Prehistoric Social Organization in the American Southwest: Theory and Method. In *Reconstructing Prehistoric Pueblo Societies,* edited by W. A. Longacre, pp. 11–58. School of American Research, University of New Mexico Press, Albuquerque.

Hillier, Bill, and Julienne Hanson

1984 *The Social Logic of Space.* Cambridge University Press, London.

Hinkes, Madeline J.

1983 Skeletal Evidence of Stress in Subadults: Trying to Come of Age at Grasshopper Pueblo. Unpublished Ph.D. dissertation, Department of Anthropology, University of Arizona, Tucson.

Hough, Walter

1919 *Archaeological Exploration in Arizona.* Smithsonian Miscellaneous Collections 70(2):3–90. Smithsonian Institution, Washington, D.C.

1920 *Archaeological Excavations in Arizona.* Smithsonian Miscellaneous Collections 72(1):64–66. Smithsonian Institution, Washington, D.C.

1930 *Exploration of the Ruins in the White Mountain Apache Indian Reservation,* Arizona. Proceedings, U.S. National Museum, 78(2865):1–21. Washington, D.C.

Hunter-Anderson, Rosalind L.

1977 A Theoretical Approach to the Study of House Form. In *For Theory Building in Archaeology,* edited by L. R. Binford, pp. 287–315. Academic Press, New York.

Jacobs, David

1997a *A Salado Platform Mound on Tonto Creek. Roosevelt Platform Mound Study. Report on the Cline Terrace Mound.* Roosevelt Monograph Series No. 7, Anthropological Field Studies No. 37. Arizona State University, Tempe.

1997b Intensively Sampled and Tested Sites in the Vicinity of Casa Bandolero. In *Salado Residential Settlements on Tonto Creek. Roosevelt Platform Mound Study. Report on the Cline Mesa Sites, Cline Terrace Complex, Part* 1, by Theodore J. Oliver and David Jacobs, pp. 73–146. Roosevelt Monograph Series No. 9, Anthropological Field Studies No. 38. Arizona State University, Tempe.

James, Steven R.

1994 *Regional Variation in Prehistoric Pueblo Households and Social Organization: A*

Quantitative Approach. Ph.D. dissertation, Department of Anthropology, Arizona State University, Tempe. University Microfilms, Ann Arbor.

1997 Change and Continuity in Western Pueblo Households during the Historic Period in the American Southwest. *World Archaeology* 28:429–456.

Johnson, Alfred E.

1965 The Development of Western Pueblo Culture. Unpublished Ph.D. dissertation, Department of Anthropology, University of Arizona, Tucson.

Judd, Neil M.

1927 *Archaeological Investigations in Chaco Canyon, New Mexico.* Smithsonian Miscellaneous Collections 78(7):158–168. Smithsonian Institution, Washington, D.C.

1964 *The Architecture of Pueblo Bonito.* Smithsonian Miscellaneous Collections 147(1). Smithsonian Institution, Washington, D.C.

Kent, Susan

1990 Activity Areas and Architecture: An Interdisciplinary View of the Relationship between Use of Space and Domestic Built Environments. In *Domestic Architecture and the Use of Space: An Interdisciplinary Cross-Cultural Study,* edited by Susan Kent, pp. 1–8. Cambridge University Press, Cambridge.

Kidder, Alfred V.

1958 *Pecos, New Mexico: Archaeological Notes.* Papers of the Peabody Foundation for Archaeology 5. Phillips Academy, Andover, Massachusetts.

1962 *An Introduction to the Study of Southwestern Archaeology.* Revised edition. Yale University Press, New Haven. Originally published 1924, Yale University Press, New Haven.

Kintigh, Keith W.

1985 *Settlement, Subsistence and Society in Late Zuni Prehistory.* Anthropological Papers of the University of Arizona 44. University of Arizona Press, Tucson.

Klie, Barbara J., Alan H. Simmons, and Susan Jackson

1982 AZ P:6:10. In *Cholla Project Archaeology, Volume 2, The Chevlon Region,* edited by J. Jefferson Reid, pp. 33–53. Archaeological Series No. 161. Arizona State Museum, Tucson.

Kluckhohn, Clyde

1940 The Conceptual Structure in Middle American Studies. In *The Maya and Their Neighbors,* edited by C. L. Hay et al., pp. 41–51. Appelton-Century, New York.

Kostof, Spiro

1995 *A History of Architecture: Settings and Rituals.* 2d ed. Oxford University Press, New York.

Kus, Susan, and Victor Raharijaona

1990 Domestic Space and the Tenacity of Tradition among Some Betsileo of Madagascar. In *Domestic Architecture and the Use of Space: An Interdisciplinary Cross-Cultural Study,* edited by Susan Kent, pp. 21–33. Cambridge University Press, Cambridge.

Lange, Richard C., Craig P. Howe, and Barbara A. Murphy

1993 A Study of Prehistoric Roofing Systems in Arizona Cliff Dwellings. *Journal of Field Archaeology* 20:485–498.

Lawrence, Denise L., and Setha M. Low

1990 The Built Environment and Spatial Form. *Annual Review of Anthropology* 19:453–505.

Layne, Linda L.

1987 Village Bedouin: Patterns of Change from Mobility to Sedentism. In *Method and Theory for Activity Area Research,* edited by Susan Kent, pp. 345–373. Columbia University Press, New York.

Lee, Richard B.

1979 *The !Kung San: Men, Women, and Work in a Foraging Society.* Cambridge University Press, Cambridge.

Lefebvre, Henri

1991 *The Production of Space.* Basil Blackwell, Oxford.

Lekson, Stephen H.

1984 *Great Pueblo Architecture of Chaco Canyon, New Mexico.* University of New Mexico Press, Albuquerque.

Lekson, Stephen H. (editor)

1983 *The Architecture and Dendrochronology of Chetro Ketl, Chaco Canyon, New Mexico.* Reports of the Chaco Center 6. Division of Cultural Research, National Park Service, Albuquerque.

Lemonnier, Pierre

1986 The Study of Material Culture Today: Towards an Anthropology of Technical Systems. *Journal of Anthropological Archaeology* 5:147–186.

1993 Introduction. In *Technological Choices: Transformation in Material Culture since the Neolithic,* edited by Pierre Lemonnier, pp. 1–35. Routledge, London.

Lindauer, Owen

1995 *Where the Rivers Converge. Roosevelt Platform Mound Study. Report on the Rock Island Complex.* Roosevelt Platform Mound Study No. 4, Anthropological Field Studies No. 33. Arizona State University, Tempe.

1996 *The Place of the Storehouses. Roosevelt Platform Mound Study. Report on the Schoolhouse Point Mound, Pinto Creek Complex.* Roosevelt Platform Mound Study No. 6, Anthropological Field Studies No. 35. Arizona State University, Tempe.

Lindsay, Alexander J., Jr.

1987 Anasazi Population Movements to Southeastern Arizona. *American Archaeology* 6:190–199.

Longacre, William A.

1970a *Archaeology as Anthropology: A Case Study.* Anthropological Papers of the University of Arizona 19. University of Arizona Press, Tucson.

1970b A Historical Review. In *Reconstructing Prehistoric Pueblo Societies,* edited by W. A. Longacre, pp. 1–10. School of American Research, University of New Mexico Press, Albuquerque.

1975 Population Dynamics at Grasshopper Pueblo, Arizona. In *Population Studies in Archaeology and Biological Anthropology: A Symposium,* edited by Alan C. Swedlund, pp. 71–74. Memoirs of the Society for American Archaeology 30.

1976 Population Dynamics at Grasshopper Pueblo, Arizona. In *Demographic Anthropology: Quantitative Approaches,* edited by Ezra B. W. Zubrow, pp. 169–183. University of New Mexico Press, Albuquerque.

Longacre, William A., and Michael W. Graves

1982 Multidisciplinary Studies at Grasshopper Pueblo. In *Multidisciplinary Research at Grasshopper Pueblo, Arizona,* edited by W. A. Longacre, S. J. Holbrook, M. W. Graves. Anthropological Papers of the University of Arizona 40:1–4. University of Arizona Press, Tucson.

Longacre, William A., and J. Jefferson Reid

1974 The University of Arizona Archaeological Field School at Grasshopper: Eleven Years of Multidisciplinary Research and Teaching. *Kiva* 40:3–38.

Lorentzen, Leon H.

1993 From Atlatl to Bow: The Impact of Improved Weapons on Wildlife in the Grasshopper Region. Unpublished master's report, Department of Anthropology, University of Arizona, Tucson.

Lowell, Julie C.

1991 *Prehistoric Households at Turkey Creek Pueblo.* Anthropological Papers of the University of Arizona 54. University of Arizona Press, Tucson.

1994 Illuminating Fire-Feature Variability in the Grasshopper Region of Arizona. *Kiva* 60:351–370.

McGuire, Randall H., and Michael B. Schiffer

1983 A Theory of Architectural Design. *Journal of Anthropological Archaeology* 2:277–303.

Marshall, Michael P., John R. Stein, Richard W. Loose, and Judith E. Novotny
1979 *Anasazi Communities of the San Juan Basin.* Public Service Company of New Mexico, Albuquerque.

Martin, Paul S.
1967 Description of Architectural Details. In *Chapters in the Prehistory of Eastern Arizona, III,* by Paul S. Martin, William A. Longacre, and James N. Hill, pp. 16–55. Fieldiana: Anthropology 57. Field Museum of Natural History, Chicago.

Martin, Paul S., and John B. Rinaldo
1950 *Sites of the Reserve Phase, Pine Lawn Valley, Western New Mexico.* Fieldiana: Anthropology 38(3). Field Museum of Natural History, Chicago.
1960 *Table Rock Pueblo, Arizona.* Fieldiana: Anthropology 51(2). Field Museum of Natural History, Chicago.

Martin, Paul S., John B. Rinaldo, and William A. Longacre
1961 *Mineral Creek Site and Hooper Ranch Pueblo, Eastern Arizona.* Fieldiana: Anthropology 52. Field Museum of Natural History, Chicago.

Metzger, Todd R., Larry V. Nordby, and Susan F. Eininger
1989 *Wupatki National Monument Prestabilization Architectural Documentation Manual for Prehistoric Masonry Sites.* Southwest Cultural Resources Center, National Park Service.

Mills, Barbara J.
1998 Migration and Pueblo IV Community Reorganization in the Silver Creek Area, East-Central Arizona. In *Migration and Reorganization: The Pueblo IV Period in the American Southwest,* edited by Katherine A. Spielmann, pp. 65–80. Arizona State University Anthropological Research Papers No. 51. Arizona State University Press, Tempe.

Mills, Barbara J., Sara Herr, and Scott Van Keuren (editors)
1999 *Living on the Edge of the Rim: Excavations and Analysis of the Silver Creek Archaeological Research Project* 1993–1998. Arizona State Museum Archaeological Series No. 192. Arizona State Museum, Tucson.

Mindeleff, Cosmos
1900 *Localization of Tusayan Clans.* 19th Annual Report of the Bureau of American Ethnology for the Years 1897–1898, Pt. 2, pp. 635–653. Washington, D.C.

Mindeleff, Victor
1891 *A Study of Pueblo Architecture: Tusayan and Cibola.* Annual Report of the Bureau of American Ethnology 8:3–228. Smithsonian Institution, Washington, D.C.

Montgomery, Barbara K.
1992 Understanding the Formation Processes of the Archaeological Record: Ceramic Variability at Chodistaas Pueblo, Arizona. Unpublished Ph.D. dissertation, Department of Anthropology, University of Arizona, Tucson.

Montgomery, Barbara K., and J. Jefferson Reid
1990 An Instance of Rapid Ceramic Change in the American Southwest. *American Antiquity* 55:88–97.

Morgan, Lewis Henry
1965 *Houses and House-Life of the American Aborigines.* Reprinted. University of Chicago Press, Chicago. Originally published 1881 as "Contributions to North American Ethnology," vol. 4, U.S. Government Printing Office, Washington, D.C.

Morris, Don P.
1986 *Archaeological Investigations at Antelope House.* National Park Service, U.S. Department of the Interior, Washington, D.C.

Morrow, Baker H., and V. B. Price (editors)
1997 *Anasazi Architecture and American Design.* University of New Mexico Press, Albuquerque.

Odland, John
1988 *Spatial Autocorrelation.* Scientific Geography Series. Sage, Newbury Park, California.

Olsen, Stanley J.
1982 Water Resources and Aquatic Fauna at Grasshopper Pueblo. In *Multidisciplinary*

Research at Grasshopper Pueblo, Arizona, edited by W. A. Longacre, S. J. Holbrook, and M. W. Graves. Anthropological Papers of the University of Arizona 40:61–62. University of Arizona Press, Tucson.

Olson, Alan P.

1959 An Evaluation of the Phase Concept in Southwestern Archaeology: As Applied to the Eleventh and Twelfth Century Occupations at Point of Pines, East Central Arizona. Unpublished Ph.D. dissertation, Department of Anthropology, University of Arizona, Tucson.

Pfaffenberger, B.

1992 Social Anthropology of Technology. *Annual Review of Anthropology* 21:491–516.

Plog, Stephen E.

1977 *A Multivariate Approach to the Explanation of Ceramic Variation.* Ph.D. dissertation, University of Michigan, Ann Arbor. University Microfilms, Ann Arbor.

1980 *Stylistic Variation in Prehistoric Ceramics: Design Analysis in the American Southwest.* Cambridge University Press, Cambridge.

Potter, James M.

1998 The Structure of Open Space in Late Prehistoric Settlements in the Southwest. In *Migration and Reorganization: The Pueblo IV Period in the American Southwest,* edited by Katherine A. Spielmann, pp. 137–164. Arizona State University Anthropological Research Papers No. 51. Arizona State University Press, Tempe.

Prudden, T. Mitchel

1903 The Prehistoric Ruins of the San Juan Watershed in Utah, Arizona, Colorado, and New Mexico. *American Anthropologist,* n.s., 5(2):224–288.

1914 The Circular Kivas of Small Ruins in the San Juan Watershed. *American Anthropologist* 16(1):33–58.

Rapoport, Amos

1969 *House Form and Culture.* Prentice-Hall, Englewood Cliffs, New Jersey.

1980 Vernacular Architecture and the Cultural Determinants of Form. In *Buildings and Society,* edited by D. King, pp.283–305. Routledge and Kegan Paul, London.

1982 *The Meaning of the Built Environment: A Nonverbal Communication Approach.* Sage, Beverly Hills.

1990 Systems of Activities and Systems of Settings. In *Domestic Architecture and the Use of Space: An Interdisciplinary Cross-Cultural Study,* edited by Susan Kent, pp. 9–20. Cambridge University Press, Cambridge.

Reed, Erik Kellerman

1956 Types of Village-Plan Layouts in the Southwest. In *Prehistoric Settlement Patterns in the New World,* edited by G. R. Willey. Viking Fund Publications in Anthropology 23:11–17. Wenner-Gren Foundation for Anthropological Research.

1958 Comment on "Evidence at Point of Pines for a Prehistoric Migration from Northern Arizona." In *Migrations in New World Culture History,* edited by Raymond H. Thompson, pp. 7–8. University of Arizona Bulletin 27. University of Arizona Press, Tucson.

Redman, Charles L.

1993 *People of the Tonto Rim: Archaeological Discovery in Prehistoric Arizona.* Smithsonian Institution Press, Washington, D.C.

Reid, J. Jefferson

1973 Growth and Response to Stress at Grasshopper Pueblo, Arizona. Unpublished Ph.D. dissertation, Department of Anthropology, University of Arizona, Tucson.

1989 A Grasshopper Perspective on the Mogollon of the Arizona Mountains. In *Dynamics of Southwestern Prehistory,* edited by Linda Cordell and George Gumerman, pp. 65–97. Smithsonian Institution Press, Washington, D.C.

1998 Return to Migration, Population Movement, and Ethnic Identity in the American Southwest: A Peer Reviewer's Thoughts on Archaeological Inference. In *Overview, Synthesis and Conclusions,* edited by Stephanie M. Whittlesey, Richard Ciolek-Torrello, and Jeffrey H. Altschul, pp. 629–638. Vanishing River: Landscapes and Lives of the Lower Verde Valley: The Lower Verde Archaeological Project. SRI Press, Tucson.

Reid, J. Jefferson, and Barbara K. Montgomery

1998 The Brown and the Gray: Pots and Population Movement in East-Central Arizona. *Journal of Anthropological Research* 54:447–459.

Reid, J. Jefferson, and Charles R. Riggs

1995 The Dynamics of Pueblo Architecture. Paper presented at the 60th Annual Meeting of the Society for American Archaeology, Minneapolis, Minnesota, May 3–7.

Reid, J. Jefferson, Michael B. Schiffer, Stephanie M. Whittlesey, Madeleine J, Hinkes, Alan P. Sullivan, Christian E. Downum, William A. Longacre, and H. David Tuggle

1989 Perception and Interpretation in Contemporary Southwestern Archaeology: Comments on Cordell, Upham, and Brock. *American Antiquity* 54:802–814.

Reid, J. Jefferson, and Izumi Shimada

1982 Pueblo Growth at Grasshopper: Methods and Models. In *Multidisciplinary Research at Grasshopper Pueblo, Arizona,* edited by W. A. Longacre, S. J. Holbrook, M. W. Graves. Anthropological Papers of the University of Arizona 40:12–18. University of Arizona Press, Tucson.

Reid, J. Jefferson, John R. Welch, Barbara K. Montgomery, and Maria Nieves Zedeño

1996 A Demographic Overview of the Late Pueblo III Period in the Mountains of East-central Arizona. In *The Prehistoric Pueblo World:* A.D. 1150–1350, edited by Michael A. Adler, pp. 73–85. University of Arizona Press, Tucson.

Reid, J. Jefferson, and Stephanie M. Whittlesey

1982 Households at Grasshopper Pueblo. *American Behavioral Scientist* 25:687–703.

1990 The Complicated and the Complex: Observations on the Archaeological Record of Large Pueblos. In *Perspectives on Southwestern Prehistory,* edited by Paul E. Minnis and Charles L. Redman, p. 184–195. Westview Press, Boulder.

1999 *Grasshopper Pueblo: A Story of Archaeology and Ancient Life.* University of Arizona Press, Tucson.

Reynolds, William E.

1981 Ethnoarchaeology of Pueblo Architecture. Unpublished Ph.D. dissertation, Department of Anthropology, Arizona State University, Tempe.

Riggs, Charles R.

1994a Dating Construction Events at Grasshopper Pueblo: New Techniques for Architectural Analysis. Unpublished master's thesis, Department of Anthropology, University of Arizona, Tucson.

1994b Organizational Characteristics of Mogollon Pueblos in East-Central Arizona. In *Mogollon VII: The Collected Papers of the* 1992 *Mogollon Conference Held in Las Cruces, New Mexico,* edited by Patrick H. Beckett, pp. 9–18. COAS Publishing and Research, Las Cruces, New Mexico.

1998 *The Social Process of Migration and Its Influence on Community Organization: An Example from East-Central Arizona.* Prepared for the Symposium: A Revolt against Hierarchical Authority: Alternative Models of Prehistoric Social Organization at the 63d Annual Meeting of the Society for American Archaeology, Seattle, Washington, March 25–29.

1999a Spatial Variability in Room Form at Grasshopper Pueblo, Arizona. In *Sixty Years of Mogollon Archaeology: Papers of the Ninth Mogollon Conference, Silver City, New Mexico* 1996, edited by Stephanie M. Whittlesey, pp. 3–11. SRI Press, Tucson.

1999b *The Architecture of Grasshopper Pueblo: Dynamics of Form, Function, and Use of Space in a Prehistoric Community.* Ph.D. dissertation, Department of Anthropology, University of Arizona, Tucson. University Microfilms, Ann Arbor.

Rinaldo, John B.

1959 *Foote Canyon Pueblo, Eastern Arizona.* Fieldiana: Anthropology 49(2). Field Museum of Natural History, Chicago.

1964 Architectural Details, Carter Ranch Pueblo. In *Chapters in the Prehistory of Eastern Arizona II,* by Paul S. Martin, John B. Rinaldo, William A. Longacre, Leslie G. Freeman Jr., James A. Brown, Richard H. Hevly, and M. E. Cooley, pp. 15–58. Fieldiana: Anthropology 55. Field Museum of Natural History, Chicago.

Rock, James T.

1974 The Use of Social Models in Archaeological Interpretation. *Kiva* 40:81–92.

Rohn, Arthur H.

1965 Postulation of Socio-Economic Groups from Archaeological Evidence. In *Contributions of the Wetherill Mesa Archaeological Project,* assembled by Douglas Osbourne, Memoirs of the Society for American Archaeology, no. 19, pp. 65–69.

1971 *Mug House.* Washington: National Park Service.

Sackett, James R.

1990 Style and Ethnicity in Archaeology: The Case for Isochrestism. In *The Uses of Style in Archaeology,* edited by M. W. Conkey and C. A. Hastorf, pp. 32–43. Cambridge University Press, Cambridge, England.

Saile, David G.

1985 Many Dwellings: Views of a Pueblo World. In *Dwelling, Place and Environment: Towards a Phenomenology of Person and World,* edited by David Seamon and Robert Mugerauer, pp. 159–182. Martinus Nijhoff, Dordrecht, The Netherlands.

Sánchez, Arturo G.

1986 *Arqueología del área de las Cuarenta Casas, Chihuahua.* Serie Arqueología, Instituto Nacional de Antropología e Historia, Mexico.

Sanders, Donald

1990 Behavioral Conventions and Archaeology: Methods for the Analysis of Ancient Architecture. In *Domestic Architecture and the Use of Space: An Interdisciplinary Cross-Cultural Study,* edited by Susan Kent, pp. 43–72. Cambridge University Press, Cambridge.

Scarborough, Robert, and Izumi Shimada

1974 Geological Analysis of Wall Composition at Grasshopper with Behavioral Implications. *Kiva* 40:49–66.

Schiffer, Michael B.

1995 Archaeological Context and Systemic Context. In *Behavioral Archaeology: First Principles,* pp. 25–34. Reprinted. University of Utah Press, Salt Lake City. Originally published 1972, *American Antiquity* 37:156–165.

1986 Radiocarbon Dating and the "Old Wood" Problem: The Case of the Hohokam Chronology. *Journal of Archaeological Science* 13:13–30.

1987 *Formation Processes of the Archaeological Record.* University of New Mexico Press, Albuquerque.

Shapiro, Jason S.

1997 *Fingerprints on the Landscape: Space Syntax Analysis and Cultural Evolution in the Northern Rio Grande.* Ph.D. dissertation, Pennsylvania State University. University Microfilms, Ann Arbor.

Shipman, Jeffrey H.

1982 Biological Relationships among Prehistoric Western Pueblo Indian Groups Based on Metric and Discrete Traits of the Skeleton. Unpublished Ph.D. dissertation, Department of Anthropology, University of Arizona, Tucson.

Smiley, Terah L.

1955 The Geochronological Approach. In *Geochronology: With Special Reference to Southwestern United States,* edited by Terah L. Smiley. University of Arizona Bulletin 26(2), Physical Science Bulletin 2, pp. 15–28. University of Arizona Press, Tucson.

Smith, Adam T., and Nicholas David

1995 The Production of Space and the House of Xidi Sukur. *Current Anthropology* 36(3):441–471.

Sofaer, Anna

1997 The Primary Architecture of the Chacoan Culture: A Cosmological Expression. In *Anasazi Architecture and American Design,* edited by B. H. Morrow and V. B. Price, pp. 88–132. University of New Mexico Press, Albuquerque.

Spielmann, Katherine A. (editor)

1998 *Migration and Reorganization: The Pueblo IV Period in the American Southwest.* Arizona State University Anthropological Research Papers No. 51. Arizona State University, Tempe.

Spier, Leslie

1919 *Ruins in the White Mountains, Arizona.* Anthropological Papers of the Museum of Natural History 18(5):363–387. Museum of Natural History, New York.

Stark, Miriam T.

1998 Technical Choices and Social Boundaries in Material Culture Patterning: An Introduction. In *The Archaeology of Social Boundaries,* edited by Miriam T. Stark, pp. 1–11. Smithsonian Institution Press, Washington, D.C.

Stark, Miriam T., Jeffery J. Clark, and Mark D. Elson

1995 Causes and Consequences of Migration in the 13th Century Tonto Basin. *Journal of Anthropological Archaeology* 14:212–246.

Stark, Miriam T., Mark D. Elson, and Jeffery J. Clark

1998 Social Boundaries and Technological Choices in Tonto Basin Prehistory. In *The Archaeology of Social Boundaries,* edited by Miriam T. Stark, pp. 208–231. Smithsonian Institution Press, Washington, D.C.

Steadman, Sharon

1996 Recent Research in the Archaeology of Architecture: Beyond the Foundations. *Journal of Anthropological Research* 4:51–93.

Steward, Julian H.

1955 Lineage to Clan: Ecological Aspects of Southwestern Society. In *Theory of Culture Change,* by Julian Steward, pp. 151–172. University of Illinois Press, Urbana. Revised version of paper originally published in 1937 as "Ecological Aspects of Southwestern Society," *Anthropos* 32:87–104.

Sullivan, Alan P., III

1974 Problems in the Estimation of Original Room Function: A Tentative Solution from the Grasshopper Ruin. *Kiva* 40:93–100.

Swartz, Deborah L., and Brenda G. Randolph

1994 The Griffin Wash Site: AZ V:5:90/96 (ASM/TNF). In *The Roosevelt Community Development Study. Volume 2: Meddler Point, Pyramid Point, and Griffin Wash Sites,* by Mark D. Elson, Deborah L. Swartz, Douglas B. Craig, and Jeffery J. Clark, pp. 297–416. Center for Desert Archaeology Anthropological Papers No. 13. Tucson.

Swentzell, Rina

1990 Pueblo Space, Form, and Mythology. In *Pueblo Style and Regional Architecture,* edited by Nicholas C. Markovich, Wolfgang F. E. Preiser, and Fred G. Strum, pp. 23–30. Van Nostrand Reinhold, New York.

Taylor, Walter W.

1948 *A Study of Archaeology.* Memoirs of the American Anthropological Association No. 69.

Thomas, Reginald W., and Richard J. Hugget

1980 *Modelling in Geography.* Barnes and Noble, Totowa, New Jersey.

Thompson, Raymond H., and William A. Longacre

1966 The University of Arizona Archaeological Field School at Grasshopper, East-Central Arizona. *Kiva* 31:255–275.

Titiev, Mischa

1992 *Old Oraibi: A Study of the Hopi Indians of Third Mesa.* University of New Mexico Press, Albuquerque. Reprinted. Originally published 1944 as Papers of the Peabody Museum of American Archaeology and Ethnology 22(1), Harvard University, Cambridge, Mass.

Triadan, Daniela

1989 Defining Local Ceramic Production at Grasshopper Pueblo, Arizona. Unpublished Master's thesis (photocopy), Lateinameikainstitut, Freie Universität Berlin, Germany.

1997 *Ceramic Commodities and Common Containers: Production and Distribution of White*

Mountain Red Ware in the Grasshopper Region, Arizona. Anthropological Papers of the University of Arizona 61. University of Arizona Press, Tucson.

Tuggle, H. David

1970 *Prehistoric Community Relationships in East-Central Arizona.* Ph.D. dissertation, University of Arizona, Tucson. University Microfilms, Ann Arbor.

1982 Settlement Patterns in the Q Ranch Region. In *Cholla Project Archaeology, Volume 3, The Q Ranch Region,* edited by J. Jefferson Reid, pp. 151–175, Archaeological Series No. 161. Arizona State Museum, Tucson.

Tuggle, H. David, J. Jefferson Reid, and Robert C. Cole Jr.

1984 Fourteenth Century Mogollon Agriculture in the Grasshopper Region of Arizona. In *Prehistoric Agriculture Strategies in the Southwest,* edited by S. F. Fish and P. R. Fish. Anthropological Research Papers 33:101–110. Arizona State University, Tempe.

Upham, Steadman

1982 *Polities and Power: An Economic and Political History of the Western Pueblo.* Academic Press, New York.

Upham, Steadman, and Fred Plog

1986 The Interpretation of Prehistoric Political Complexity in the Central and Northern Southwest: Toward a Mending of the Models. *Journal of Field Archaeology* 13:223–238.

Uphil, Eric

1972 The Concept of the Egyptian Palace as a "Ruling Machine." In *Man, Settlement, and Urbanism,* edited by Peter J. Ucko, Ruth Tringham, and G. W. Dimbleby, pp. 721–733. Schenkman, Cambridge, Massachusetts.

Van Dyke, Ruth M.

1999 Space Syntax Analysis at the Chacoan Outlier of Guadalupe. *American Antiquity* 64:461–474.

Vanderpot, Rein

1994 AZ U:8:187/918: Porter Springs Marina Site. In *The Roosevelt Rural Sites Study. Volume 2: Prehistoric Rural Settlements in the Tonto Basin,* edited by Richard S. Ciolek-Torrello, Steven D. Shelley, and Su Benaron, pp. 127–165. Statistical Research Technical Series No. 28. Tucson.

Walker, William

1995 Ritual Prehistory: A Pueblo Case Study. Unpublished Ph.D. dissertation, Department of Anthropology, University of Arizona, Tucson.

Watson, O. Michael

1970 *Proxemic Behavior: A Cross-Cultural Study.* Approaches to Semiotics Vol. 8. Mouton, The Hague.

Welch, John R.

1996 The Archaeological Measures and Social Implications of Agricultural Commitment. Unpublished Ph.D. dissertation, Department of Anthropology, University of Arizona, Tucson.

Wells, Susan J., and Keith M. Anderson

1988 *Archaeological Survey and Architectural Study of Montezuma's Castle National Monument.* Publications in Anthropology 50. Western Archaeological and Conservation Center, National Park Service, Department of the Interior.

Wendorf, Fred

1950 *A Report on the Excavation of a Small Ruin Near Point of Pines, East-Central Arizona.* University of Arizona Bulletin 21(3), University of Arizona Social Science Bulletin 19. University of Arizona, Tucson.

Wheat, Joe Ben

1952 Prehistoric Water Sources of the Point of Pines Area. *American Antiquity* 17:185–196.

1954 *Crooked Ridge Village.* University of Arizona Bulletin 25(3), Social Science Bulletin 24. University of Arizona, Tucson.

1955 *Mogollon Culture Prior to* A.D. 1000. Memoirs of the American Anthropological Association 82, Memoirs of the Society for American Archaeology 10.

Whiting, John W. M., and Barbara Ayers

1968 Inferences from the Shape of Dwellings. In *Settlement Archaeology,* edited by K. C. Chang, pp. 117–133. National Press Books, Palo Alto, California.

Whittlesey, Stephanie M.

1974 Identification of Imported Ceramics through Analysis of Attributes. *Kiva* 40:101–112.

1978 Status and Death at Grasshopper Pueblo: Experiments toward an Archaeological Theory of Correlates. Unpublished Ph.D. dissertation, Department of Anthropology, University of Arizona, Tucson.

1982 Examination of Previous Work in the Q-Ranch Region: Comparison and Analysis. In *Cholla Project Archaeology, Volume 3, The Q Ranch Region,* edited by J. Jefferson Reid, pp. 123–150. Archaeological Series No. 161. Arizona State Museum, Tucson.

Whittlesey, Stephanie M., Eric J. Arnould, and William E. Reynolds

1982 Archaeological Sediments: Discourse, Experiment, and Application. In *Multidisciplinary Research at Grasshopper Pueblo, Arizona,* edited by W. A. Longacre, S. J. Holbrook, and M. W. Graves. Anthropological Papers of the University of Arizona 40:28–35. University of Arizona Press, Tucson.

Wiessner, Poly

1984 Reconsidering the Behavioral Basis for Style: A Case Study among the Kalahari San. *Journal of Anthropological Archaeology* 3:190–234.

Wilcox, David R.

1975 A Strategy for Perceiving Social Groups in Puebloan Sites. In *Chapters in the Prehistory of Arizona IV,* by Paul S. Martin, Ezra B. W. Zubrow, Daniel C. Bowman, David A. Gregory, John A. Hanson, Michael B. Schiffer, and David R. Wilcox, pp. 120–159. Fieldiana: Anthropology 65. Field Museum of Natural History, Chicago.

1982 A Set-Theory Approach to Sampling Pueblos: The Implications of Room-Set Additions at Grasshopper Pueblo. In *Multidisciplinary Research at Grasshopper Pueblo, Arizona,* edited by W. A. Longacre, S. J. Holbrook, and M. W. Graves. Anthropological Papers of the University of Arizona 40:19–27. University of Arizona Press, Tucson.

Wilcox, David R., Thomas R. McGuire and Charles Sternberg

1981 *Snaketown Revisited.* Arizona State Museum Archaeological Series 155. Tucson.

Wilk, Richard R., and William L. Rathje

1982 Household Archaeology. *American Behavioral Scientist* 25:617–639.

Wobst, H. Martin

1977 Stylistic Behavior and Information Exchange. In *Papers for the Director: Research Essays in Honor of James B. Griffin,* edited by C. E. Cleland, pp. 317–342. Anthropological Papers No. 61. Museum of Anthropology, University of Michigan, Ann Arbor.

Zedeño, Maria Nieves

1994 *Sourcing Prehistoric Ceramics at Chodistaas Pueblo, Arizona: The Circulation of People and Pots in the Grasshopper Region.* Anthropological Papers of the University of Arizona 58. University of Arizona Press, Tucson.

Index